Comics and Pop Culture

Comics and Pop Culture

Adaptation from Panel to Frame

EDITED BY BARRY KEITH GRANT
AND SCOTT HENDERSON

University of Texas Press Austin

Copyright © 2019 by the University of Texas Press
All rights reserved
Printed in the United States of America
First edition, 2019

Requests for permission to reproduce material from this work should be sent to:
    Permissions
    University of Texas Press
    P.O. Box 7819
    Austin, TX 78713-7819
    utpress.utexas.edu/rp-form

♾ The paper used in this book meets the minimum requirements of
ANSI/NISO Z39.48-1992 (R1997) (Permanence of Paper).

Library of Congress Cataloging-in-Publication Data

Names: Grant, Barry Keith, 1947–, editor. | Henderson, Scott, 1965–, editor.
Title: Comics and pop culture : adaptation from panel to frame / edited by
Barry Keith Grant and Scott Henderson.
Description: First edition. | Austin : University of Texas Press, 2019. |
Includes bibliographical references and index.
Identifiers: LCCN 2019007789
    ISBN 978-1-4773-1938-3 (cloth : alk. paper)
    ISBN 978-1-4773-1939-0 (pbk. : alk. paper)
    ISBN 978-1-4773-1940-6 (library e-book)
    ISBN 978-1-4773-1941-3 (nonlibrary ebook)
Subjects: LCSH: Film adaptations—History and criticism. | Comic strip characters in
motion pictures. | Comic strip characters on television. | Comic books, strips, etc.—
Film adaptations. | Motion pictures and comic books. | Mass media and culture.
Classification: LCC PN1997.85 .C636 2019 | DDC 791.43/6—dc23
LC record available at https://lccn.loc.gov/2019007789

doi:10.7560/319383

*In memory of Scott's daughter, Paige,
and the comics and films they enjoyed together
and
in memory of Barry's father, Sumner, who created
his own comic strip while serving during World War II*

Contents

Acknowledgments

The editors wish to thank the Office of the Dean of Social Sciences at Brock University and the Council for Research in Social Sciences for research grants to complete this book. Graduate students Malcolm Matthews and Cory Maddalena helped with preparation of the manuscript and images, as did our Brock Fine Arts colleague Amy Friend and her student assistant Sarah Martin. Malisa Kurtz prepared the index with her usual thoroughness. At the University of Texas Press, senior acquisitions editor Jim Burr was supportive from the beginning. Assistant editor Sarah McGavick ably steered the manuscript through the acquisitions process, and Lynne Chapman and Abby Webber provided the careful copyediting.

Comics and Pop Culture

Introduction

BARRY KEITH GRANT AND SCOTT HENDERSON

It is hard to conceive of the contemporary film industry without consider-ing the impact of comic book adaptations, particularly given their current dominance at the box office. Superhero adaptations now make up a sizeable portion of Hollywood's blockbuster releases. The year 2017 witnessed yet another successful wave of superhero movies, including *Guardians of the Galaxy Vol. 2*, *Spider-Man: Homecoming*, and *Wonder Woman*, the highest-grossing film of the summer; and 2018 continued the trend with *Avengers: Infinity War*, *Aquaman*, and, of course, *Black Panther*, which shattered opening box-office records. There is no doubt that today film adaptations of comic source texts are among the most high-profile blockbuster attractions produced by Hollywood.

Yet while the current prevalence of such adaptations is notable, film and comics are cultural forms that have had transmedia connections almost from the beginning. As John L. Fell observed in his 1974 book, *Film and the Narrative Tradition*, the emergence of newspaper comics "accompanied the development of the motion picture. After the creation of the animated car-toon, the most successful comic artists worked both fields" (89). Fell goes on to show how Winsor McCay, who moved from comics to film with some of the first animated films, *Little Nemo* (1911) and *Gertie the Dinosaur* (1914), and other early comic artists developed visual narrative strategies and shift-ing points of view that paralleled the development and techniques now re-ferred to as the classic Hollywood or classic narrative style.

As Blair Davis notes, "hundreds of silent shorts and animated films based on comic strips were produced in the dawn of the twentieth century, like *The Katzenjammer Kids*, *Happy Hooligan*, *Buster Brown*, *Dream of the Rarebit Fiend*, *Mutt and Jeff*, *Krazy Kat*, and many others" (*Comic Book Movies* 3). Then, in the 1930s, appeared the adventure strips produced by "a new generation of hard-edged melodramatists who pilfered movie techniques" (Fell 89), even as the strips themselves were being adapted to cinema. This was the case for the fantasy adventures of Flash Gordon, as well as the domestic misadventures of Blondie, who first appeared in 1930 and generated a nationally syndicated radio show and a series of twenty-eight films produced by Columbia, both of which spanned the 1940s.

Since then, comic strip and book characters from L'il Abner and Superman to Peanuts and the Watchmen have been adapted to television, stage, and of course cinema. In 1978 Richard Donner's version of *Superman* became the first comic book movie blockbuster. While comic book adaptations had driven earlier serials, one-off films, and series, the arrival of *Superman* and the development of much-improved special effects (for which *Superman* was given a Special Achievement Academy Award for Visual Effects) heralded a new boom. Although the genre developed in fits and starts over the ensuing decades, the success of *Superman* did suggest that comic book adaptations offered filmmakers great potential for success. *Superman* was followed not only by its sequels but by other adaptations, such as *Flash Gordon* (Mike Hodges, 1980), *Swamp Thing* (Wes Craven, 1982), and, memorably, Lucasfilm's critically panned *Howard the Duck* (Willard Huyck, 1986).

Superhero adaptations received a significant boost from Tim Burton's 1989 film *Batman* and its three sequels, *Batman Returns* (Burton, 1992), *Batman Forever* (Joel Schumacher, 1995), and *Batman & Robin* (Joel Schumacher, 1997). The poor critical reception of the latter led to the cancellation of a sequel and might have suggested that comic book adaptations had run their course. Yet there were many other films adapted from comic books within this same period, including some derived from lesser-known comic franchises. One of the most successful was *Men in Black* (Barry Sonnenfeld, 1997), loosely adapted from the comic book series of the same name. The comics originated with a small publisher, Aircel, which was in turn bought out by another small publisher, Malibu, which itself was subsequently purchased by Marvel, who owned the property at the time of the adaptation. There was also critical and cult success in the adaptation of *Ghost World* (Terry Zwigoff, 2001), adapted from Daniel Clowes's 1997 graphic novel (collected from a series of stories he had published between 1993 and 1997). *Ghost World*, in both media, depicted aspects of late-1990s youth culture, particularly notions of suburban alienation via its two central characters, recent high school graduates Enid (portrayed in the film by Thora Birch) and Rebecca (Scarlett Johansson).

The use of familiar tropes drawn from youth films also contributed to the appeal and success of *Spider-Man* (Sam Raimi, 2002). The film's focus on the high school trials and tribulations of Peter Parker (Tobey Maguire), his transformation into Spider-Man, and his blossoming romance with Mary Jane Watson (Kirsten Dunst) allowed the story to resonate with more than a core group of comic book fans. While it had been preceded by a successful adaptation of *X-Men* (Bryan Singer) in 2000, the phenomenal blockbuster success of *Spider-Man* and its sequels, *Spider-Man 2* (Raimi, 2004) and *Spider-Man 3* (Raimi, 2007), took comic book adaptations determinedly into the mainstream.

The earlier critical and commercial failure of *Batman & Robin* did not spell the end of the Batman franchise, which was revitalized in Christopher Nolan's *Batman Begins* (2005). Nolan's version and its sequels, *The Dark Knight* (Nolan, 2008) and *The Dark Knight Rises* (Nolan, 2012), took inspiration and adapted some story lines from the Alan Moore–written DC Comics graphic novel *The Killing Joke* (1998), while also borrowing elements from Frank Miller's 1987 *Batman: Year One*. Miller's 1986 miniseries *The Dark Knight* revitalized the *Batman* franchise and provided some inspiration for Tim Burton's earlier effort.

The most recent explosion of comic book adaptations is most closely linked to the emergence of the Marvel Cinematic Universe (MCU). Marvel Studios, itself a subsidiary of Walt Disney Studios, has created a transmedia universe of intersecting properties across film, television, online content, comic books, and other media formats. The first MCU film was *Iron Man* (Jon Favreau, 2008), which inaugurated an initial phase that culminated in *The Avengers* (Joss Whedon, 2012). Subsequent phases have culminated in further Avengers films, *Avengers: Age of Ultron* (Joss Whedon, 2015), and *Avengers: Infinity War* (Anthony Russo and Joe Russo, 2018). The universe has continued to expand as new properties emerge, including *Black Panther* (Ryan Coogler, 2018), *Ant-Man* (Peyton Reed, 2015), and *Guardians of the Galaxy* (James Gunn, 2014). While each property does work autonomously in terms of narrative, there is overlap among story lines, both between films as well as with other media, including television and comics. More recently DC has attempted to emulate this process with its own DC Extended Universe (DCEU). This universe has included the Superman film *Man of Steel* (Zack Snyder, 2013), *Suicide Squad* (David Ayer, 2016), *Wonder Woman* (Patty Jenkins, 2017), and DC's answer to the Avengers, *Justice League* (Snyder, 2017), in addition to crossovers in other media. As these films, particularly the Marvel franchises, continue to dominate the box office, television ratings, and streaming platforms, there seems to be little indication that the popularity of comic book adaptations will wane anytime soon. So, while there have been ebbs and flows, comic book adaptations have always been part of the cinematic and cultural landscape. As Davis writes about the appeal of these texts, "Adaptation was an integral part of film, television, and comics from very early in the history of each medium. Adapting comics to film and television (as well as vice-versa) demonstrates our collective desire to experience the same stories and characters in more than just one form, be it pen and ink, four-color printing, celluloid, or broadcast signal" (*Movie Comics* 2).

The current popularity of these adaptations may be credited to the fact that cinema has had to become increasingly dependent on its relationship with spectacle as it struggles to compete with other forms of entertainment, including streaming television services and online media. Comic books provide an obvious source for spectacular narratives, often offering action-packed story lines and other visual and sonic flourishes that seem to propel much of contemporary cinema. This approach allows films to employ the myriad digital technologies for both sound and image that are at filmmakers' disposal. As has frequently been the case in film history, rivalry with other entertainment media has meant that cinema needs to reinforce its own distinct assets in order to retain audiences. As television increasingly moves toward streaming, the corresponding "quality television" texts that emerge offer complex narratives and detailed character development that exceed what is possible within the duration of most films. While there have been television adaptations of a number of comic book characters and franchises, including the Netflix shows *Jessica Jones*, *Luke Cage*, and *Daredevil*, these have tended to be more character driven, with less emphasis on the full-blown spectacle of cinematic adaptations.

In the summer of 2017 Netflix made its first acquisition of another media producer—in this case, Millarworld, a Scotland-based comic publishing company whose creations include *Kick-Ass* and *Kingsman*, both of which have been featured in recent film adaptations. This acquisition suggests that the growth potential of comic book adaptations continues unabated, while it also reinforces the notion that the transmedia nature of popular entertainment is very much the way of the future. Online media also pose a threat to film, with easy access to a wide variety of short- and longer-form narratives, games, and myriad other options for visual entertainment that fill the leisure time of the twenty-first-century consumer. Comic book reading itself has become more high-tech with the advent of digital formats such as the Amazon-owned ComiXology. Cinema's unique assets remain in the realm of spectacle, large screens, and booming sound systems that increasingly emphasize action and special effects, particularly for films aiming for mainstream, blockbuster appeal.

As M. Keith Booker has suggested, "until very recently, the technology available to filmmakers simply did not allow them the range and scope that have always been available to comic artists, whose creativity was limited only by their imaginations" (ix). Advances in digital technology have permitted the fantasy worlds of comic books to be brought to life on screen more vividly, and more believably, than ever before. The promotional tagline for *Superman*, the movie that inaugurated the comic book adaptation blockbuster, was "You'll believe a man can fly." This development is part of an evolution that has its origins in the emergence of both media forms at the end of the nineteenth century. Jared Gardner suggests that adaptation is an intrinsic part of the connection between film and comics: "Far from being an aberration or dilution of their 'true' formal properties, the convergence of film and comics can be understood as an embrace of the genetic links that once bound film and comics together when they emerged as the new media modes of storytelling in the early years of the twentieth century" (181). Developments in film technology have allowed for a re-embrace, as film is now able to more believably adapt the fanciful worlds of comic books. The formal properties of comic books can now be aligned with the visual effects made possible by digital cinema, permitting adaptations to provide more seamlessly the same sorts of thrills found on the comic page. Indeed, it might be argued that this recent convergence of film and comics is in fact evidence of André Bazin's famous claim regarding the myth of total cinema, that it had only to wait for the technological means to make it so for it to happen.

This greater convergence permitted by new technology is not limited to the bombastic narratives of the superhero story line. Comic books and graphic novels that do not feature superheroes also rely on flights of fancy and visual permutations that are rendered more believably on screen using newer technologies. This is evident, for example, in Matt Yockey's chapter on *American Splendor* (Robert Pulcini and Shari Springer Berman, 2003) in this collection. The film, based on the autobiographical graphic novel by Harvey Pekar, follows the author's relatively uneventful daily life. Despite being about the apparently mundane life of a file clerk, the film still actively employs numerous visual tropes derived from comic books, including thought balloons, captions, comic-style frames, and other traces of the materiality of the comic medium. Yockey relates these elements to the source material's efforts to provide an affective experience for viewers/readers. Pekar's story underlines the fact that comic book and graphic novel tropes are not limited to the more recent superhero boom in cinema. While superheroes, such as those of the Marvel and DC Universes, tend to dominate the popular perception of comic book adaptations, the relationship between the two forms of popular media, as the various chapters in this book show, is far more extensive and nuanced.

Fell's claims about the intertwined histories of film and comics are reinforced by Liam Burke's recognition, in his book *The Comic Book Film Adaptation: Exploring Modern Hollywood's Leading Genre*, that Louis Lumière's *L'arroseur arrosé* (1895), "often celebrated as the first narrative film . . . is also cinema's first adaptation of a comic" (Burke 3). Indeed, early cinema provides numerous examples of the interplay between film and comics. Fell's consideration of Winsor McCay's visual trickery underlines this connection. Fell identifies McCay's comic strip *Little Nemo in Slumberland*, first published in 1905, as sharing many similarities with issues of movement and perspective simultaneously being developed in cinema. McCay's earlier strip *Dream of the Rarebit Fiend* was adapted into a live-action short in 1906 by Edwin S. Porter, while McCay himself created animated films, including *Little Nemo* and an adaptation of a *Rarebit Fiend* strip, *How a Mosquito Operates* (1912). This intertwined history of the two media is also evident in J. P. Telotte's consideration in this volume of the various adaptations of Felix the Cat. Telotte identifies that animation is about space, and particularly the manipulations of the space(s) in which narratives take place. The antics of Felix, often involving the hero cat shifting shapes and manipulating his surroundings, were adapted from page to screen via animation. While Telotte notes the changes in the depictions of Felix's antics over time, we are also reminded of the inherent pliability allowed by animation, something that "live-action" cinema has only more recently been able to effectively match.

Comic books have also endeavored to bring film techniques to the printed page, as is evident in Scott Bukatman's examination of the ways in which special effects are employed in both media. In his contribution to this volume, Bukatman reserves special attention for the comic book adaptation of Stanley Kubrick's *2001: A Space Odyssey* (1968). In comparing the film effects created by special effects supervisor Douglas Trumbull to the comic book effects drawn by writer/artist Jack Kirby, Bukatman explains how the comic version employs the tools of its medium, mobilized by the unique style of Kirby, to recreate the effect felt by viewers of the film. Again, the intersections between the two media are writ large, indicating that both attempt to replicate techniques of the other in reaching their audience, in finding the means of providing an affective experience for viewers and readers.

Where Bukatman focuses more precisely on the effects in *2001*, Blair Davis considers more widely the history of comics that have been adapted from films and the manner in which the narrative world of the film could be extended for audiences. As he notes in his chapter, this is a process that has been going on for over one hundred years, but it is one that has become more prominent since the 1970s. As transmedia storytelling has grown, and as the industrial structures of the entertainment industries have increasingly been driven by convergence, the extension of film narratives into other media forms such as comic books has grown in significance. Davis aptly situates this within the wider history of such adaptations in a manner that underlines how franchises have become an integral part of the contemporary entertainment industry.

The influence of transmedia storytelling is a recurring notion throughout this collection. The shared visual nature of film and comics and the expanding diegetic universes of key comic franchises allow for the easy transference of characters, imagery, and even continuing story lines from one medium to the other. Liam Burke's chapter explores the concept of the comic book tie-in and the ways such tie-ins have often functioned as extensions of narratives from one medium to the other. Not only do they encourage ongoing engagement with story worlds by the audience, but they also encourage increased consumption of a variety of entertainment products, to the obvious benefit of the industry. Aesthetically and structurally, as Burke notes, these adaptations offer "a window onto the creative and formal fluidity that marks today's industries." Where once comic book tie-ins had a more "throwaway" quality and seemed inspired mainly to wring whatever money they could from consumers interested in a character or franchise, more recently they have become an integral part of a wider universe that extends across a range of media platforms.

The multimedia franchise is also the concern of James Chapman in his consideration of how the character of Modesty Blaise was adapted across three different media: newspaper comic strip, novel, and film. As Chapman suggests, the various *Modesty Blaise* texts were products of their time, all first appearing in the 1960s and indicative of the social change of the era, particularly in regard to gender. Yet Chapman concludes that the 1966 film is a missed opportunity that failed to connect with fans of the comic strip or novel, and that the filmmakers, including notable director Joseph Losey, failed to understand the nuances and tone of the source material. For Chapman, the case of *Modesty Blaise* serves as a reminder of the difficulties of adaptation as well as the need to please fans of a franchise that already has an established visual presence.

The history of comic book to film (and sometimes vice versa) adaptation is significant, and the first section of this book focuses on aspects of that history alongside analyses of the aesthetics of adaptation. In addition to the chapters already mentioned, this section includes Aaron Taylor's chapter examining issues of genre classification in superhero cinema. For Taylor, this includes consideration of the link between superhero films and the broader "comic book movie" as a genre. Again, the issues of transmedia forms of storytelling as well as consumption play a significant role in any understanding of the genre traits of superhero cinema. As Taylor points out, industry practice, the formal and structural properties of the films themselves, and the dynamics of reception all serve to imply some forms of genre cohesiveness, while at the same time raising important questions about the ways in which films are classified and how the long-held notions of genre categorization are being challenged by the changing nature of the film and entertainment industries. Taylor recognizes that the interplay between film and comics, along with other media, means that comic books themselves have often borrowed from other genre traditions throughout their history.

One area of adaptation in which tremendous interplay can be found is in the relationship between the print medium of Japanese manga and its film and television form of anime. As Chris Reyns-Chikuma outlines in his chapter, the relationship between manga and anime in Japan is long-standing, complex, and unique. Reyns-Chikuma's chapter serves as a reminder that comic-to-film adaptations are not limited to Hollywood or even to other Western film industries. Indeed, the conventions and histories of diverse national industries reveal striking differences in terms of aesthetic, economic, and ideological motivations such as those Reyns-Chikuma identifies within the Japanese context. By providing a history that addresses industry attributes, such as authorship and the role of studios, alongside a consideration of social issues, Reyns-Chikuma uses select case studies to provide insight into the uniqueness of this Japanese form of adaptation and cultural production. With its global reach and influence, the Japanese industry highlights distinct practices that reaffirm the complexity of adaptation.

Industry convention is also a concern in Miriam Kent's chapter, which focuses specifically on Marvel superhero narratives in both film and comics and examines how these narratives partake in and reinforce dominant social constructions related to gender and heterosexuality. Kent identifies the ways in which superhero films make use of action-genre conventions, aligning with Aaron Taylor's noting of the ways that comic books are indebted to other genres. As these texts and their adaptations replicate dominant genre conventions, they also have a tendency to rearticulate the dominant heteronormativity aligned with those conventions. Among the ways of reading superheroes, Kent points out that they tend to be "exceptional beings" whose "coming out" is one of the many ways in which their relationship to mainstream society is "queered." Yet this aspect of superheroes is routinely elided in both the comics as well as the adaptations, where in all but the most exceptional cases the narratives, with their use of familiar genre tropes, actively function to maintain heteronormative identities and more traditional roles. The 2017 success of *Wonder Woman* suggests that superhero films focused on strong women may have viability, but at the time of this writing it is much too early to tell whether *Wonder Woman* will remain exceptional or prove to be the beginning of more significant change. After all, *Wonder Woman* still relies on a heterosexual love interest to drive much of its plot as Diana Prince / Wonder Woman (Gal Gadot) is convinced to save humankind because of her love for Steve Trevor (Chris Pine), whose depiction as a buff fighter pilot and spy reinforces traditional masculine ideals.

The impressive impact of Marvel's *Deadpool* (2016) and *Deadpool 2* (2018) also suggests the possibility of moving away from heteronormative superheroes. The comic books from which the first film was adapted suggest a fluidity to Deadpool's sexuality as he indicates a sexual desire for both men and women, although the 2016 film adaptation is far less overt about the pansexual nature of the main character, played in the film by Ryan Reynolds. It offers joking hints about Wade Wilson's / Deadpool's possible attraction to men, but this is offset by the presence of his fiancée, Vanessa (Morena Baccarin), a romanticized character who is very distinct from the "mutant" Vanessa (a.k.a. Copycat) who appears in the comics, and by the fact that the plot is motivated by his desire to reunite with her. Again, *Deadpool* provides an exception, and the film adaptation indicates that Kent's arguments remain salient, as the active foregrounding of heterosexual romance and desire that drives the film's narrative militates against the potential queerness of the superhero.

Jeffrey A. Brown's chapter on *Black Panther* also provides a reminder of ways in which dominant culture has not provided significant room for diverse voices. In the concluding chapter to this volume, Brown reminds readers that the history of mainstream comics, and of film adaptations, has provided very few black role models. The massive success of the recent *Black Panther* adaptation thus raises some interesting questions, as the titular character serves as an object of identification for a wide range of fans and thus, as Brown notes, "exposes the cultural and political tensions that arise at the intersections of admiration and appropriation." While the representation of Black Panther challenges many racial stereotypes, the character's initial emergence in Marvel Comics came amid the civil rights movement, and his present-day adventures align him with Afrofuturism and provide strong connections to the concerns of contemporary black communities. The dearth of black heroes in mainstream comics and their corresponding adaptations means that heroes such as Black Panther take on a greater cultural weight. At the same time, the film's and character's place at the heart of the Marvel Cinematic Universe create a wide appeal, opening up the debates about appropriation and cultural exploitation that Brown interrogates.

The role of fan agency, and fan identification with favorite franchises, means that changes within adapted texts raise concerns about fidelity to the source material, which is often of greatest concern to dedicated fans of a franchise. While this has always been an issue for film adaptations, particularly of well-known literary works, the shared visual and structural elements in film and comics, as well as the highly devoted nature of many fans — as witnessed in numerous annual comic cons and similar fan events — means that fidelity may have even greater importance in the comic-to-film adaptation process than in others. As Ian Gordon, Mark Jancovich, and Matthew P. McAllister have posited, "comics and films both have audiences, but comics have core audiences of fans that engage with characters over longer periods of time, and . . . these fans have distinct opinions on how characters should be adapted for film" (xi).

The second section of this collection addresses the processes of adaptation and the myriad questions they raise. J. Mark Percival's chapter examines the issue of fidelity in relation to two adaptations of the British comic character Judge Dredd. Percival acknowledges that questions of authenticity invoke a social construction and that this can vary depending upon varied interest groups as well as other social and historical contexts. As already alluded to, comic book fans are very much a devoted interest group, and with the advent of ever-increasing online forms of communication there is much opportunity for its members to share their pleasure or lack of it regarding the perceived fidelity of any given adaptation. Judge Dredd, though, has the further distinction of being a cult comic book character, regularly appearing in the weekly UK science-fiction anthology comic *2000 AD*; its cult fan base, one might argue, is even more heavily invested in the character and his story lines than most fans. While both adaptations, *Judge Dredd* (1995) and *Dredd* (2012), were commercial failures, Percival notes that the latter was accepted as more authentic than the former by the comic's creators and particularly by devoted fans of the character, who expressed their opinions in online formats such as blogs and other modes of social media. While neither film adequately captures the satirical tone of the comic, the discourse around the more recent film, including that of fans and critics, suggested that Karl Urban's portrayal of Dredd was regarded as being much more authentic than the earlier performance by Sylvester Stallone. Yet, perhaps because of Stallone's star power, the earlier film was more commercially successful, though neither could be termed a commercial success.

Fidelity is also the focus of the chapter by Jason Rothery and Benjamin Woo, who recognize that adaptations are unlikely to be fully faithful to their source text in any case. Indeed, they suggest that in instances when attempts are made to recreate the original text, more attention is then drawn to the changes that are made. Rothery and Woo argue instead that adaptations are discourses about texts, and that fidelity thus can operate on many levels. They point out that fidelity can include adherence to plot, or to style, or to tone—either that of the original author's "vision" or of the "spirit" of the source material. Essentially, Rothery and Woo uncover the notion that authenticity can mean different things in different contexts, particularly in relation to the adapting of different types of source comic books or graphic novels, each with its own particular relationships with its readership or audience. Examining the divergent strategies and relationships to source texts within indie, cult, and blockbuster comic book movies, the authors show how audiences and fan bases are a significant factor of adaptation, stressing that filmmakers "are not adapting a text alone but a *relationship* between text and audience."

The concerns in both Percival's and Rothery and Woo's chapters serve as reminders of the complexities involved in adaptation even though both cinema and comics are intensely visual modes of storytelling. The act of bringing the visual world of comic books, with their allusions to motion and reliance on written text, to film, where actual motion and the use of sound are key components, is far from straightforward. In their contributions, both James C. Taylor and Julian Hoxter interrogate more specific aspects of the complex adaptation process. Taylor focuses on the employment of digital special effects, while Hoxter concentrates on the development of the screenplay. Taylor's examination of digital effects aligns with the insights offered by Rothery and Woo in terms of the divergent aspects of fidelity on offer. Taylor considers how hand-drawn images on the comic page are brought into motion on the screen via newer technologies. He points out that it is not only an aesthetic fidelity that is achieved, but that, as in the case of Sam Raimi's *Spider-Man* trilogy (2002, 2004, 2007), film's employment of CGI can convey themes derived from the comic book source. CGI also poses problems in the way it blurs the lines between the verisimilitude expected of cinema and the wider variation of artistic styles permitted in drawing, which range from simple and cartoonish to highly realist. Taylor explores this tension between fantasy and reality found when a superhero comic book character such as Spider-Man exists in a real-world setting such as New York City. (This tension is also intrinsic to the Marvel Universe, which situates its characters in real-world locales, as opposed to the DC Universe, which employs fictional equivalents, such as Gotham City and Metropolis.) Thematically,

Peter Parker's all too familiar real-world anxieties contrast with his other-worldly abilities as Spider-Man, a dichotomy made manifest in the distinction between reality and CGI.

Hoxter identifies that screenplay adaptations of comic books differ from those deriving from other source material. He pays particular attention to issues of franchise development and, again, to the transmedia elements of the contemporary entertainment industry. Through analysis of examples from several tentpole comic book films, Hoxter demonstrates that screenplay adaptation of comic book material is often markedly different from that of other scripts, and that its practices are derived from the very nature of comic book collaboration between artists and writers. Additionally, individual comic book issues are most often part of longer story lines and broader universes. As these are brought to the screen, Hoxter's insights regarding the contemporary screenwriting process are both practical, in terms of understanding the mechanics of the screenwriting and development process, and also theoretically insightful for interrogating the nature of contemporary cinema production, the entertainment industry, and the central role that these tentpole superhero films play.

As noted earlier, the expanding transmedia universes of comic book worlds are not limited entirely to film. Television provides another space for the extension and development of story lines and characters. Sherryl Vint's chapter addresses both the promises and the challenges in adapting comic book serial narratives to the seriality of television. In this so-called golden age of quality television, shows that focus on narrative and storytelling have become increasingly dominant. In relation to the spectacle of cinema, these television adaptations offer the potential for greater story development and fleshing out of characters with their various backstories. As a component of transmedia storytelling, these more complex narratives work alongside film spectacle in extending the universe in which that spectacle may take place. Vint focuses on *Powers*, an adaptation that originally appeared for Sony's PlayStation gaming console and its PlayStation Vue programming before being released on the Amazon Prime streaming service. She examines the ways in which *Powers* both extends aspects of the Marvel Universe (the original comic books appeared in Image Comics, before moving to Marvel subsidiary Icon) as well as interrogates the superhero genre. The seriality afforded via streaming enables *Powers* to focus on longer character arcs. Indeed, as Vint points out, the series does not follow the same narrative trajectory as the comic book, instead using backstory from later in the comic book series as the first televised season before introducing the story line that made up the first issue of the comic. The thematic changes that such adaptation creates allows for fuller understanding of different audience expectations for different media.

Aviva Briefel's chapter focuses on Double Take Comics' *Ultimate Night of the Living Dead*, an extension of a well-known film property into the comic book medium that allows for the development of possible stories that exist on the margins of George Romero's 1968 film, *Night of the Living Dead*. Briefel uses her analysis of these comics to assess how these tales from the margins ask important questions, raising political issues regarding marginalization while simultaneously interrogating the genre limitations of the source text. Arguably, Romero's original film (and its subsequent sequels) offered political allegory relating to issues such as race, class, and consumerism; and in extending the stories that inhabit the margins of the film, *Ultimate Night of the Living Dead* is able to make these issues resonant for contemporary audiences and alert us, as Briefel suggests, "to the productive possibilities of adaptations as aesthetic and critical fields of inquiry."

Transmedia storytelling also enables engagement with other forms of media beyond film and comic books. Such interaction extends the possibilities of critical engagement with a variety of sociocultural concerns, drawing such concerns into the film or comic book text through cultural reference. Scott Henderson, in his chapter, shows this dynamic at work in his consideration of the impact of punk and post-punk culture on representations of gender, and the ways in which subcultural style and fashion inform both the comic books and the film adaptation of *Tank Girl*. References to punk and post-punk subcultures bring with them existing cultural meaning, which then inform the narrative and aid both thematic and character development, particularly for audiences familiar with those subcultures. Henderson explores the representation of women in three comic books that emerged in the early to mid-1980s—*Love and Rockets*, *The Ballad of Halo Jones*, and *Tank Girl*—while then considering how references to music and the use of the soundtrack become central to the representation of gender and the foregrounding of a strong female protagonist in the 1995 film adaptation of the latter title.

Such engagement with other texts is central to John Bodner's analysis of the *Scott Pilgrim* series of graphic novels and the corresponding 2010 film adaptation, *Scott Pilgrim vs. the World*. The *Scott Pilgrim* series invokes the transmedia nature of contemporary narrative, with Bodner pointing out that the "original" graphic novels were themselves filled with a postmodern array of extratextual references as part of their meaning making. These include, among many others, copious references to video games, popular music, other comic book narratives, and Japanese manga. *Scott Pilgrim*, as a text, calls attention to many of the components of contemporary transmedia adaptation, so that the film becomes an adaptation of a text that is, in many ways, itself a cultural adaptation calling attention to its own source material in its overt employment of many techniques derived from the aesthetic of comic books. As Bodner concludes, the intertwined nature of the *Scott Pilgrim* books and film are indicative of the current nature of cultural production, where the boundaries between media continue to erode as storytelling extends onto multiple platforms, and audiences are expected to bring to these texts their own cultural knowledge in order to assemble meaning.

Certainly, not all filmgoers are comic book readers. Box-office numbers in comparison to comic book sales attest to that fact. Yet, as Jared Gardner suggests, "the DVD and the digital age has made us all comic readers now, even if we never pick up a comic book" (183). With no indication that the comic book film is on the wane, but rather is a pivotal component of the contemporary multimedia entertainment industry, it is crucial, indeed necessary, for film and cultural studies to continue to explore the dense and evolving interplay between these media forms. Back in 1924 the cultural critic Gilbert Seldes declared that "of all the lively arts the comic strip is the most despised, and with the exception of the movies it is the most popular" (193). Although something similar might be said of comic book movies, there is nevertheless a growing body of work that has begun to explore this area seriously, often drawing on the initial insights John L. Fell offered over forty years ago. The present collection provides a diverse set of case studies, histories, and analyses that point to the continually evolving and growing area of comic-to-film adaptation and, we hope, that contribute significantly to understandings of this cultural phenomenon. With such rich terrain, there is room for growth in this field as adaptions of comic books and graphic novels continue to be central to film-production strategies and to provide sources of film narratives. The essays gathered herein provide concepts, models, and approaches that themselves are readily adaptable to the myriad of emerging and fascinating texts that continue to push the boundaries of both panel and frame.

Works Cited

Booker, M. Keith. *"May Contain Graphic Material"*: *Comic Books, Graphic Novels, and Film*. Westport, CT, Praeger, 2007.

Burke, Liam. *The Comic Book Film Adaptation: Exploring Modern Hollywood's Leading Genre*. Jackson, University Press of Mississippi, 2015.

Davis, Blair. *Comic Book Movies*. New Brunswick, NJ, Rutgers University Press, 2018.

————. *Movie Comics: Page to Screen/Screen to Page*. New Brunswick, NJ, Rutgers University Press, 2017.

Fell, John L. *Film and the Narrative Tradition*. Berkeley, University of California Press, 1974.

Gardner, Jared. *Projections: Comics and the History of Twenty-First-Century Storytelling*. Stanford, CA, Stanford University Press, 2012.

Gilmore, James N., and Matthias Stork, editors. *Superhero Synergies: Comic Book Characters Go Digital*. Lanham, MD, Rowman and Littlefield, 2014.

Gordon, Ian, Mark Jancovich, and Matthew P. McAllister, editors. *Film and Comic Books*. Jackson, University Press of Mississippi, 2007.

Mendelson, Scott. "Box Office: 'Wonder Woman' Tops 'Iron Man 3,' Is Now Fifth-Biggest Superhero Movie Ever." *Forbes*, 4 September 2017, https://www.forbes.com/sites/scottmendelson/2017/09/04/box-office-wonder-woman-ends-summer-by-soaring-past-iron-man-3/#279ebe1f346a.

Seldes, Gilbert. *The 7 Lively Arts*. New York, Sagamore Press, 1957.

PART ONE

ISSUES AND DEBATES

The Crossroads of Infinity, or *Universum Incognitum*

SCOTT BUKATMAN

Comics and cinema are gloriously different media, but there's no reason to deny all that they share, from visual vocabularies to storytelling imperatives. Both, in my experience, have excelled at producing a sense of wide-eyed wonder. Here I will consider special effects in both media and their evocation of encounters with cosmic unknowns, *universum incognitum*. Stanley Kubrick's *2001: A Space Odyssey* (1968), in its cinematic and comics incarnations, will be my central point of reference, and special effects supervisor Douglas Trumbull and comics writer and artist Jack Kirby my favored fabulists.[1]

A photographic collage from *Fantastic Four* #51 from 1966 ("This Man, This Monster"), gives us Mister Fantastic himself, Reed Richards, who has used a glorious Kirby contraption to "create a dimensional entrance to subspace," for reasons I need not go into here—I'll just trust Reed when he claims it to be "the area I must explore." A few pages later, and there he is, hovering in space as Stan Lee's hyperbole pours from his mouth: "I've done it!!" he double-exclamation-point exclaims. "I'm drifting into a world of limitless dimensions!! It's the crossroads of infinity—the junction to everywhere!"

Words like *limitless*, *infinite*, and *everywhere* of course evoke the sublime—they are some of the very qualities that Edmund Burke saw as its attributes in his 1757 treatise on the subject. The sublime, briefly, was an experience of something beyond the realm of human comprehension or even full apperception: the vastness of the Himalayas, the violence of a storm crashing against the shore, volcanic eruptions transforming the landscape, spectacular waterfalls. That these were natural phenomena was no accident, for nature was a place where one experienced a power that could only be God's, and one's incomprehension or terror or sense of helplessness were all appropriate responses to the experience greater than one's own. At the same time, the sublime elevated the human, who alone was able to contemplate and conceive the power of nature and the divine, and could thereby feel exalted (perhaps after the feeling of terror subsided).

Jack Kirby's art surely constituted my first experience of the sublime, through his cosmic images of interstellar space, the monumentality of Asgard at the end of the Rainbow Bridge, and the Negative Zone, to say nothing of such titanic figures as Galactus, who ate planets, and (most sublimely of all) Ego the Living Planet. Kirby's cosmos was all large panels and crackling energies, his machines (including the one that propelled Reed into the Negative Zone) abstract arrays of geometric forms (and more "Kirby Krackle"). These energies were inescapable, and the knowledge that all emanated from the mind and the hand of Kirby—a human motor if ever there was one[2]—added its own level of sublime shock and awe.

The "Star Gate" sequence in *2001* depended upon an in-camera technological effect, slit-scan photography. The sequence, overseen by Douglas Trumbull, renounced traditional representation in favor of abstract forms that somehow evoked, at once, outer space; the streaking, strobing neon of a nighttime car trip; and the filmic experiments of Stan Brakhage and Oskar Fischinger. Dave Bowman's face is frozen in contorted terror, his incomprehension evoking Arthur C. Clarke's axiom: "Any sufficiently advanced technology is indistinguishable from magic" (Clarke was, of course, *2001*'s coauthor). Arrayed lines of light emanate from the vanishing point along the screen's center horizon, and the effect is one of infinite expansion combined with relentless enclosure. Later in the eleven-minute sequence, tinted tracking shots above tundra, volcanic fields, and Monument Valley suggest our arrival at another world, unpopulated, caught between seismic upheaval and luminist repose.

The sequence additionally recalls the brightly colored fragments seen tumbling in a kaleidoscope. The kaleidoscope was an important model of modernist perception, and its ephemeral collages possessed an immediate metaphorical value. Baudelaire, for example, was fascinated by them because, as Jonathan Crary reminds us, kaleidoscopes "coincided with modernity itself." The kaleidoscope was a machine that disintegrated any fixed perspective: "shifting and labile arrangements" became the new, and very appropriate, point of view (Crary 113–114).[3]

What I've called *kaleidoscopic perception* is comprised of equal parts delirium, kinesis, and immersion, and it characterized many popular entertainments of the later nineteenth century, from expositions to magic-lantern shows, panoramas, and travel tours (Bukatman, *Matters of Gravity*). The descriptions surrounding immersive environments such as fairgrounds and

2001: A Space Odyssey (1968): delirium, kinesis, and immersion in the "Star Gate" sequence.

amusement parks—distilled urban realms—were rife with delirious liberation, and while planners of vast world's fairs were inspired by rationalist visions of progress, the midway nevertheless still beckoned, and a pleasurable cacophony carried the day. John Kasson, writing of Coney Island, fabulously captures its fundamental multisensory bombardment:

> As visitors entered the amusement area, they encountered an environmental phantasmagoria, combining characteristics of the beer garden, county fair, Chicago Midway, vaudeville, and circus. . . . We must try to imagine the smells of circus animals, the taste of hot dogs, beer and seafood, the jostle of surrounding revelers, the speed and jolts of amusement rides, and, what especially impressed observers, the din of barkers, brass bands, roller coasters, merry-go-rounds, shooting galleries, and hundreds of other attractions—above all, the shouts and laughter of the crowd itself. . . . Coney Island plunged visitors into a powerful kinesthetic experience that, like the surf itself, overturned conventional restraints, washed away everyday concerns, buoyed and buffeted participants as they participated to its sway." (49)

Engaging with delirium, kinesis, and immersion allowed mass culture to soothe some anxieties. But its consumers also demonstrated a developing *taste* for these sensations. At a time of increasing concentration of power and control, popular recreations offered oceans of irrational pleasures. Technology was usually the vehicle for these effects, but here technology was unleashed against itself, against the rationalist control that usually adhered to technological culture.

Cinematic special effects, usually nested within the rational discourse of science fiction narratives, possess a similar gesture toward an antirationalism. They redirected the spectator to the visual (and auditory and even kinesthetic) conditions of the cinema and, in so doing, brought principles of perception to the foreground of consciousness.

Before the seamless integration of live footage and generated images made possible by digital technologies, cinematic special-effects sequences constituted something of a space apart. Compositing footage of human figures with effects footage posed all kinds of problems in the predigital world, including the introduction of visible grain, color and lighting mismatches, and wobble. It was easier simply to cut from a human observer to the wondrous effect. At these separate and spectacular sites, technological anxieties (the fear of newly experienced technological might) and technological hopes (dazzling views of potential technological progress) were simultaneously on display and perhaps even partly reconciled. *2001* contains many such sequences: the docking of a spaceship with a vast rotating and orbiting space station is one; another is of course Douglas Trumbull's abstract Star Gate sequence, in which Dave Bowman, the lone remaining astronaut, is conducted through a radically other space within which human perception and cognition are woefully inadequate to the newness of the experience. Here, the film moves into a different mode of representation and production to suggest the worlds that lie, as a supertitle puts it, "Beyond the Infinite."

"Beyond the Infinite" not only summons thoughts of the sublime, it echoes Stan Lee's language of two years earlier. This leads to the realization that Kirby's collages constituted special-effects sequences of their own; here it's the collage form that alludes to those spaces beyond human comprehension, *even* when that human is the intellectually formidable Reed Richards. As with the Star Gate sequence, which moves from realist imagery to, well, a kind of light show through which astronaut and spectators together hurtle, Kirby's collages also present interdimensional movement through the shift to another mode of production and perception.[4] The flat lines and color of the drawn comics page yield to an assemblage of objects, presented through the medium of photography.

Reed floats in familiar form: blue uniform, pronounced outline, naturalistic perspective. But what he floats *before* is something else again. Circles and spheres surround him, some clearly suggesting planetary bodies, clustered in ways never before experienced by human eyes, while others are just flat concentric forms with a metallic sheen. A geodesic dome with some evocation of three-dimensional volume dominates the lower space of the collage, but immediately behind it is a flat array of concentric circular shapes that, upon a closer look, don't entirely connect with one another, creating a more Cubist interplay of forms. There are some alterations to the print version: Reed floats more centrally in the original, while on the published page the center position is (ha!) taken up by Lee's word balloon. The colors also have changed, shifting the palette toward a blue that might connote outer space; the original is drenched in copper tones that suggest the inside of a watch or something more unfamiliar. And so this collage, in its language, its purpose, and its mode of production, anticipates, by two years, Kubrick's (and Trumbull's) visual strategies.

The Star Gate sequence and the Negative Zone epitomize what science fiction writer and theorist Samuel Delany has termed the *paraspace*. The paraspace exists parallel to the normal space of the diegesis—it is a rhetorically heightened "other realm." Further, "conflicts that begin in ordinary space are resolved in this linguistically intensified paraspace" (Delany 31). Indeed, the notion of a paraspace might be endemic to the genre of science fiction, as even the earliest texts permit such a linguistic intensification directed toward the exotic spaces of, for example, outer space or the future. The language in such works transcends the descriptive, instead offering the reader an experience of explicit "otherness." The breakneck cyberspace sequences in William Gibson's *Neuromancer* (1984) exemplify the literary strategies at work: "Get just wasted enough, find yourself in some desperate but strangely arbitrary kind of trouble, and it was possible to see Ninsei [a hub location in the novel] as a field of data. . . . Then you could throw yourself into a high-speed drift and skid, totally engaged but set apart from it all, and all around you the dance of biz, information interacting, data made flesh in the mazes of the black market" (Gibson 16).

Delany limits his precepts to the operations of literary texts, but it is easy to find analogues in other media. Cinema is rife with such "heightened rhetoricity," especially in the paraspaces presented by the special-effects work of the science fiction film. In her extensive phenomenological analysis of *2001*, Annette Michelson has demonstrated the breakdown of linear narrative in favor of a spectacularity and sensuality of form, and it is her implicit contention that much science fiction film operates in a similar (if less sustained) fashion. There are profound moments of kaleidoscopic perception in many science fiction films that preceded *2001*—in "The Ultimate Trip" (Bukatman, *Matters of Gravity*, chap. 5), I explored the significance of a slight but similar camera roll in both *Forbidden Planet* (1956) and *The Incredible Shrinking Man* (1957), but it takes over completely that "ultimate trip" of *2001*'s Star Gate sequence, which was anticipated by Kirby's collages of two years before.

It's no kind of exegetical stretch to see Kirby's collages as attempts to rep-

Jack Kirby's collage in *Fantastic Four* #51 (1966) anticipates the visual strategies of *2001*.

resent the movement into another dimension: the scripts tell us so. In one, Johnny, Crystal, Sue, and Ben stand before a vast viewing screen, contemplating the cosmic collage of the Negative Zone; in another, "countless light years away, in a far distant galaxy, a strange shimmering ray shoots out from a planet whose name we of Earth could never even learn to pronounce" (here our linguistic inability stands in for our cognitive limitations); in still one more, "unable to control his capsule-prison, Clark Kent gazes helplessly as he drifts past awesome wonders that stagger all imagination!"— and there are plenty of other examples. At Marvel Comics in the 1960s and during Kirby's tenure at DC Comics in the 1970s, the collage was used most often in the "cosmic" comics for all the stuff the comics themselves used to label "Senses-Shattering!"—at Marvel in *Fantastic Four* and *Thor*[5] and at DC within Kirby's fabled Fourth World saga. Oddly, though, the most, and the most audacious, collages were featured not in *New Gods* or *The Forever People* (sublimely titled comics if ever there were) but in *Superman's Pal Jimmy Olsen*.

In a way, that should not surprise. The book was the first of Kirby's new line to appear, and that first issue in 1970 was famously jammed with new concepts. While it's common wisdom that *Jimmy Olsen* was the most lunatic of Kirby's books,[6] it's surprising to realize that it was also perhaps the most formally audacious as well. In that first issue, two pages of photocollages (three in total, a full page and two half-page images) are introduced by a caption (now written by Kirby himself) that announces: "Without warning, Jimmy Olsen and the Newsboy Legion find their Whiz Wagon careening madly through a nightmare of kaleidoscopic form and color!" In a later issue, Clark (Superman) Kent is "hurled into the unknown." Collages featuring incomprehensible technologies and other-dimensional weirdness continue in the shift from Marvel to DC: in fact, Kirby doubles down.

But let's get back to *Fantastic Four* #51, and Reed floating before a cosmos that even he cannot fully comprehend. Along with special-effects sequences, the circles and spirals, the jumble of shapes and forms, put me in mind of kaleidoscopes. Kaleidoscopic perception is at work in these Kirby collages: characters find themselves "careening madly through a nightmare of kaleidoscopic form and color," after all. As with the slightly later Star Gate sequence, the work moves into another mode of representation ("slit-scan" photography for *2001*, photographic collage for Kirby) to confront another mode of existence. While the photocollages are not marked by the signifiers of movement that characterize a more typical Kirby page—there are no motion lines, for example—there is every sense that the field is in flux; Reed and the others are not gazing upon a landscape painting of the Nega-

A "senses-shattering" Kirby collage in issue #1 of *Superman's Pal Jimmy Olsen* (1970).

tive Zone, for example, but at the pulsations and shifts of an unstable register that cannot be completely known. The kaleidoscopic "trip" through the Star Gate similarly presents an experience that is almost entirely characterized by movement—there are no fixed elements, no anchors to provisionally orient the protagonists.

I wonder what Kirby felt upon seeing *2001* for the first time—did he recognize some of his own strategies at work? Well, something must have resonated, for in 1976, having returned to Marvel, Kirby produced a large-format adaptation of the film, followed by a comic book series that took a host of other characters "beyond the infinite" (one per issue!), evolving each of them into . . . something more. Kirby's adaptation is, unsurprisingly, different from the film that Kubrick and Arthur C. Clarke produced: where the film presented breathtaking images to which the spacefaring protagonists were, until the end, oblivious, Kirby just cannot *do* banal, and neither can his characters. The large-scale pages are drenched in sublime energies—large panels, full-page images, double-page spreads; everything is spaceships, primordial lunar landscapes, and Kirby Krackle. The book also features some of the most abstract imagery Kirby produced within the confines of a comic book, and there is even a collage, illustrating the title page of part two, "The Thing on the Moon."

This collage is unique, however, in depicting the space shuttles, satellites, and space stations in Earth orbit (using photographed elements from the film). For the only time, then, photographic elements are used to represent what they already are, rather than being détourned in the direction of something altogether different. The collage uniquely anchors the reader in plausibility and comparative stability—indeed, banality—while it's Kirby's dynamic, large-scale drawing that moves readers "beyond the infinite." As Dave Bowman enters the other-dimensional realm, the Kirby-written caption sounds like all the collage captions ("It is a *savage* and continuous disorientation which smashes *all* memory and identification with the individual self"), but here this transcendental moment emanates from Kirby's own hand.

The kaleidoscope of swirling forms and nonnaturalistic colors, with the suggestion of a planet-scape in upheaval toward the background, speaks to the film's own brand of psychedelia. That page is preceded by a two-page spread showing the astronaut's pod, tiny in the frame and seemingly floating before an abstract onslaught that suggests planetary forms and tumultuous motion, but, again, Kirby eschews the kind of collage that placed Reed, floating, against the abstract photographed form and instead allows his pen to go wild. Figure and ground are presented in the same visual language, which perhaps suggests that there will be no return for Dave Bowman, *2001*'s astronaut, at least not *as* Dave Bowman. After all, Reed was figured as something apart from Negative Zones and some other briefly visited other-dimensions, while Bowman is now fundamentally and irrevocably a part of whatever he is experiencing. This is reality, and on page after page, Kirby's pen renders this new real, this kinetic, immersive, delirious real, this kaleidoscopic real(m), with explosive energy, simultaneously giving us something apocalyptic and euphoric.

I have so far simply demonstrated artists' recourse to a different representational register to mirror protagonists' encounters with worlds beyond the known or even the knowable. The movement away from mimesis and toward heightened visual rhetoric suggests, or even performs, the failure of the human's perceptual and cognitive abilities to make sense of these paraspatial worlds beyond the infinite. Delany-esque paraspaces are where limits are confronted and where conflicts are resolved; often, they are sites for the redefinition of the human. But I think that more than disorientation is at work in these instances.

Tom Conley has written much on what he calls "cartographic writing" in early modern Europe in terms that seem applicable to paraspaces, comics, and sites of human (re)definition. He notes that maps were unique concatenations of graphic and linguistic elements, places where visual design impacted semantic meaning. They offered up definitions of the self, frequently aligned with the centered subject-position generated by nationalism. They placed the known against the unknown and even posited relations between them, between self-knowing subject and unknown territory. "The unknown, graphically inscribed as *terrae incognitae* on the western and southern horizons of early maps," writes Conley, "was . . . an important element of the maps' overall depictions. It was to be conquered, or at least to become known insofar as the gain of knowledge would assure the discoverer's founding illusion of immortality" (8). Disorientation, then, or defamiliarization, was a step on the road to some form(s) of mastery.

"For the first time," Conley writes, viewers "were able to see the totality of the world *from without while within* its confines, with effects no less dazzling than those of our first reception of images"—wait for it—"of the earth taken from the moon in 1968" (12, emphasis in the original). Conley has unwittingly returned us to the time not only of Apollo 8 but of *2001* and Kirby's *Fantastic Four*. The specifics of his language merit a lengthy excerpt:

> Spectators could imagine themselves in the midst of a mystical voyage
> beyond the confines of a well-beaten space by means of newly known areas

IT IS A *SAVAGE* AND CONTINUOUS DISORIENTATION WHICH SMASHES *ALL* MEMORY AND IDENTIFICATION WITH THE INDIVIDUAL *SELF*-- DAVE BOWMAN *CANNOT* REMEMBER WHO HE IS -- OR HOW HE CAME TO BE... HE HAS BECOME COMPLETELY TRAUMATIZED...

Kirby's rendering of astronaut Dave Bowman entering the "other-dimensional realm" in the 1976 comic book adaptation of *2001*.

being distorted onto flat planes that yielded illusions of a universe of infinite curvature. The viewer of these early maps could thus broach the unknown all the while he or she was leading the grounding paradox of the outside-inside into areas that, at least in narrative and literary domains, could probe conditions of sexual identity, of parentage, of authority, and of kinship within the body of the self. (12)

The Cinerama or 70 mm large-screen viewing conditions under which *2001* was originally experienced also permits, I think, spectators "to imagine themselves in the midst of a mystical voyage beyond the confines of a well-beaten space," using different—but not so different—technical means. Mystical? If we return to Clarke's dictum that "any sufficiently advanced technology is indistinguishable from magic," then yes. The Star Gate sequence, a journey into a cosmic *incognitae,* is presumably abstract simply because Bowman's (and our) cognitive and sensorial apparatus are not up to the task of making it make sense. Throughout *2001,* a projection of "newly known areas being distorted onto flat planes" yields "illusions of a universe of infinite curvature"—curvature being a fundament, as Annette Michelson notes, of the Cinerama screen on which the film was initially projected (58).[7]

But what, exactly, does *2001* map? For Michelson, in her signal appreciation of the film, the film maps for its viewers a new relation between perception, cognition, and corporeality. Michelson's language, steeped in the sensibility of Merleau-Ponty, repeatedly invokes a kind of cartographic mission. "Kubrick's masterwork," she writes, "is designed as an instrument of exploration and discovery" (56). This work about movement, with its forward-tracking shots continually moving us toward enigmas and mysteries, becomes a "voyage of discovery, a progress towards disembodiment" (56). In the scenes that play with gravity and relational movement (docking, stewarding, jogging) haptic disorientation becomes "an agent of cognition." The viewer's own body becomes, Michelson argues, itself weightless, forced to relearn its relationship to the world: "Viewing becomes, as always but as never before, the discovery, through the acknowledgement of disorientation, of what it is to see, to learn, to know, and of what it is to be, seeing. Once the theatre seat has been transformed into a vessel, opening out onto and through the curve of a helmet to that of the screen as into the curvature of space, one rediscovers, through the shock of recognition, one's own body living in its space" (58). *2001,* then, creates a space of viewing in which perception becomes a recognized (re-cognized) and active experience. To align it with Conley's cartographic mode, what gets mapped here (or remapped, reconfigured) is the viewer's own relation to the world and the body—the film creates (maps?) a phenomenological rebirth for the viewer. *Terra incognita* becomes *universum incognitum* becomes *corpus incognitum* and *mentes incognitae*.[8]

So something more than dazzlement *is* at stake in this encounter with the unknown; the unknown becomes a challenge, a demonstration that borders cannot contain everything, cannot resolve all questions—and may indeed pose as many questions as answers. As with the sublime, a paradoxical positioning of human power occurs: on the one hand, the map containing unknown territory constitutes "a language of enigmas—rebuses, ideograms, hieroglyphics—[that] can convey the incommunicability and fascination that the unknown seems to be offering," while at the same time, this mystical unknowability is contained "insofar as the printed and drafted character of the account has been rationalized, proofread, set in letterpress, and distributed" (Conley 12). The diagrammatic and pictographic aspect of maps "affords a new consciousness and a sense of animation that comes with a subject's feeling of depreciation and freedom from confining areas of language" (19).

Cinema and the comics might be understood as particularly invested in some form of cartographic reasoning (Conley leans in this direction when he writes that "cartographic reasoning inspires both the graphic and the imaginary forms of literature" [2]).[9] In both, narration is simultaneously a spatial exploration—whether in the form of an embodied camera navigating space, or in the reader's eye tracing action across the trajectory of the comics page. In both, a tension between the linguistic and the pictorial obtains in such a way that linguistic meaning is challenged and revealed as incomplete. And in some genres of films and comics—science fiction and horror, primarily—human limitations are brought to the fore: in cinema, the limits of human perception and knowledge are engaged, as André Bazin notes, by an embodied camera limited to a single, if mobile, perspective upon a complex world; and in comics, the pictorial treatment of language and the semantic values of pictures complexly interweave. The profoundly descriptive and navigational nature of Trumbull's special-effects sequences—whether in *Close Encounters of the Third Kind* (1977), *Blade Runner* (1982), or even *Star Trek: The Motion Picture* (1979)—betray a cartographic impulse (and the plots of all of these hinge upon exploration and discovery), as do the experiments with page layout and flow that characterize comics innovation from Winsor McCay to Neal Adams, J. H. Williams III, and beyond.

Much of the particular power of comics to map space and time is exemplified by a single page of the alternate-world *Watchmen* by Alan Moore and Dave Gibbons (DC Comics, 1986). The omnipotent superpowered Doc-

tor Manhattan has abandoned Earth to its chaotic and insignificant inhabitants and retreated to Mars, where he contemplates both the universe and
an old photograph. "All we ever see of stars are their old photographs." His
internal monologue links the malleability of memory and Einsteinian space-
time. "The photograph is in my hand," he begins, and the frame shows us
his hand, holding the photo. "It is the photograph of a man and a woman.
They are at an amusement park, in 1959." The photograph is of the person
he once was, and the woman he once loved. The second panel shows the tat-
tered photo fallen to the pinkish sands of Mars.[10] "In twelve seconds time, I
drop the photograph to the sand at my feet, walking away. It's already lying
there, twelve seconds into the future."

Using all nine panels of the three-by-three grid that structures every page
of *Watchmen*'s twelve issues, Moore conflates the time of looking, the time
of the photograph, the time, twenty-seven hours ago, when Doctor Manhattan came upon the photograph hanging on a forgotten wall ("It's still there,
twenty-seven hours into the past. . . . I'm still there, looking at it"), the future
moment of dropping the photograph to the alien soil, which by page's end
is now some seconds in the past. Doctor Manhattan has taken a few steps
away, aware of his helplessness (as well as his lack of interest). Grandly dis-
passionate, he surrenders the photograph and goes off to look at the stars,
whose light "takes so long to reach us." The last panel repeats the second: the
photo on the sand, Doctor Manhattan's footprints, traces of time, the caption "All we ever see of stars are their old photographs." Extradiegetically, the
page demonstrates the comic book's fundamental ability to hold multiple,
sequential images in a simultaneous array. Each image continues to exist on
the page as our eye moves past it. All moments, all images, are contemporary; all moments, all images, have already happened.

Each medium, cinema and comics, has its own affordances. As I argue
throughout *Hellboy's World: Comics and Monsters on the Margins*, cinema's
address to the body, and its engagement with technology, is more fundamental and more profound than it is in the comics. Cinema's impact is frequently a consequence of the embodied act of perceiving; Stan Brakhage
writes of a prelinguistic world that is known through an eye "unruled by
man-made laws" and that "does not respond to the name of everything."
Without the filter of language, the infant encounters everything anew in an
"adventure of perception" (Brakhage). Brakhage's own nonnarrative films
surely exist as such adventures: they fragment time and space, distort optical
norms, and include nonphotographic materials, all to break down habitu-
ated modes of seeing in favor of something more exploratory and uncertain,
less linguistic and "meaningful." Few filmmakers have followed his lead, but

my own experience as a film viewer suggests that many more films hold the *potential* to become perceptual adventures, at least in part, and that an active and creative spectator holds the possibility of unleashing that potential.

Consider Joseph Cornell's hallucinatory *détournement* of the 1931 Hollywood film *East of Borneo* that is his *Rose Hobart* (1936). In jettisoning footage and rearranging the sequence of the rest, in replacing its soundtrack with Brazilian pop music, in slowing it down to silent speed and screening it through colored glass, Cornell demonstrated that beneath the surface of narrative film lurked something altogether more strange. If few films manage to tap into that potential strangeness in any sustained way, they often do in part—witness the special-effects sequences of Douglas Trumbull in such films as *2001* and *Close Encounters of the Third Kind*, or the spectacle of Fred Astaire dancing on the ceiling in *Royal Wedding* (1951).

The cinematic viewer is immersed in that adventure of perception in which perceptual and corporeal limits are both recalled and transcended. But comics are, I think, more *engrossing* than *immersive* and present instead what I've called a complex adventure of *reading* in which syntheses of word and image, image sequences, and serial narratives are continually performed. Comics bring principles of reading to the foreground, as cinema does for perceptual experience.

Despite my great love of both, I cannot possibly make identical claims for the impact of Kirby's collages and *2001*'s special effects: the radicalism of the film's technique makes a point-by-point comparison seem almost silly. But I'm nevertheless struck by Kirby's attempts, both before and after Kubrick's, to make the comics page do something different, making it speak to—perform, actually—altered conditions of existence, perception, cognition, and corporeality—as I'm always struck by popular media's presentation of alternative bodies and alternative ways of being in the world. Kirby's is the pulp version (as are, in film, *Forbidden Planet* and *The Incredible Shrinking Man*), and what it lacks in sensory overload and perceptual reconfiguration it makes up for with crackling energy, visual invention, and just plain punch.

2001 was the first film I saw all by myself—nobody I knew wanted to see it. I went in knowing that it was supposed to be difficult to understand, and I remember calling my father excitedly during intermission to tell him that, hey, I understood it so far. Then, of course, the Star Gate sequence and finale blew my eleven-year-old mind. Yet my confusion didn't disturb me, as it so often does my students. Why didn't the obscurantism of the film bother me? From where did my willingness to go with Kubrick, Clarke, and Trumbull's flow originate? I can't be sure, but I'd like to hazard a guess that Lee and

Kirby had indeed paved the way, and that Kirby's superheroic imagination and otherworldly collages had prepared me for the first profound cinematic experience of my life. Writing now, I am beyond tickled to discover that Kubrick with Trumbull performed an act of aesthetic estrangement not so different, in either purpose or means, from the ones Kirby performed with Lee. These were figures on a common voyage, even as their maps manifested in different media.

Notes

1. This essay takes me back to my earlier writing on cinematic special effects and science fiction's evocation of sublimity and my later writing on the operations of comics — I'm struck by how much of my thinking is synthesized here. See, in particular, "The Ultimate Trip: Special Effects and Kaleidoscopic Perception" and "The Artificial Infinite: On Special Effects and the Sublime," both in *Matters of Gravity: Special Effects and Supermen in the 20th Century* (Duke University Press, 2003); *Terminal Identity: The Virtual Subject in Postmodern Science Fiction* (Duke University Press, 1993); *Blade Runner* (BFI Palgrave, 1997); and *Hellboy's World: Comics and Monsters on the Margins* (University of California Press, 2016). A shorter and rather different version of this essay appeared as "Kirby, Collage, and Kaleidoscopes," in *Comic Book Apocalypse: The Graphic World of Jack Kirby*, edited by Charles Hatfield and Ben Saunders (IDW, 2015), pp. 89–103, and I thank them both for allowing me to repurpose that essay here and for inviting me to participate in the catalogue for their wonderful Jack Kirby exhibition at California State University, Northridge, on display from August 24–October 10, 2015.
2. For the history and implications of the "human motor" concept, see Anson Rabinbach, *The Human Motor: Energy, Fatigue, and the Origins of Modernity* (University of California Press, 1990).
3. *2001*'s vertiginous effects can recall *Ballet mécanique*, the 1924 film by Fernand Léger and Dudley Murphy, of which Jean Epstein growled, "Anyone enchanted by this abstract cinema should buy a kaleidoscope."
4. This is extended in the collages Kirby produced for the later *Spirit World* magazine, though the collages destined for *In the Days of the Mob* provided something more like a gritty documentary authenticity.
5. Beginning in *Journey into Mystery*, which introduced the character in 1962.
6. The infamous two-part Don Rickles homage is exhibit A for the prosecution. Suffice to say the story involves the insult comic's dichotomous twin, "Goody" Rickles, and the minions of Darkseid.
7. Michelson's was one of the first positive assessments of the film.
8. Thanks to Catherine Kearns for the Latin.
9. As well, of course, in his *Cartographic Cinema* (University of Minnesota Press, 2006).
10. This is a visual reference to the iconic photograph Buzz Aldrin took of a footprint on the moon in 1969.

Works Cited

Bazin, André. "The Evolution of the Language of Cinema." *What Is Cinema? Vol. 1,* edited by Hugh Gray, Berkeley, University of California Press, 1967, pp. 23–40.

Brakhage, Stan. *Metaphors on Vision. Film Culture*, no. 30, Fall 1963.

Bukatman, Scott. *Hellboy's World: Comics and Monsters on the Margins.* Berkeley, University of California Press, 2016.

———. *Matters of Gravity: Special Effects and Supermen in the 20th Century.* Durham, NC, Duke University Press, 2003.

———. *Terminal Identity: The Virtual Subject in Postmodern Science Fiction.* Durham, NC, Duke University Press, 1993.

Burke, Edmund. *A Philosophical Enquiry into the Origin of Our Ideas of the Sublime and Beautiful.* Harvard Classics, vol. 24, part 2. New York, Collier, 1909–1914.

Conley, Tom. *The Self-Made Map: Cartographic Writing in Early Modern France.* Minneapolis, University of Minnesota Press, 1996.

Crary, Jonathan. *Techniques of the Observer: On Vision and Modernity in the Nineteenth Century.* Cambridge, MA, MIT Press, 1990.

Delany, Samuel R. "Is Cyberpunk a Good Thing or a Bad Thing?" *Mississippi Review,* nos. 47/48, 1988, pp. 28–35.

Gibson, William. *Neuromancer* (Terry Carr edition). New York: Ace, 1984.

Kasson, John. *Amusing the Million: Coney Island at the Turn of the Century.* New York, Hill and Wang, 1978.

Michelson, Annette. "Bodies in Space: Film as 'Carnal Knowledge.'" *Artforum,* vol. 7, no. 6, 1969, pp. 54–63.

Rabinbach, Anson. *The Human Motor: Energy, Fatigue, and the Origins of Modernity.* Berkeley, University of California Press, 1990.

From Adaptation to Extension: A History of Comics Adapting Films, 1974–2015

BLAIR DAVIS

While the term "comic book movie" is ubiquitous in modern cinema, "movie comics" are not nearly as well known, despite their growing role in the comics industry. Comics have been adapting and extending cinematic narratives and their characters for more than a century, but the relationship between the comics and film industries has evolved significantly in recent decades. With media conglomerates such as WarnerMedia and Disney now owning comic book publishers such as DC and Marvel, the ways in which comics handle cinematic content have become subject to a much different corporate logic than in the early-to-mid twentieth century. In turn, comic books' adaptations and extensions of films have increasingly reflected new industrial and aesthetic concerns since the 1970s.

By tracing the evolution of movie comics from the mid-1970s through the modern era, cyclical patterns emerge surrounding the economic and creative choices behind their production. The history of media in the twentieth century is one of constant intersection, mediation, and cross adaptation, with cycles of adaptation and extension existing throughout. As transmedia storytelling takes hold, and as media conglomerates seek to develop franchises, extensions have now surpassed adaptations as the most popular way to bring films to comics readers.

Bringing films to comics is not a new phenomenon, however. As I've chronicled elsewhere, comics have adapted and extended films for over a hundred years (Davis). Comic strips featuring new adventures of Charlie Chaplin first appeared in 1915, while British series like *Film Fun* and *The Kinema Comic* used stars such as Harold Lloyd, Ben Turpin, Fatty Arbuckle, and Buster Keaton throughout the 1920s (see King and Saxby). The classical era saw comic book series like *Movie Comics* (1939 and 1946), *Fawcett Movie Comics* (1949–1952), *Hollywood Film Stories* (1950), *Motion Picture*

Comics (1950–1953), and *Movie Love* (1950–1953) adapt new films into panel form. Stars such as John Wayne, Alan Ladd, Roy Rogers, Gene Autry, Tim Holt, Buster Crabbe, Bob Hope, and Jerry Lewis all had their own comic books chronicling their further adventures, as did such comedy teams as Abbott and Costello, Our Gang, and the Three Stooges. Comic books based on films and their stars were among the most popular titles with readers in the 1950s and were especially vital to publishers in between the demise of horror comics early in the decade and the resurgence of superhero titles as the 1960s began.

Dell Comics also regularly adapted films in their *Four Color* series, starting with Disney's *The Reluctant Dragon* (1941), *Dumbo* (1941), and *Bambi* (1942). *Four Color* also offered readers the continuing antics of Mickey Mouse, Donald Duck, Felix the Cat, Popeye, Andy Panda, Porky Pig, Woody Woodpecker, and other animated characters, all of whom regularly appeared on movie screens during the era of the double bill. Such feature films as *The Sword and the Rose* (1953), *The Searchers* (1956), *Around the World in 80 Days* (1956), *The Vikings* (1958), *Hercules* (1959), *Rio Bravo* (1959), *Ben-Hur* (1959), *The Time Machine* (1960), *Spartacus* (1960), and *Mysterious Island* (1961) were brought to the pages of *Four Color*, while Dell's *Movie Classics* series offered readers adaptations of *Jason and the Argonauts* (1963), *The Raven* (1963), *Santa Claus Conquers the Martians* (1964), *The Masque of the Red Death* (1964), *Beach Blanket Bingo* (1965), *The Sons of Katie Elder* (1965), and *The Dirty Dozen* (1967). Gold Key Comics' *Movie Comics* adapted Disney films such as *Mary Poppins* (1965), *The Jungle Book* (1967), and *The Love Bug* (1968), along with *Mutiny on the Bounty* (1962), *How the West Was Won* (1962), *X: The Man with the X-Ray Eyes* (1963), *The Fall of the Roman Empire* (1964), *Yellow Submarine* (1968), and *Beneath the Planet of the Apes* (1970).

Films from a wide range of genres and studios (representing both A films and B movies alike) were readily found in comics form on newsstands throughout the 1940s, 1950s, and 1960s. By the time Marvel Comics began offering readers movie-related titles in the 1970s, comics readers had long been able to find their favorite films adapted into panel form. But the strategies by which films were brought to the comics page would evolve over the decades to come.

The 1970s: Apes, Odysseys, and Galaxies Far, Far Away

By the mid-1970s, the comic book marketplace was a very different one than that of a generation prior. Dell Comics stopped publishing titles in 1973, while Gold Key was in decline throughout the decade (eventually ending distribution to newsstands in 1981) (Barrier 346–349). Feature-film adaptations became harder to find on newsstands throughout much of the decade. Just as Hollywood underwent significant industrial and creative changes by the early 1970s (leading to the rise of "New Hollywood"), so too did the comics industry. Marvel Comics had recently positioned itself as a leading publisher, while long-established companies began to fold, and the ways in which readers experienced cinematic content through comics also started to change.

In 1974, Marvel launched *Planet of the Apes* magazine, a black-and-white, magazine-sized title that included comics material alongside articles and photos. After adapting the series' five films, Marvel gave readers new story lines set in the *Apes* world that took place in different eras. The magazine was quickly followed by the comic book *Adventures on the Planet of the Apes*, which lasted for eleven issues between 1975 and 1976 and adapted the first two films in the series. With a low-rated *Planet of the Apes* television series canceled after fourteen episodes in 1974, and a 1975 animated series (*Return to the Planet of the Apes*) that only lasted one season, there was no longer any need for a tie-in comic book. Without new films or episodes to fuel newsstand sales, Marvel canceled *Planet of the Apes* magazine in 1977.

While the ongoing popularity of *Star Trek* reruns helped Gold Key sustain a comic book series based on the show, licensed properties generally lacked value to comics publishers throughout most of the twentieth century (although this would change by the early twenty-first century) if they were not actively supported with sequels and new seasons of episodes. This logic was tested in 1976, however, when Marvel gave renowned writer/artist/editor Jack Kirby the task of first adapting Stanley Kubrick's *2001: A Space Odyssey* and then extending its narrative in bold new directions. Kirby began by creating a *Marvel Treasury Special* of the film, which was twice the physical size of a regular comic book and at eighty-two pages was nearly four times as long. Known for his detailed renditions of cosmic images in *The Fantastic Four* and *The New Gods*, Kirby was naturally suited to adapting Kubrick's film. As with any adaptation, the source material is altered to fit the strengths and limitations of the new medium. The comic uses third-person narrative passages to explain the events from the long, silent stretches of the film. The famous match-cut edit of a bone thrown into the air contrasted with a floating spacecraft becomes multiple panels, with the words, "Moonwatcher sees his enemy fall! He feels a sense of great power. He is master of the world! As the surge of elation sweeps through him, Moonwatcher shouts in victory and throws his weapon to the sky!! Higher and higher it sails—aimed at the infi-

A double-page spread, the comic book equivalent of 70 mm widescreen cinema, in Jack Kirby's 1976 *Marvel Treasury Special* adaptation of *2001: A Space Odyssey* (1968).

nite where the countless stars wait for the coming of man—and man comes to space!! Across the agonizing ages he follows the destiny bequeathed to him by the monolith—for, the second leg of his journey awaits him . . . the time has arrived to take it!!" (Kirby, *Marvel Treasury Special* 12).

While such narration resembles the bombastic descriptions found in other Marvel books like *Thor* and *The Avengers*, the strength of Kirby's adaptation is in how he translates Kubrick's images through his own inimitable visual style, using the book's larger page dimensions to full advantage in his detailed renditions of futuristic technologies, epic vistas, and kaleidoscopic imagery. Numerous full-page panels convey the majestic scope of Kubrick's cinematic compositions and Arthur C. Clarke's concepts, often accompanied by the artist's "krackle" effect using innumerable small black dots to suggest cosmic energy.[1] Even more impressive are the double-page spreads—the comic book equivalent of 70 mm widescreen projection, given how large the book's pages are—depicting the moon's surface, the spacecraft *Discovery One*, and Dave Bowman's journey through the monolith and its ensuing vortex.

Kirby's unique art style, his strategic use of large-scale images, and his kaleidoscopic use of color make this adaptation of *2001: A Space Odyssey* one of the most memorable comics adaptations of a film ever produced. Perhaps even more remarkable is how Kirby followed up this adaptation with an ongoing series in which he explored the "awesome secrets!" of the monolith and its effects on various civilizations in different eons. Each issue declares the series to be "based on concepts from the MGM/Stanley Kubrick production," while the covers include the tagline "Begin a New Journey to the Stars—And Beyond!"

The film's characters never appear in the comics, which instead use the basic premise of the monolith transforming members of primitive societies. In the first issue, for example, a caveman known as the "Beast-Killer" learns how to fashion a spearhead out of stone after encountering the monolith. Kirby reinvents the film's juxtaposition of the bone and the spacecraft by offering matching panels of the Beast-Killer throwing a spear and an astronaut named Decker in the year 2001 throwing an artifact away while marooned on an asteroid. At the end of the story, Decker similarly travels through the monolith, "traumatized by the visual battering of the spectacle! In his present form he cannot survive the experience! Decker must be changed!! As Beast-Killer became man, Decker must become something else!!" the narration decrees (Kirby, *2001* 26; no. 1). Much like Dave Bowman, Decker appears to age rapidly before us, eventually transforming into a "New Seed" (better known as a "Star Child") and soaring away into space in the final panel: "The New Seed answers the call of the beckoning cosmos, as the monolith waits for the maturing of the next to come" (Kirby, *2001* 31; no. 1).

The last three issues of the series focus on a sentient robot named X-51, a.k.a. Mister Machine. The cosmic scope of earlier issues gave way to the more straightforward adventures of a robotic hero, with the radical shift in tone unable to stave off the series' impending cancellation. After ten issues, *2001: A Space Odyssey* came to an end, but not before the final panel promised an upcoming series featuring Mister Machine. Rebranded as Machine Man the following year, the character has had a steady presence in the Marvel Universe ever since (even occasionally serving as an auxiliary member of the Avengers), although his ties to *2001* have been largely forgotten.

Marvel might have been less committed to the *2001* series by 1977 once they received the license to publish comics based on an upcoming new film—*Star Wars*. An editorial printed in all of the publisher's books with a July 1977 cover date (including the eighth issue of *2001: A Space Odyssey*) noted that if the *Star Wars* comic book released that same month "sounds familiar, it might be because we've plugged it a bit in the past, but a much better bet is that you've been hearing about the multi-million dollar, super science-fiction film from 20th Century Fox upon which our comic is based." The editorial mentions that "to do it justice in graphic story format, Mr. Lucas handpicked Marvel for the awesome adaptation task," and "to guarantee [that] the power and scope of the original film are preserved, the adaptation is going to be done in six parts, one issue per month" ("Marvel Bullpen Bulletins" 28). Marvel's use of multi-issue film adaptations was a major shift away from the single-issue approach common at Dell, Fawcett, and Gold Key. By extending cinematic narratives across more than one hundred pages in their *Star Wars* and *Planet of the Apes* books, Marvel dramatically changed the adaptive strategies used to bring movies to comics in the 1970s. The narrative pace of their adaptations was more akin to that of cinema than to the comic books of the 1950s (in which patterns of film-to-panel adaptation were cemented).

With this new approach came occasional liberties on the covers in order to sensationalize the film's events further for prospective readers. The fifth issue's cover shows Luke Skywalker and Chewbacca, surrounded by rebel pilots and an X-Wing fighter, rushing toward the *Millennium Falcon* while the Death Star fires laser blasts at them. "Hurry, Chewbacca! We're being attacked by the Death Star!" yells Luke. The scene never occurs in the film, nor does it appear in the issue itself. Similarly, the cover to issue six depicts Luke and Darth Vader locked in a lightsaber duel, which the two characters never have in the film.

Despite such glaring inconsistencies, the series was well received by readers and ran for over nine years at Marvel. After the initial six issues adapted the film, writer Archie Goodwin (who also penned the *Star Wars* newspaper strip) began telling new stories about the film's characters. "At Last! Beyond the Movie! Beyond the Galaxy!" proclaimed the series' covers. The first page also declared, "Continuing the saga begun in the film by George Lucas," as a way of letting readers know that these were new adventures found only in the pages of Marvel Comics. But these new story lines placed Lucas's characters in some at times bizarre circumstances. By the eighth issue, Han Solo and Chewbacca were fighting space pirates alongside an aging librarian named Don-Wan Kihotay, who believed he was a Jedi Knight, as well as a giant, green, bounty-hunting rabbit named Jaxxon (who describes himself as a "lepus carnivorous") (*Star Wars* 11; no. 8). A few years later, Darth Vader attempts to sabotage Princess Leia's plans to obtain a bank loan for new X-Wing fighters. Rather than kill or kidnap Leia, Vader merely threatens her credit score while advising against reporting his schemes to the local authorities: "It would only do evil things to your credit rating," muses the Dark Lord of the Sith (*Star Wars* 22; no. 48).

Such preposterous aspects aside, Marvel's *Star Wars* series was notable in how it extended the film's narrative in new directions while still attempting to adhere to the continuity established by Lucas. In prior decades, comics featuring John Wayne, Gene Autry, Bob Hope, and Jerry Lewis offered the new adventures of famous stars without tying them to specific films. While it was common for 1960s comic books based on television series like *Star Trek* to feature stories tied to (and taking place in between) particular episodes, given the serialized nature of the source material, comics based on specific films in this era relied primarily on adaptation rather than narrative extension. Narrative continuity became increasingly important to readers of movie comics in later decades, with Marvel's work in the 1970s proving to be a turning point in how the comics industry handled Hollywood films.

As with *Star Wars*, Marvel made another early attempt at negotiating the line between creative liberty and existing continuity with *Godzilla: King of the Monsters*, an ongoing series that ran between 1977 and 1979. Notably, the series takes place within the confines of the regular Marvel Universe, with Godzilla crossing paths with SHIELD, the Fantastic Four, and the Avengers. Marvel was unable to retain the publication rights to the character (Japanese studio Toho is notoriously difficult to deal with in copyright matters), but along with *Planet of the Apes* magazine, *2001: A Space Odyssey*, and *Star Wars*, *Godzilla: King of the Monsters* proved that comics could extend cinematic content through serialized storytelling.

The 1980s and 1990s: Super Specials, Further Adventures, and the Franchise Floodgates

Along with series that offered the continuing adventures of popular film characters and concepts, Marvel also began adapting popular films with its *Marvel Super Special* series. From 1978 to 1986, readers could enjoy such Hollywood blockbusters as *Close Encounters of the Third Kind* (1977), *Jaws 2* (1978), *Star Trek: The Motion Picture* (1979), *Raiders of the Lost Ark* (1981), *Blade Runner* (1982), *Octopussy* (1983), *Dune* (1984), *The Muppets Take Manhattan* (1984), and *Labyrinth* (1986) in panel form. Each issue featured a longer page count than the average comic book, was printed in a larger magazine size, and regularly included promotional photos and "behind the scenes" features about the making of the film. All of these features were designed to make each issue feel more like a collectible souvenir from the film rather than just the mere adaptations found in similar books of prior decades.

DC similarly published what they called a "Collector's Album" for both

Superman (1978) and *Superman II* (1980), with the covers promising a look at the "Stars/Costumes/Set Designs/Special Effects" rather than an adaptation of each film's narrative. With the demise of Dell and Gold Key, adaptations of films were no longer a regular fixture on newsstands, so these "Super Specials" and "Collector's Albums" became a novelty for curious comics fans, because a whole generation had passed since the days in which comic book versions were regularly tied to the release of new films.

As part of their *Super Special* edition of *Blade Runner*, Marvel offered a brief editorial called "Behind the Comics Adaptation" explaining how they approached bringing films to comics readers: "Translating a movie into the comics format takes a bit of doing. While the two forms share some similarities—both use close-ups, establishing shots, etc.—one difference can't be ignored. Films move; comics don't. Unless you have unlimited pages, there is no way to even begin to duplicate the film experience. But, given the right talent, it is possible to convey the feeling and flavor contained in the original work. That's what we set out to do with this magazine" ("Behind the Comics Adaptation" 52).

These ideas of conveying the "feeling" and the "flavor" of the source material are variations on how film creators have long sought to capture the essence or the spirit of a text when adapting it to cinema (see Davis 26, 89–90). All of these are vague terms, of course, but allude to retaining key images, narrative elements, and aspects of characterization. By using enough of these factors in a comic book adaptation of a film, the emotional pleasures (i.e., feelings generated) and resultant tone (or flavor) of the source material can be carried over to a new medium. As the previously quoted editorial implies, it is impossible to fully recreate the content of one medium in another, given the different aesthetic and industrial practices involved, but it is still possible to create a satisfying variation that plays to the new medium's strengths. In this case, *Blade Runner*'s cyberpunk costumes, futuristic cityscapes, and neo-noir lighting work well in the static imagery of comics panels, allowing the reader's gaze to linger upon the contrasts in color, texture, and illumination that make the film such a memorable (but transient) experience.

Marvel also reprinted some *Super Special* issues as limited series (themselves a novelty in the early 1980s), with *Blade Runner* divided into two issues and *The Muppets Take Manhattan* into three standard-size comic books, for instance. DC offered single-issue adaptations of films based on their own characters, such as *Swamp Thing* (1982), *Superman III* (1983), and *Supergirl* (1984), along with occasional versions of such science-fiction/fantasy films as *Little Shop of Horrors* (1986), *Alien Nation* (1988), and the third through seventh entries of the *Star Trek* franchise. After their *Super Special* comics

The comics page conveys the feeling and flavor of the futuristic cityscapes in *Blade Runner* (1982).

ended in 1986, Marvel adapted a few films, such as *House II: The Second Story* (1987), *Who Framed Roger Rabbit* (1988), and *Willow* (1988). But as their ongoing *Star Wars* series enjoyed continuing success through the early-to-mid 1980s, Marvel launched other titles, such as *The Further Adventures of Indiana Jones*, *Star Trek*, and *Freddy Krueger's A Nightmare on Elm Street*, that extended the narrative world of those film franchises.

By the end of the decade, Marvel saw new competition from independent publishers that were licensing the rights to other popular film franchises. Now Comics adapted such films as *Fright Night* (1985), *Fright Night Part 2* (1988), and *Ghostbusters II* (1989), while Dark Horse Comics acquired the rights to publish comics based on the *Aliens* franchise in 1988. While first adapting James Cameron's 1986 film, *Aliens*, Dark Horse soon began offering numerous miniseries taking place in various new settings while creating new characters to fight (and be killed by) the aliens. These were soon followed by numerous comics based on *Predator* (1987), as well as the team-up series *Aliens vs. Predator*—the latter leading to numerous follow-up series from Dark Horse (including those in which the creatures fought Superman, Batman, Judge Dredd, and the Terminator) and even inspiring two feature films in which the two eponymous creatures do battle.

As media theorist Derek Johnson notes, "executives, agents and creators alike" began contemplating ways of growing media franchises by the mid-1980s, with comic books seen as an important part of this process (54). As the 1990s began, independent publishers actively pursued the rights to turn popular films into comic books. The short-lived publisher Topps Comics offered adaptations of *Bram Stoker's Dracula* (1993), *Jurassic Park* (1993), *Jason Goes to Hell* (1993), *Mary Shelley's Frankenstein* (1994), *GoldenEye* (1995), and *The Lost World: Jurassic Park* (1997), hoping to use the popularity of these films as a way of building a larger line of titles (including ones featuring noncinematic characters) that might rival the top companies in the comics industry. While Topps Comics folded in 1998, Dark Horse thrived with their new takes on *Aliens, Predator, The Terminator* (1984), and *Starship Troopers* (1997).

Dark Horse also acquired the publication rights to *Star Wars* in 1991, feverishly expanding the narrative world of Lucas's films with series taking place before, after, and in between the original film trilogy's events. This included chronicling the prehistory of the Jedi in such titles as *Dawn of the Jedi* and *Tales of the Jedi*, the latter taking place "approximately 5000 years before the battle of Yavin," an event depicted in *Star Wars* (1977) (*Star Wars Omnibus*). The scope of the stories being told in such comics was far beyond anything imagined by Marvel in prior decades and correctly anticipated the coming demand for film prequels fleshing out smaller character details, plot points, and backstories.

Conclusion: The 2000s and Beyond

Smaller publishers like Now Comics and Topps Comics failed because they focused exclusively on adaptation, while Dark Horse and newer publishers, such as BOOM! Studios and IDW, have thrived over the past decade by offering extensions of films and film franchises like *Godzilla, Planet of the Apes, Ghostbusters, Back to the Future, Hellraiser, Die Hard*, and *28 Days Later* in ongoing series. While Marvel and DC offered occasional adaptations of blockbuster films and those based on their own characters in the 1990s and early 2000s, such comics are not among their top-selling titles in the same way that licensed books are at Dark Horse and IDW. Smaller publishers have used licensed titles based on movies (and, increasingly, television series) as a way of building their companies and offsetting the potential creative risks taken with nonlicensed titles.

Since the rise of the Marvel Cinematic Universe with *Iron Man* (2008),

A prequel comic book encourages readers to continue the story by watching *Iron Man 3* (2013) in theaters.

however, both Marvel and DC have increasingly used comic books as a way to offer prequels to specific films in the hope of building audience anticipation for their theatrical release. DC's prequel comic for *Man of Steel* (2013) depicts life on Krypton before the planet's destruction, while prequel issues for *Green Lantern* (2011) show the backstories of various characters. Marvel has offered prequel issues (regularly called "Preludes") for all of their feature films since 2008, such as 2011's *Captain America: First Vengeance* and 2015's *Marvel's Avengers: Age of Ultron Prelude—This Scepter'd Isle*. The prequel books typically tie together plot details between films, explore details of a character's past, or foreshadow a new film's villain.

Such comic books are prime examples of transmedia storytelling, which has become an ever more important way to build and maintain media franchises in recent years. As various media corporations have merged in recent decades, the narratives, characters, and concepts of film and television properties have become increasingly extended across multiple media platforms. Many audiences have appreciated the resultant complexity in narrative continuity of a shared "universe" existing across particular films, programs, comics, and video games, while media producers reap the benefits of increased brand awareness and market presence. With Disney acquiring both Marvel and Lucasfilm in recent years, new opportunities for media convergence now exist with both the rise of the Marvel Cinematic Universe and the rebirth of the *Star Wars* film franchise. After taking over the license from Dark Horse in 2015, Marvel published numerous *Star Wars* comics set between *Star Wars* (1977) and *The Empire Strikes Back* (1980), along with series connected to *Star Wars: The Force Awakens* (2015) and the *Star Wars Rebels* television series (2014–2018). With the same parent company owning both Lucasfilm and Marvel, new possibilities emerge for using comics to support and extend cinematic narratives.

As actual adaptations become harder to find from comics publishers, books that offer the further (or prior) adventures of beloved screen characters have become the dominant way in which movies are handled in panel form. The shift to extended narratives is part of a larger pattern in popular culture, such as television viewers embracing "complex" storytelling practices in both cable and network programs favoring serialization over self-contained stories (see Mittell). Movies and comics have a long history of adapting each other, but the balance between adaptation and extending film narratives has shifted to varying degrees over the last hundred years. The patterns that Marvel set in motion in the 1970s have been embraced by most contemporary publishers as newly created stories have largely replaced adapted ones. The interplay between movies and comic books has played an increasingly important role in Hollywood over the past four decades; as the corporate and creative patterns of modern media culture continue to evolve, movie comics will prove ever more vital to publishers and studios alike.

Note

1. For more about the use of "Kirby Krackle," see Charles Hatfield, *Hand of Fire: The Comics Art of Jack Kirby* (University Press of Mississippi, 2012).

Works Cited

Barrier, Michael. *Funnybooks: The Improbable Glories of the Best American Comic Books*. Berkeley, University of California Press, 2015.
"Behind the Comics Adaptation." *Marvel Super Special*, no. 22. Marvel Comics, September 1982, p. 52.
Davis, Blair. *Movie Comics: Page to Screen / Screen to Page*. New Brunswick, NJ, Rutgers University Press, 2017.
Johnson, Derek. *Media Franchising: Creative License and Collaboration in the Culture Industries*. New York, New York University Press, 2013.
King, Graham, and Ron Saxby. *The Wonderful World of Film Fun, 1920–1962*. London, Clarke's New Press, 1985.
Kirby, Jack. *Marvel Treasury Edition: 2001: A Space Odyssey*. New York, Marvel Comics, 1976.
———. *2001: A Space Odyssey*. 10-issue series. Marvel Comics, December 1976–September 1977.
"Marvel Bullpen Bulletins." *2001: A Space Odyssey*, no. 8. Marvel Comics, July 1977, p. 28.
Mittell, Jason. *Complex TV: The Poetics of Contemporary Television Storytelling*. New York, New York University Press, 2015.
Star Wars. 107-issue series. Marvel Comics, July 1977–May 1986.
Star Wars Omnibus: Tales of the Jedi, Vol. 1. Dark Horse Comics, 2007.

Take the Movie Home! How the Comic Book Tie-In Anticipated Transmedia Production

LIAM BURKE

As *Superman Returns* (2006) races toward its third act, criminal mastermind Lex Luthor stops to taunt a weakened Superman by revealing that he was responsible for the false information that sent the Man of Steel on a futile five-year journey to find his home planet of Krypton. In *X2* (2003) Jean Grey survives the climactic action sequence to join her fellow mutants in Washington, DC, where they confront the US president. And in Tim Burton's *Batman* (1989) the money the Joker throws onto the streets of Gotham is revealed to be counterfeit currency with his face on the one-dollar bill. These moments would be unfamiliar to cinema audiences, because they never appeared on screen. Instead, they can be found in the "Official Comic Adaptation" of these blockbusters. Ironically, these films were based on comic books by the same publishing companies that were now (re)adapting them to the page.

Released alongside big-budget films, comic book tie-ins are often quickly produced and just as quickly forgotten. Yet, as demonstrated by Jonathan Gray's popularization of "off-screen studies" (4), the academy is paying greater attention to spin-offs, promotional materials, and other previously ignored paratexts. Nonetheless, the focus tends to be spread across the larger franchises, with some iterations receiving little sustained interest. For instance, the few scholars who have studied novelizations describe the research area as "marginalized" (Mahlknecht 139), "ignored" (Baetens, "From Screen to Text" 226), and deserving of "more detailed critical appreciation than its current reputation suggests" (Allison). The scholar who has perhaps written most widely on the topic, Jan Baetens, argues that the study of novelizations "bring[s] to the fore a certain number of crucial issues in the film and literature field" and "foregrounds the internal hybridization of contemporary media" ("From Screen to Text" 237).

Baetens concedes that novelizations have garnered some interest outside the academy ("Novelization" 45). For instance, the format is regularly the subject of trade paper articles, most of which question the novelization's relevance in an era of home video and streaming services (Suskind; Sloan; Alter). Novelization writers also have an industry body, the International Association of Media Tie-In Writers; however, despite recognizing short stories and audio plays alongside novelizations at their annual Scribe Awards, the association does not have a category for comic books.[1] This omission is made even more glaring by the fact that the ceremony takes place at the annual San Diego Comic-Con. Thus, while some scholars may bemoan the lack of attention the novelization has received, comic book tie-ins have received little interest within the academy or anywhere else.[2]

Yet the comic book adaptation, like its slightly more respectable sister form, the novelization, offers a window onto the creative and formal fluidity that marks today's media industries. Through creator interviews and close analysis of the texts, this chapter positions comic book tie-ins as antecedents to today's transmedia practices and provides a better understanding of why comics, their characters, and their creators form the connective tissue of many modern media conglomerates. To bring this analysis into sharper focus, the key examples in this chapter will be those texts that close the loop between comics and cinema: comic book adaptations of comic book movies.

The Process and Purpose of Comic Book Adaptations

Since the earliest days of the US comic book industry publishers have adapted popular films (and later TV shows), with DC Comics' precursor National Allied Publications releasing *Movie Comics* in 1939, which promised "a full movie for 10¢" and featured imperial adventure *Gunga Din* (1939) on the cover of the first issue.[3]

This long-standing practice has often seen films that were based on comics, such as *Batman, Teenage Mutant Ninja Turtles* (1990), and *Judge Dredd* (1995), return to their originating form via comic book adaptations.[4] Yet despite the volume and longevity of this practice, these comic book adaptations have been given little scholarly attention. This lack of interest may stem from the mistaken belief that a comic book adaptation's source material is the film. As Thomas Leitch suggests, "adapting texts that are largely visual to begin with seems so easy, simple, or natural that the process has limited theoretical interest" (180). However, as *Batman* comic book

Movie Comics, first published in April 1939 by National Allied Publications, adapted popular films such as *Gunga Din* (1939).

writer and editor Dennis O'Neil explains, "the conventional wisdom on those things is that the comic book and the movie have to come out on the same release date" (O'Neil, interview), with the tie-in more often based on a draft of the screenplay rather than the finished film. This reliance on pre-production material is often responsible for the inconsistencies that emerge between the final film and its otherwise faithful comic book tie-in.

This emphasis on release dates has also contributed to the low cultural standing of media tie-ins, with Linda Hutcheon noting how tie-ins are often considered "commercial grabs, unmitigated commodifications, or inflationary recyclings" (119), while Pillai describes how licensed comics are "dismissed as distant echoes of either of their parent media" (103). The production studios and publishers have done little to dispel this reputation, with these media tie-ins serving two key functions: promotion and merchandise. Baetens describes the novelization's ability to "give the movie more visibility in places where it is less advertised, such as bookshops and newsstands," as its "raison d'être" ("Expanding the Field" 71–72). Similarly, most comic book adaptations reuse the film's promotional art for the comic's cover alongside straplines like "Official Movie Comic Book Adaptation" (*X2*). Thus, like film posters smuggled onto the shelves of comic stores, these carefully timed adaptations help build awareness of these new releases.[5]

In addition to their promotional role, these comic book adaptations also provide an additional revenue stream, and if the publisher is a subsidiary of the same conglomerate as the studio, as in the case of WarnerMedia companies DC Comics and Warner Bros., then there is an even greater incentive for such synergy. Comic book creators are also enticed by the economic potential of these adaptations, as well as the control it offers them as fans and creators. For instance, reflecting on his experience of the 1989 *Batman* adaptation, writer Dennis O'Neil recalled, "I think I got more money than I'd made on anything up to that point. I don't know that anybody expected it to be the big hit that it was" (O'Neil, interview). O'Neil would go on to write the comic book adaptations for the film's three sequels, as well as the novelizations of *Batman Begins* (2005) and *The Dark Knight* (2008).

While also identifying making a living as a motivation for working on projects such as the *Star Wars* (1977) novelization, prolific tie-in writer Alan Dean Foster points to his interest as a fan: "I got to enlarge on the characters; if there was a scene I particularly liked, I got to do more of it, and I had an unlimited budget" (Suskind). A number of scholars have described how media tie-in creators are steeped in fan culture (Baetens, "From Screen to Text" 229; Gough 42; Alter), with M. J. Clarke quoting his interview with a writer of the *24* comic book tie-in in which the comic creator identified the porous boundary between "enthusiastic professional" and "fan fiction" writer (*Transmedia Television* 40). Thus, many media tie-in creators are professional writers attracted to tie-ins by the opportunity to work on their objects of interest. In this way these enthusiasts become examples of the textual poachers Henry Jenkins famously described, in that they borrow elements from their object of devotion and repurpose them for a new context.

For some media tie-in writers, however, their interest extends beyond fandom to a greater sense of ownership and responsibility. Jeremy Strong notes how the author of *First Blood*, David Morrell, used his role as the writer of the novelization of the film's sequel, *Rambo: First Blood Part II* (1985), to reclaim "authorial control" over a character that had become a right-wing action hero in the films (331). Similarly, longtime *Dick Tracy* writer Max Allan Collins adapted the 1990 film version as a novelization, noting that "I sought the job because at the time I was the writer of the comic strip. . . . So I had a proprietary attitude" (Collins). Years later Collins would adapt the screenplay based on his own graphic novel *Road to Perdition* (2002) as a novelization, explaining, "With *Road to Perdition*, I really had a proprietary attitude because it was my story—I created it, writing the graphic novel (Richard Piers Rayner was the artist, a brilliant one). I lobbied for that job because I didn't want anybody else doing a novel version" (Collins).

Fundamentally, the financial benefit coupled with the opportunity to work on a favorite property entices creators to contribute to media tie-ins even if the process might not always be aesthetically satisfying. However, what attracts customers to these seemingly redundant cash-ins? Comic book adaptations tend to serve three broad functions for consumers: souve-

nirs for fans, especially completists; proxies for those who missed the original or want to reexperience it; and summaries prior to the next installment.

John Fiske describes how collecting in fan culture "tends to be inclusive
rather than exclusive. . . . The individual objects are therefore often cheap,
devalued by the official culture, and mass-produced" (44). Thus, despite the
low cultural standing of media tie-ins, for the avid consumer these branded
products are collected alongside T-shirts, action figures, and Pez dispensers.
As Dennis O'Neil reflects, "I always assumed when writing those things that
one of my jobs was to provide a souvenir for the movie[;] in fact on that first
Batman in 1989, I think the comics were sold in movie lobbies" (O'Neil,
interview).

However, O'Neil later added, "It's a tricky job because you have to provide
that souvenir, but you also have to assume that some of your readers will not
have seen the movie" (O'Neil, interview). Indeed, for some audiences these
media tie-ins may be the only way to experience a text that is not available
to them. For instance, in 1992 DC Comics published a comic book adaptation of the Fox television show *Batman: The Animated Series* (1992–1995).
The fifth issue of *The Batman Adventures* included a letter from a Canadian
reader in which he explained, "Us poor, unlucky souls in Montreal will not
be able to see the new Batman animated series since we don't have a Fox af-
filiate here. As such, quite a few of us are thrilled to at least be reading stories
based on the series." Even those audiences who manage to see the original
films or TV shows turn to tie-ins for "repetition of the pleasure experienced
while watching the film" (Mahlknecht 143) and as a means of "staying in
touch with the movie" (Baetens, "From Screen to Text" 227). Indeed, this
experience is promised by the books, with the *Daredevil* (2003) comic book
adaptation assuring readers that "this adaptation captures all the cinematic
excitement of the new movie."

Baetens links the emergence of the novelization in early cinema partly to
the popularization of the "one-reel format centered around the same character having a new adventure in each installment" ("Novelization" 53). Today,
with the dominance of media franchises, tie-ins have gained renewed purpose as mid-installment summaries. For instance, the four-part *Captain
America: Civil War Prelude* comic series was actually a direct adaptation
of earlier films *Iron Man 3* (2013) and *Captain America: The Winter Soldier*
(2014), but rather than position these comics as adaptations, promotional
copy invited readers to "Follow the road to Marvel's CAPTAIN AMERICA:
CIVIL WAR."[6]

Despite low cultural standing and limited critical attention, comic book
tie-ins serve a number of important and interrelated functions for pro-

ducers, creators, and consumers. Yet there are a number of different types of books produced under the broad heading of comic book adaptation, with the dominant book produced at any one time symptomatic of the shifting relationship between comics and cinema.

A Taxonomy of Comic Book Adaptations

Adaptation studies is rife with categories offered by scholars hoping to bring precision to a topic that is often diffuse, with Brian McFarlane suggesting of these taxonomies that the scholar "will need to understand what kind of adaptation he is dealing with if his commentary on an individual film is to be valuable" (11). While the limitations of such categories have been well argued (Cartmell 24), they do provide a standard by which wider determinants might be understood. Drawing on past taxonomies, I argue for four broadly identifiable categories of comic book adaptations.

The first and perhaps most recognizable category includes comics based directly on films. In these *direct adaptations* a premium is placed on fidelity, as the stated goal is to replicate the film experience, or, as the cover of the *Batman Returns* (1992) comic book adaptation announced, to "take the movie home!" Accordingly, this group tallies with the category of adaptation that Dudley Andrew describes as "transformation," where the assumed task is reproducing "something essential about an original text" (100). These direct adaptations were particularly important in the 1980s and early 1990s, when the blockbuster paradigm had been established but the films were not as readily accessible following their initial release. In an era of digital distribution platforms, direct adaptations are less frequently produced. For instance, after *Batman Begins*, neither of the film's sequels received a comic adaptation. Today direct adaptations have been superseded by tie-ins that extend a film's narratives.

A 2015 *New York Times* article describes how novelizations have "taken on a patina of respectability," as they no longer directly adapt the narrative of the film but rather fill in gaps in the story (Alter). Anticipating today's transmedia franchises, comics have a long history of *transmedia extension*. For instance, with the seventh issue of the original series, Marvel's *Star Wars* comics transitioned from the first category, direct adaptation, to the second, transmedia extension. The issue (cover dated January 1978) was the first following the conclusion of the film's narrative and included a "Special Note to Star Warriors," in which the editor described how the comic's creators had "become the first team to carry forward the legend of Luke Skywalker, Han

Solo, Princess Leia, and company beyond the storyline of the blockbusting 20th Century Fox movie release." Through this and similar examples (*Alien*, *The Terminator*, *RoboCop*), comics have served as an important site for producers and fans looking to continue the adventures of their favorite screen heroes. For instance, *Batman: The Animated Series* writer Paul Dini described how the comic book tie-ins were not "a simple knock-off," but afforded him the opportunity "to do *Mad Love*, a graphic novel that not only revealed [popular villain] Harley Quinn's heretofore unknown origin, but also won the comic industry's highest award, the Eisner, for the best single issue in 1994" (Dini and Kidd).

While media convergence made the original texts more accessible and direct adaptations somewhat superfluous, it also found audiences becoming migratory. This environment placed an emphasis on media tie-ins that extend the central narratives. As comic book publishing is steeped in such transmedia extensions, Marvel is unsurprisingly at the vanguard of this transition, rounding out the Marvel Cinematic Universe with books like *Marvel's the Avengers Prelude: Fury's Big Week*. The comic's blurb excitedly announces, "The newest installment of the official Marvel Cinematic Universe tie-in comics is here just in time for the Avengers movie!" with the story following superspy Nick Fury as he orchestrates the various events that link stand-alone Marvel movies *Iron Man 2* (2010), *Thor* (2011), and *Captain America: The First Avenger* (2011).

While the direct adaptations of the 1980s and 1990s might have been considered transformations, the films themselves tended to be what Andrew would describe as "borrowing" (98), in that they were looser reworkings of the comic book characters. This infidelity left a space for direct adaptations, as there was little overlap with the ostensive urtext. However, as I argue in *The Comic Book Film Adaptation*, the post-2000 boom in comic book film adaptations was marked by increased fidelity (159). This shift included the first comic book film transformations, such as *Sin City* (2005), *300* (2007), and *Watchmen* (2009), which faithfully followed their source texts. Accordingly, direct (re)adaptations of these films would have been redundant, with publishers instead repackaging the original comics to take advantage of the renewed interest.

Even within the larger category of film borrowings, the source became an increasingly important determinant. For instance, when promoting *Batman Begins*, director and cowriter Christopher Nolan identified the 1989 origin story "The Man Who Falls" as a "jumping off point" for the adaptation ("Genesis of the Bat"). The Dennis O'Neil comic opens with a young Bruce Wayne falling down a well before retelling key moments in Batman's origin, a narrative device Nolan's film also employs.[7] The importance of this comic was reinforced when "The Man Who Falls" was collected alongside the film's direct adaptation and "Other Tales of the Dark Knight" in a *Batman Begins* trade paperback. Readers riffling through the paperback must have experienced a certain sense of déjà vu as the sequence of Bruce falling down the well opens the direct adaptation only to reappear sixty-six pages later in "The Man Who Falls."[8]

This repackaging of key comics as a primer for audiences brings us to the third category of comic book adaptations, *digests*. André Bazin, citing Sartre, describes film adaptation as a "digest," explaining that it is "literature that has been made more accessible through cinematic adaptation . . . as if the aesthetic fat, differently emulsified, were better tolerated by the consumer's mind" (49). Similarly, for readers enticed by the film, a trade paperback such as *Ant-Man: Scott Lang*, released to coincide with the cinematic debut (2015) of the character, cherry-picks the most relevant stories from decades of the character's publication history. These digest comics, alongside more faithful comic book movies, are reflective of the growing importance of comics within the conglomerate structure and the culture more generally. Where once the original comics were so poorly regarded that they were ignored by producers, and new tie-in comics were created to accompany a release, today the films follow the comics so closely that direct adaptations are often unnecessary, with studios and publishers instead opting to repackage the original comics as the "source material."

The fourth major category of comic book adaptations, *pastiche*, has become increasingly popular in recent years and demonstrates how the hand-crafted nature of the form allows comics to avoid some of the limitations of live-action production. In 2013 Adam West's Batman swung back into action forty-five years after the television series (1966–1968) went off the air. The intervening decades had done little to dampen the hero's verve, as the character was now paper and ink. *Batman '66* is a monthly comic replete with retro styling and pun-laden dialogue that promises "new stories inspired by the classic TV series!"

In charting the evolution of the novelization, Baetens identifies the "elite or highbrow" novelization that is produced long after a film has been released and is thus "totally disconnected from the marketing context" ("Expanding the Field" 55). He goes on to explain that rather than attempt to produce direct adaptations, writers of these highbrow novelizations offer "a personal viewpoint on the world of the cinematic images" (55). Similarly, *Batman '66* writer Jeff Parker, who identifies himself as a "fan" of the TV series, describes how he eschews fidelity and prides himself "on being able to step away from [the series] and realize what's just slavish mimicking, and what gets the spirit of it" (Sims). While the "spirit" of the source is impossible to quantify, Parker's interpretation of the series chimed with critics, with reviews describing how the pastiche "might just fit right in with the spirit of the show's better episodes" (Cecchini).

The success of *Batman '66* saw the tie-in joined by a growing roster of postmodern pastiches that includes the TV show adaptations *Wonder Woman '77* and *X-Men '92*. A number of scholars have noted how adaptations serve a nostalgic function for their knowing audience (Cartmell 26; Corrigan 36; DeBona 41). Freed from the marketplace demands that beset synchronous tie-ins, these pastiche books have met that desire for the industry's aging, more self-aware readership who have exhausted episodes of the show but still want to relive those earlier experiences.

How these four categories of comic book adaptations rise and fall in popularity and relevance is symptomatic of the changing relationship between comics and cinema. When home video was limited and the original comics were roundly ignored by unfaithful feature films, direct adaptations dominated, but as digital distribution has seen the creative industries embrace transmedia narratives, a process comics have been engaged in for decades, the emphasis has shifted to transmedia extensions. The visibility gained by the comic book industry and its readership in the digital age resulted in more faithful adaptations that rendered direct adaptations redundant, with the source elevated through new editions and carefully curated digests. Bringing a number of these interests together, the popularity of pastiche adaptations of long-canceled shows demonstrates the aging readership of comics and the ability of comics to revisit stories no longer available to film and television.

Key Considerations

From their cover blurbs to their publication dates, most comic book adaptations of films explicitly position themselves as media tie-ins. While this might result in them being dismissed as opportunistic cash-ins, these synergistic productions provide unobstructed insight into the key interactions between comics and cinema, including authorship, continuity, and medium specificity.

Authorship

M. J. Clarke describes how the production of tie-ins is orchestrated "to minimize contact and interaction between all the participants," such as producers, licensors, editors, and writers ("Strict Maze" 439). Describing the type of material tie-in writers tend to receive prior to working on an adaptation, *Road to Perdition* creator Max Allan Collins remarked that "it varies greatly. On some of the big action films, like [the] *Mummy* movies, I occasionally got the same promo reel shown to the people deciding whether or not to do a Happy Meal or a lunch box or whatever. Usually I got some photographic material. Occasionally I got nothing at all" (Collins). Within that vacuum creators respond as all adapters do, by being "first interpreters and then creators" (Hutcheon 18).

For instance, Dennis O'Neil explained how the limited page count of a standard comic book necessitated removing a subplot from his *Batman Forever* (1995) adaptation that detailed the reasons for Bruce's guilt over his parents' death: "It wasn't necessary to understand the story, and you've got to cut more than 100 pages from somewhere" (O'Neil, interview). Ironically, while the scenes were shot (with footage appearing in the promotional trailer), the subplot was also largely removed from the theatrical release. In the DVD special features, screenwriter Akiva Goldsman explains that the sequences showed a young Bruce reading his father's last diary entry, in which he described feeling compelled to go on the family's ultimately fatal trip to the movies to placate his son—a subplot the screenwriter describes as a "much darker version of the movie" ("Shadows of the Bat"). Thus, in this instance, the comic creator and the filmmakers independently arrived at the same result.

Such creative harmony is rare, however. For instance, O'Neil recalls how while working on *Batman* (1989) he tried to predict, based on the preproduction script, "what they were likely not to cut and proceed accordingly. In that case, there is a scene in the movie where the Joker drops dollar bills from a balloon onto the streets of Gotham, and they turn out to have his picture on them. I thought 'surely this will make the final cut of the movie.' But it didn't, bad guess" (O'Neil, interview).

Some interactions can prove even more stifling. Collins describes the "terrible experience" of writing the novelization of the 2003 film *Road to Perdition*, which was based on his own graphic novel. He explains, "I was forced to cut my 75,000-word novel to 40,000 words, making me remove anything said or done by my characters that [wasn't] in their movie" (Collins). Given the dangers of deviating too far from the corporate line, most creators strive to exploit what Clarke describes as "leeway": "a matter of finding space either in the script (in the case of artists' layouts) or in editorial mandates (in the case of writers)" (*Transmedia Television* 48). Some creators use this leeway to reassert authorial control and comment on the adaptation process. For instance, *Teenage Mutant Ninja Turtles* creators Kevin Eastman and Peter Laird wrote the comic book adaptation of the 1990 film based on their original series, which included an epilogue in which reporter April O'Neil pitches the story to a publisher at "Mega Comics," with the publisher deeming the idea "too far-fetched" to work "as the basis for a comic book."

In the absence of clear corporate supervision, many creators rely on their knowledge as fans or their experiences working on the original comics to fill in the narrative gaps provided by the limited guidelines and sparse production materials.[9] For instance, describing the experience of adapting the DC Comics video game *Injustice: Gods Among Us* back to comics, writer Tom Taylor remarked, "As a huge DC fan I know how Batman and Superman have the *World's Finest* friendship at their core, and they don't just want to punch each other in the face" (Taylor).

While comic book tie-ins might provide creators with some leeway to assert their authorial control, there is an acceptance that their work serves a greater corporate function. As O'Neil comments, "You focus on the job. You don't focus on what a wonderful writer you are or that you hope to be recognized as because that's irrelevant to what you're doing" (O'Neil, interview). This pragmatism is prized in tie-in creators. Clarke quotes one tie-in writer who noted, "Reliability and dependability is almost more important than sheer talent" ("Strict Maze" 441). Such adherence to a larger mandate has been a cornerstone of mainstream comic book publishing for decades, where creators would conform to house styles and coordinate with many other creators working in the same shared universe. Transmedia producer Jeff Gomez notes that within today's transmedia franchises, filmmakers, showrunners, and comic book creators often serve as "I. P. Stewards" for a larger vision. Comic book tie-ins presaged this shift toward collaborative authorship, and thus it is unsurprising to find multiple comic book properties and their creators at the key junctures of today's transmedia franchises. As Bart Beaty points out, the high volume of comic publishing "has a great deal to teach us about collaborative authorship, audience knowledge, and editorial oversight in the culture industries" (109).

Continuity

Linda Hutcheon describes how "recognition and remembrance are part of the pleasure (and risk) of experiencing an adaptation; so too is change" (4). Adapters must contend with this tension between maintaining a connection with the source, so that audiences can view the adaptation as an *adaptation*, while also navigating the changes that inevitably occur when a story is reworked for a new context. The strict commercial and industrial pressures of comic book tie-ins intensify these issues for the creators, but for the critic it can sharpen an understanding of the key tensions in the intersection between comics and cinema.

J. Mahlknecht believes that "with novelization, repetition is arguably more important than variation" (144). Yet while cover blurbs may promise, for example, "the comic adaptation of the blockbuster motion picture" (*Fantastic Four*), many scholars are quick to point out that tie-ins tend to be based on a film's screenplay and early production material (Allison; Baetens, "From Screen to Text" 230; Clarke, *Transmedia Television* 37; Mahlknecht 141). Consequently, faithfulness to the script can actually result in a comic book adaptation that is unfaithful to the finished film. For instance, while *X2* concludes with Jean Grey sacrificing her life to save her fellow mutants, this was a midshoot change to the screenplay that was not included in the comic, which sees the hero survive.

The issue of fidelity is compounded for those creators who have worked on the urtext. Mahlknecht notes how tie-in writers will often try to eliminate "plot holes in the script" that might have occurred due to "limited running time" or "sloppy screenwriting" (153). For instance, after thirteen years writing the *Dick Tracy* strip, Max Allan Collins describes how the novelization was "a rough job because they fought me when I would put in references to the strip that weren't in the movie. Later, however, I was told by one of the producers that I had solved plot-hole problems and written dialogue that they used in the final film" (Collins). Similarly, longtime *Batman* writer and editor Dennis O'Neil established the "Bat-bible," an editorial guide that ensured character consistency across the hero's many titles. One of the key tenets of the bible was that "Batman never kills. . . . If he did not consider human life inviolable, he would not be the Batman" (O'Neil, "Bat-bible"), a rule Tim Burton's *Batman* films frequently ignore. Yet in the tie-ins, which O'Neil wrote, the writer is careful to avoid explicit depiction of Batman killing his villains, going so far as to change sequences in the otherwise faithful (re)adaptations. For instance, in one memorable sequence from *Batman Returns* the hero repurposes a villain's bomb by affixing it to an otherwise unstoppable strongman. In the film the bomb explodes, presumably killing the strongman, while in the comic book adaptation Batman safely disposes of the explosive by throwing it down an empty sewer.

Within the narrow fidelity of direct adaptations, however, creators are limited in their ability to rework the script. O'Neil included an inventive "visual cue to our regular readers that this is not the Batman you're used to" (O'Neil, interview). The comic book adaptation of *Batman* opens on a movie

The first page of the comic book adaptation of *Batman* (1989) opens with a visual cue that the story falls outside regular comic book continuity.

theater audience, with the story emerging from a film reel while a caption reads, "It's just a movie, for heaven's sake." The *Batman Forever* tie-in acknowledges the comic's true source, with the first panel emerging from the film's script, replete with a slug line, "EXT. ARKHAM ASYLUM—NIGHT," while the *Batman & Robin* (1997) comic opens on the set of the film, where the director Joel Schumacher (identifiable by his long, gray hair) is positioning costume-clad actors in front of a green screen—an implicit critique of the franchise's increasing reliance on computer-generated imagery (CGI).

The move from direct adaptations to transmedia extensions has seen a shift from strict fidelity to a more fluid continuity, where the focus is on uniformity between the differing versions rather than adherence to a particular story. Such continuity has been the bedrock of shared comic book universes for decades, but it is now the goal of transmedia franchises. To reconcile the need for fidelity and variation in transmedia extensions, many creators exploit plot points in tie-ins that were ignored or skirted over in the main texts. Clarke calls these opportunities "unexplored gems" ("Strict Maze" 447). As more and more gems are unearthed, the boundaries between what were once paratexts and the main text have become unclear, a liminal condition Peter Lunenfeld anticipated in 1999 when he suggested conglomerate strategies have "bloated the paratext to such a point that it is impossible to distinguish between it and the text" (14). But the long-standing continuity of comics, exemplified by their transmedia extensions, provides a model for how to traverse this environment and further underscores why comics lend themselves so readily to today's transmedia franchises.

Medium Specificity

Robert Stam notes that a "variation on the theme of fidelity suggests that an adaptation should be faithful not so much to the source text, but rather to the essence of the medium of expression" (58). Baetens, however, describes the novelization as "anti-adaptation," as it "goes out of its way to adopt a low profile and to avoid marking the semiotic rupture that the change from film to book entails" ("Novelization" 49). Similarly, Dennis O'Neil notes how industrial pressures limit a medium-specific approach in comic book tie-ins: "Movies, comic books, and novels are different story delivery systems and they all have their strengths and weaknesses. And so in a perfect world, you would rethink the story that the movie people wrote in terms of your own medium. But I didn't feel I should do that, or I'm not sure I would have been permitted to do that. I had to stick pretty closely to the movie" (O'Neil, interview). Accordingly, to cement the relationship between the adaptation and the source, a premium is often placed on visual and narrative fidelity in the comic at the expense of embracing the form's unique means of expression.

But this faithfulness is made more difficult by the limited resources available to writers and artists who begin working on their tie-ins during the feature film's production. Therefore, early promotional material available to the artist tends to be faithfully recreated in the comic. For instance, one of the first promotional images released for *X2* was the villain Magneto in his plastic prison holding a guard in midair, a scene diligently replicated in the comic down to the positioning of the villain's toothbrush.

Clarke describes how a number of the artists he interviewed use photographs, screen grabs, and image editing software to ensure a greater likeness in their adaptations while working on comic book tie-ins. Such techniques might be more faithful, but they are at odds with one of the "principle characteristics of narrative drawing" identified by Thierry Groensteen: "synecdochic simplification" (134–135). Groensteen contends that narrative drawing "often evacuates that which is not necessary to the intelligibility of the represented situation" (135). For instance, artist David Yardin, who has adapted the DC Comics video game *Injustice: Gods Among Us* as a comic, described how faithfulness chafed against the comic form's proclivity toward more selective imagery: "People ask me what I don't like to draw, it's usually licensed video games or movie designs. . . . In comics, traditionally it's been kind of a streamlined representation of the costumes, Superman is just the underwear on the outside. . . . So it can be a bit of a chore incorporating all these elements that work well in other mediums [to comics]. They can translate across, but it's a lot of work to make them look the same as they do in the other mediums" (Yardin).

Comic book adaptations will often import filmic devices to strengthen their link to the film. For instance, the 2003 film *Hulk* features a sequence in which Betty Ross recalls a childhood memory of an explosion at an army desert base. The flashback uses saturated colors and panel-like shot transitions, in keeping with the film's larger comic aesthetic. However, in a pattern that is both ironic yet commonplace, while the film is striving for a comic aesthetic, the comic itself adopts filmic devices. In the comic book adaptation of *Hulk* the flashback sequence is realized in sepia tones that replicate antiquated photography rather than more medium-specific devices, such as Ben-Day dots.

This "*indirect contamination* of one media regime by another" (Baetens, "Novelization" 44) has been identified in tie-ins by a number of scholars, who describe these adaptations as blurring "inherent medial difference" (Mahlknecht 143), as "complex examples of medium hybridity" (Pillai 103),

Where possible, comic book tie-in artists emphasize visual fidelity in their adaptations by faithfully replicating early promotional images (*X2*: film and comic).

and as foregrounding "the internal hybridization of contemporary media" (Baetens, "From Screen to Text" 237). I have previously articulated the cross-pollination between the comics and film languages in comic book movies as a relay: "In moving between comics and cinema, these codes knit the forms closer together thereby widening the overlap and increasing the opportunity for further semiotic exchange" (Burke 172). Although the comic book adaptation is an explicit example of this type of exchange in which specificity is diminished to facilitate the flow of content across multiple media platforms, it can be found across many creative industries.

Baetens suggests that the "contemporary novel tends to be read as itself already a novelization, albeit an imaginary one" ("Novelization" 56). Similarly, comic book publishers have often sought for their books to be viewed as film adaptations in waiting. For instance, Marvel Comics primed many of its characters for adaptation in the early 2000s with a streamlined Ultimate imprint. Through the use of widescreen panels and black gutters, the Ultimate comics compelled readers (and filmmakers) to imagine what a film version might look like. It should therefore be unsurprising that when the adaptations were eventually produced, Ultimate books appeared in the digest collections that accompanied releases such as *Daredevil* (2003), *Hulk* (2003), and *Spider-Man 2* (2004).[10]

Modern entertainment conglomerates favor content that spreads across multiple platforms. While this ambition does invite moments of semiotic exchange, it can also lead to the erosion of medium specificity. In this respect comic book tie-ins, which were born of two media, were the canary in the transmedia coal mine.

Conclusion

In the October 1992 issue of the *Batman: The Animated Series* tie-in comic, *The Batman Adventures*, one reader wrote of *The Batman Adventures*, "It's not the original comics, nor is it the TV series. The animators have adapted the animated series by stretching the original comics creation. The comics series further stretches the TV series so that we have a third generation work." By describing the tie-in comic as a "third generation work" in active engagement with other versions, the reader articulates a more dialogic view of adaptation favored by many scholars (Brooker 62; Hutcheon 8; Stam 31). The wider creative industries have now embraced this fluidity as part of larger shifts to cross-platform paradigms. However, as the 1992 letter suggests, comic book adaptations have long been a fertile site of collaborative authorship, fluid continuity, and semiotic exchange, anticipating the transmedia turn in today's creative industries.

Notes

1. Max Allan Collins, cofounder of the International Association of Media Tie-In Writers, explained in an email to me, "Our focus has been prose. Also, the comic book industry has plenty of awards to cover them, in my view. I can't think of one tie-in novel nominated for a [Mystery Writers of America] Edgar [Award] or the science-fiction Hugo Award—[cofounder] Lee Goldberg and I wanted to remedy that" (Collins).

2. The limited attention comic book tie-ins have received within the academy has tended to focus on their function as brand extensions and licensed properties within larger transmedia franchises—for example, M. J. Clarke's analysis of *Heroes* and *24* comic book spin-offs in *Transmedia Television*; Kerry Gough's analysis of the Dark Horse comics based on the *Alien* franchise; and Nicolas Pillai's article on the *X-Files* comic book tie-ins, "'What Am I Looking At, Mulder?'"

3. Like DC, Marvel Comics also made judicious use of film adaptations. For instance, in one licensing coup Marvel secured the rights to publish the *Star Wars* comic book adaptation on the eve of the film's record-breaking release in 1977.

4. Film and television adaptations have formed the backbone of many publishers that lack the intellectual property (IP) of Marvel and DC Comics, such as Gold Key Comics (*Star Trek*, *The Twilight Zone*, and *Walt Disney's Mickey Mouse*), Dynamite Entertainment (*Army of Darkness*, *The Terminator*, and *RoboCop*), and Dark Horse Comics (*Aliens*, *Buffy the Vampire Slayer*, and *Star Wars*). The appeal of these comic book adaptations for such IP-deprived publishers is simple; the licenses offered ready-made characters with a built-in audience. Even publishers with recognizable characters, such as Marvel and DC Comics, will try to siphon off the interest generated by these blockbuster films, with direct comic book adaptations of the films simply one of the more explicit examples.

5. The importance of these books as promotional paratexts is further evident in how rarely they are republished or made available from online comic distributors. As Mahlknecht notes of the comic book adaptation's sister form, "since novelizations are so closely linked to the film's cinematic release, once a film's run in theaters is over the novelization's duty has been fulfilled" (151).

6. Fans anticipating the next franchise installment often scour promotional comics in case they might provide insider knowledge of the upcoming film. For example, a number of websites posted articles on possible "Easter eggs" in the *Batman v Superman* prequel comics distributed exclusively by soft drink maker Dr. Pepper (Burlingame).

7. Commenting on the comic book fidelity of the Christopher Nolan *Batman* adaptations, O'Neil remarked, "The last three Batman movies, not counting the *Batman v Superman* thing, in their own way, they were very faithful to what we had done and often when I was reading through the scripts that involved Ra's al Ghul, I was thinking, 'Wow, they really understand this character, they really got it'" (O'Neil, interview).

8. Like *Batman Begins*, later Nolan films were indebted to fan-favorite comics. For instance, *The Dark Knight* includes the doomed partnership between Batman, Com-

missioner Gordon, and District Attorney Harvey Dent from *The Long Halloween*, while the Joker's origin (or lack thereof) recalls *The Killing Joke*. Thus, it should be unsurprising that the later films did not receive direct comic adaptations.

9. Often creators working on the monthly comics will also be hired to produce the comic book adaptations: for example, Bruce Jones was writing the *Incredible Hulk* book at the time he adapted the 2003 *Hulk* film; Chuck Austen adapted *X2* and wrote *X2 Prequel: Nightcrawler* while serving as Marvel's writer on *Uncanny X-Men*; and Dennis O'Neil adapted the four Burton/Schumacher films as comics during his tenure as *Batman* editor.

10. The digest collection published to coincide with the theatrical release of *Daredevil* included the film's direct adaptation alongside *Ultimate Daredevil and Elektra* #1; the *Hulk* digest included both *The Ultimates* #5 and *Ultimate Marvel Team-Up* #2 and #3 alongside the "Official Movie Adaptation"; and the *Spider-Man 2* collection included *Ultimate Spider-Man* #14 and #15.

Works Cited

Allison, Deborah. "Novelisations and *Capricorn One*." *M/C Journal*, vol. 10, no. 2, 2007, http://journal.media-culture.org.au/0705/07-allison.php.

Alter, Alexandra. "Popular TV Series and Movies Maintain Relevance as Novels." *New York Times*, 4 January 2015, http://www.nytimes.com/2015/01/05/business/media/popular-tv-series-and-movies-maintain-relevance-as-novels.html?_r=0.

Andrew, Dudley. *Concepts in Film Theory*. Oxford, UK, Oxford University Press, 1984.

Baetens, Jan. "Expanding the Field of Constraint: Novelization as an Example of Multiply Constrained Writing." *Poetics Today*, vol. 31, no. 1, 2010, pp. 51–79.

———. "From Screen to Text: Novelization, the Hidden Continent." *The Cambridge Companion to Literature on Screen*, edited by Deborah Cartmell and Imelda Whelehan, Cambridge, UK, Cambridge University Press, 2007, pp. 226–238.

———. "Novelization, a Contaminated Genre?" Translated by Pieter Verrmeulen. *Critical Inquiry*, vol. 32, no. 1, 2005, pp. 43–60.

Bazin, André. "Adaptation, or the Cinema as Digest." *Bazin at Work: Major Essays and Reviews from the Forties and Fifties*, edited by Bert Cardullo, translated by Bert Cardullo and Alain Piette, New York, Routledge, 1997, pp. 41–52.

Beaty, Bart. "Comic Studies: Fifty Years after Film Studies." *Cinema Journal*, vol. 50, no. 3, 2011, pp. 106–110.

Brooker, Will. *Hunting the Dark Knight: Twenty-First Century Batman*. London, I. B. Tauris, 2012.

Burke, Liam. *The Comic Book Film Adaptation: Exploring Modern Hollywood's Leading Genre*. Jackson, University Press of Mississippi, 2015.

Burlingame, Russ. "Batman V Superman: Easter Eggs and Clues in the Dr. Pepper Prequel Comics." *Comicbook*, 12 March 2016, http://comicbook.com/2016/02/16/batman-v-superman-easter-eggs-and-clues.

"The Business of Novelization & Tie-Ins Part Three: The Characters." *International Association of Media Tie-In Writers*, 22 June 2013, http://iamtw.org/articles/business-part-three-characters/.

Cartmell, Deborah. "Text to Screen: Introduction." *Adaptations: From Text to Screen,*

Screen to Text, edited by Imelda Whelehan and Deborah Cartmell, London, Routledge, 1999, pp. 23–28.

Cecchini, Mike. "Batman 66 #1 (DC Comics) Review." *Den of Geek*, 5 July 2013, http://www.denofgeek.com/us/books-comics/batman/147713/batman-66-1-dc-comics-review.

Clarke, M. J. "The Strict Maze of Media Tie-In Novels." *Communication, Culture and Critique*, vol. 2, no. 4, 2009, pp. 434–456.

———. *Transmedia Television: New Trends in Network Serial Production*. New York, Bloomsbury, 2013.

Collins, Max Allan. Interview by Liam Burke. 31 July 2016.

Corrigan, Timothy. "Literature on Screen, a History: In the Gap." *The Cambridge Companion to Literature on Screen*, edited by Deborah Cartmell and Imelda Whelehan, Cambridge, UK, Cambridge University Press, 2007, pp. 29–44.

DeBona, Guerric. "Dickens, the Depression, and MGM's David Copperfield." *Film Adaptation*, edited by James Naremore, New Brunswick, NJ, Rutgers University Press, 2000, pp. 106–128.

Dini, Paul, and Chip Kidd. *Batman Animated*. New York, Harper Entertainment, 1998.

Duncan, Randy, and Matthew J. Smith. *The Power of Comics: History, Form and Culture*. New York, Continuum, 2009.

Fiske, John. "The Cultural Economy of Fandom." *The Adoring Audience: Fan Culture and Popular Media*, edited by Lisa A. Lewis, London, Routledge, 1992, pp. 30–49.

"Genesis of the Bat: A Look at the Dark Knight's Incarnation and Influences on the Film." DVD bonus content. Performed by Christopher Nolan. *Batman Begins Two-Disc Deluxe Edition*, Warner Home Video, 2005.

Gomez, Jeff. "Transmedia Storytelling Masterclass." Lecture, Australian Centre for the Moving Image, Melbourne, 10 October 2014.

Gough, Kerry. "Translation Creativity and Alien Econ(c)omics: From Hollywood Blockbuster to Dark Horse Comic Book." *Film and Comic Books*, edited by Ian Gordon, Mark Jancovich, and Matthew P. McAllister, Jackson, University Press of Mississippi, 2007, pp. 37–63.

Gray, Jonathan. *Show Sold Separately: Promos, Spoilers, and Other Media Paratexts*. New York, New York University Press, 2010.

Groensteen, Thierry. *The System of Comics*. Jackson, University Press of Mississippi, 2007.

Hutcheon, Linda. *A Theory of Adaptation*. New York, Routledge, 2006.

Jenkins, Henry. *Textual Poachers: Television Fans and Participatory Culture*. New York, Routledge, 1992.

Leitch, Thomas M. *Film Adaptation and Its Discontents: From "Gone with the Wind" to "The Passion of the Christ."* Baltimore, MD, Johns Hopkins University Press, 2007.

Lunenfeld, Peter. *The Digital Dialectic: New Essays on New Media*. Cambridge, MA, MIT Press, 1999.

Mahlknecht, J. "The Hollywood Novelization: Film as Literature or Literature as Film Promotion?" *Poetics Today*, vol. 33, no. 2, 2012, pp. 137–168, doi:10.1215/03335372-1586572.

McFarlane, Brian. *Novel to Film: An Introduction to the Theory of Adaptation*. Oxford, UK, Clarendon Press, 1996.

O'Neil, Dennis. "Bat-bible." Unpublished document received by Liam Burke via email, 26 September 2010.

————. Interview by Liam Burke. 7 June 2016.

Pearson, Robert E., and William Uricchio. "I'm Not Fooled by That Cheap Disguise." *The Many Lives of the Batman: Critical Approaches to a Superhero and His Media*, edited by Roberta E. Pearson and William Uricchio, London, BFI, 1991, pp. 182–213.

Pillai, Nicolas. "'What Am I Looking At, Mulder?'" *Science Fiction Film and Television*, vol. 6, no. 1, 2013, pp. 101–117.

"Shadows of the Bat: The Cinematic Saga of the Dark Knight; Part 5, Reinventing a Hero." DVD bonus content. Performed by Akiva Goldsman. *Batman Begins Two-Disc Deluxe Edition*, Warner Home Video, 2005.

Sims, Chris. "'Batman '66' Writer Jeff Parker and Artist Colleen Coover: The Comics Alliance Interview, Part One." *Comics Alliance*, 2 April 2014, comicsalliance.com /batman-66-jeff-parker-colleen-coover-interview-part-one/.

Sloan, Will. "The Endangered Art of the Movie Novelization." *Hazlitt*, 20 February 2014, http://hazlitt.net/feature/endangered-art-movie-novelization.

Stam, Robert. "Beyond Fidelity: The Dialogics of Adaptation." *Film Adaptation*, edited by James Naremore, New Brunswick, NJ, Rutgers University Press, 2000, pp. 54–78.

Strong, Jeremy. "Rambo on Page and Screen." *A Companion to Literature, Film, and Adaptation*, edited by Deborah Cartmell, Chichester, UK, John Wiley, 2012, pp. 330–341.

Suskind, Alex. "Yes, People Still Read Movie Novelizations . . . And Write Them, Too." *Vanity Fair*, 27 August 2014, http://www.vanityfair.com/hollywood/2014/08 /movie-novelizations-still-exist.

Taylor, Tom. Interview by Liam Burke. 17 April 2016.

Yardin, David. Interview by Liam Burke. 17 April 2016.

Manga, Anime, Adaptation: Economic Strategies, Aesthetic Specificities, Social Issues

CHRIS REYNS-CHIKUMA

The practice of adapting manga (Japanese comics) to anime (Japanese animation) is historically as long-standing as that of Western comics-to-animation adaptation. Beyond being merely forms of cultural production, *manga* and *anime* refer to an aesthetic, economic, and ideological world with key differences from its American counterpart. These differences are often difficult to understand because of the ways in which anime and manga reflect their distinctive culture's ethnocentric biases and economic interests. This chapter considers the key specificities of manga, anime, and their adaptations by discussing some of the major authors and studios, events and activities, characters and aesthetics (seriality, interactivity), as well as the social issues that inform them, arguing that these vibrant cultural forms are inextricably tied to and part of the larger landscape of cultural production in Japan. Overall, I want to show that manga and anime are fundamentally more transmedial than North American animation was, at least from the start.

Some Cultural Specificities

As shown by Scott McCloud, mangas[1] have some formal specificities, such as a slightly different ratio of "frame-to-frame transition" categories (e.g., more "aspect-to-aspect transitions"), more depictions of the environment, and more subjective views that can be seen, for example, in the subjective speed lines (McCloud 74–82, 112–114). Mangas also tend to be more visual, as in the *chibi* (extremely deformed traits) and other specific facial conventions, like "blood gushing from the nose when sexually aroused." Additionally, a great number of onomatopoeias are more ostensibly spread on the page. This extravisuality might be attributed to the fact that mangas are usually printed in black and white instead of color and therefore must deploy alternative techniques to visually distinguish different elements. Hence, in order to distinguish one character from another, hair is emphatically spiky or features hair antennae instead of being black, brown, or blond. This perspective on Japanese specificities has also been theorized by Neil Cohn under the designation of "Japanese Visual Language" (JVL), in which most Japanese, and Japanese artists in particular, learn to practice a similar visual language as opposed to the West, where one is pushed to learn his or her own visual language from elementary school (Cohn).

Also, although creating mangas is first an individual activity, work organization for commercial publication is more a collective effort in Japan. Publishing studios tend to be structured with a complex set of horizontal and vertical relations between members and are headed by a leader, usually the editor (Kinsella). Working conditions are hard, with long hours, strict deadlines, and low wages. But in spite of these conditions, collaborative creativity is effective, as it provides an encouraging sense of accomplishment and unity to workers and has led to economic success for many artists and their industry. Finally, manga is fundamentally serial and is prepublished first in weekly or monthly magazines on cheap paper (i.e., pulp) and then, sometimes, if commercially successful, in a small-book format on better-quality paper (*tankôbon*).

Likewise, Japanese animation, which inherited numerous aesthetic conventions from manga, also has its specificities. If most of the symbols are similar (e.g., the big eyes to express emotions or the little finger up to refer to an affair), in anime they are set in motion (e.g., anger signs pulsing above characters' heads). But anime creates the impression of movement instead of representing it. Some foreigners still regard this limited animation as a flaw or limitation (which it was at the beginning, when it was done for economic reasons) instead of a stylistic choice with specific meaningful possibilities (which it quickly became, given the necessity to develop strong characters, among other things, to compensate). The tradition of *kamishibai* (paper theater)[2] and the regular reading of manga before watching the anime made it easier for the Japanese to accept this limited movement, which implies bigger blank spaces (gutters) between the pictures. Most of these techniques (using a subjective point of view, creating the impression of movement, bigger blank spaces, etc.) tend to invite viewers to participate more actively with their imagination than does Western animation. It also allows fans to build their own new stories by buying and positioning action figures, cosplaying, or creating anime music videos and other remixes. Finally, contrary to Western animation, voices in anime are recorded after the visuals. The result is that speech and mouth movement are less synchronized, which can be jarring to and poorly received by some Westerners. To compensate, greater emphasis is placed on expressive vocal performance, reinforcing the strong emotional aspects of the drawing through *chibi* and the like.

As of 2010, anime accounts for 60 percent of Japanese film production. The 1990s and 2000s are considered to be "Japanese Cinema's Second Golden Age," due to the immense popularity of anime, both in Japan and abroad.[3] However, anime is basically serial through its main medium, television, often as an adaptation from serial magazines. Nevertheless, if television production dominates, profit overwhelmingly comes from DVD and tie-in sales rather than through television advertisement. Most animes are based on mangas, so that these animes were for a long time called "TV manga," but many are also based on video games (such as *Final Fantasy* and *Pokémon*) or other media, such as "light novels" (i.e., a short novel illustrated with manga/anime-style pictures). Many of these animes differ to some degree from their original sources, even if the author of the manga is also the director of the anime. This is mainly because films and television series are different media with different constraints, namely time and money: it costs much less to publish a manga than to produce an anime. It is also due to the fact that far from the auteurist dogma, the studio closely adapts mangas and animes to the consumers' demand and the social context. Some anime series are original, but most are also intended to promote other products, such as an ongoing manga or video game series. Because they refer to other Japanese products (e.g., toys) not sold outside Japan, or because they are too specifically Japanese (e.g., featuring Japanese mythology), most do not make it to the US or Western markets.

All these industries have also promoted, early and systematically, phenomena like manga clubs, cosplays, and manga and anime conventions. These phenomena spread abroad through "fansub" (i.e., anime subtitled by fans rather than licensed translators) and "scanlation" (i.e., fan-made scanning, translating, and editing of manga), two activities that disseminated their products first through VHS and then through posting on the internet. Manga, anime, and the connections between them are much more dominant in Japanese culture than comic books, animation, and their various transmediations are in Western cultures. Hence, cultural anthropologist Ian Condry defines anime as referring to "Japanese animated film and television, but the worlds of anime extend well beyond what appears on the screen. Anime is characteristic of contemporary media in its interconnected webs of commercial and cultural activities that reach across industries and national boundaries" (1). As the industrial structures of the entertainment industries have increasingly been driven by convergence, the extensions of narratives into diverse media formats such as comic books and films have grown in significance. But in Japan, this convergence took place earlier and more systematically (Steinberg).

Despite fierce competition, especially with American cultural industries (e.g., Hollywood, Walt Disney Studios), Japan's own cultural industry flourished after three decades of successfully developing almost only electronic hardware such as radios, TV sets, and computers. Hence, contrary to DC and particularly Marvel in the 1960s, which created few new cultural products after the 1970s, Japanese studios have been at the forefront of technological and software innovation since the 1980s, and more dynamically so, as I later will demonstrate with the case of *Pokémon*.

Explaining Success

There are many interconnected factors to explain the success of manga and anime and the connections between them in Japan. One factor is certainly the long and rich tradition of the publishing industry in Japan, including books that resembled manga in as early as the eighteenth century (Kern). A second factor might be the less disruptive separation between written and visual signs in Japanese traditions. The written Japanese language comprises mostly kanjis,[4] that is, Japanese ideograms. These are drawn as much as they are written; this is readily apparent in the country's strong calligraphy heritage, still very much alive today in schools and private clubs. Similarly, and as a third factor, for a long time pictures and words were not as systematically separated in Japan's painting conventions and its printing industries, compared to the more radical split between pictures and words from the sixteenth century onward in the West that led to logocentrism and theorizations of art specificities (Lessing's *Laocoon*, 1767). Another, related factor in manga and anime's popularity in Japan is the cultural necessity of constantly reinforcing reading and writing skills. Japanese ideograms are much harder to remember than Western alphabets, and they need to be practiced as often as possible. Hence, many educators and children find that reading them in any format, especially in manga, is not only entertaining but also useful and engaging.[5]

Another reason for manga and anime's success might be that in artistic studios, like in many Japanese companies, work organization mixes both horizontal relations emphasizing collaboration among colleagues and vertical relations accepting hierarchy based on an ideology of consensus (Kinsella). Evaluating the industry ten years later, Condry further emphasizes a "soul" of anime created through "collective social energy" (2). This might have led to a more unified "Japanese Visual Language" (Cohn) than in the Western comic world, one that is easier to produce and reproduce, teach and learn, and gain the acceptance of consumers, "prosumers," and "produsers" (consumer-producers). Yet another factor is that lingering traditional practices and modern protectionist rules, as well as the convergence of industries and collaboration with administration and government (i.e., MITI, the Ministry of International Trade and Industry) facilitated a unified market, which quickly and systematically catered to many audiences through age segmentation (child, teen, and adult), while still producing cross-age series (for families).

Genre categories are also broad, so that almost anything can be the topic of manga and anime — comedy, detective stories, fantasy, sci-fi, history, war, martial arts, sports, economics, instructional or educational material, experimental genres, underground subject matter, porn — while including genre crossings, like slapstick humor in the detective anime *The Castle of Cagliostro* (1979). Some genres are specific to manga and anime, such as "mecha" (stories with robots, often giant ones), which is extremely popular in Japan, most notably in *Astro Boy* (1950s–1960s) and *Gundam* (1980s) as well as the recent *Gurren Lagann* (2007–2013). Markets have also been segmented according to clearly delineated gender categories (*shôjo*/girl, *shônen*/boy, *seinen*/male adult, *josei*/female adult). For instance, *shôjo* uses *bishônen* protagonists (beautiful boys) drawn mainly for female audiences, while it is also more open to other genre classifications and to cross-gender genres like male gay romance (BL/boy love) and female gay love for women (*shôjo-ai*). Japanese society as reflected in manga and anime tends therefore to be more tolerant than US society, which is influenced by a more conservative and superior morality, still visible today in most superhero stories (McLelland 1).

Another factor might seem paradoxical, but in a country where public demonstrations of emotions are more controlled (Araki and Wiseman), more emotions are explicitly shown in mangas and animes than in Western comics and animation, through facial and gestural exaggerations and caricature-like expressions next to realistic representations — hence, a more systematic use of the big eyes and *chibi*. Often, this extreme expression is even more emphasized by the absence of background. These exaggerated features could be interpreted as a way to facilitate catharsis or as an emotional escape valve due to the fact that Japan is a "high context culture" in which people tend to communicate implicitly through facial expressions,

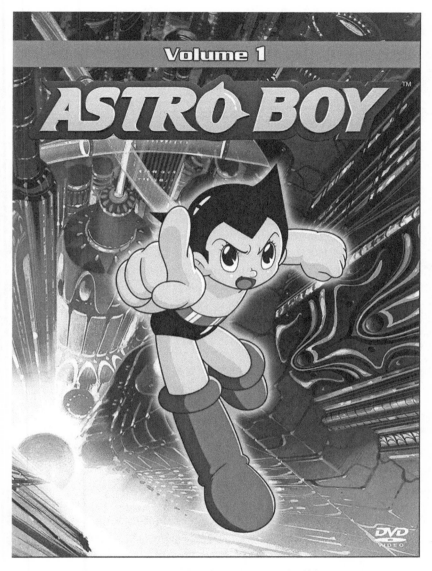

Astro Boy's anime style and sci-fi origins are evident on the DVD cover.

gestures, silence, and tone of voice rather than through explicit verbal messages (Hall).

Also, the Japanese tend to read manga in weekly or monthly magazine formats anywhere and at any time, although especially during usually long and frequent train and bus commutes. These magazines can be found everywhere in bookstores, libraries, and convenience stores located at every street corner. Moreover, readers often have easy access to the copies in these stores, so that they can test if the mangas are pleasing without the intervention of cultural gatekeepers (e.g., critics). In the last decades, animes are also easily accessible, thanks to portable electronic devices. Manga and anime appear on many different platforms, such as computers, phones, and tablets, which also gave rise to digital mangas.[6]

The role of television is also more dominant, especially in its relation to animation in Japan, than it is in Western countries. Although the last two decades have been thought to mark the end of the television era in the world, some critics have shown that this is not the case in Japan. Rather, the television industry there quickly took advantage of streaming (both legal and illegal) through the internet. The completion of the 634-meter-tall Tokyo Skytree broadcast tower in 2012 (the tallest in the world) further testifies to television's enduring importance in Japanese society (Lamarre 54).

Traditional binary distribution between movie theaters and "TV" has been challenged by new post-television technologies such as the internet and with particular vigor in Japan, given that the country is more connected in terms of infrastructure and devices than anywhere else in the world. In the same way, it is essential to emphasize that the split between anime and live-action film is less clear in the digital age in terms of its production and distribution. Many live-action films produced today, especially the ones inspired by comic books (American and Japanese), use computer generated images (CGI). Effects that were once specific to comic books because they were easy to draw and were much more difficult to represent in realistic live-action movies are now used regularly in these movies. But since the United States dominates the global market of live-action movies and TV with its special effects and live-action fare, Japan seems to have chosen the manga-anime path, enabling successful competition with American animation.

Also, in Japanese culture the divide between production and consumption is less pronounced than in American culture and has given birth to a lively, very productive "prosumer" culture, with manga conventions, cosplays, fansubs, and *dôjinshi* (mangas produced by fans). This is partly due to the fact that in manga and anime "the principle of creativity revolves around characters, which in turn encourages extensions by not limiting anime worlds to one story" (Condry 83) and makes merchandising easier (Steinberg).

Finally, contrary to what is often thought in the West, and in spite of a more unified "Japanese Visual Language" (Cohn), manga and anime represent a great diversity of styles, both in drawing and narration. For example, not all creators use big eyes (e.g., Miyazaki and *mangaka* Taniguchi Jirô do not), and this diversity further manifests in the presence of several underground-comics worlds (Quigley).

Histories of Manga

As it is possible to trace the history of comics back to the Middle Ages (e.g., to the Bayeux Tapestry and stained glass) and even beyond (to murals in Egyptian pyramids) (McCloud 13–15), manga is sometimes ahistorically and nationalistically connected to the eleventh-century *e-makimono* (such as the picture scroll of the *Genji monogatari*), the twelfth-century *toba-e* (Buddhist scrolls like the *Chôju-giga* that feature animal caricatures), and *ukiyo-e* (woodblock prints like Hokusai's *The Great Wave off Kanagawa*) produced in the seventeenth to nineteenth centuries.[7] A more precise historization, however, goes back to the eighteenth and nineteenth centuries. Backed by a long and rich tradition of drawing and painting that from the seventeenth century onward was itself influenced by Western arts and sciences (mainly through Deshima, the Edo Dutch trading post), and later both by native forms of animation like the *kamishibai* and by Western comic strips, modern manga appeared first in Japanese newspapers (Kern). The first modern manga were often editorial cartoons and were published in newspapers and magazines like *Puck* at the end of the nineteenth century and *Tokyo Puck* from 1905. From then on, Japanese comics and animation were a mixture of Eastern (Japanese, Chinese, Indian) and Western (American, European) influences in their technology, techniques, forms, conventions, and content (from local and Eastern folktales to new Western topics and genres like sci-fi).

Almost contemporary with the Lumières' *L'arroseur arrosé* (1895) (a comics-to-movie adaptation) and Winsor McKay's *Little Nemo* (1911) (a comics-to-animation adaptation), the first adaptations in Japan date from the beginning of the twentieth century. As early as 1913, US and European animations arriving in Japan were immediately imitated. The earliest commercial animation dates to 1917.

If not much happened, in terms of comics adaptation and animation, between the two wars, during World War II foreign films were banned. Pop culture had been deemed futile, and shortages of material limited further development of the industry; thus, it was only by the end of the war, in January 1945, that propaganda animes came out, of which the two films on Momotaro (Peach Boy) were the first theatrical feature-length releases in Japan.

After some years of slow production during the postwar period, when Japan was in ruins, the anime industry developed quickly. Berndt writes that "in the 1950s, the Tôei Dôga Studio aimed to become the 'Disney of the East' and aligned itself with the national cinema. Yet since around 1970, the main format for anime production has not been the single work for a more or less universal audience, but TV series addressed to specific taste groups" (86).

The King of Manga: Fame and Issues

The typical anime style with which Americans are now familiar emerged in the 1960s with Tezuka Osamu's work. It is with him that both the manga and the anime industries and art fully developed. Being from a wealthy family, Tezuka was able to watch Walt Disney animations like *Snow White and the Seven Dwarves* (1937) many times in a private setting even before the war started.[8] After abandoning his career as a doctor, he published his first manga, *New Treasure Island*, in 1947 and *Kimba the White Lion* in 1950. Then in February 1952, his most famous and recognizable manga, *Astro Boy*, began serialization in *Weekly Shônen Magazine*, and in 1953 he published what was the first *shôjo* manga, *Princess Knight*, serialized in *Shôjo Club* until 1956. In 1961 he founded his own company, Mushi Production, as a competitor of the then powerful Toei Animation studio. It produced his first anime, adapted from his manga *Astro Boy*, in 1963, which became his first national, then international, success and catalyzed the golden age of Japanese manga and anime. Seeing how Disney's animations could be understood in different countries, he believed that manga and anime could also become international languages. As a result of these factors, many young Japanese artists began to emulate his style as early as the 1960s (Schodt, *Dreamland Japan* 223–274; Lunning).

Astro Boy tells the story of a highly advanced robot boy created by a scientist to replace his deceased son. The robot fights criminals, monsters, and other bad robots but always for peace. The *Astro Boy* success was followed by many others, most of which were first manga then anime produced for children. Later, under pressure of the younger generation, Tezuka also strongly contributed to the more mature adult manga of the period, includ-ing *gekiga* (dramatic genre) titles such as *Phoenix* (1967–1988), *Black Jack* (1970s), *Ayako* (1972), and *Buddha* (1972–1983). However, out of the more than 150,000 pages (seven hundred volumes) that he drew, some mangas were not adapted to anime, such as the famous *Message to Adolf* (1983–1985).

As for anime's aesthetic aspects, Tezuka experimented early on with cine-matic techniques, such as slow motion in a single panel to quick changes between two panels, zooming in from distance to close-up shots and vari-ous angles. At the beginning, he devised a system of limited animation in which only one part of the image—a character's eyes or lips—moved, saving on cells and costs. He also started an "animation bank" of cells with typical poses and expressions that could be used several times, further cutting down the cost and allowing him to compete in foreign markets (hence *Astro Boy* was on American TV screens as early as the mid-1960s).

Also, he was the first to use manga and anime's typical big eyes, a fact that is often a topic of debate. Some say that he drew big eyes under the influence of cartoon characters like Betty Boop and Mickey. However, the single influ-ence of US cultural production is contested in this case since the visual style might have come from the big-eyed dolls produced industrially in Japan in the 1920s. As well, even if big eyes are meant to embody ideal beauty and are often presented as connected either to Asian and Japanese self-hatred or to the desire to more easily sell the big-eyed characters, I believe they could also be interpreted as a way to better express emotions, which is essential in Japanese manga and anime.

Following his death at sixty in 1989, Tezuka's reputation grew to reach the status of "god or king of manga" (*manga no kami*). In 1994, a museum was built in his honor, and a Tezuka theme park (supposedly twice the size of Tokyo Disneyland!) opened in 2003.

Studio Gainax: New Mecha and the *Otaku* Debates

In addition to Tezuka's studio, other studios, such as Gainax, developed suc-cessfully. Officially founded in 1984 by four university students and fans of science fiction, Gainax produced big successes, such as *Royal Space Force: The Wings of Honneamise* (1987) and more recently the *Diebuster* saga (2004–2006). Gainax seems to take pleasure in creating stories that resist "monolithic readings" (Cavallaro, *Art of Studio Gainax* 6) and therefore en-courages readers/viewers to be prosumers of meaning. Similarly, its incor-poration of kanjis and both syllabaries "attests to the studio's allegiance to a semiotic sensibility steeped in Eastern tradition, and particularly in pictographic and ideographic forms of writing" (18). Furthermore, it redefined genres, such as mecha, from what was often a simple glorification of virile heroism to stories "lacerated by insecurity and doubt" (12). Gainax's history was for a long time "a story of continual failure, yet the company built enough of a reputation that it was asked to help on a variety of projects" (Condry 132).

In December 1994, almost one year before the release of the TV broadcast *Neon Genesis Evangelion*, a mecha anime, director Anno Hideaki worked on a manga with artist Sadamoto Yoshiyuki with the common explicit goal of using it to induce public interest in the anime, scheduled for release in October 1995. While the anime series ended in March 1996, the manga ended in 2013, fifteen years after the conclusion of the TV anime. The TV series ending, which was ambiguous and unsatisfying for many fans, was then followed by a first feature-length film entitled *The End of Evangelion*, released in 1997. This was followed by two more films in 2003 and 2007, both of which provided alternative endings.

As in many mangas and animes, *Neon Genesis Evangelion* is set years after a worldwide apocalypse in the futuristic fortified city of Tokyo. As Napier (*Anime*) explains, Japan regularly goes through cataclysmic natural events, such as tsunamis and earthquakes, and is also the only country that was the victim of the atomic bomb (see also the manga *Akira*). The protagonist, Shinji, is a teenage boy who was recruited by his father to pilot a giant bio-machine called an Evangelion into combat with alien beings called Angels. The story explores the experiences and emotions of Evangelion pilots as they try to prevent the Angels from causing another cataclysm and undertake their quest of finding out the truth behind events.

There are many robots in Japanese manga and especially anime, such as *Tetsujin 28-go/Gigantor* in the 1960s (mixing elements from Wagner's operas and Chinese epics), *Voltes* (1977), *Daimos* (1979), and *Gundam RX-78* (1980), which feature cyborgs. During these years Japan became a powerful industrial then postindustrial nation, but at the same time its fertility and aging crisis started. In an attempt to meet its growing labor demand, the country allowed more foreigners (including many Brazilians and Americans of Japanese descent) to seek unskilled jobs and some skilled ones, such as nursing. But opening the foreign-labor market was strongly opposed, and this protectionist attitude partly contributed to fueling the production of robots, which were seen as a viable solution to the manpower shortage.[9] This might also explain the more positive interpretations of robots and cyborgs, like Otomo Katsuhiro's *Akira* (1980s) and Shirô Masamune's *Ghost in the Shell*

(1989, weekly; 1992, book; 1995, anime) and the *Power Rangers* and *Trans-formers* series, in contrast with the more negative *Frankenstein* follow-ups in the West (Allison 93–127, 102). This positive interpretation of human-machine symbiosis, to which collective collaboration and Shinto animism should be added, could also be seen as a continuation of Prime Minister Nakasone's 1980s-era revenge politics and policies (i.e., technonationalism).

It is not surprising that Gainax was founded by four fans who created stories that encouraged fan participation. In Japan, the whole manga and anime industry is complemented by fans' extensive and intensive activities before, during, and after the comikets (comic markets). These fans prolifically "copy" their favorite heroes and stories. But contrary to the legal-ist American system, in Japan there tends to be an unspoken and implicit agreement allowing fans to "copy." The Japanese copyright owners understand first that there are now too many people, projects, and venues to police fully, and that mass copying and transforming can increase sales of the original products rather than hinder them. Copying activities are allowed and even sometimes encouraged, provided that certain basic ethical principles are maintained, such as not copying for profit and not explicitly hurting the producers (Condry 23–25). As a result, the borders between amateurs and professionals are not so clear, as one can see in the example of *dôjinshi* (fan-zine mangas), made outside of the traditional publishing industry in a "do-it-yourself" manner. The same vaguely differentiated producer-consumer relationship can be observed in fansubbing and scanlation. As Lawrence Lessig wrote, Japan is a model of the "read/write culture" as opposed to a "read only culture."[10]

But this fan participation has a darker side that has been often and ex-cessively emphasized, especially in the West. A fan is referred to in Japa-nese as an *otaku*, the term often associated in the West, and in Japan until recently, with a fetishistic addiction to manga, anime, or video games. Not-withstanding its prevalence, this negative reputation is largely undeserved. *Otaku* obsessiveness is usually not nearly as extreme or unhealthy as often portrayed, and most *otaku* are not actually lonely or isolated; rather, they form communities that gather together to (re)create fan fiction as an escape from the many formal obligations of Japanese society. Poitras notes that but for brief relapses, the word *otaku* started to lose its negative connotation in Japan in the 1990s, when businesses started to understand that there was a lot of money to earn by protecting these avid buyers. Contrary to the strong reactions against comics in the 1950s in the United States, in Japan, except around a few negative, highly publicized cases,[11] such scapegoating à la Wer-tham of the violence in manga, anime, and more recently video games never led to antimanga laws (Schodt, *Manga!* 27; Brenner 100–101). Indeed, not only is there no empirical proof of the causal connection between fictional and real violence, but one could also easily argue that on the contrary, fictional violence is often cathartic and therefore prevents the manifestation of violence in the real world.

CLAMP and the Representation of Women in Manga and Anime

Preceded by the all-female Fabulous 49ers, who produced content in the 1970s, CLAMP is one more example of a positive way in which Japanese manga differs from the Western comics world. An all-female manga artist group created in the mid-1980s, CLAMP never worked as assistants to other *mangaka*, male or female, and learned first from high school courses and then through collaboration. Their work is based on a collaborative model in which specific functions and roles are equally shuffled (Cavallaro, *CLAMP in Context* 10).

CLAMP is interesting first because of its success story, with its mangas being quickly adapted into animes and the group creating a multiverse with titles such as *RG Veda* (1989–1996), *Tsubasa: Reservoir Chronicle* (2003–2009), and many others. Cavallaro explains that *Tsubasa* is especially reliant on crossovers (*CLAMP in Context* 8–9), and that when CLAMP entered the process of adaptation of the original manga *Tsubasa* into an anime series, "the challenges faced by the saga's creators reproposed themselves with something of a vengeance . . . [that] consisted of the release of the OVA [original video animation] *X: An Omen*" (*CLAMP in Context* 80).

But CLAMP is also interesting because it is a group of committed women artists whose many protagonists are heroines, and mostly positive ones. Although both the economic and the creative aspects of the cultural industry are still dominated by patriarchy, it is important to emphasize that there are more women manga and anime artists than women comics and animation artists in the Western world. However, if proportions are clearly in Japanese favor, roles (subaltern, leader, or independent)[12] might not be as favorable for women. Similarly, more stories with more female characters have been made in Japan than in America and have uninterruptedly been created by either male or female artists, from Tezuka's *Princess Knight* (1953) to female author Takeuchi Naoko's *Sailor Moon* (1991) to CLAMP's *Magic Knight Rayearth* (1997) and Miyazaki's amazing heroines. Almost consequently, representation of gender and women's issues is richer than in Western comics, where female artists and characters are fewer and continue to be infamously and systematically sexualized. To some extent this is surprising, since Japan is not especially famous for feminism or women's independent voices, especially in the workplace, where once married and/or pregnant, women quit their jobs.

This does not mean that manga and anime are not often sexist, even violently so.[13] First, one has to confront the fact that the vast majority of these heroines are girls and not adult women. Second, in many cases, they are also sexualized in various ways. This is obvious not only in the very successful genres like porno and subgenres such as *ero*, *hentai* (perverted), *ecchi* (softcore), *harem* (many girls involved with single boy or man), *lolicon* (Lolita complex; i.e., attraction to young and even prepubescent girls), and *kogal* (female high schooler with suggestive clothes and attitudes).[14] There is actually a term for the Japanese version of sexism in the manga and anime worlds, "fan service," which encompasses all the elements that do not further the plot but instead pander to readers, especially sexually, with panty shots and cleavage close-ups, especially in *shônen*/boy and *seinen*/adult male categories.

Therefore, the positive representation of women, quantitatively and qualitatively (positive heroines), reveals one more apparent paradox about Japanese society, because if explicit graphic sexualization of girls and young women is a regular feature in many male-oriented genres, real violence as officially reported (e.g., in the streets) is much rarer in Japan than it is in the United States. Therefore, as previously explained about the exaggerated expressions in facial and gestural representations, seeing these violent scenes might play the same role of emotional escape valve.

Ambivalent genres with ambiguous genders are also very successful in Japan and are often denounced or censored in the United States. Take Takahashi Rumiko's *Ranma ½* (1987–1996) as an example, in which the male martial art trainee protagonist, Ranma, is cursed to become a girl when accidentally splashed with water. The series started as a manga and was so successful that it was made into an anime and even a live-action series. For Napier, "one may deplore their stereotyping, but at the same time one cannot help admitting that all aspects of the female persona have a far wider play in Japanese popular culture than they do in the West" (Napier, "Vampires" 105–106). However, Allison sounds less optimistic in describing "magical girls" as ambivalent icons of sexuality and consumerism (Allison 134–142). I believe that these views are not mutually exclusive. While Japanese mangas and animes do present a much wider and richer array of female roles, many are still sexualized and exploitative. Simultaneously, and shockingly for most Westerners, but clearly working in Japanese society, it is that same psychological dynamic that allows male readers to fantasize and that also discourages them from being violently sexist.

Ghibli and Miyazaki Hayao

By the mid-1980s, when Japan's economy was on the verge of becoming "Number One" (Vogel), a new split in the manga and anime studio organization appeared. After creating movies with other studios, Miyazaki co-founded Studio Ghibli in 1985 with three others. If the others produced some memorable movies (e.g., Takahata Isao directed *Grave of the Fireflies* [1988]), Miyazaki was clearly the studio's leading figure for several reasons (McCarthy; Drazen 253–279). The studio is special because it is guided by an overall auteurist philosophy much closer to European auteur theory than to American studios (from Walt Disney to Pixar), while still working within the consensus-based and master-guided ideology of Japanese studios. Contrary to most animes, Ghibli's films are dedicated to movie theaters rather than TV. Hence Jacqueline Berndt can say, "One remembers very well, that the director of these prestigious films did not want his works to be named anime. Indeed, there is a certain irony to the fact that Miyazaki's films[,] which have pursued a different path than anime since the 1980s, helped anime to get acknowledged beyond subcultural communities and commercial necessities" (84). Moreover, Miyazaki usually draws his characters by hand and only uses computers for the background. He, too, does not want to be part of the anime world fundamentally based on convergence, with its ties to toys and TV ads (Condry 151). In an interview just after the release of *Spirited Away* (2001), Miyazaki presented the movie as being clearly against what the manga and anime worlds are today, especially where producing tie-ins is concerned. As he stated in an interview, "Children are losing their roots, being surrounded by high technology and cheap industrial goods" (qtd. in Drazen 278).

Yet if his animated films are considered artistically valuable, they are also extremely popular in Japan and abroad. Moreover, "sometimes, as was the case with *Princess Mononoke* [1997] and other films by its director . . . anime cuts across generational lines to be embraced by everyone from children to grandparents" (Napier, *Anime* 7). In 1984, *Nausicaa* (which, exceptionally, was first a manga) became a "groundbreaking masterpiece" anime (Drazen 259). Parallel to the many popular anime TV series, Ghibli went on producing twenty more animated films, most by Miyazaki, such as *Laputa: Castle in the Sky* (1986), *My Neighbor Totoro* (1988), and *Kiki's Delivery Service* (1989). There is no doubt that in a Japan that is more and more sensitive to female issues, Miyazaki's strong, independent heroines play a key role in his films' success. Similarly, *Nausicaa*'s powerful environmental themes also resonated with audiences, since such concerns are pervasive in Japanese cul-

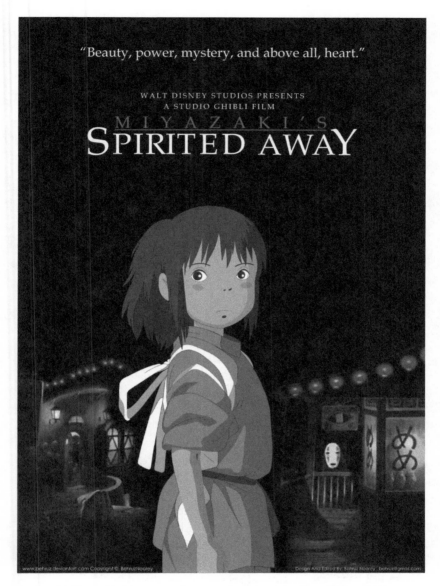

Studio Ghibli's worldwide renown draws particularly on the films of Miyazaki Hayao, such as *Spirited Away* (2001).

ture, which features various contemporary pop adaptations of animism (e.g., technoanimism, magical animistic personalities or traits).

Princess Mononoke became the top film of all time in Japan, surpassing *E.T.: The Extra-Terrestrial* (1982) and only surpassed later by *Titanic* (1998). Then *Spirited Away* (2001) won the Golden Bear at the Berlin Film Festival and the Academy Award for Best Animated Feature. Although he produced three more films (*Howl's Moving Castle* in 2004, *Ponyo* in 2008, and *The Wind Rises* in 2013), to some extent Miyazaki's official retirement in 2016 and Takahata's death in 2018 might have foreshadowed the end of an anime studio like Ghibli, progressive on the one hand (with its strong female protagonists and environmental messages) and traditional and conservative on the other (with a one-way communication from a master to a fascinated audience) in a new interactive, prosumers' media world.

Pokémon and the Tie-in Debate

Although the *Pokémon* (po[c]ke[t] mon[sters]) story could be told by emphasizing the authorship of its creator, Tajiri Satoshi (Buckingham and Selton-Green 17), the studio that accepted his project, OLM Inc., contrasts somewhat with an author-oriented studio like Ghibli.

In the last years of the millennium a new consumer phenomenon developed in Japan and swept across the globe. *Pokémon*, which began life as a piece of software to be played on Nintendo's Game Boy (a handheld video gaming console), quickly diversified into a comic book, a television show, a movie, stickers, small toys, trading cards, and other tie-ins, such as T-shirts and backpacks (Tobin). A publisher noticed that his readers had taken a real liking to the new video game, and he bought the comic book rights to *Pokémon*. All that activity itself reignited sales of the *Pokémon* cartridges, which in turn had TV Tokyo enter an agreement with Nintendo to produce a show, further encouraging sales of the cartridges and inciting the broadcasting company to produce the movie *Poketto Monsutô* (*Pocket Monster*, 1999). This cycle of mounting success shows the synergy between intermedia activities like hardware, software, toys (mainly produced by the Bandai company), TV, movies, and cards.

Hence, one can see that this new world of manga, anime, and their adaptations has changed in Japan quite quickly. On the one hand, "the manga provided character development and back story for the trainers, the pocket monsters and their adversaries," while on the other, "anime has been the source of inspiration behind a plethora of video games for decades[;] a more

Pokémon: consumerist ideology or speaking to childhood experience?

recent development is the reverse trend, namely the adaptation of games as animations" (Cavallaro, *Anime* 8). Moreover, instead of introducing all the characters at the beginning (as did *The Smurfs*), *Pokémon*'s creators gradually added new ones, keeping consumers engaged.

Some saw the *Pokémon* phenomenon as a typical example of the emerging consumerist ideology in which companies take advantage of consumers, especially young ones, who make easy targets. However, this phenomenon might be interpreted in a less negative way. Others see "*Pokémon* [as] a cultural practice, something you *do* [even if it is] within a field of forces" (Buckingham and Sefton-Green 12). Furthermore, while its success was briefly interrupted in 1997 by the photo-epileptic-seizure incident caused by the rapid flashing lights in one TV episode, *Pokémon* presented parents with an appealing alternative to violent games. Unlike American games such as *Mortal Kombat* (1992) or Japanese games like *Street Fighter* (1987), *Pokémon* was based on a quest that nurtured cooperation and healthy competition between friends. Buckingham and Sefton-Green conclude that "the global success of *Pokémon* is partly a result of its ability to 'speak' to shared aspects of childhood experience, and of the ease with which it can be integrated within the routines of children's everyday lives" (13). However, this positive interpretation does not preclude the previous one emphasizing the commercial aspect of the whole Pikachu business and even beyond, of the whole video game business, especially in a way to avoid traditional conservative critics that see video games and Japanese anime as violent.

Today it is generally acknowledged that "the interval between production and consumption seems [to be] shrinking, compressing, or collapsing. Fan cultures are one prime example because the fan mode of consumption is so productive that it scarcely feels like consumption at all; it feels like a mode of production in itself" (Lamarre 20). But at the same time, to produce their own content, fans need to consume and to be part of consumerist society. Moreover, in contrast with the local 1970s *Doraemon*, the millennial *Poké-mon* is global and virtual, where anybody can play and identify.

Conclusion

I have shown how the deeply interconnected Japanese worlds of manga, anime, and adaptation quickly became fundamentally more transmedial than their North American counterparts and, with few exceptions, such as Miyazaki, more oriented toward TV. I have also noted how issues around representations of women, pornography, violence, artists' hard working conditions (long hours, low salaries), and interpretations of copyright laws are perceived differently, that is, more openly, in Japan, while such concerns are still quite hotly debated and controversial in the West.

Beyond the mangas and animes by Tezuka, Gainax, CLAMP, Ghibli/ Miyazaki, and *Pokémon*'s multiple producers, many more came out and were successful in Japan and abroad. This cultural success, which ironically began just at the start of what is called the "lost decade," a decade of economic stagnation in Japan in the 1990s, was supported by fan prosumers first in Japan and then beyond. Even if Japan could become the "Number One" neither economically nor militarily (because of its constitution), at least it could become a global soft power, influencing other countries and people without coercion on a global scale, including old enemies like Korea and China, and competing with American cultural production. In the recent decades, Japan has become a real cultural force in the worlds of manga and anime, not only in terms of business (quantitatively) but also qualitatively as an innovative power. Many (including the Japanese themselves!) did not see this "cool Japan" (McGray) coming, because the West has frequently framed Japanese success within the stereotype of a good copycat with a weak creative culture. Manga and anime were so successful and important for the Japanese economy that in the 1990s the Japanese government tried to play a role in orienting their cultural production in various ways (offering subsidies, prizes, etc.). Interestingly, however, "neither the Japanese culture industries nor the Japanese government (or indeed teachers) have any control over how, in today's 'remix' world, cultural content is accessed, [re]interpreted and [re]distributed among networks of fans and consumers" (McLelland 6).

Moreover, ironically, since 1994, because manga in Japan is slowly declining and anime is less and less lucrative, they have been quickly displaced by the newer popular entertainment of video games, which is much more rewarding financially, and now culturally and socially (Gonsalvo). Hence, manga and anime are more and more playing a subaltern role of supplying storyboards and characters to be adapted for video games.

Notes

1. I will sometimes use the plural for mangas and animes as a way to emphasize the diversity of these two media in spite of a certain unity.

2. *Kamishibai* refers to a storyteller roaming the streets, telling stories and showing drawings on paper.

3. See Dave Kehr, "FILM; Anime, Japanese Cinema's Second Golden Age," *New York Times*, 20 January 2002, https://www.nytimes.com/2002/01/20/movies/film -anime-japanese-cinema-s-second-golden-age.html.

4. The kanji system is complemented with two syllabaries called hiragana and katakana.

5. This is similar to the way comics have been promoted by some educators as a tool to help kids read, and beyond, to motivate them to learn (Brenner xii–xiv).

6. See Kyodo, "Sales of Digital Manga Overtake Print Editions in Japan for First Time," *Japan Times*, 26 February 2018, https://www.japantimes.co.jp/news/2018/02/26 /national/sales-digital-manga-overtake-print-editions-japan-first-time/#.Wug9x NOFNbU.

7. See Cavallaro, *Japanese Aesthetics and Anime*. The dominance of one trend might vary according to the author but also the period; hence Tezuka was definitively influenced by the West at the beginning of his career in the 1940s to 1950s, while in the 1980s to 1990s, during the ascending years of Japan as a global economic power, the group CLAMP was increasingly Eastern oriented (drawing from Hindu, Buddhist, and Shinto traditions).

8. For the influence of Disney in Japan, see Condry 95–96.

9. See Daniel Moss, "Graying Japan Wants Automation, Not Immigration," *Japan Times*, 28 August 2017, https://www.japantimes.co.jp/opinion/2017/08/28/commentary /japan-commentary/graying-japan-wants-automation-not-immigration/#.WurN4 NOFNbU.

10. See Daniel H. Pink, "Japan, Ink: Inside the Manga Industrial Complex," *Wired*, 22 October 2007, https://www.wired.com/2007/10/ff-manga/.

11. See, among several, the Miyazaki Tsutomu case in 1988–1989 and the "Kobe School Killer" case in 1997 (Brenner 79, 100–101); see also Galbraith, Kam, and Kamm. For the mockumentary on *otaku*, see Reyns-Chikuma 111–119; and Cavallaro, *Art of Studio Gainax* 53–58.

12. "Few were in the top positions. Female animators were clearly on staff, but [in] the meetings between those with power—such as producers, scriptwriters, directors, and key frame artists—I estimate that about one in five or six (at most, one in three) were women" (Condry 6).

13. It is difficult to gauge how often, since statistics are not readily available.

14. It is worth noting that all these genres also exist in the United States and now on the global market through the internet.

Works Cited

Allison, Anne. *Millennial Monsters: Japanese Toys and the Global Imagination.* Berkeley, University of California Press, 2006.

Araki, Fumiyo, and Richard Wiseman. "Emotional Expressions in the United States and Japan." *Intercultural Communication Studies,* vol. 6, no. 2, 1996, pp. 13–32.

Berndt, Jacqueline. "Postcritical Anime: Observations on Its 'Identities' within Contemporary Japan." Osaka City University, Osaka, Japan, 14–16 September 2010, www.academia.edu/1193996/Postcritical_Anime_Observations_on_its_Identitie _within_Contemporary_Japan.

Brenner, Robin. *Understanding Manga and Anime.* Westport, CT, Libraries Unlimited, 2007.

Buckingham, David, and Julian Sefton-Green. "Structure, Agency, and Pedagogy in Children's Media Culture." *Pikachu's Global Adventure: The Rise and Fall of Pokémon,* edited by Joseph Tobin, Durham, NC, Duke University Press, 2004, pp. 12–33.

Cavallaro, Dani. *Anime and the Art of Adaptation.* Jefferson, NC, McFarland, 2010.

———. *The Art of Studio Gainax.* Jefferson, NC, McFarland, 2009.

———. *CLAMP in Context.* Jefferson, NC, McFarland, 2012.

———. *Japanese Aesthetics and Anime: The Influence of Tradition.* Jefferson, NC, McFarland, 2013.

Cohn, Neil. "Japanese Visual Language: The Structure of Manga." *Manga: An Anthology of Global and Cultural Perspectives,* edited by Toni Johnson-Woods, London, Bloomsbury, 2010, pp. 187–203.

Condry, Ian. *The Soul of Anime: Collaborative Creativity and Japan's Media Success Story.* Durham, NC, Duke University Press, 2013.

Drazen, Patrick. *Anime Explosion: The What? Why? and Wow! of Japanese Animation.* Berkeley, CA, Stone Bridge Press, 2003.

Galbraith, Patrick, Thiam Huat Kam, and Björn-Ole Kamm, editors. *Debating Otaku in Contemporary Japan: Historical Perspectives and New Horizons.* London, Bloomsbury, 2015.

Gonsalvo, Mia. *Atari to Zelda: Japan's Videogames in Global Contexts.* Cambridge, MA, MIT Press, 2016.

Hall, Edward T. *Beyond Culture.* Garden City, NY, Anchor Press, 1977.

Iwabuchi, Koichi. "'Soft' Nationalism and Narcissism: Japanese Popular Culture Goes Global." *Asian Studies Review,* vol. 26, no. 4, 2002, pp. 447–469.

Kern, Adam L. "East Asian Comix: Intermingling Japanese Manga and Euro-American Comics." *The Routledge Companion to Comics,* edited by Frank Bramlett, Roy T. Cook, and Aaron Meskin, New York, Routledge, 2017, pp. 106–116.

Kinsella, Sharon. *Adult Manga: Culture and Power in Contemporary Japanese Society*. Surrey, UK, Curzon, 2000.

Lamarre, Thomas. *The Anime Ecology: A Genealogy of Television, Animation, and Game Media*. Minneapolis, University of Minnesota Press, 2018.

Lunning, Frenchy. "Tezuka's Manga Life." *Mechademia*, vol. 8, 2013.

MacWilliams, Mark W., editor. *Japanese Visual Culture: Explorations in the World of Manga and Anime*. Armonk, NY, M. E. Sharpe, 2008.

McCarthy, Helen. *Hayao Miyazaki: Master of Japanese Animation*. Berkeley, CA, Stone Bridge Press, 1999.

McCloud, Scott. *Understanding Comics: The Invisible Art*. New York, William Morrow, 1994.

McGray, Douglas. "Japan's Gross National Cool." *Foreign Policy*, no. 130, 2002, pp. 44–54.

McLelland, Mark, editor. *The End of Cool Japan: Ethical, Legal, and Cultural Challenges to Japanese Popular Culture*. New York, Routledge, 2017.

Napier, Susan J. *Anime: From Akira to Princess Mononoke; Experiencing Contemporary Japanese Animation*. New York, Palgrave, 2001.

———. "Vampires, Psychic Girls, Flying Women and Sailor Scouts: Four Faces of the Young Female in Japanese Popular Culture." *The Worlds of Japanese Popular Culture: Gender, Shifting Boundaries, and Global Cultures*, edited by D. P. Martinez, Cambridge, UK, Cambridge University Press, 1998, pp. 91–109.

Poitras, Gilles. *Anime Essentials: Every Thing a Fan Needs to Know*. Berkeley, CA, Stone Bridge Press, 2001.

Quigley, Kevin, editor. *Comics Underground Japan*. New York, Blast Books, 1996.

Reyns-Chikuma, Chris. "*Otaku no video*: Portraits animés de Japons méconnus." *CinémAction*, no. 123, 2006, pp. 111–119.

Schodt, Frederik L. *Dreamland Japan: Writings on Modern Manga*. Berkeley, CA, Stone Bridge Press, 1996.

———. *Manga! Manga! The World of Japanese Comics*. Tokyo, Kodansha International, 1983.

Steinberg, Marc. *Anime's Media Mix: Franchising Toys and Characters in Japan*. Minneapolis, University of Minnesota Press, 2012.

Thompson, Jason. *Manga: The Complete Guide*. New York, Ballantine Books, 2007.

Tobin, Joseph, editor. *Pikachu's Global Adventure: The Rise and Fall of Pokémon*. Durham, NC, Duke University Press, 2004.

Vogel, Ezra F. *Japan as Number One: Lessons for America*. Cambridge, MA, Harvard University Press, 1978.

Genre and Superhero Cinema

AARON TAYLOR

Superhero cinema is noteworthy for the considerable impact a relatively small, but growing, body of movies may prove to have on familiar and long-standing ideas about film genre. While some might wish to nominate the superhero film as a genre unto itself, the focus here instead will be to suggest that the category proposes other, more provocative, ways of considering and engaging with genre. The effects of superhero cinema—particularly their formal, structural, and industrial dimensions—are deserving of closer scrutiny. The following taxonomical notes address some of these facets: the categorical problem of the "comic book movie"; the limitations of empirical efforts to identify unifying features; and the economics of superhero cinema's fluid conventionality.

Contending with the "Comic Book Movie"

It has become commonplace to refer to the expansive number of adaptations of superhero comic properties as a "genre." Undoubtedly, the adoption of the nomenclature was prompted by the accelerated production of big-budget films featuring superhero properties in the early 2000s. The historical emergence of this category as an identifiable genre is most comprehensively argued by Liam Burke, who identifies the year 2000 as the marker of the genre's "classical" phase—achieved after a "long period of articulation" (109–110). It should be noted that Burke's generic label goes beyond super-hero titles; he regards the comic book film adaptation as a genre unto itself (84). This distinction will be discussed shortly, but first the subject to consider is one of numbers—specifically, the quantitative dimensions of generic designation and recognition.

Between 2000 and 2018, approximately 153 American feature films adapted from comics were theatrically released in North America, and roughly seventy-five titles with a wide theatrical release were based on pre-existing superhero properties. An additional twenty-one titles featured superhero-related original content (with nineteen others receiving limited release).[1] Despite frequent media complaints about the perceived oversaturation of this production cycle, one could claim that the number of titles seems relatively low to qualify as a distinct generic category.[2] In 2015, for example, only 2.2 percent of 158 wide releases qualified as superhero titles (Mendelson).[3] And in 2016—the year with the historically highest number of superhero productions to date—the percentages also remained fairly low: roughly 6 percent of all wide releases were superhero films.[4] These numbers are obviously lower than other more prolific genres, such as action (11 percent of wide releases in 2015), biography/history (14 percent), crime (7 percent), comedy (22 percent), drama (10 percent), horror (8 percent), and sci-fi (8 percent).[5] Another way of countering the oversaturation argument would be to point out that of the roughly 3,027 wide-release films produced from 2000 to 2018, 2.47 percent of them are superhero films (and if we account for all 11,380 theatrical releases, they account for a mere 0.01 percent).[6]

Claims of superhero exhaustion have little to do with numbers, then. Rather, they bespeak broader criticisms indirectly aimed at the disproportionate amount of media attention and box office receipts that superhero films receive compared with other forms of cinema. In 2018, for example, films adapted from comics captured an 18.55 percent market share of works categorized by source material (a gross of over $2.36 billion), and superhero properties grossed over $2.15 billion, representing a remarkable market share of 20.32 percent of works categorized by creative type ("Domestic Theatrical Market"). As Thomas Schatz points out, *The Dark Knight* (2008) "grossed more in its opening weekend ($158 million) than [the Oscar-winning] *Slumdog Millionaire* returned in its entire six-month run" that same year (213). Complaints about oversaturation also tend to be veiled but familiar criticisms of blockbuster filmmaking as a whole. Indeed, in the same essay, Schatz lambasts superhero films as being "emblematic of . . . an industry increasingly wed to formulaic fantasies and infantile spectacles designed and dumbed down for an all-too-receptive worldwide audience" (214).

But these concerns with numbers and critical complaints beg a larger question: How many works does it take before a set of films with evident similarities are dubbed a "genre"? That is, one might ask whether a group of films needs to achieve a substantial enough critical mass before achieving the designation "genre"—a label that actually serves as a kind of honorific. Semantics aside, it has been suggested that such groupings are more distinctive than "modes" (e.g., nonfiction, melodrama, experimental), more durable than temporally discrete "cycles" (e.g., the Freed/MGM musicals, spaghetti westerns, blaxploitation), and more generative of influential/ prototypical exemplars than short-lived or uninspiring "clusters" (e.g., reality TV adaptations, the Friedberg/Seltzer spoofs, or films about pets or food) (Grindon 44–45). Clearly, post-2000 superhero cinema represents an identifiable production trend, or "cycle." But what is gained by calling the grouping a "genre"? And why now?

Adaptations of superhero comics (or masked adventurer pulps) represented a substantial percentage of the serials produced between 1930 and 1956. Approximately fifty-five serials produced during this time were adaptations of pulp or comics properties, and roughly twenty-three of these feature superheroic or masked-avenger types—nearly 10 percent of all 232 serials produced during this period.[7] Comparatively, during the same period, roughly eighty-five features and/or B-film programmers were adapted from pulp- or comics-based properties, with only one title featuring a super-powered character proper: *Superman and the Mole Men* (1951). Indeed, only twenty-eight adapted superhero titles and seventeen films featuring original superhero material were produced in the United States before 2000. But the serials' prolific production levels are not an anomaly: fifty-five of the ninety live-action American televisual adaptations of comics material produced since 1950 are superhero titles, with an additional thirty titles based on original superhero content.[8]

The larger point here is that the contemporary superhero cycle, or Burke's "comic book film," only apparently gains "generic" status after 2000 once it is "legitimized" by the machinery of big-budget feature filmmaking. In so doing, dozens of silent one-reelers, B films, serials, and serialized dramas for television are treated as mere prototexts rather than contributors to a generic canon. None of these examples are referenced or analyzed by Burke. Nor are their own particular aesthetics or thematics deemed worthy of contributing to the characteristics or tropes of the "genre."

In short, the category does not spring fully formed from the head of Zeus.[9] Just as Saige Walton reminds us that the origin of the superhero was a "decidedly intergeneric and transmedia formation," so too is it worth noting that contemporary superhero cinema is merely an expensive and already familiar byproduct of earlier, less grandiose media formations (88). Thus, the reintroduction to a third cinematic Spider-Man in *Captain America: Civil War* (2016) is an occasion for pleasure for those accustomed to the character's many previous animated, televisual, video game, and print in-

A cryptic cameo from the Flash (Ezra Miller) in *Batman v Superman: Dawn of Justice* (Warner Home Video, 2016).

carnations. Indeed, this mediated variegation is itself the very subject of Marvel Comics' "Spider-Verse" saga (2014) and subsequent 2018 animated adaptation, which showcases every version of the wall crawler ever depicted.

And while Bruce Wayne observes cryptic images of his future JLA colleagues for the first time in *Batman v Superman: Dawn of Justice* (2016), fans greet fleeting shots of the Flash, Aquaman, and Cyborg like reappearances of old, familiar friends. Generic self-consciousness has always been a preoccupation of superhero fiction, and not just in its later periods, as Burke or Geoffrey Klock would have it (Klock 25–26). The Spider-Man or Batman reboots are merely the film industry's appropriation of comics' long-running explorations of alternate continuities, "retconned" story lines, and interwoven parallel fictional dimensions.[10] These are not the markings of generic exhaustion; they are the workings of superhero storytelling's essential structure and economic impetuses.

Burke also claims that "effective" superhero spoofs only arose during the "stationary phase" of 2008 (114). But the implication that earlier parodies like *Mystery Men* (1999) lacked "viewers literate in generic protocol" is untenable (110). It is necessary to remember that genres can be almost instantly self-conscious, and there is often almost no temporal lag between parody and target group.[11] Audiences were already familiar with superheroes through their extensive cross-media appearances. Indeed, superhero cinema has a robust parodic tradition, arising as early as the mid-1960s, and was largely synonymous with camp aesthetics prior to the renewed production cycle of the early 2000s. Just as superhero comics were skewered in *Mad*'s

"Superduperman" stories in the 1950s and subjected to satirical perversities by 1960s comix artists (for example, Gilbert Shelton's *Wonder Wart-Hog*), the popular success of superhero camp on film and television is unsurprising. Not only are the first two nonadapted superhero features camp outings (*The Wild World of Batwoman* [1966] and *Fearless Frank* [1967]), so too are a number of the most influential and lucrative pre-2000 comic book adaptations (*Batman: The Movie* [1966], *Barbarella* [1968], *Flash Gordon* [1980], and *Batman Forever* [1995]).

It might even be asserted that seriousness does not come naturally to the televised or cinematic superhero. Nearly two-thirds of films and TV programs featuring original superhero content is of an explicitly comedic or satirical bent. One could anticipate that compared to other genres, the ratio of satirical-to-straight productions would almost certainly be quite high. Self-ridicule seems built into superhero cinema. It is not uncommon for action to be accompanied by its own disavowal, with characters explicitly commenting on the improbability of their situations or the ludicrousness of their appearance (e.g., the Joker's digs at Batman's outfit in *Batman* [1989], the yellow-spandex cracks in *X-Men* [2000], the title character's homophobic slurs against costumes in *Hancock* [2008]). Thus, on the one hand, Deadpool's wisecracks at the affected, conventionalized posturing of action stars ("She's gonna do a superhero landing!") in *Deadpool* (2016) are themselves affected, conventionalized expressions. But on the other, his cheap shot at Twentieth Century Fox ("It's like the studio didn't have enough money for any more X-Men") is not mere lily gilding; it extends superhero cinema's innate satirical impulses outward, acknowledging viewers' awareness of Hollywood's complex and often restrictive political economy.

Given superhero cinema's inherent and necessary self-awareness, then, it seems to be the ideal demonstration of Celestino Deleyto's claim that generic "change is not particularly transgressive" (229). The alleged reflexivity of contemporary entries is really just an inevitable attempt to expand generic parameters. For example, the much-maligned "grimdark" tendencies of post–*Batman Begins* (2005) productions are to be understood as reactionary responses to superhero cinema's extended affinities with camp. Thus, our reintroduction to the Fantastic Four in 2015, for example—with Mister Fantastic's rubberized limbs pinned in cruciform to a surgical table—does not just nod to Cronenbergian body horror (Weintraub). It is also a stylistic effort at cultural legitimization—the "genrefication" of a formerly low-rent and unserious production cycle.

To genrefy, then, is also to gentrify. Subsuming superhero cinema within the broader, taxonomic structure of Burke's "comic book movie" accom-

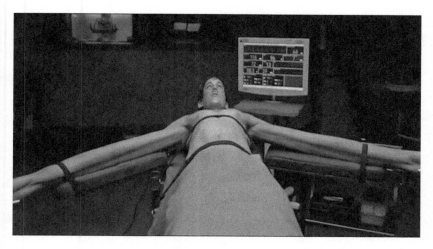

Superhero film as Cronenbergian body horror: Miles Teller in *Fantastic Four* (Twentieth Century Fox Home Entertainment, 2015).

plishes the same qualitative act of upscaling. Indeed, Burke gives pride of place to the superhero within his definition of the comic book movie, which is said to depict "a vigilante or outsider character engaged in a form of revenge narrative, and is pitched at a heightened reality with a visual style marked by distinctly comic book imagery" (106). Never mind that there are far too many exceptions to prove his rule: the titular characters of *Josie and the Pussycats* (2001), *Bulletproof Monk* (2003), and *Garfield* (2004) aren't particularly vengeful, and the style of crime films like *Road to Perdition* (2002), *A History of Violence* (2005), and *Whiteout* (2009) conform more closely to hard-boiled tropes.

Perhaps Burke's prescriptivism would exclude such frequent "aberrations." But to do so perpetuates the stultifying popular confluence of comics and superhero fare. Given that comic retailers generally reported that roughly 55 percent of direct market sales in 2014 were superhero titles, such synonymy is unsurprising.[12] The interchangeability of terms is partly a symptom of the North American tendency to imagine comics as a lowbrow genre rather than a medium (Chute and Dekoven 157). Admittedly, the perception is changing, largely due to the migration of comics into libraries, bookstores, and short lists for prestigious literary awards. Nevertheless, if comics themselves are saddled with a categorical misapplication—one that directly shapes popular perception of the medium—granting the "comic book movie" generic status implicitly seeks to counter inevitable socio-historic assumptions of juvenility, escapism, disposability, and simplicity.

With genrefication to the rescue, then, we can strike up yet another chorus of "POW! BIFF! Comics Aren't Just for Kids Anymore!"

Certainly, superhero cinema frequently addresses its own broader categorical designation reflexively. *Batman: The Movie* (1966), *Superman* (1978), *Hulk* (2003), *Spider-Man 2* (2004), *Watchmen* (2009), and many others explicitly contend with the specificity of their medium by directly adopting filmic analogues for the aesthetics of the comics from which they are adapted. In so doing, they remind us how adaptations can themselves "function similarly to genres": they fulfill certain key expectations—that is, they acknowledge their own hypertextual relation to their source material (Hutcheon 121). And yet, this notion is very different from saying that adaptations *are* a genre. As articulated, Burke's definition offers us the descriptive markers of content and style but lacks the crucial, cohesive thematic or philosophical dimensions necessary for a robustly defined genre. More to the point, for those interested in sketching out just such dimensions for the superhero film, one need first query what exactly is to be gained by granting the category generic status, not to mention why pride of place seems to be given to contemporary productions with reflexive tendencies.

Instead, and at best, heavily stylized superhero films signal how self-conscious processes of adaptation play a defining role in what one, at first, might be tempted to dub *genres of remediation*. Such categories apply to films that directly contend with the formal features of the medium whose content they appropriate. In this sense, one might speak of the "video game movie" in the same vein as the "comic book movie," for both share a similarly low cultural regard. But the lowly status of these two genres of remediation should also make us mindful of the fact that their more prestigious relatives—literary or theatrical adaptations—are not categorized in generic terms. One doesn't speak of "book movies" or "theater movies," despite the fact that these adaptations are often just as preoccupied with novelistic or dramaturgical conventions.

This discussion of numbers and nomenclature, ancestry and adaptation, should help reinforce a useful lesson: labeling a body of works as a genre is neither a neutral nor an objective designation. Rather, like the distinctive creation of "film noir" (an unacknowledged taste category) or the "western" (an unacknowledged subset of historical fiction), the "superhero genre" enables certain business, critical, and viewing praxes. It is not that superhero cinema is better referred to as a cycle or cluster. Nor is it to imply that calling the "comic book movie" a genre echoes the perceived pretentiousness of indiscriminately substituting the term "graphic novels" (a mode or format) for "comics" (a medium). Instead, we need to be alert to the propensity toward *genre fixity*. That is, "generic description must always avoid slipping into evaluation by reifying generic patterns of a historical period as norms" (Grant 10). To partake in genre is to engage in taste making, and so we would do well not to minimize the seventy years of often comical comic book films and serials preceding the blockbusters of the twenty-first century.

Hellblazers, Swamp Things, Vampire Slayers, and Other Problems

Earlier, it was noted that Burke's "comic book movie" lacked a coherent set of thematic preoccupations. By extension, then, identifying the structural dimensions of superhero cinema is necessary if a persuasive argument is to be made for the category's generic status. That is, in accordance with Rick Altman's robust linguistic approach to genre, the distinctiveness of the superhero film partly rests on identifying its unique semantic and syntactic elements (i.e., its iconography and "meaning-bearing structures") ("Semantic/Syntactic Approach" 10–11). One ought to consider, then, why Altman's approach to genre remains a crucial one and what challenges it poses for normative approaches to defining superhero cinema. But one should also consider why the efforts to identify the distinctive features of this "genre" are potentially more important than the features themselves.

An oft-rehearsed difficulty with generic definitions is the "question of corpus" — that is, the criteria one applies in arguing for this or that film's belongingness within a given genre (Grant 22). In other words, if one is to identify a genre's essential features, one can only do so on the basis of analyzing works that have already been identified as exemplars of the genre in question. In order to avoid this empirical conundrum, many theorists have taken up Andrew Tudor's influential claim that categorization is ultimately defined by "common cultural consensus" (138). The superhero genre, then, is what we collectively imagine it to be, and it achieves generic status by virtue of a demonstrable number of stakeholders (viewers, filmmakers, producers, distributers, critics, and so on) agreeing to identify it as such. Correspondingly, Burke undertakes audience research to argue that both fans and nonfans are now beginning to refer to "comic book movies" as a genre (88).

However, there are important limitations to Tudor's "social convention method" of generic identification (Staiger 205). Naturally, it is tempting to declare that generic labels arise via social usage. After all, many erroneously claim that a tomato is a vegetable (or are unclear about its botanical identity) simply because it makes for a better savory *arrabiata* sauce than a sweet sundae topping. In this case, culinary practice supplants the taxonomi-

cal schemes of scientific classification based on material, biological qualities. Resisting the unreserved default to such a casual approach to generic
labels—no matter how widespread—is not just a scholarly insistence on
pedantic accuracy, as Burke would have it (93); no matter how many people
refer to a "comic book movie genre," they still are risking categorical confusion by treating form and content as synonyms.

One might counter by proffering genres of form (novels, poems, plays)
and genres of content (the popular story groups arising in the wake of mass
literacy and publication methods). But there are reasons to restrict "genrefication" to content categories. For one, I have already asserted that comics
have been perceived as a vulgar genre, which has had a long, stultifying
effect on the medium's public perception and reception. Similarly, describing animation as a genre (as IMDb does, for example) also reinforces the
pervasive association of this production method with kiddie fare. If genre
can and does manage expectation, definition by consensus can and does
lead to conservative and conventionalized beliefs about what a medium or
form "ought" to look like—hence the crushing generic uniformity of American comics adaptations in both the twentieth and the twenty-first centuries
(which perhaps explains Burke's centralization of vigilantes and revenge
narratives in his definition of comic book movies). Just as fifty-six of the
ninety-three films produced during the sound era's first wave of feature-
length comics adaptations (1930–1959) were based on humorous newspaper strips (60 percent), 49 percent of post-2000 adaptations are superhero titles.[13] Content so easily can become dictated by cultural consensus as
well. Scott Bukatman is correct to complain that "superhero films are even
more obsessed with origin stories than the comics themselves" (121). Out
of the seventy-five post-2000 superhero adaptations, thirty-three of them
(44 percent) are essentially introductions to their titular characters. And
even Burke demonstrates the considerable pressure put upon adaptations
of "nonmainstream" comics like *The League of Extraordinary Gentlemen*
(2003) and *Watchmen* (2009) to ensure these filmed versions conform to
formulaic templates (122–127).[14]

For these reasons, one ought not to defer unreservedly to Tudor's definition by consensus. By contrast, Altman's early linguistic model has the
advantage of requiring thoroughgoing attention to the content of a category's members. So, one might itemize superhero semantics: the category's
"common traits, attitudes, characters, shots, locations, sets," and recurring
narrative preoccupations (Altman, "Semantic/Syntactic Approach" 10). A
prominent example is Tim Dirks's catalogue of such semantic elements as
secret identity, special powers, main enemy, unique costume, accessories,

mission, sidekick/team, origin story, home/location (Dirks). Other prescriptive check boxes are compiled by Peter Coogan, who argues that to qualify as a superhero, a character must have "a selfless, pro-social mission," be equipped with extraordinary powers, and have a superhero identity "embodied in a codename and iconic costume, which typically express his biography, character, powers, or origin" (30).[15]

Just as vital are attempts to enumerate superhero cinema's syntax: the "constitutive relationships between undesignated and variable placeholders" (Altman, "Semantic/Syntactic Approach" 10). Popular attempts at articulating superhero cinema's syntactic dimensions tend to be pragmatically oriented. For example, popular wikis (e.g., TV Tropes) or blogs (e.g., *Superhero Nation*) catalogue recurring tropes, conventions, and themes for aspiring writers — narrative dos and don'ts, as it were.[16] Or, more abstractly, one might identify the philosophical resonance of superhero cinema's persistent semantic details. Referring to Dirks's list, one might note superhero cinema's preoccupation with such analogous subjects as the divided self (secret identity), posthumanism and the body (special powers), Manichean morality (main enemy), masquerade (costume), technophobia/philia (accessories), existentialism and teleology (mission), communal obligation (team), and environmental determinism (origin/home).

And yet this discussion of possible superhero semantics and syntax is not articulated in the interest of articulating a distinctive generic definition; it is intended only to remind us that attempts to define genres would do well to remain open, expansive, and fluid. For example, a popular fannish enterprise is to play the "Character X Isn't Really a Superhero" game.[17] Even creators participate, as exemplified by Max Landis's vociferous assertions that his own work *Chronicle* (2012) shouldn't be considered a superhero film by virtue of its lack of required semantic features (i.e., an altruistic, empowered character with an alter ego) ("Max Landis"). One might dispute him with syntactic rejoinders — for example, *Chronicle* reworks familiar tropes by representing a posthuman protagonist who buckles under the conditions that typically produce heroes. One of *Chronicle*'s protagonists is, instead, eventually driven insane by his altered body, existentially meaningless life, and wretched treatment at home and school.

But such a rebuttal would be beside the point. The discursive flurry surrounding the categorization of superhero cinema reminds us of Altman's crucial revision to his classic semantic/syntactic approach: that genre formation is also a matter of pragmatics. The arguments, debates, and discussions surrounding the possibility of superhero cinema's generic distinctiveness perfectly embody "the competition among multiple users that characterize genres" (Altman, *Film/Genre* 210). For, clearly, none of the aforementioned lexical elements cited here can or ought to be taken as sacrosanct. Otherwise, one runs the risk of tautological generic definitions. For example, Coogan argues that costumed-but-non-powered tough guys like Batman or rampaging beasts like the Hulk are still counted as superheroes because their stories are marked off from other related genres "by a preponderance of generic conventions" (30). Not only is his logic circular, but he also inexplicably outlaws liminal generic oddballs like the sorcerous *Constantine* (2005), the horrific *Swamp Thing* (1982), the militaristic *Nick Fury: Agent of SHIELD* (1998), or the monster-stomping martial arts of *Buffy the Vampire Slayer* (1992) (48).

That is, if we are hesitating to call superhero cinema sui generis here, such hesitation acknowledges that its parameters are debatable. More importantly, it also acknowledges that such debate is a crucial dimension of pragmatic generic production. The passionate classificatory discussion generated by superhero cinema differs from other, older forms of debate because it largely acknowledges the category's fundamental *fan-oriented* ontology. Superhero cinema is predicated upon the fan discourses it appropriates from comic book culture. Continuity-based superhero comics by mainstream publishers have cultivated a generic identity via their strategic courtship of fans' collective intelligence. Indeed, expertise in narrative arcana largely defines and limits the audience of superhero comic books — the consumptive pleasure of which lies in one's expert knowledge of narrative continuity and ability to contribute to fan debates (Pustz 129). Engaging in informed discussion about the boundaries, parameters, or generic distinctiveness of superhero cinema, then, is a means of acquiring subcultural capital. Moreover, Hollywood has appropriated this genre-enabled pleasure from comics fandom. Not only do the studios rely on fan networks to promote their superhero productions, but both Warner Bros. and Marvel Studios cultivate generic cohesiveness by rewarding fan knowledge of comic book (and filmic) intertextuality. In-jokes, throwaway references, and (most importantly) shared cross-continuities are all strategies co-opted from mainstream comics publishing. Crucially, they serve as studio efforts to establish, reinforce, and manage "official" generic boundaries.

Heroes for Hire: Brand Continuity and Generic Grafting

A final point of consideration involves the subsuming of this manufactured intertextuality within new and evolving industrial praxes of generic formation. Two significant developments are noteworthy here: *brand con-*

tinuity and *generic grafting*. The first concept refers to the corporate and narrative strategies that established the so-called DC Extended Universe, Disney's Marvel Cinematic Universe, and Fox's separate Marvel franchises. The second concept denotes the relatively novel trade discourses that situate superhero cinema in relation to other genres. Both suggest a new managerial hyperconsciousness of genre, and a concentrated effort to employ it in order to stake out brand identities within a competitive marketplace.

Because superhero films are among the most profitable of a given studio's tentpole productions, it is obviously within a company's best financial interest to establish a recognizable brand identity for these franchises.[18] Barry Langford, for example, argues that superhero franchises achieve box office viability due to their narrative and stylistic affinity with the effects-driven, science fiction blockbusters of the late twentieth century—a veritable master genre, financially speaking (182). If these blockbusters exemplify a kind of master or meta genre, then unlike the other popular genres with which it is associated (action/adventure, crime, fantasy, science fiction), superhero cinema is both beyond and about the conventions, formulae, rules, systems, and traditions in which audiences are most economically invested.

Indeed, it may prove instructive to consider superheroes as the most idealized of figures from the respective genres with which they are associated. As figurative paragons, they operate within exaggerated or specialized versions of particular subgenres: fantasy/heroic epic (Doctor Strange, Thor, Wonder Woman); hard-boiled crime/detective (Batman); heist (Ant-Man); horror (Blade, Ghost Rider, Hellboy, Hulk); sci-fi space opera (Green Lantern, Guardians of the Galaxy, Superman); teen pic (Spider-Man); urban crime/vigilante (Daredevil, Deadpool, Punisher); war (Captain America, Peggy Carter, Suicide Squad); western (Jonah Hex, Lone Ranger). As the "Dark Knight Detective," it is not simply that Batman is just another representative of the hard-boiled mystery subgenre; as a grim crime buster, he is the zenith of his respective tradition. What is more, his influence is felt on the now superhuman mental faculties and street-fighting prowess of his Victorian predecessor in *Sherlock Holmes* (2009). Similarly, Blade and Buffy inspire Van Helsing (2004) to hit the gym, the Hulk mandates a more monstrous Mr. Hyde in *The League of Extraordinary Gentlemen* (2003), the angst of Donnie Darko (2001) rivals Spider-Man's, Daredevil and the Punisher push Harry Brown (2009) to more desperate measures, the Suicide Squad could give the mercenaries of *The Expendables* (2010) a run for their money, and, to this day, no cowboy rocks a ten-gallon hat like the Lone Ranger. These heroes are "super" insofar as they represent the apex fantasy objects, or figures of wish fulfillment, within long-running popular story categories.

Little surprise, then, that these heroes recur as established generative transmedia brands, and contemporary studios clamor to hitch their wagons to these lucrative generic stars. But it is not enough for a given studio to establish an expertise within a given genre in order to presell the franchises in which it invests. That is, unlike companies during the studio era, we do not see studios aligning a "house style" with a specialty genre, as was the case with Warner Bros.' "urban crime" films, MGM's "quality musicals," and Universal's horror output. Rather, a studio often positions its franchise series within larger brands — usually associated with preexisting media companies or author figures. Box Office Mojo's "Franchise Index" precisely exemplifies this development, listing not just profitable comics "series" but also such lucrative "brands" as "Alan Moore," "Dark Horse Comics," "DC Comics," and "Marvel Comics" ("Franchises").

In concrete terms, then, Warner Bros. does not simply perpetuate the *Batman* franchise; the Caped Crusader must be situated — both narratively and as a brand — under the in-house umbrella of a DC Extended Universe. Intellectual properties licensed from DC Entertainment are no longer adapted within self-contained titles or microcycles; they comingle within serialized, cross-referencing stories. Such cross-pollination within the DC adaptations thus helps establish Warner's *brand equity*: a tactic that "informs an audience's consumption of its series, resulting not only in [Warner] delivering a reliable type of product, but to a receiver who is already predisposed to watch it" (Tait 54). Prior to its absorption by Disney, the briefly independent Marvel Studios ushered in this transformative strategy by successfully managing its own cinematically underexploited properties — both in-house and within a shared narrative and corporate continuity (Johnston 9–14). Appropriating comic book seriality and continuity in this fashion helps concretize quasi-generic stability (as staple aesthetic features of the superhero genre) and brand equity (as unifying guarantors of durability). Continuity is thus market driven, and it contributes to the windfall profits enjoyed by the larger parent companies (i.e., WarnerMedia and the Walt Disney Company) that own both the publishers and the studios that traffic in superhero fare.

In filmic terms, if Marvel adaptations still currently outpace DC in number, it is not simply a matter of centralized control — that is, of DC Entertainment licensing fewer of its properties to studios unassociated with its parent company. Indeed, with Marvel Studios' efforts to reacquire most of the licenses for its affiliated product, Disney is obviously not overly concerned with cannibalizing its own audience. The company's lack of concern is due to Marvel Studios' ongoing practice of *generic grafting*: the tendency to explicitly align its intellectual property with already recognizable cinematic genres and/or production cycles. Largely taking its cue from such

Suicide Squad as war film (Warner Home Video, 2016).

early generic conservatism as New Line's foregrounding of horror in *Blade* (1998) and Fox's science-fictional emphasis in its first *X-Men* outing, Marvel Studios continues to court a diversified, undifferentiated audience with its hybridized approach to genre. Thus, space opera helps to sell the D-listers who populate *Guardians of the Galaxy* (2014), and *Captain America: The Winter Soldier* (2014) is a throwback to the conspiracy thrillers of the 1970s. Indeed, comedic trappings more or less remain a staple throughout Marvel's productions, while also serving as a brand distinction from Warner Bros.' alleged "no jokes" policy.[19]

But despite continually trafficking in the "grimdark" treatment of its properties, the "Distinguished Competition" has taken note of Marvel's strategic generic hybridity and the underplaying of its association with juvenile pulp. Greg Silverman, Warner Bros. president of creative development, asserted that "the filmmakers who are tackling these properties are making great movies about superheroes; they aren't making superhero movies" (qtd. in McClintock). For example, if *Suicide Squad* (2016) is not "really" a superhero film, it is not because its battalion is populated by supervillains. Rather, Silverman and director David Ayer would be just as pleased if older viewers were preoccupied by comparing squad members with the assorted badasses in *The Guns of Navarone* (1961), *Where Eagles Dare* (1968), *Kelly's Heroes* (1970), or *Inglourious Basterds* (2009). The filmmakers' strategic undermining and confusing of generic boundaries does not simply reinforce Janet Staiger's important assertion that Hollywood genres have never been pure. On the one hand, Staiger is correct to declare that post-Fordian movies aren't any more hybridized than their predecessors (203–204). If *Suicide Squad* is a war film that just happens to feature superpowered characters, it certainly "broadens the film's appeal" (Staiger 213).

But on the other hand, superhero cinema most clearly illustrates Celestino Deleyto's even more radical claim that films "participate in genres but don't belong to them" (223). Instead, individual works make use of generic conventions in particular ways, and this participation in a genre is not to be equated with static membership (227). Rather, belongingness is continually subjected to a process of negotiation. Superheroes are forever marked as outsiders, then. And if superhero cinema's generic parameters remain contested, then it is largely because its most prominent representatives both court and refute the designation.

All categorical uncertainty aside, however, the impact of this expanding body of films on the conceptualization, practice, and reception of generic moviemaking continues to be felt. Hollywood's adaptation of the narrative content, aesthetics, and commercial tactics of comics' most prominent and profitable genre has had expansive ramifications, which are still evolving. While its distinctiveness as a film genre remains in question, the formal, structural, and industrial features of superhero cinema represent potentially far-reaching revisions to long-held notions about the systematizing and classifying of popular categories.

Notes

1. These statistics are based on an IMDb Power Search of American feature films based on comic books, strips, and graphic novels and released between 1911 and 2018, slightly modified for accuracy and known omissions. To date, there have been approximately 318 feature-length adaptations.

2. Such complaints are now almost too numerous to catalogue, but for recent examples see Agar; Blake; and Ulanoff.

3. I have modified Mendelson's statistics for accuracy and known omissions.

4. This statistic can be generated by cross-referencing superhero titles against the numbers of wide releases for 2016 listed in Box Office Mojo's Yearly Box Office charts. The annual charts are available at http://www.boxofficemojo.com/yearly/.

5. The generic labels referenced here are those employed by IMDb. The statistics were generated through an IMDb Power Search of feature films in 2015 that grossed over $1.5 million domestically and Box Office Mojo's box office chart for 2015. IMDb allows for a film to have multiple generic designations, and so crossover or hybrid entries are inevitable. In each case, however, I tried to ensure that each film was only placed within a single generic entry for comparative purposes—recognizing, of course, that making such hard-and-fast distinctions is often a problematic enterprise. Other genres include documentary (2 percent), fantasy (6 percent), musicals (2 percent), romance (4 percent), and thrillers (4 percent). For descriptions of each genre recognized by IMDb, see "Genres."

6. This statistic was generated by cross-referencing the aforementioned IMDb Power Search (of American feature films released between 1911 and 2018 based on

comics) against the compiled number of wide releases tabulated under Box Office Mojo's Yearly Box Office charts. The total percentage of works adapted from comics since 2000 would be 1.37 percent.

7. These numbers were produced by referring to the titles compiled in Kinnard. For ease of reference, a fairly comprehensive list of serials produced and distributed in the USA can be found at https://en.wikipedia.org/wiki/List_of_film_serials.

8. These statistics are based on an IMDb Power Search of live-action American television programs released between 1950 and 2018 based on comics or featuring superhero content.

9. It should also be stressed that short-lived or apparently minor cycles can sometimes "contaminate" the straightforward generic identity of other contemporaneous films, and in turn, these cycles incorporate influences from adjacent concurrent clusters (Neale 253–254). Recent examples include: the heist undertaken by magically empowered con artists in *Now You See Me* (2013) and its sequel (2016); *Birdman*'s (2014) situation as a film about theater but also the superheroic struggle between ego and alter ego; *Midnight Special*'s (2016) young, telekinetic (and science-fictional) fugitive with pronounced superheroic connotations (a habit of wearing goggles while reading *Superman* comics).

10. "Retconning" (short for "retroactive continuity") is a comics industry neologism that refers to the revision of past canonical story events within a series in light of new narrative developments. Filmic examples include *X-Men: Days of Future Past* (2014), with its strategic efforts to excise the narrative continuities of *X-Men: The Last Stand* (2006) and *X-Men Origins: Wolverine* (2009) via convoluted time-travel machinations.

11. See the following: Gallagher 304; Harries 287; Neale 212; and Williams 123–124.

12. For one example, see Fantom Headquarters.

13. These numbers were culled from the titles listed in Kinnard and additional titles listed in the aforementioned IMDb Power Search of American feature films released between 1911 and 2018 that were based on comics.

14. For a summary of popular resistance to the latter film, see Ryan.

15. See also Reynolds (16).

16. For examples, see McKenzie; and "Superhero Tropes."

17. For a typical example, see the "Why Batman Isn't a Superhero" discussion board at http://comicvine.gamespot.com/forums/gen-discussion-1/why-batman-isn-t-a-superhero-1477465/.

18. For a brief survey of the centrality of superhero properties within franchise filmmaking, see Balio (26–28).

19. For a discussion of this brand distinction, see McWeeny.

Works Cited

Agar, Chris. "Are There Too Many Superhero Movies for Hollywood to Handle?" *Screen Rant*, 8 November 2014, http://screenrant.com/superhero-movies-box-office-release-dates.

Altman, Rick. "A Semantic/Syntactic Approach to Film Genre." *Cinema Journal*, vol. 23, no. 3, 1984, pp. 6–18.

———. *Film/Genre*. London, BFI, 1999.

Balio, Tino. *Hollywood in the New Millennium*. Basingstoke, UK, Palgrave Macmillan, 2013.

Blake, Corey. "Too Many Superhero Movies?" *CBR*, 29 October 2014, https://www.cbr.com/too-many-superhero-movies/.

Bukatman, Scott. "Why I Hate Superhero Movies." *Cinema Journal*, vol. 50, no. 3, 2011, pp. 118–122.

Burke, Liam. *The Comic Book Film Adaptation: Exploring Modern Hollywood's Leading Genre*. Jackson, University Press of Mississippi, 2015.

Cawelti, John. "*Chinatown* and Generic Transformation in Recent American Films." *Film Genre Reader IV*, edited by Barry Keith Grant, Austin, University of Texas Press, 2012, pp. 279–297.

Chute, Hillary, and Marianne Dekoven. "Comic Books and Graphic Novels." *The Cambridge Companion to Popular Fiction*, edited by David Glover and Scott McCracken, Cambridge, UK, Cambridge University Press, 2012, pp. 175–195.

Coogan, Peter. *Superhero: The Secret Origin of a Genre*. Austin, TX, MonkeyBrain Books, 2016.

Deleyto, Celestino. "Film Genres at the Crossroads: What Genres and Films Do to Each Other." *Film Genre Reader IV*, edited by Barry Keith Grant, Austin, University of Texas Press, 2012, pp. 218–236.

Dirks, Tim. "Superheroes on Film." *Filmsite*, n.d., http://www.filmsite.org/superheroesonfilm.html.

"Domestic Theatrical Market Summary for 2018." *The Numbers*, 28 December 2018, http://www.the-numbers.com/market/2018/summary.

Fantom Headquarters. "2014 in Review: Comic Book Sales Trends for Fantom Comics." *Fantom Comics*, 5 May 2015, http://fantomcomics.com/blog/2015/05/05/comicbooksalestrends/.

"Franchises [2016]." *Box Office Mojo*, n.d., http://www.boxofficemojo.com/franchises/.

Gallagher, Tag. "Shoot-Out at the Genre Corral: Problems in the 'Evolution' of the Western." *Film Genre Reader IV*, edited by Barry Keith Grant, Austin, University of Texas Press, 2012, pp. 298–312.

"Genres: Genre Definitions." *IMDb*, n.d., https://help.imdb.com/article/contribution/titles/genres/GZDRMS6R742JRGAG?ref_=helpms_helpart_inline#.

Grant, Barry Keith. *Film Genre: From Iconography to Ideology*. London, Wallflower, 2011.

Grindon, Leger. "Cycles and Clusters: The Shape of Film Genre History." *Film Genre Reader IV*, edited by Barry Keith Grant, Austin, University of Texas Press, 2012, pp. 42–59.

Harries, Dan. "Film Parody and the Resuscitation of Genre." *Genre and Contemporary Hollywood*, edited by Steve Neale, London, BFI, 2002, pp. 281–293.

Hutcheon, Linda. *A Theory of Adaptation*. New York, Routledge, 2006.

Johnston, Derek. "Cinematic Destiny: Marvel Studios and the Trade Stories of Industrial Convergence." *Cinema Journal*, vol. 52, no. 1, 2012, pp. 1–24.

Kinnard, Roy. *The Comics Come Alive: A Guide to Comic Book Characters in Live-Action Productions*. Metuchen, NJ, Scarecrow Press, 1991.

Klock, Geoff. *How to Read Superhero Comics and Why*. New York, Continuum, 2002.

Langford, Barry. *Film Genre: Hollywood and Beyond*. Edinburgh, UK, Edinburgh University Press, 2005.

"Max Landis and James Gunn at MorrisonCon." YouTube video, uploaded by Mark Warner, 5 October 2012, https://www.youtube.com/watch?v=oQmJTvokyjQ.

McClintock, Pamela. "Warner Bros. Film Chief on 'Wonder Woman,' J. K. Rowling's 'Fantastic Beasts' Script and How DC Will Compete with Marvel." *Hollywood Reporter*, 3 June 2015, http://www.hollywoodreporter.com/news/warner-bros-film-chief-wonder-799408.

McKenzie, Brian. "List of Superhero Cliches, Tropes, and Conventions." *Superhero Nation*, 18 December 2011, http://www.superheronation.com/2011/12/18/cliches-in-superhero-stories/.

McWeeny, Drew. "Why Superman and Batman May Lose the War to Marvel Before They Even Begin." *Hitfix*, 26 August 2014, https://uproxx.com/hitfix/why-dcs-serious-superman-may-give-marvel-the-big-screen-edge/.

Mendelson, Scott. "No, There Are Not Too Many Comic Book Movies." *Forbes*, 7 January 2015, http://www.forbes.com/sites/scottmendelson/2015/01/07/batman-iron-man-and-wolverine-arent-taking-over-hollywood/.

Neale, Steve. *Genre and Hollywood*. New York, Routledge, 2000.

Pustz, Matthew J. *Comic Book Culture: Fanboys and True Believers*. Jackson, University Press of Mississippi, 1999.

Reynolds, Richard. *Superheroes: A Modern Mythology*. Jackson, University Press of Mississippi, 1992.

Ryan, Kyle. "Mass *Watchmen* Walk-Outs?" *The A.V. Club*, 10 March 2009, http://www.avclub.com/article/mass-watchmen-walk-outs-24907.

Schatz, Thomas. "Movies and a Hollywood Too Big to Fail." *American Cinema of the 2000s*, edited by Timothy Corrigan, New Brunswick, NJ, Rutgers University Press, 2012, pp. 194–215.

Staiger, Janet. "Hybrid or Inbred: The Purity Hypothesis and Hollywood Genre History." *Film Genre Reader IV*, edited by Barry Keith Grant, Austin, University of Texas Press, 2012, pp. 203–217.

"Superhero Tropes." *TV Tropes*, n.d., https://tvtropes.org/pmwiki/pmwiki.php/Main/SuperheroTropes.

Tait, R. Colin. "The HBO-ification of Genre." *Cinephile*, vol. 4, no. 1, 2008, pp. 50–57.

Tudor, Andrew. *Theories of Film*. New York, Viking, 1974.

Ulanoff, Lance. "Enough, Already, with the Superhero Movies." *Mashable*, 15 July 2015, http://mashable.com/2015/07/15/too-many-superhero-movies/#lz6g8aO8WPqn.

Walton, Saige. "Baroque Mutants in the 21st Century? Rethinking Genre through the Superhero." *The Contemporary Comic Book Superhero*, edited by Angela Ndalianis, New York, Routledge, 2009, pp. 86–106.

Weintraub, Steve. "Exclusive: Josh Trank and Simon Kinberg Talk *Fantastic Four*." *Collider*, 26 January 2015, http://collider.com/the-fantastic-four-movie-details-josh-trank/.

Williams, Alan. "Is a Radical Genre Criticism Possible?" *Quarterly Review of Film Studies*, vol. 9, no. 2, 1984, pp. 121–125.

"Yearly Box Office." *Box Office Mojo*, 1 August 2016, http://www.boxofficemojo.com/yearly/.

Destroying the Rainbow Bridge: Representations of Heterosexuality in Marvel Superhero Narratives

MIRIAM KENT

The focus of this chapter is recent adaptations of Marvel comic book super-hero narratives, as well as the comics on which they are based. Noting the parallels between mainstream comics and Hollywood industry conventions, I discuss the construction of heterosexual superheroism as informed by discussions of postfeminism and gender constructionism within these narratives. Recent forays into gender issues and superhero narratives have proved valuable in both comics studies (Lavin; Ricca; Robinson; DiPaolo; Brown; Stuller; Gibson) and film studies (Schubart; Stasia; Waites; Purse; Kaklamanidou; Gray), but few of these studies have considered the ways in which heterosexuality is constructed as a constituent of superheroism, and few address both comics and film. This chapter aims to address these gaps and provide new avenues for considering the role of heterosexuality in super-hero narratives.

Given the significance of the (male) superhero's apparent sexual and heroic subjectivity, then, this chapter interrogates Marvel adaptations' discursive and cinematic constructions of a superheroic sexuality that is by default hetero. Indeed, while superhero comics have portrayed characters who can be considered queer (as defined by Michael Warner's use of the term as denoting nonnormative sexualities "at odds with straight culture" [38]), such characters remain conspicuously absent from adaptations of Marvel comics. Compulsory heterosexuality is a component of hegemonic masculinity, which is "built upon the assumption of men's natural supremacy over women (and effeminate men)" (Charlebois 24). To add to this dynamic, though, is the equally pervasive issue of postfeminist culture, which also promotes the supposedly natural binary opposition between men and women and a reaffirmation of traditional gender roles, including that of "protective paternalism" enacted by male heroes (Godfrey and Hamad). Postfeminism involves a series of contemporary cultural discourses that rely on notions of feminine empowerment put forward by second-wave feminism while ultimately denouncing politicized movements calling for women's equality (McRobbie). This chapter therefore takes the form of a textual analysis informed by feminist critiques of postfeminist culture, as well as reaching to the established field of queer theory to enable a reading of the construction of Marvel characters' heterosexualities within both comics and films. I ultimately determine the ways in which both media utilize a superheroic narrative resting on a naturalized heterosexuality that functions in tandem with the superhero subjectivity. Throughout this chapter, "heterosexuality" is referred to as an institution that shapes media discourses, affecting the representation of both gender and sexuality.

Gender Dynamics in Marvel Comics and Film

The Hero's Journey, the key narrative identified by Joseph Campbell on which many major Hollywood blockbusters have been based since the 1970s, predicates that the central protagonists of such films must be male (Campbell). Developments in the conventions of the contemporary blockbuster likewise call for a male protagonist, or, in the words of Thomas Schatz, an "utterly naïve man-child" (32). Furthermore, recent revelations from leaked emails sourced from Sony, the studio that has produced numerous films based on Marvel's Spider-Man, clearly marked a number of "mandatory" traits of the character, including that he be male and "not a homosexual" (Biddle).

Superhero films are said to broadly partake of action genre conventions (Lichtenfeld 254). Interestingly, action cinema has followed a remarkably similar trajectory to mainstream comic books in terms of how gender representations have been discussed. Since the late 1960s, male audiences have been the main demographic for big-budget Hollywood blockbusters, including those in the action genre (Chapman 190–191). Given the prevalence of gendered discourses regarding the content of Hollywood industry knowledge, "men's films" are considered to focus on action and violence, whereas "women's films" prioritize character and emotion (Krämer). Efforts are often made to reconcile the two, resulting in action films containing romance elements, while still centralizing the narrative of the male protagonist (Maltby 21). Like comics, action cinema has had a noted tendency to marginalize feminine characters, such as those who suffer kidnapping, rape, and even death to provide the hero with the motivation needed to defeat the villain

(Tasker 16). Such narrative mechanisms are significantly similar to the infamous "women in refrigerators" trope, a term coined by comic book writer Gail Simone, who noted the prevalence of tragedies inflicted upon women in superhero comics "in service of male superhero narratives" (Mandville 206).

Both comics and films are sites of struggle in terms of the subjectivities presented (or not presented) therein. Like the mainstream films critiqued in seminal works by authors such as Laura Mulvey, popular comic books have been characterized as male dominated (Pustz 101). While feminist comics scholars have been combatting this perception recently, suggesting that women's reading habits and representations are more complex than has been previously argued (Healey; Scott), the notion that superheroes are "for boys" remains ingrained in the Western cultural consciousness. Indeed, superhero comics have been noted for their fetishization of violence inflicted upon women by men (DiPaolo 119; Robbins 216; McDaniel 88). In this sense superhero comics are considered masculine territory.

As noted, the established trope of the victimized superhero girlfriend has lent itself particularly well to the contemporary action cinema in terms of its gender dynamics. The death of Gwen Stacy in the *Spider-Man* comics of the 1970s marked a watershed moment for comics, heralding darker, more "adult" story lines (Blumberg). In the narrative, Peter Parker's heroic alter ego, Spider-Man, seeks revenge on his archnemesis, the Green Goblin, after the villain kidnaps Gwen, the love of Peter's life, and drops her off the George Washington Bridge. Though Peter supposedly unwittingly caused Gwen's death with the force of the web he used to catch her, he is motivated to kill the Goblin. Notably, in accordance with the character's heroism, Spider-Man does not immediately cause his nemesis's death; the Goblin dies instead when he is impaled by his own flying device (Conway and Kane). Gwen's death represents the epitome of women's victimization in mainstream comics of that era, particularly when considering the assertions of the editors, who argued that the only narrative alternative to Gwen's death would have been marriage (Blumberg).

The contemporary blockbuster's need for a romantic subplot is then happily wedded to the comic books on which Marvel adaptations are based. Films such as Sam Raimi's *Spider-Man* trilogy (2002, 2004, 2007), *The Punisher* (1989) and its 2004 remake, *The Amazing Spider-Man 2* (2013) — which directly depicts the death of Gwen Stacy — and, to an extent, *Iron Man* (2008), all feature major plot points in which the wives or girlfriends of the central heroes are kidnapped, tortured, or killed, propelling the hero into action. This is constructed using cinematic conventions as well as through

Masculine action and feminine victimization in *Spider-Man* (2002).

the narrative. For instance, in *Spider-Man* (2002), while Peter (Tobey Maguire) and the Green Goblin (Willem Dafoe) engage in a climactic fight, Spider-Man is shown finally defeating the Goblin with all of his strength after the Goblin taunts Spider-Man by saying, "I'm going to finish her nice and slow," referring to Peter's girlfriend, Mary Jane Watson (Kirsten Dunst). Importantly, Spider-Man's masculinity is cinematically highlighted through shots of Peter's exposed face, which is covered in blood, sweat, and saliva after having been beaten by the Goblin. This is presented in slow motion in order to highlight the physical assault on the masculine body that the hero is forced to endure. Peter likewise emits a series of manly cries as he finally pushes the Goblin away. The masculine body in action cinema is inextricably linked with markers of physical exertion, such as bodily fluids and battle cries (Purse 81), and thus Peter's overcoming the Goblin via the threats made to Mary Jane is portrayed as an act of explicitly masculine action motivated by the endangered heterosexual union. It is in such ways that conventional superhero narratives reify traditional gender roles of masculine action and feminine victimization via dominant discourses of heterosexuality.

Heterosexual Dysfunction in Marvel Superhero Narratives

There is more to be said about heterosexuality in Marvel superhero narratives. If heteronormativity, which signifies "the institutions, structures of understanding, and practical orientations that make heterosexuality seem not only coherent—that is, organized as a sexuality—but also privileged" (Berlant and Warner 548), is present everywhere and not just in sexual acts, it is worth determining the relationship between superheroism and heterosexuality. Likewise, given the inextricable link between how gender and sexuality are conceived, as well as the apparent reliance by superhero narratives on binaristic notions of gender, it is useful to triangulate Marvel's portrayals of heterosexuality, gender, and superheroism and account for the impact on these representations by both comics and film within the palimpsestic web of texts. Herein, the filmic Marvel superhero text can be positioned as a "recontextualization" (Casetti 83) of the prior comic book text that has been reassembled in correspondence with cultural factors.

Theorists supporting a constructionist notion of gender note that both gender and sexuality are socially constructed. Judith Butler in particular has argued for an understanding of gender as constituting cultural discourses and behaviors that are repeated over time (*Gender Trouble* 43). Judith Lorber similarly notes that the gender binary is one of the foundational elements of society, in which biological sex and other factors such as race are used as "crude markers" of "ascribed social statuses" (43). The gender binary thus functions within political, hierarchical terms, maintaining the gender order. Such discourses, which promote an essentialized notion of gender, constitute what Michael Kimmel refers to as an "interplanetary" approach to gender in which men and women are discursively constructed as so inherently different that they may as well hail from different planets (usually Mars and Venus) (1). This perspective, as Kimmel notes, ignores the myriad similarities between genders, while only privileging the perceived differences.

Likewise, postfeminist culture, which is often considered to mark a return to traditionalist modes of gender, also capitalizes from such essentialist notions. Diane Negra, for example, argues that portrayals of women's life stages focus predominantly on the quest for finding heterosexual love and starting a family (173). Rosalind Gill likewise notes the postfeminist effort behind the "reassertion of sexual difference" in the media since the 1990s (158). Gill ultimately argues that "discourses of natural gender difference can be used to freeze in place existing inequalities by representing them as inevitable" (159). As I will suggest, this "inevitability" of sexual difference, through which heterosexuality is also articulated, plays a considerable role within Marvel superhero narratives.

The maintenance of the binaristic gender order informs what Butler terms the "heterosexual matrix" (*Gender Trouble* 9), maintaining masculine dominance through the "culturally intelligible grids of an idealized and compulsory heterosexuality" (185). This creates meaning out of the interlocking notions of sexuality and gender, which serve patriarchal hierarchies of gender dominance. Here, we can see the interlocking of notions of sexuality and gender culminating to maintain gender order. Furthermore, Butler argues that it is crucial for heterosexuality to be constantly repeated and emphasized in order to perpetuate the heterosexual matrix. Heteronormative structures present heterosexuality as the "original" sexuality, while homosexuality is merely a copy (Butler, "Imitation and Gender"). However, Butler argues, this only occurs as a result of heterosexuality's compulsory nature, and thus heterosexuality will only ever be a copy of itself. This is because heterosexuality is constantly reproducing copies of itself to allay the anxiety that it could be questioned and rendered optional instead of compulsory (Butler, "Imitation and Gender" 313). Thus, heterosexuality can be hard to "see" or make sense of when represented in media texts, since such representations occupy "an unspoken invisible centrality" (Griffin 13).

As noted by Negra, heterosexual marriage is often centralized in postfeminist culture. However, the furor over marriage in Marvel comics has been notably present throughout the publisher's history. *Fantastic Four Annual* #3 was declared "the most sensational super-spectacular ever witnessed by human eyes!!" (Lee and Kirby, "Bedlam"). While hyperbole was part and parcel of Marvel's output at the time, this issue was deemed particularly noteworthy because it featured Fantastic Four members Reed Richards (Mister Fantastic) and Susan Storm (the Invisible "Girl") tying the knot. In the issue the wedding is such a phenomenon that it occupies the front page of the news, which is begrudgingly read by a furious Doctor Doom, who aims to seek revenge on Reed for defeating him previously. Similarly, Spider-Man's wedding to Mary Jane in *Amazing Spider-Man Annual* #21 is gratuitously displayed on the cover of the issue, with the happy couple beaming in front of the heart-shaped Spider-Man emblem and the wedding attendees (an alternate cover shows Peter in his Spider-Man costume and replaces the wedding guests with an assortment of Marvel heroes and villains in confrontational poses) (Michelinie, Shooter, and Ryan). Here we can see a union (or marriage) of familiar wedding and superhero iconographies.

Recent portrayals of heterosexuality have become increasingly complex. In her analysis of heterosexuality in the science fiction television series *Star Trek: The Next Generation* (1987–1994), Lee Heller suggests that heterosexuality occupies a discursive space that is marked explicitly as both utopic and unfulfilling. She ultimately argues that the series "tries to imagine utopian romantic configurations and ideal sexual others, only to tell us, first, that such relationships are necessarily heterosexual, and second, that heterosexuality is inherently unable to fulfil the desire it is supposed to serve" (Heller

Familiar wedding and superhero iconographies merge in *Amazing Spider-Man Annual* #21 (1987).

226). This paradox is based dually on the idea that men and women are complementary (Hunter 311), but also draws from the interplanetary perspective described by Kimmel. In this sense, Heller notes, media texts offer a view of men and women as "made for each other" because they are different, and yet totally incompatible—also because they are different. She continues that "in popular media accounts of heterosexual gender trouble, the key term is not just difference, but difference that divides" (Heller 227). This dividing difference is a foundational element of Marvel's representations of heterosexual romance and is interestingly intertwined with the superheroic narratives.

Numerous films based on Marvel comics draw on the idea that the central characters—the romantic couple—are "meant to be together." The dysfunctional-utopic nature of heterosexuality is highlighted in both *The Incredible Hulk* (2008) and *Captain America: The First Avenger* (2011), and both films similarly intermingle the heterosexuality with the superheroic narratives. *The Incredible Hulk* incorporates this as an element of dysfunction within its utopian heterosexuality. Bruce Banner (Edward Norton), who turns into the Hulk when he gets angry after being infected by gamma radiation, lives in Brazil, desperately trying to find a cure for his condition. In the opening of the film, during which Bruce is concocting a potential cure, the film indicates that he is so eager to find it because he is in love with his former associate, Betty Ross (Liv Tyler). This is intercut with frequent shots of a newspaper clipping Bruce keeps that includes a picture of Betty. Meanwhile, Betty is also unconditionally devoted to Bruce. This narrative arrangement clearly reaches to what Bordwell, Staiger, and Thompson refer to as the double plot of classical Hollywood cinema (16). Here, two strands of action intertwine within the film and unite a group of characters. The authors note that "almost invariably, one of these lines of action involves heterosexual romantic love" (16). Thus, the composition of these films and the characters therein are arranged according to dominant notions of sexuality and gender.

The characters' mutual yearning for each other is highlighted in a scene in which both lie in their beds in separate rooms. An aerial shot of Betty gradually zooms in as she is lying in her bed, looking concerned. It cuts to a similar shot of Bruce, then back to Betty, who is close to crying, then back to Bruce. The next shot is of Betty, touching her face and closing her eyes. The concern, here, is presented as the dilemma of the great danger they face—Betty harbors a known fugitive; Bruce is on the run from the US Army—but it is framed within the heterosexual conundrum asking, "However will their love survive?" Thus, Betty and Bruce are destined to be together as complementary soul mates but ultimately cannot be together because he is the

Hulk. Bruce's status as the Hulk also contributes to the heterosexuality's dysfunction, which is explicitly expressed during a would-be sex scene: Bruce and Betty are unable to have sex because it would increase his heart rate, which essentially causes him to "Hulk out."

At the end of the film, Bruce must bid farewell to Betty in order to defeat the film's villain, Emil Blonsky (Tim Roth), who has turned himself into a sort of mega-Hulk (the Abomination). This farewell takes place in a helicopter that is transporting the two to safety while Blonsky goes on a rampage in the city. Bruce tells Betty he has to be the one to stop Blonsky, while Betty begs him not to go. The night sky with violent clouds indicates both the peril in which the heterosexual union is placed and the danger that Bruce is putting himself into as they finally kiss goodbye in close-up. This is followed by a medium shot of Bruce allowing himself to drop to the ground. Again, the heterosexual union and danger of the narrative amalgamate and become almost inseparable.

Captain America: The First Avenger is also a notable example of the way in which heterosexuality's dysfunction is intertwined with the narrative alongside its utopic principles. The film's romance narrative focuses on the potential love between British agent Peggy Carter (Hayley Atwell) and Captain America, Steve Rogers (Chris Evans). Significantly, they are made for each other because they both, on separate occasions, state that they are looking for the right partner to dance with. This first happens when Peggy and Steve discuss Steve's love life, or lack thereof, and how Peggy is going to go dancing with him, and then again in a subsequent scene in which Steve's friend Bucky makes a pass at Peggy in a bar, only to be rejected because Peggy is only interested in Steve. However, Steve and Peggy will never be united, as Steve, after becoming Captain America and defeating the evil Nazi the Red Skull (Hugo Weaving), finds himself alone on an aircraft carrying weapons of mass destruction over which he has lost control. With the plane heading to New York, he calls Peggy over the radio and explains that he must land the plane in the sea, leaving slim chance of his survival. Soft music plays in the background of these shots, which cut between Peggy at the army headquarters and Steve in the plane. After an emotional exchange, Steve is cut off just as he expresses worries about stepping on Peggy's feet when they finally dance. Peggy repeats Steve's name before being shown in a long shot, hunched over her desk, with sad music in the background. These final scenes are a culmination of the inseparability of the heterosexuality and the heroic narrative. Further, Peggy and Steve's complementarity is again coupled with the unfulfilled union — this time, Peggy and Steve will never be together, as Peggy will be an old woman by the time Steve is thawed out of the ice that preserves his body after he crashes into the sea.

In these narratives, heterosexuality is intertwined within the form of the film's narrative, characters, and composition, rather than being an isolated plot or subplot. Simultaneously, this functions both to showcase the utopic ("they were meant for each other") yet dysfunctional ("they can never be together") nature of heterosexuality, making it appear natural and invisible. Whereas the "women in refrigerators" narratives explicitly implicate the superhero girlfriends within the action by utilizing them as plot points, the intermeshing that the heterosexuality and the narrative peril undertake is a more covert formation of dominant ideologies, drawing the gender in as part of the overall representation of heterosexuality. The heterosexual matrix thus becomes even more naturalized when the perils of heroism and the dysfunction of heterosexuality are presented as one naturally occurring, commonsensical phenomenon.

This bond between the heroic narrative and heterosexuality is so strong that when male characters enter the world of superheroics (that is, when they acquire their powers), they actually enter the world of heterosexual dysfunction. The most notable example of this occurs in *Captain America: The First Avenger*. When Steve is introduced in the film, he is portrayed as small, weak, and sickly, unable to join the army. This is framed by heterosexual discourses in the aforementioned scene with Peggy. Peggy escorts Steve to the secret lab where he will receive the Super Soldier Serum that turns him into Captain America. In the car on the way there, Steve and Peggy talk about women. Steve is flustered, and Peggy interjects, "You have no idea how to talk to a woman, do you?" to which he replies, "I think this is the longest conversation I've had with one. Women aren't exactly lining up to dance with a guy they might step on," which leads to the exchange about dancing. Importantly, Steve's status as a weak, powerless man is also presented as what makes him unattractive to women. He thus exists outside of heterosexual dysfunction, or even any sort of sexuality. It therefore follows that after Steve receives the Super Soldier treatment, he immediately becomes attractive to women, which is signaled by Peggy quite clearly eyeing up his newly muscular body, even touching his chest, after he is removed from the machine that grants him his powers. Now taller, stronger, and more conventionally attractive, Steve has entered the world of (masculine) superheroics, but he has simultaneously entered the world of heterosexual dysfunction.

The parallel introduction of male characters to the realm of heroism and heterosexuality has been present in Marvel narratives for some time. Joseph Willis, for example, notes that in Spider-Man's origin story in *Amazing Fantasy* #15 (Lee and Kirby, "Spider-Man"), pre-spider-bite Peter Parker is shown as being specifically unattractive to women, with his female classmates making unkind comments toward him (Willis). In this sense, he has

Peggy Carter (Hayley Atwell) eyes the newly muscular body of Steve Rogers (Chris Evans) in *Captain America: The First Avenger* (2011).

been barred from partaking of heterosexuality (and hence from any sexuality, since heteronormativity dictates the invisibility of alternatives). After he acquires his powers, however, he becomes more integrated into the group of teens and is admired by women while in his Spider-Man persona. Willis thus argues that after he acquires his powers and becomes a hero, he also realizes his heterosexual potential: "With powers come a superhero identity, and a sexual identity. However, in the superhero narrative, this development of a sexual identity is framed in a specifically hetero-normative construct and subject to patriarchal power structures of strict gendered performances" (Willis). This twinning of superheroic narratives with heterosexuality has thus been maintained throughout the decades and throughout both film and comic book media. It also speaks to the coming-of-age elements of the Sam Raimi *Spider-Man* trilogy's narrative, which are framed both by the responsibility discourses in Uncle Ben's death and Peter's emergence within the arena of heterosexual coupling. However, I would suggest that these heroes not only enter the world of heterosexuality on receiving their powers, but that it is a world in which heterosexuality is dually utopic and dysfunctional, thus indicating an adaptation of the material to contemporary postfeminist rhetoric.

Such sentiments are further evident in contemporary Marvel comics, particularly a recent story line centering on Peter Parker's marriage to Mary Jane. After the couple got married in 1987, Marvel subsequently decided to erase the story from existence in the late 2000s. Here, Peter makes a deal with the demon Mephisto in order to save Aunt May's life. In return, Mephisto removes the marriage from living memory (Straczynski and Quesada). The story line disrupts the utopic constitution of Peter and MJ's marriage. Further, statements leading up to the story's publishing by Marvel's then editor in chief and artist of the story line, Joe Quesada, are quite illuminating. Chronicling his loathing for the wedding since the story was told in the 1980s, Quesada expresses a duty toward the character to undo the marriage, stating, "Are Peter and MJ okay as is, sure, but a lot of the drama and soap opera that was an integral part of the Spider-Man mythos is gone" (qtd. in "Joe Fridays"). Hence, Quesada's reasoning with regard to the marriage is that a married couple is too utopic, which results in a lack of drama, which he perceives as a main attraction of Peter's story lines. However, Quesada continues: "I always hated the portrayal of the marriage, and by that I mean that for years after they were married they were never really portrayed as truly happy[;] I don't understand in a way why that was done. I believe it was an attempt by the creators back then to bring back a much-needed tension to the relationship side of Peter's world that was now missing because he was no longer single. It was an attempt to bring back the soap opera" (qtd. in "Joe Fridays").

Here Quesada expresses what he perceives as an inconsistency in Peter's marriage—that marriages should be perfect, that there is no room for "soap opera" in representations of a marriage. The incongruities of heterosexual romance resurface. Marriage, which is perceived as the ultimate, perfect heterosexual union, was considered inappropriate for Peter Parker. Rather, it was preferred that he partake of the combined dysfunctional-utopic heterosexuality that accompanies single life. The heterosexual utopia must be fulfilled, but at the same time, it cannot flourish.

Heller's overarching argument is that the characters in *Star Trek: The Next Generation* are prevented from fulfilling their heterosexual desires because men and women, despite being complementary, are presented as being just too different. Subsequently, Heller extends this argument in terms of postfeminist discourses, arguing that postfeminist rhetoric has resulted in a call on the part of men for a return to traditional gender roles (229). It has also resulted in a resurgence of a demand for women to be accommodating of men's flaws and not prevent men from embodying their "natural" desires (230). Only then can heterosexual relationships be made to "work." Thus, she states, women are encouraged to "tolerate, rather than challenge, difference as an essential component of heterosexual relationships" (228). Significantly, it is the different-yet-made-for-each-other qualities of heterosexuality that are stressed as being crucial, even necessary, elements of heterosexual romance. Thus, this reading of heterosexuality in Marvel superhero narratives is not necessarily performing a "queering" function of banal romance; rather, it is in postfeminist culture's interest to present such relationships as desirable.

Through this lens it is possible to consider the implications of the superhero narrative within wider discourses of sexuality and gender and how these come to the fore through the act of adaptation. In such a context it becomes clear that the superhero narrative, in whichever medium, elaborates these relationships. Further, the palimpsestic relationship between comics and their film adaptations is perhaps unexpectedly tied to the institution of heterosexuality. This should be considered alongside readings of superheroes as elaborating queer identities (see for instance Lendrum; Purse; Fawaz). While superheroes, as exceptional beings who often undertake experiences that resonate with queer milestones (such as "coming out" as superheroes), certainly speak to notions of queer identity, it should not be understated that superhero narratives overwhelmingly partake of dominant structures of heterosexual coupling. Such narratives rigorously reassert heterosexuality in an age where LGBTQ identities are becoming more widely accepted in Western culture.

Note: This essay was supported by the Arts and Humanities Research Council, United Kingdom.

Works Cited

Berlant, Lauren, and Michael Warner. "Sex in Public." *Intimacy*, vol. 24, no. 2, 1998, pp. 547–566.
Biddle, Sam. "Spider-Man Can't Be Gay or Black." *Gawker*, 19 June 2015, http://gawker.com/spider-man-cant-be-gay-or-black-1712401879.
Blumberg, Arnold T. "'The Night Gwen Stacy Died': The End of Innocence and the Birth of the Bronze Age." *Reconstruction: Studies in Contemporary Culture*, vol. 3, no. 4, 2003, https://reconstruction.eserver.org/034/blumberg.htm.
Bordwell, David, Janet Staiger, and Kristin Thompson. *The Classical Hollywood Cinema: Film Style and Mode of Production to 1960*. New York, Columbia University Press, 1985.
Brown, Jeffrey A. *Dangerous Curves: Heroines, Gender, Fetishism, and Popular Culture*. Jackson, University Press of Mississippi, 2011.
Butler, Judith. *Gender Trouble*. New York, Routledge, 1990.
———. "Imitation and Gender Insubordination." *The Lesbian and Gay Studies Reader*, edited by Henry Abelove, Michèle Aina Barale, and David M. Halperin, New York, Routledge, 1993, pp. 307–320.
Campbell, Joseph. *The Hero with a Thousand Faces*. 3rd ed., Novato, CA, New World Library, 2012.
Casetti, Francesco. "Adaptation and Mis-Adaptations: Film, Literature, and Social Discourses." *A Companion to Literature and Film*, edited by Robert Stam and Alessandra Raengo, Chichester, UK, Wiley Blackwell, 2004, pp. 81–91.
Chapman, James. *Cinemas of the World: Film and Society in the Twentieth Century*. London, Reaktion, 2004.

Charlebois, Justin. *Gender and the Construction of Dominant, Hegemonic, and Oppositional Femininities*. Lanham, MD, Rowman and Littlefield, 2011.

Conway, Gerry, and Gil Kane. "The Goblin's Last Stand!" *The Amazing Spider-Man* #122, July 1973, Marvel Comics.

DiPaolo, Marc. *War, Politics and Superheroes: Ethics and Propaganda in Comics and Film*. Jefferson, NC, McFarland, 2011.

Fawaz, Ramzi. *The New Mutants: Superheroes and the Radical Imagination of American Comics*. New York, New York University Press, 2016.

Gibson, Mel. "Who Does She Think She Is? Female Comic-Book Characters, Second-Wave Feminism and Feminist Film Theory." *Superheroes and Identities*, edited by Mel Gibson, David Huxley, and Joan Ormrod, New York, Routledge, 2014, pp. 135–146.

Gill, Rosalind. "Postfeminist Media Culture: Elements of a Sensibility." *European Journal of Cultural Studies*, vol. 10, no. 2, 2007, pp. 147–166.

Godfrey, Sarah, and Hannah Hamad. "Save the Cheerleader, Save the Male: Resurgent Protective Paternalism in Popular Film and Television after 9/11." *The Handbook of Gender, Sex, and Media*, edited by Karen Ross, New York, Wiley, 2011, pp. 157–173.

Gray, Richard J. "Vivacious Vixens and Scintillating Super Hotties: Deconstructing the Superheroine." *The 21st Century Superhero: Essays on Gender, Genre and Globalization in Film*, edited by Richard J. Gray and Betty Kaklamanidou, Jefferson, NC, McFarland, 2011, pp. 75–93.

Griffin, Sean. "Introduction." *Hetero: Queering Representations of Straightness*, edited by Sean Griffin, Albany, State University of New York Press, 2009, pp. 1–17.

Healey, Karen. "When Fangirls Perform: The Gendered Fan Identity in Superhero Comics Fandom." *The Contemporary Comic Book Superhero*, edited by Angela Ndalianis, New York, Routledge, 2009, pp. 144–163.

Heller, Lee E. "The Persistence of Difference: Postfeminism, Popular Discourse, and Heterosexuality in *Star Trek: The Next Generation*." *Science Fiction Studies*, vol. 24, no. 2, 1997, pp. 226–244.

Hunter, Erika. *Introducing the New Sexuality Studies*. 2nd ed., New York, Routledge, 2011.

Hutcheon, Linda. *A Theory of Adaptation*. New York, Routledge, 2006.

"Joe Fridays: Week 48." *Newsarama*, May 2006, http://web.archive.org/web/200605250 15750/http://www.newsarama.com/JoeFridays/JoeFridays48.html.

Kaklamanidou, Betty. "The Mythos of Patriarchy in the X-Men Films." *The 21st Century Superhero: Essays on Gender, Genre and Globalization in Film*, edited by Richard J. Gray and Betty Kaklamanidou, Jefferson, NC, McFarland, 2011, pp. 61–74.

Kimmel, Michael. *The Gendered Society*. New York, Oxford University Press, 2000.

Krämer, Peter. "Women First: *Titanic* (1997), Action-Adventure Films and Hollywood's Female Audience." *Historical Journal of Film, Radio and Television*, vol. 18, no. 4, 1998, pp. 599–618.

Lavin, Michael R. "Women in Comic Books." *Serials Review*, vol. 24, no. 2, 1998, pp. 93–100.

Lee, Stan, and Jack Kirby. "Bedlam at the Baxter Building!" *Fantastic Four Annual* #3, October 1965, Marvel Comics.

———. "Spider-Man!" *Amazing Fantasy* #15, August 1962, Marvel Comics.

Lendrum, Rob. "Queering Super-Manhood: The Gay Superhero in Contemporary

Mainstream Comic Books." *Journal for Arts, Sciences, and Technology*, vol. 2, no. 2, 2004, pp. 69–73.

Lichtenfeld, Eric. *Action Speaks Louder: Violence, Spectacle, and the American Action Movie*. Westport, CT, Praeger, 2004.

Lorber, Judith. "'Night to His Day': The Social Construction of Gender." *The Social Construction of Difference and Inequality*, edited by Tracy E. Ore, New York, McGraw-Hill, 2000, pp. 54–65.

Maltby, Richard. *Hollywood Cinema*. Oxford, UK, Blackwell, 2003.

Mandville, Alison. "Out of the Refrigerator: Gail Simone's Wonder Woman, 2008–2010." *The Ages of Wonder Woman: Essays on the Amazon Princess in Changing Times*, edited by Joseph J. Darowski, Jefferson, NC, McFarland, 2014, pp. 205–222.

McDaniel, Anita K. "Comics, 1960–2005." *Women in Science Fiction and Fantasy*, edited by Robin Anne Reid, New York, Oxford University Press, 2008, pp. 84–93.

McRobbie, Angela. "Post-Feminism and Popular Culture." *Interrogating Postfeminism: Gender and the Politics of Popular Culture*, edited by Yvonne Tasker and Diane Negra, Durham, NC, Duke University Press, 2007, pp. 27–39.

Michelinie, David, Jim Shooter, and Paul Ryan. "The Wedding!" *Amazing Spider-Man Annual* #21, June 1987, Marvel Comics.

Mulvey, Laura. "Visual Pleasure and Narrative Cinema." *Film Theory and Criticism: Introductory Readings*, 6th ed., edited by Leo Braudy and Marshall Cohen, New York, Oxford University Press, 2006, pp. 837–848.

Negra, Diane. "Time Crisis and the New Postfeminist Heterosexual Economy." *Hetero: Queering Representations of Straightness*, edited by Sean Griffin, Albany, State University of New York Press, 2009, pp. 173–189.

Purse, Lisa. *Contemporary Action Cinema*. Edinburgh, UK, Edinburgh University Press, 2011.

Pustz, Matthew J. *Comic Book Culture: Fanboys and True Believers*. Jackson, University Press of Mississippi, 2000.

Ricca, Brad J. "The Female Hero in Comics." *Women in Science Fiction and Fantasy*, edited by Robin Anne Reid, New York, Oxford University Press, 2008, pp. 182–184.

Robbins, Trina. "Feminism." *Encyclopedia of Comic Books and Graphic Novels*, edited by M. Keith Booker, Westport, CT, Greenwood, 2010, pp. 212–218.

Robinson, Lillian S. *Wonder Women: Feminisms and Superheroes*. New York, Routledge, 2004.

Schatz, Thomas. "New Hollywood, New Millennium." *Film Theory and Contemporary Hollywood Movies*, edited by Warren Buckland, New York, Routledge, 2009, pp. 19–46.

Schubart, Rikke. *Super Bitches and Action Babes: The Female Hero in Popular Cinema, 1970–2006*. Jefferson, NC, McFarland, 2006.

Scott, Suzanne. "Fangirls in Refrigerators: The Politics of (In)Visibility in Comic Book Culture." *Transformative Works and Cultures*, vol. 13, 2013, http://journal.transformativeworks.org/index.php/twc/article/view/460/384.

Stam, Robert. "Introduction: The Theory and Practice of Adaptation." *Literature and Film: A Guide to the Theory and Practice of Film Adaptation*, edited by Robert Stam and Alessandra Raengo, Oxford, UK, Blackwell, 2005, pp. 1–51.

Stasia, Cristina L. "'My Guns Are in the Fendi!': The Postfeminist Female Action Hero." *Third Wave Feminism: A Critical Exploration*, 2nd ed., edited by Stacy Gillis, Gillian

Howie, and Rebecca Munford, Basingstoke, UK, Palgrave Macmillan, 2007, pp. 237–249.

Straczynski, J. Michael, and Joe Quesada. *Spider-Man: One More Day*. Marvel Comics, 2008.

Stuller, Jennifer K. "What Is a Female Superhero?" *What Is a Superhero?*, edited by Robin S. Rosenberg and Peter Coogan, New York, Oxford University Press, 2013, pp. 19–24.

Tasker, Yvonne. *Spectacular Bodies: Gender, Genre and the Action Cinema*. New York, Routledge, 1993.

Waites, Kate. "Babes in Boots: Hollywood's Oxymoronic Warrior Woman." *Chick Flicks: Contemporary Women at the Movies*, edited by Suzanne Ferriss and Mallory Young, Milton Park, UK, Taylor and Francis, 2008, pp. 204–220.

Warner, Michael. *The Trouble with Normal: Sex, Politics, and the Ethics of Queer Life*. Cambridge, MA, Harvard University Press, 2000.

Willis, Joseph. "Female Sex and Sexual Identity in the Superhero Narrative." Transitions 5: New Directions in Comics Studies, 25 October 2014, Birkbeck, University of London.

Mutatis Mutandis: Constructing Fidelity in the Comic Book Film Adaptation

JASON ROTHERY AND BENJAMIN WOO

In a short article for *Literature/Film Quarterly*, David T. Johnson named the summer of 2006 the "Summer of Adaptations": "This summer, the studios have once again relied heavily on adaptations to generate audiences [with] television shows, comic books, and novels all providing ample stores of material" (170). Yet this heavy reliance on adaptations was not the seasonal fad Johnson implied. A decade later, cinemas remain full of remakes, reboots, sequels, prequels, and other species of adaptations, and comic books and graphic novels remain common sources of intellectual property among filmmakers and studios. If Johnson's "Summer of Adaptations" demonstrated "the continued relevance of adaptation studies" (170), then the persistence of adaptations from more popular sources, including comic books and graphic novels, creates opportunities to rethink some of the field's preconceptions.

Initially configured as "film and literature," adaptation studies has pursued a relatively narrow range of questions about a narrow range of objects. Analyses traditionally focused on adaptations of canonical literature through comparisons between book and movie—what Leitch calls "the chimerical quest for fidelity" (100). Adaptation scholars have thoroughly—almost obsessively—rejected this quest for some time now (Andrew; Cartmell and Whelehan; Stam), yet comic book film adaptations seem to suggest a recentering of faithfulness. There is, for instance, a perceived similarity between the visual storytelling employed in comics and the cinema, and faithfulness remains a key criterion of value for audience members, whether they identify as comic book fans or not (Burke). But the more closely adaptors attempt to recreate the original text, the more attention they invite to the changes they do make (Furlong 188). Thus, critics are caught between the "chimerical" and theoretically unfashionable notion of fidelity and the summary dismissal of one of the audience's most important interpretative categories.

But what if we didn't have to choose? The contradictions of fidelity can be transcended if it is seen as a *discourse* about texts rather than a quality they possess. The question is not whether adaptations are faithful to their sources but how that relationship is constructed so that the changes screenwriters, directors, and designers introduce are accepted as *necessary*. As Robert Stam contends, before speaking of fidelity one ought first to ask, "Fidelity to what?" Should filmmakers "be faithful to the plot in its every detail . . . to the physical descriptions of characters? . . . Or is one to be faithful to the artist's intentions? But what might they be, and how are they to be inferred? . . . Or is the adapter-filmmaker to be true to the style of a work? To its narrative point of view? Or to its artistic devices?" (Stam 57–58). Stam means to demonstrate the fundamental instability of commonsense notions of fidelity, but in doing so he also points to its rich, multivalent possibilities. Following Stam's provocations, then, "fidelity" can be separated into at least four distinct frames: *narrative* fidelity (i.e., following preexisting plotlines and characters); *stylistic* or *visual* fidelity (i.e., modeling shots and sequences on the original visual text); *authorial* fidelity (i.e., following the authentic "vision" of the original author or authors); and a looser *essential* fidelity (i.e., staying true to the "spirit" of the source material). These frames may be deployed at any stage in the circuit of production, circulation, and reception. However, we are principally interested in promotional strategies embodied in a range of paratexts. They are not only key sites for articulating fidelity discourses but also the ones that most clearly indicate how producers want audiences to understand the films. This chapter explores the discursive strategies enacted by media producers to achieve or secure the chimerical but valuable perception of "fidelity" in cinematic adaptations of comic books and graphic novels.

Fidelity in the Field of Comics/Film

Louis Lumière's *L'arroseur arrosé* (1895), adapted from early comic art sources, including an 1887 comic strip by Hermann Vogle, could arguably be called the first "comic book movie" (Burke 3). Comics and film have had a promiscuous relationship ever since, with characters and techniques frequently moving between the two media. While this has been most clearly exemplified by the superhero adaptations of the last fifteen years, "comic book–related films have done much to [establish] *both* . . . the action-oriented mega-blockbuster *and* the thematically and/or visually innovative art film" (McAllister, Gordon, and Jancovich 109; emphasis added). As fields of cultural production, comics and film are homologously structured, split between a heteronomously oriented subfield of general production (i.e., pursuing large audiences for economic profits) and an autonomously oriented subfield of restricted production (i.e., pursuing small audiences for cultural profits) (Bourdieu). However, recent shifts in the political economy of media industries have led to ever greater levels of synergy between film and comics (Beaty). While one can still conceptualize a field of film without comics, the reverse is much harder.

We analyzed the framing of ten films produced and distributed over a span of fifteen years and sorted them into three groups based on their positions within this hybridized field of cultural production: namely, independent films based on alternative comics; smaller studio films based on independent comics; and blockbuster franchise films based on "mainstream" superhero comic books. In the first category, we looked at *Ghost World* (2001), *American Splendor* (2003), and *Persepolis* (2007); in the second, *Sin City* (2005), *Watchmen* (2009), and *Scott Pilgrim vs. the World* (2010); and in the third, *Spider-Man* (2002), *The Amazing Spider-Man* (2012), *The Avengers* (2012), and *Man of Steel* (2013). For each film, we examined a range of sources, including bonus features on DVD and Blu-ray releases, public panels at venues such as the San Diego Comic-Con, and reviews in the *New Yorker*, the *New York Times*, and the popular "fanboy" film gossip and criticism blog *Ain't It Cool News*. We anticipated that there would be marked shifts in the discursive strategies employed as we moved across these categories, which combine both industrial criteria (e.g., production and marketing budgets) and aesthetic ones (e.g., the audiences and taste cultures interpellated by them). While neither the categories nor the frames are entirely discrete, we posit that these three groups of cinematic adaptations experience broadly similar "problems" owing to their positions in the field of cultural production and that the strategies they adopt respond to these problems.

The Indie Comic Book Movie

While *American Splendor, Persepolis,* and *Ghost World* expected and enjoyed critical adulation, their relatively modest budgets meant that they would never see wide release in the North American market but rather circulate in a subfield of "indie" cinema.[1] *American Splendor,* based on Harvey Pekar's long-running, independently published underground comic of the same name, was adapted by the writer-director team of Shari Springer Berman and Robert Pulcini. The duo had previously made documentaries, and the film mixes fictional and documentary modes. *Ghost World* was also a first foray into fiction filmmaking for director Terry Zwigoff, who had previously directed the documentary *Crumb* (1994). Meanwhile, Marjane Satrapi's adaptation (with codirector Vincent Paronnaud) of her own two-part graphic novel *Persepolis* was her first film ever. As memoirs or biographies of real people, *American Splendor* and *Persepolis* are obviously less fantastical than the films in the other two categories; *Ghost World*'s narrative is also relatively "realistic," concerning several weeks in its protagonists' lives following their high school graduation. Further, they are the only films included in this study to be nominated for Academy Awards in a major "creative" category (Best Adapted Screenplay in all three cases).[2] In order to secure their place within the field of independent cinema, adaptors had to "domesticate" their source material, distancing it from prejudices about comic books as low culture that might still have been active among potential audiences in this subfield.

In order to do so, paratexts repeatedly highlight their cartoonist authors, simultaneously figuring the source material in an auteurist frame and securing authorial fidelity for its adaptation. For instance, Satrapi codirected *Persepolis* and is foregrounded in reviews and DVD special features, including a half-hour-long making-of featurette and a filmed panel at Cannes. In *Ghost World*'s spare DVD special features, Daniel Clowes (who is credited as co-screenwriter) receives attention similar to director Zwigoff and lead actor Thora Birch. Indeed, critics tended to treat Zwigoff and Clowes as a de facto duo, as in comments like, "Zwigoff and Clowes still haven't quite solved the problem of how to make a great film from a graphic novel" (Denby).[3] However, neither Satrapi nor Clowes is as central to their films as Pekar is to *American Splendor*. Already a quasi celebrity thanks to recurring appearances on *Late Night* and the *Late Show with David Letterman*, the real-life Pekar is a constant presence in the film itself and in the discourses surrounding it. He provides voice-over narration and appears in several "documentary" interludes. In one such scene, actor Paul Giamatti, who plays Pekar, takes a break from his performance and shares the frame with Pekar while grabbing food from the craft services table. Pekar stares into the camera with trademark disdain—indeed, he functions as a kind of bad conscience for the adaptors, noting for instance that Giamatti "don't look nothin' like me."

In these examples, authorial fidelity is supported by the filmmakers' use of visual or stylistic fidelity. In addition to its usual work of linking source material and adaptation, stylistic fidelity evokes the author by simulating their "graphiation," the distinctive and communicative "trace" of the artist's hand (Baetens). This is most evident in the animated feature *Persepolis*, which fully reproduces the aesthetic of Satrapi's drawings, though *American*

Splendor also features animated portraits of Pekar that reflect the styles of his various collaborators. In the short comic insert "My Movie Year" (written by Pekar and illustrated by Gary Dumm), codirector Shari Springer Berman claims, "We got this idea from Harvey's comics where he's drawn all kinds of ways by different artists. So we thought it'd be appropriate to give him different looks at different points in the film." Furthermore, *American Splendor* tries to evoke qualities of the comics form *in general* in addition to those specific to its source text, such as making the visual plane "curl" as if a page is being turned and using a set design intended to "resemble comic book panels" (Pulcini). More subtly, *Ghost World* author Clowes has described the film's use of color as an adaptation of his aesthetic and remarked upon Birch's "uncanny" resemblance to his drawings of her character, Enid Coleslaw (Hall; Clowes).

Yet this category is not without its tensions. Satrapi, for instance, denies a one-to-one correspondence between her graphic novel and its adaptation. Pushing back against the "storyboard" discourse that would construct comics as rough drafts for their filmic counterparts, Satrapi takes pains to preserve the autonomy of these respective media during the aforementioned panel at Cannes: "Certain people thought you just had to take the frames and film them one after another and that would give you a film. People draw a relationship between cinema and comics, but it's not true. Nor is a comic book a storyboard for filmmaking." We have already noted how Pekar serves as a reminder of the source material throughout *American Splendor*, and the fact that both it and *Persepolis* are presented as nonfiction adds another layer of "adaptation." In the commentary track for *American Splendor*, Pekar's family and friends—all of whom appear as themselves and are portrayed by actors in the film—frequently question him about the film's accuracy, up to and including anodyne details such as whether Pekar's hair was really "ever that long" (Brabner). Foregrounding the film's real-life subjects is another way of indexing its status as an adaptation, in a sense putting symbolic quotation marks around the whole film. In drawing closer to the authors, these films end up drawing attention to the ultimately unbridgeable chasm between source and adaptation.

The Cult Comic Book Movie

Turning to the second category, smaller studio films based on middlebrow comics, we find that source material is often valued for its distinctive (visual) style, a style that is tied to originating authors and must be carefully pre-

Persepolis (2000/2007) author and filmmaker Marjane Satrapi: source and adaptation.

served. The source material for films in this category tended to have devoted audiences that highly anticipated their adaptations, though none was a clear and unambiguous hit. For works seeking to occupy a space in between "quality" and the "popular" or the "independent" and the "mainstream" (Beaty and Woo 56), these strategies imply that the source material's genius can be guaranteed through the adaptation process by the active, if largely behind-the-scenes, participation of originating authors. For example, posters for *Sin City* consistently referred to the film as *Frank Miller's Sin City* despite the relatively low profile of both the work and its author outside of the comics world. Similarly, the intimate involvement of *Scott Pilgrim* cartoonist Bryan Lee O'Malley is highlighted in that film's Blu-ray special features: an hour-long featurette incorporates interviews with O'Malley, myriad shots of him on set interacting with cast and crew, and a commentary track (one of three included on the release) he recorded with director Edgar Wright. *Watchmen* is a more complicated case, as the comic's creators — writer Alan Moore and artist Dave Gibbons — took different positions on the film. The filmmakers mention Moore glowingly, if sparingly, but he famously disowned it, going so far as to refuse on-screen credit, while Gibbons seems to have performed a consultative role. However, Gibbons comes off as less central to the production than O'Malley or Miller to the films based on their work. While his presence in Blu-ray featurettes creates

Visual fidelity between comic book and film in *Watchmen* (1986/2009).

opportunities to underscore the film's visual fidelity—"It's just fantastic," Gibbons observes, "to see on the set how the colors that we used in *Watchmen* had been translated to the big screen"—he does not utter a single word during the *Watchmen* panel at San Diego.

Depicting cartoonists as collaborators apparently renders source and adaptation as coequal forms. However, attempts to signal visual fidelity perversely subordinate comics to film, with the former serving more as a guide for the latter than autonomous works. The lengths to which Robert Rodriguez went in order to have Miller credited as *Sin City*'s codirector, including quitting the Directors Guild of America in protest, are well known by now, but the fact that the film credits no writer other than Miller is less frequently remarked upon. That is, we are supposed to believe that there was no screenplay other than Miller's comics. While Satrapi refused to reduce comics to mere storyboards, this comparison has been a key discourse in framing comics' reception among filmmakers and studio executives (Burke 170). Indeed, Rodriguez refers to Miller's novels as "the best directed movies never seen on a movie screen" and to their film as a transcription rather than an adaptation. *Sin City* is almost ostentatious in its narrative and stylistic fidelity: dialogue is lifted nearly verbatim from the comics, and the film uncannily reproduces Miller's visual aesthetic. Throughout his commentary, Rodriguez repeatedly declaims that shot after shot is "straight out of the book." Zack Snyder and Edgar Wright are prone to similar declarations, though this holds slightly less true for *Pilgrim* because the series was still incomplete when the adaptation went into production.[4] O'Malley has said that the series' concluding installments incorporated "changes" made by the filmmakers, not to bring the comic in line with the film but because he thought they were better artistic solutions. Similarly, although some production elements were not derived directly from O'Malley's illustrations, he nonetheless credits them as capturing the *feeling* of his work. Intriguingly, there are elements whose origins neither O'Malley nor Wright can identify. At one point, Wright says, "I can't even remember what's yours and what's mine," and O'Malley replies, "Same here. . . . Looking through volume one the other day I'm like, I don't even know what I wrote anymore." As in the prior category, fidelity discourses foreground the involvement of comic creators. Here, however, these creators act more as guarantors of stylistic fidelity than as something to which adaptations must be faithful as such.

The Blockbuster Comic Book Movie

If adaptations in the first two categories protect—or perhaps project— fidelity by mobilizing their sources' creators and aesthetics, what options are available when an "adaptation" arguably has no source? Whereas *Scott Pilgrim* displays a somewhat unusual intertwining of source and adaptation around a conception of the work's "essence" that is fully embodied in neither text, this is the generalized condition in our final category. Blockbuster comic book films rarely adapt a single source; instead, they are based on franchises or properties. This "database" of characters, settings, premises, and themes typically comprises the products of many creators working more or less independently of one another over extended periods of time. Consequently, there is no single standard against which the cinematic versions' faithfulness may be measured.

Thus, all four films in this category devote significant resources to preparing audiences for deviations from their own prior interpretations (Furlong). The framing of Superman, Spider-Man, or the Avengers as "modern myths," for instance, implies they have transcended their comic book origins, deemphasizing the authority of any individual iteration and creating an imperative for repeated adaptations. Myths are meant to be retold. *Man of Steel* director Zack Snyder contends that "as a . . . student of comic books . . . Superman was the kind of golden god up on a hill you couldn't touch," yet this also provides screenwriter David S. Goyer with the rationale for a reinterpretation: "Part of what we had to do is get [the audience] comfortable with the fact that we were actually going to change the mythology a little bit." Filmmakers and studio executives appear acutely aware of the ongoing need to court fans, and we read these discourses as attempts to defuse the potential negative reactions to new interpretations. One *Spider-Man* (2002) DVD feature—a "pop-up" option whereby comic book–style captions appear throughout the film—serves just such a preemptive purpose, not only identifying deviations but locating them in specific issues or story arcs. Director Sam Raimi states on a commentary track that he hopes a direct reference to the early comics will satisfy "that one of one thousand fan requirements." Over a decade later, his successor on the franchise, Mark Webb, celebrates the return of Spider-Man's mechanical web-shooters (a notorious quasi controversy regarding Raimi's *Spider-Man*) in his commentary, stating, "I hope the fanboys appreciate [it]."

Among the blockbuster adaptations, narrative, authorial, and visual fidelity are all far less significant than in the other two categories. Rather than central features of promotional discourse, they are largely referenced in an effort to secure what we have called essential fidelity. The special edition release of Raimi's *Spider-Man*, for example, situates the film as an extension of a still-expanding universe, and several featurettes trumpet the contributions of a host of authors and illustrators, foregrounding various interpretations of the character over his fifty-year history. While both this film and Webb's *The Amazing Spider-Man* feature the obligatory cameo by former Marvel editor in chief Stan Lee, the earlier iteration makes an effort to recognize contributions from numerous authors involved in *Spider-Man*'s success and longevity. Lee serves more as an embodiment of the Marvel *brand* than a traditional authorial figure, and his presence in Marvel movie adap-tations anticipates the discursive alloying of the brand *as* author. By 2012, for instance, *Avengers* director Joss Whedon seemed acutely aware of his role as the steward of a sprawling megafranchise. Despite referencing cre-ators he considers especially influential (e.g., Jim Starlin), he frames Marvel Studios itself as a crucial influence. Indeed, he cites decisions imposed by the Disney-owned studio—what might once have been taken as corporate interference or intrusion into his creative process—as the insightful contri-butions of a key collaborator.

But the most important strategy for convincing audiences of these films' fidelity to the spirit of the "original" is the construction of filmmakers them-selves as what Suzanne Scott calls "fanboy auteurs."[5] By the time Whedon and Snyder were hired to direct *Avengers* and *Man of Steel*, respectively, both this category in general and their fannish credentials in particular were well established. In 2002, by contrast, the paratexts surrounding *Spider-Man* worked hard to establish Raimi's bona fides. Both Raimi himself and pro-ducer Avi Arad recount a story about Raimi's parents hiring a local artist to paint a Spider-Man mural on the wall of his childhood bedroom, and Raimi is repeatedly credited with insisting that the film retain Spider-Man's iconic costume design. Actors like Andrew Garfield and Henry Cavill are also occasionally enrolled into this job: the former made a surprise appear-ance at a Comic-Con panel in a Spider-Man costume prior to filming *The Amazing Spider-Man*, and Cavill assured an enthusiastic crowd that every-one involved in *Man of Steel* had "great respect for the canon." This "respect" is often communicated through the use of "Easter eggs." These may be well-known catchphrases (e.g., "Avengers assemble!"), the use of creators' or re-lated characters' names in unobtrusive spots (e.g., place-names, background signage, or background newscasts), or the visual "quotations" of well-known images from comics that Burke calls "peak moments" (165), such as *Amazing Spider-Man*'s final shot of the hero swinging over the city, which Webb de-scribes as "that great iconic frame from the comics." Such references may be incorporated into relatively "free" adaptations to bolster the sense of fidelity. A strategy for reassuring fan audiences, these "Easter eggs" presuppose that the filmmakers know what they are doing, even as they deviate from fan expectations. In the absence of an "original" or "author" as locus of fidelity, filmmakers (usually directors) are framed as franchise stewards who love and understand the characters just as the fans do, because they are them-selves fans. They are thus empowered to act as curators, selecting elements from the database and harmonizing them into a new interpretation that remains true to the franchise's "core" in some important but ineffable way.

Conclusion

Let us again emphasize that we are interested in how ideas of faithfulness are discursively constructed in and around adaptations. Despite occasional protestations to the contrary, audiences expect changes will be made from page to screen, so long as they're the "right" ones. For example, in a suggestive comparison between *Harry Potter and the Sorcerer's Stone* (2001) and *The Lord of the Rings: The Fellowship of the Ring* (2001), Cartmell and Whelehan note that the former was criticized for being *too* faithful to the book and thus an inferior cinematic experience compared with Peter Jackson's freer adaptation of Tolkien's novel (75). Ultimately, faithfulness is a matter of interpretation and, as such, is in the eye of the beholder.

But fidelity discourses do important work for media producers. George Bluestone, who is often named as the founder of fidelity criticism, asserts that "film-makers still talk about 'faithful' and 'unfaithful' adaptations without ever realizing that they are really talking about successful and unsuccessful films. Whenever a film becomes a financial or even a critical success the question of 'faithfulness' is hardly given any thought" (180). Despite fidelity's theoretical incoherence, it often suits producers to act as though adaptation is a straightforward process. A range of the possible fidelity discourses was present in each of the three categories we examined; however, films tended to organize the discourses around a central frame in response to particular strategic problems. For indie films based on alternative comics, it was most important to foreground the author and their vision in order to appeal to the regimes of value active among audiences for indie/independent cinema. Adaptations of middlebrow graphic novels tended to be pitched to audiences already committed to the original work, and the participation of the author was a means to guarantee the film's visual aesthetic in its translation from page to screen. Finally, blockbuster adaptations of long-running superhero comics suffer from too much, often conflicting, source material. Without a singular text, author, or aesthetic to be compared to, filmmakers have a freer hand to seek the property's "essence," and the "original comics" are mobilized to prop up the filmmaker's authority.

As long as filmmakers draw on preexisting properties, they must acknowledge—in one way or another—that they are not adapting a text alone but a *relationship* between text and audience. Fidelity discourses are an important part of the process of extending, and ideally expanding, that relationship. They operate, perhaps, as countermeasures against criticisms commonly levied against adaptations: lack of originality, privileging special effects spectacle over diegetic substance, seemingly endless sequels, and so on. Is fidelity, therefore, a discursive smoke screen, distracting audiences from this supposed paucity by highlighting how filmmakers "borrow" originality from their source material, or does a masterful use of fidelity discourses help the individual adaptation stand out (as a particularly faithful or artful interpretation) from its competitors? Either way, fidelity discourses are a potent resource for attempting to (re)secure the devotion of a preexisting audience while bringing new acolytes into the fold. Returning briefly to Stam's query—"Fidelity to what?"—perhaps the only honest answer is: Fidelity to fidelity.

Notes

1. While the political economy of these films is hardly independent, "indie" remains a potent label that positions films, filmmakers, and studios within the field (Perren).

2. Raimi's *Spider-Man* was nominated for Sound and Visual Effects.

3. They took another crack at it with their 2006 adaptation of Clowes's *Art School Confidential*.

4. The script was finished in part based on O'Malley's notes for the unpublished volumes.

5. Scott develops this concept with specific reference to Snyder, the adaptor of *Watchmen* and *Man of Steel*, as well as Frank Miller's *300*.

Works Cited

The Amazing Spider-Man. Directed by Mark Webb. DVD. Columbia Pictures, 2012.

American Splendor. Directed by Shari Springer Berman and Robert Pulcini. DVD. Dark Horse Entertainment, 2003.

Andrew, Dudley. "Adaptation." *Film Adaptation*, edited by James Naremore, New Brunswick, NJ, Rutgers University Press, 2000, pp. 28–37.

The Avengers. Directed by Joss Whedon. Blu-ray. Marvel Studios, 2012.

Baetens, Jan. "Revealing Traces: A New Theory of Graphic Enunciation." *The Language of Comics: Word and Image*, edited by Robin Varnum and Christina T. Gibbons, Jackson, University Press of Mississippi, 2001, pp. 145–155.

Beaty, Bart. "The Recession and the American Comic Book Industry: From Inelastic Cultural Good to Economic Integration." *Popular Communication*, vol. 8, no. 3, 2010, pp. 203–207.

Beaty, Bart, and Benjamin Woo. *The Greatest Comic Book of All Time: Symbolic Capital and the Field of American Comic Books*. New York, Palgrave Macmillan, 2016.

Bluestone, George. "Word to Image: The Problem of the Filmed Novel." *Quarterly of Film Radio and Television*, vol. 11, no. 2, 1956, pp. 171–180.

Bourdieu, Pierre. "The Field of Cultural Production, Or: The Economic World Reversed." *Poetics*, vol. 12, nos. 4–5, 1983, pp. 311–356.

Brabner, Joyce. "Commentary." *American Splendor*. DVD. Dark Horse Entertainment, 2003.

Burke, Liam. *The Comic Book Film Adaptation: Exploring Modern Hollywood's Leading Genre*. Jackson, University Press of Mississippi, 2015.

Caldwell, John Thornton. *Production Culture: Industrial Reflexivity and Critical Practice in Film and Television*. Durham, NC, Duke University Press, 2008.

Cartmell, Deborah, and Imelda Whelehan. *Screen Adaptation: Impure Cinema*. Basingstoke, UK, Palgrave Macmillan, 2010.

Cavill, Henry. "'Man of Steel' Panel - Comic Con 2012." YouTube video, uploaded by Superman Homepage, 16 July 2012, www.youtube.com/watch?v=Ea0r7x0piOg.

Clowes, Daniel. "Making of *Ghost World*." *Ghost World*. DVD. Metro-Goldwyn-Mayer, 2001.

Denby, David. "Misanthropes: Apes and Teens." *New Yorker*, 6 August 2001, www.newyorker.com/magazine/2001/08/06/misanthropes.

Furlong, Anne. "'It's Not Quite What I Had in Mind': Adaptation, Faithfulness, and Interpretation." *Journal of Literary Semantics*, vol. 41, no. 2, 2012, pp. 175–191.

Garfield, Andrew. "The Amazing Spider-Man Panel at San Diego Comic Con 2011 - Part 1." YouTube video, uploaded by GalacticGod, 23 July 2011, www.youtube.com/watch?v=KJ4y1kdicDg.

Ghost World. Directed by Terry Zwigoff. DVD. Metro-Goldwyn-Mayer, 2001.

Gibbons, Dave. "Maximum Movie Mode." *Watchmen* bonus content, disc 1. Blu-ray. Warner Bros., 2009.

Hall, Emily. "The Humanity of Failure: An Interview with Dan Clowes." *The Stranger*, 19 July 2001, www.thestranger.com/seattle/the-humanity-of-failure/Content?oid=8069.

Johnson, David T. "Summer of Adaptations." *Literature/Film Quarterly*, vol. 34, no. 3, 2006, pp. 170–171.

Leitch, Thomas M. "Post-Literary Adaptation." *Post Script*, vol. 23, no. 3, 2004, pp. 99–117.

Man of Steel. Directed by Zack Snyder. DVD. Warner Bros., 2013.

McAllister, Matthew P., Ian Gordon, and Mark Jancovich. "Blockbuster Meets Superhero Comic, or Arthouse Meets Graphic Novel? The Contradictory Relationship between Film and Comic Art." *Journal of Popular Film and Television*, vol. 34, no. 3, 2007, pp. 108–114.

Perren, Alisa. *Indie, Inc.: Miramax and the Transformation of Hollywood in the 1990s*. Austin, University of Texas Press, 2012.

Persepolis. Directed by Vincent Paronnaud and Marjane Satrapi. DVD. 2.4.7. Films, 2007.

Pulcini, Robert. "Commentary." *American Splendor*. DVD. Dark Horse Entertainment, 2003.

Raimi, Sam. "Commentary." *Spider-Man* special edition DVD, disc 1. Columbia Pictures, 2002.

Rodriguez, Robert. "Commentary." *Sin City* recut extended DVD. Dimension Films, 2005.

Satrapi, Marjane. "Cannes Press Conference Q&A." *Persepolis*. DVD. 2.4.7. Films, 2007.

Scott Pilgrim vs. the World. Directed by Edgar Wright. Collector's edition Blu-ray. Universal, 2010.

Scott, Suzanne. "Dawn of the Undead Author: Fanboy Auteurism and Zach Snyder's 'Vision.'" *A Companion to Media Authorship*, edited by Jonathan Gray and Derek Johnson, Malden, MA, Wiley-Blackwell, 2013, pp. 440–462.

Sin City. Directed by Frank Miller and Robert Rodriguez. Recut extended DVD. Dimension Films, 2005.

Snyder, Zack, and David S. Goyer. "Strong Characters, Legendary Roles." *Man of Steel* DVD bonus content, disc 2. Warner Bros., 2013.

Spider-Man. Directed by Sam Raimi. Special edition DVD. Columbia Pictures, 2002.

Stam, Robert. "Beyond Fidelity: The Dialogics of Adaptation." *Film Adaptation*, edited by James Naremore, New Brunswick, NJ, Rutgers University Press, 2000, pp. 54–76.

Watchmen. Directed by Zack Snyder. Director's cut Blu-ray. Warner Bros., 2009.

Webb, Mark. "Commentary." *The Amazing Spider-Man*. DVD. Columbia Pictures, 2012.

Whedon, Joss. "Commentary." *The Avengers*. Blu-ray. Marvel Studios, 2012.

Wright, Edgar, and Bryan Lee O'Malley. "Commentary." *Scott Pilgrim vs. the World*. Collector's edition Blu-ray. Universal, 2010.

"We Roller Coaster Through . . .": Screenwriting, Narrative Economy, and the Inscription of the Haptic in Tentpole Comic Book Movies

JULIAN HOXTER

In the analysis of script development for movies and comic books, writing style and format are both instructional and instructive. Both the established praxis of the professional crafts and the rhetoric of each medium inflect the way scripts are written and how they address their readers. The textuality of comic book scripts and movie screenplays also reflects and illuminates the corporate context within which development occurs, as well as the creative and literary aspirations of their writers and the professional expectations of collaborators in other crafts who will work from the documents as project development continues. Adaptations from one medium to the other involve transitions in craft scripting praxis to produce documents that address different implied readerships in distinct ways.[1]

A full examination of the impact of project development in both mediums on produced texts is beyond the scope of this project; however, this brief account will indicate how, in professional screenwriting, process is informed both by the corporate context and by the nature of the product. Historically, adaptation studies has tended to focus on the adapted text ex post facto, concerned with product rather than process and primarily with fidelity to source material, although important recent work by Brian McFarlane, James Naremore, Deborah Cartmell, Imelda Whelehan, and others has done much to transform the field, giving adaptation studies new critical focus along with an engagement with postmodernism and intertextuality. In addition, typical fan-cultural assessments of cross-media adaptation between movies and comic books are also less engaged with process than they are with product because, for many fans, the issue of fidelity still resonates powerfully.

Collaborative Scripting Paradigms

In adaptations from comic books to tentpole comic book movies, these questions are also sifted through distinct iterations of collaborative scripting authorship. Unlike literary texts in other media, feature screenplays and comic book scripts are prepared and formatted by professional writers in ways that acknowledge the syncretistic nature of the mediums and, thus, anticipate and directly enable future collaboration with fellow professionals in the production crafts, from directors and actors to artists and letterers. In both mediums the supersession and partial effacement of the writer's work in the final product is designed into the processes of development and also into production. This prefatory note from Kelly Sue DeConnick (writer of the influential *Bitch Planet* series for Image Comics) to the artists who will, in two senses, draw from her script makes her view of the relationship between script and art abundantly clear: "The pages that follow are not marching orders. The metaphor I usually go to is that these are not blue prints [*sic*] —if you change something, the whole building won't collapse; they're a map. And if you see a better way to get where we're going, please GOD, let me know. As long as we get where we're going, I don't mind changing routes" (DeConnick).

Recent scholarly work by Steven Maras, Steven Price, Kathryn Millard, and others on movie screenwriting also acknowledges the collaborative process of development and authorship. As a consequence, screenwriting studies no longer conceives of screenplays as simple blueprints to be enacted, or of the credited writer(s) as the sole or unproblematic author(s) of the script, let alone the movie.[2] Although in the Anglophone academy the scholarly literature on comic books is less established, the obsolete blueprint assumption has never achieved the same level of critical orthodoxy here. This is due in part to a long-standing reification of comic book art and artists by readers and also to the influence of the comic book writer and editor Stan Lee and his famous "Marvel method" of comic book writing—in which the writer defers much of the scripting labor to the artist—on the appreciation of the comic book development process by the fan community.

In mainstream superhero comics publishing, writers have to negotiate story from the start of the development process, producing pitch documents or story outlines in order to get assignments. Some editors require strict adherence to these preparatory documents that have also been approved at the corporate level. The published comic book, however, typically bears the direct imprint of many fewer fingers than its movie equivalent. In addition, and unlike most developed tentpole treatments, which typically specify every story beat in the movie, comic book story outlines are often "broad strokes" documents. The writer works with the series editor to tweak structure and to ensure that she is not stepping on the toes of canon or introducing contradictory developments in linked series (Bendis, *Words for Pictures* 24). In the most common iteration of comic book writing, known as "full script," writers then draft a script and hand off their prose to the artist. They then make minor revisions when the artwork is finished. This stage in the scripting process often involves an element of "writing down" the dialogue and its accompanying explanatory and dramatic text captions as the produced art demonstrates its ability to carry more of the narrative load.

Story development also predates the screenplay in Hollywood tentpole development. For freelance screenwriters it often begins with competitions, known as "bake offs" in the industry, between writers who are obliged to develop their take on a given story in depth—and without recompense—to get the gig. This is a reality of the current freelance paradigm, but it also breaks the Writers Guild of America's regulations. From the point of assignment onward, story development involves a complex and often extended interaction with groups of producers and studio executives whose commercial priorities and creative concerns are inscribed into the text of the screenplay both before and after it is "green-lit," or approved for production. After the resultant screenplay has been through enough drafts for the movie to be green-lit, the work of the screenwriter is then taken forward through overlapping processes of analog and digital previsualization (including storyboarding and the production of animatics), during which other hands—including the director's—help to refine and specify the structure of action sequences and instances of spectacle. If the screenwriter is still on the project, she may then inscribe a version of this developed cinematic and spectacular story material within her emergent document—typically with further negotiated editing in order to conform these sequences to the studio's budgetary requirements—as the spec or commissioned screenplay progresses toward its final form as a shooting script.

In Hollywood, visual development is the process through which a spec or first draft commissioned screenplay is gradually transformed into a shooting script, a screenplay form with its own precedents and standards governing formatting and the level of detail expected for some kinds of content, notably action scenes and sequences involving complex special effects. To a certain extent, the address of the screenplay also changes in its journey from spec to shooting script. Where the former is written as a kind of sales document, all departments and crafts use the latter during production. The weight of meaning in the prose can shift accordingly, and the accretion of detail can impact the persuasive power of the original text. Thus a shooting script is often somewhat more prosaic than the spec from which it is developed, even if it never truly reaches the status of blueprint. A kind of anticipatory dynamism on the page is moderated but not abandoned through the visual development process.

The focus of collaborative authorship around the inscription of the visual is also a significant marker of the status of the attraction in economic terms. Both mainstream comic books and the tentpole movies adapted and developed from them or from their brands trade centrally in spectacle. Indeed, writing the cinematic, in a sense pre-inscribing the haptic, is key to the entire tentpole paradigm—the latest refinement of the blockbuster model that currently dominates and sustains Hollywood studio production and that relies for its economic viability in large part upon the attractive power of its attractions.[3] Superhero movies in particular promise their audiences a particular kind of dynamic visual storytelling, whether or not they attempt directly to adopt a full comic book aesthetic of the sort practiced in movies like *Sin City* (2005).

The Inscription of the Spectacular

The adoption and adaptation of significant elements of the comic book aesthetic—including cinematic composition, physical performance, and the rhythms of editing—fall primarily within the provinces of other professional media crafts. In tentpole movies, however, as in superhero comic books, scripts establish at the very least the tonal and narrational foundations upon which such cinematic structures can be built. They also lay out a kind of "haptic contract" between the written word and the images to come—whether drawn, animated, or filmed—that will fulfill the promise of the writing.[4] Given the massive production and marketing budgets at stake, and the small number of tentpoles that studios commit to each year (upon which they stake their commercial reputations and profitability), the importance of the persuasive function of screenwriting prose may better be appreciated in its industrial context. This is another way of saying that when they are working for Hollywood studios, screenwriters are often operating in a fear-driven corporate environment.

The inscription of the spectacular in comic book scripts and tentpole screenplays is a literary endeavor that anticipates the visual. In the former case the writing anticipates the interpolation of the graphic, and in the latter it anticipates the cinematographic. However, in neither case is the written word able to convey the totality of the attraction to come. Professional writers working in each medium approach this communication challenge very differently. Although personal style and, especially in comic books, format on the page varies from script to script, these examples also illustrate key differences both in the address and the function of the script within project development in the two mediums. For example, Neil Gaiman's writing for *Miracleman* defers to a prosaically descriptive kind of explanation.

> Page 1 panel 2
> DAYLIGHT. OUTSIDE. IN THE FOREGROUND IS A SMALL, MALE FIGURE WITH HIS BACK TO US. HE'S GOT A BACKPACK ON, AND HAS PUT HIS HANDS ON HIS HIPS, AND IS LOOKING UPWARDS, AT THE PYRAMID. THE SIDES OF IT ARE BLACK GRANITE, WITH OCCASIONAL WINDOWS AND DOORS, IN DIFFERENT ARCHITECTURAL STYLES. IT TOWERS ABOVE HIM, VANISHES INTO THE CLOUDS WHICH MASK ITS UPPER 2/3RDS FROM US.
>
> Caption: There are some things that are just too big. You can't fit them into your head—they stop at the eyes, and won't go in. (Gaiman 3)

As a comic book writer Gaiman is primarily addressing his artist collaborators, in this case expecting Mark Buckingham's art to carry the weight of communicating the sublimity of moments that "stop at the eyes." In comparison, this short example of Joss Whedon's screenwriting in the screenplay of *The Avengers* takes on the extra burden of persuading his (fear-driven) corporate readers and his professional colleagues alike that the audience of the finished movie should, and indeed will, "roller coaster through" the Helmsley Tunnel along with Iron Man in the film. Thus the screenwriter's prose offers a promise of the affect to come.

> Still being chased, Iron Man dive-bombs towards Grand Central, leading the aliens into—
>
> INT. HELMSLEY TUNNEL—CONTINUOUS
> Where he's pursued by the remaining charioteers—who score a couple of good hits—as we roller coaster through . . . (Whedon 114)

In both cases their scripting is also mediated by the operational rhetoric of the medium in question. Put very simply, movies unfold sequentially on the screen. To a significant extent their narration is bound into this temporal constant, and the format and the prose style of mainstream screenplays both play into this linear temporality directly. By contrast, comic books present their stories spatially on the page, offering the reader an implied panel-to-panel reading track through which to follow the story (Eisner). But comic book pages are also (usually) multi-image tableaux that have their own presentational logic; they are also designed to be viewed over time and out of sequence. Thus the panel to come, representing the pyramid described in the extract from Gaiman's script, is intended to be noted by the reader and moved past as the story continues, but it may also be paused at (without the intervention of a mouse or a television remote control), returned to, and engaged with as a discrete image, evocative as a graphic encapsulation of a single story moment, but also as a component of the expressive geometry of its own page and often designed to be paired within the broader geometry of a two-page spread.

In mainstream comic book publishing the relationship between script and art is further complicated by the two established commercial formats or models of writing mentioned before: full script and the Marvel method (sometimes also referred to as "plot script"). The full script model provides the artist with clear and detailed information about the content of each image panel on each page of the comic book and the relationship between them. There are as many minor variations in format to the full script paradigm as there are comic book writers, as this comment from a para-industrial guide to writing comic books makes clear: "In comic books there is no set format. There are just things that work for each writer. Those things can change from day to day based on writers' whims or who their collaborators are" (Bendis, *Words for Pictures* 27).

The Marvel method, in which the artist assumes more of the responsibility for scripting, is less common in current comic book development. The term is derived from the pragmatic practice Marvel Comics writer/editor Stan Lee adopted in the 1960s in response to the pressure of producing multiple issues on short deadlines with little or no staff support. Under the Marvel method, "the writer gives the artist a page or two of story description. The artist then interprets the story the way he wants, and the writer comes back and constructs the dialogue to accentuate the art" (Bendis, *Powers Scriptbook* 3). This note from Stan Lee sums up his working relationship with the artist Jack Kirby: "I write the story plot—go over it with Jack—he draws it up based on our hasty conferences—then, with his drawings in front of me, I write the captions and dialogue, usually right on the original art work! It seems to work out well" (qtd. in Steibel).

Even under the rubric of the full script paradigm some writers, notably Alan Moore (*Watchmen*), are famous for the detail of their scripts, while others, like Brian Michael Bendis (*Powers*), leave more flexibility to the artists by offering briefer descriptions. Bendis indicates as much in his forward to the published scripts for his author-owned Image Comics series *Powers*: "In the following pages, you will find a number of subtle formatting inconsistencies. As time went along, I altered my style to be more communicative. Also, these scripts were never created to be seen by anyone other than [artist] Michael Avon Oeming, which means that as the book goes on, the scene descriptions become less descriptive" (Bendis, *Powers Scriptbook* 3).

In comic book publishing, however, and despite these microdistinctions of script format and address to the artist, the dynamic-persuasive function of script prose has never had the same weight as it does in spec screenplay writing. In large part this is because all full script comic book writing has to address page layout, one of Thierry Groensteen's two "fundamental operations of the language of comics" (43). As we see in the formatting of Gaiman's script for *Miracleman*, the comic book writer needs to include an interstitial layer of instructional and descriptive writing between the story and the reader to establish, specify, and clarify the often complex relationship between what Will Eisner calls the "two frames" of the comic book, the panel and the page, or, under Hannah Miodrag's grid, the page as a "semantic unit" (Eisner 41; Miodrag 221). As can be inferred from this instructional extract from Bendis's script for *Powers #5, Who Killed Retro Girl? Part Five*, this necessarily affects the flow of the comic book script as a narrative document to be read:

PAGE 14–15
I WANT TO DO SOMETHING INTERESTING WITH THESE FLASH-
BACK IMAGES.
ALL silhouetted images of the figures in combat. The body language means everything. We will use a flat red color in the background with the text down the side of the PAGE, as I am wont to do. (Bendis, *Powers Scriptbook* 159)

Thus, in a comic book script, the inscription of spectacle—and thus affect—is deferred forward to the visual in a way that even the most prosaic of shooting scripts can minimize or avoid. In addition, comic book writers commonly use instructional terminology appropriated from movies to indicate visual keys, such as "shots," "angles," "cuts," and "camera moves." While the history of the movie screenplay speaks to the elision of instruction over time, that of the comic book script speaks to the appropriation of an instructional sociolect from another medium.

The cultural critic Ta-Nehisi Coates, also a writer on Marvel's *Black Panther* superhero comic, recently expressed his investment in the rhetoric of

comic books: "Superheroes are best imagined in comic books. The union between the written word, the image, and then what your imagination has to
do to connect those allows for so much. I always feel like when I see movies,
I'm a little let down by the [digital] animation. I want to hear the voice in
my head, you know" (qtd. in Riesman). It is by enabling exactly this kind
of connective and extrapolative work of the imagination that Gaiman's full
script prose will marry with Buckingham's art to come to create the spectacular for the comic book reader. In the example from *Miracleman* one can
see how Gaiman serves the rhetoric of the comic book page by splitting his
script at the panel. By contrast, Whedon's writing serves the distinct rhetoric
of his own medium, changing scene only as his story changes location.[5] Like
many tentpole movie writers, he also takes liberties with syntax to acceler-
ate the read. He changes scene on a hyphen, in the middle of a sentence, his
prose deployed as kinesis on the page to imply a future kinesis on the screen.

Tentpole writers frequently use this kind of stylistic technique. For example, this scene from *Captain America: The First Avenger* (2011) combines
the same kind of creative disregard for conventional syntax, this time breaking a sentence on an ellipsis, with the capitalization of action and a liberal
use of white space on the page. This layout separates the individual thought-
images of story progression into the flow of discrete readable moments. Importantly, note how these moments follow the principle of the *master scene
format* of American screenwriting by indicating and implying shots and
camera positions without specifying or "calling" them.

> INT./EXT. TAXICAB—DAY
> KRUGER PULLS HIS GUN AND BLASTS AT STEVE. Steve ducks, clinging
> to the side of the car.
> They swerve through the streets.
> A HORN BLARES. KRUGER LOOKS TO SEE A TRUCK ROARING AT
> HIM. Steve sees the same thing. Kruger yanks the wheel.
> THE TRUCK SIDESWIPES THE TAXI, THROWING IT INTO A ROLL.
> KIDS LOOK OVER FROM THEIR BASEBALL GAME TO SEE . . .
> STEVE ATOP THE TUMBLING CAB, RIDING IT LIKE A ROLLING LOG.
> (Markus and McFeely 39)

Conclusion

The inscription of spectacle during project development on superhero
movies foregrounds the persuasive textuality of the current iteration of the

Hollywood screenplay. This *new spec format*, a refinement of the standard master scene format, is the product of a gradual process of stylistic development that has led Hollywood screenwriting to be increasingly unburdened by the weight of the rhetoric of its own medium.[6] The historical trajectory of screenplay format away from shot calling and descriptive specificity and toward indicative kinesis is, in part, a gradual development born of the shift to a freelance screenwriting paradigm beginning in the late 1940s and prompted by studios downsizing after the Paramount Consent Decree of 1948. This extract from Robert Riskin's "shooting draft" for *Lost Horizon* (1937) illustrates a variant of the shot-driven formats prevalent in Hollywood during the classical studio period:

EXT. NARROW TABLELAND
MED. LONG SHOT
Halfway up a mountainside. The procession is just starting around a hairpin curve. They are forced to travel on a narrow ledge overlooking a deep ravine.
CLOSE SHOT—LOVETT, BARNARD AND GLORIA
As they cling against the rocky sides and glance apprehensively down into the abyss below.
CLOSE SHOT—GLORIA
Close by to Barnard. Gloria's face is wan and haggard. Every upward move seems to require a Herculean effort. She stops and has a fit of coughing.
(Riskin)

In contrast, this action scene from the screenplay for *The Dark Knight* (2008) illustrates the new spec format in its current iteration. The flow of action is maintained for the read, and syntax and capitalization are once again deployed kinetically. Once again, note how shots are never specified, but rather they are implied through the rhetoric of the screenplay in the way of instructional lacunae. The absence of instruction is itself instructive to the reader. One action leads to the next action; each thought-image implies a shot without the writers indicating it as such.

INT. LOBBY, BANK—DAY
Bozo and Grumpy move down the line of hostages—Bozo hands each Hostage OBJECTS from a bag. A GRENADE. Grumpy follows, PULLING THE PINS.
                              GRUMPY
              Obviously, we don't want you doing any—
              thing with your hands other than holding on
              for dear life.

BLAM. Chuckles is BLOWN OFF HIS FEET—Grumpy and Bozo DIVE for cover—the Bank Manager steps out of his office, SHOTGUN in hand. (Nolan and Nolan)

Where scripts used to break on the called shot, now they articulate around the thought-image and break on the scene. Over time, the master scene format deferred the cinematic forward in one sense—no longer calling shots—while pulling it back into prose in another—expressing dynamism on the page. In short, the screenplay became less a set of camera instructions and more a literary document, its new "readability" also a necessary response to the practices of Hollywood gatekeeping under the freelance paradigm. Now writers who were no longer working on contract in the manner of their forebears in the classical system needed to grab the attention of script readers, producers, and executives with their prose. The adoption of the tentpole by Hollywood studios coincided with the culmination of the move toward a new spec format for the screenplay. As a consequence, the exemplary tentpole genre that is the new superhero movie is written in a form ideally suited to expressing the centrality of the attraction upon which that commercial paradigm rests.

Notes

1. Here I refer to Wolfgang Iser's concept of an implied reader only in the sense that the feature screenplay has long been an explicitly targeted document, designed and formatted to address (and appease) specific industrial concerns. See Wolfgang Iser, *The Implied Reader: Patterns of Communication in Prose Fiction from Bunyan to Beckett* (Johns Hopkins University Press, 1974).

2. See, inter alia, Steven Maras, *Screenwriting: History, Theory, and Practice* (Wallflower Press, 2009); Steven Price, *A History of the Screenplay* (Palgrave Macmillan, 2013); and Julian Hoxter, introduction to *Screenwriting: Behind the Silver Screen: A Modern History of Filmmaking*, edited by Andrew Horton and Julian Hoxter (Rutgers University Press, 2015).

3. I use the term *haptic* simply, in reference to the scripting of cinematic and comic book action and, in particular, the establishment and communication of a "felt" exchange between the written text and its readers or audience both within the production process and after the release of the resultant movie.

4. Here my position is broadly in concert with Liam Burke's understanding of the comic book aesthetic in movies, as well as his account of the superhero movie both as a distinct genre and as the exemplary genre of the Hollywood tentpole paradigm. Liam Burke, *The Comic Book Film Adaptation: Exploring Modern Hollywood's Leading Genre* (University Press of Mississippi, 2015). See in particular chapter 5, "How to Adapt Comics the Marvel Way," pp. 228–262.

5. For example, Benoît Peeters discusses the accommodation of panels to their con-

tent in terms of rhetoric. Benoît Peeters, *Case, planche, récit: Lire la bande dessinée* (Casterman, 1998), pp. 48–53.

6. For an examination of the development of format under the freelance paradigm in spec and commissioned screenplays, see Julian Hoxter, "The New Hollywood 1980–1999," *Screenwriting*, edited by Andrew Horton and Julian Hoxter, pp. 101–126.

Works Cited

Bendis, Brian Michael. *Words for Pictures: The Art and Business of Writing Comics and Graphic Novels*. New York, Watson-Guptill, 2014.

———. *Powers Scriptbook*. Orange, CA, Image Comics, 2001.

Cartmell, Deborah, and Imelda Whelehan. *Screen Adaptation: Impure Cinema*. London, Palgrave Macmillan, 2010.

DeConnick, Kelly Sue. Script for *Bitch Planet* #3, "Too Big to Fail," 14 January 2015. *Comic Book Script Archive*, http://www.comicsexperience.com/dev/wp-content/uploads/2017/01/BITCH-PLANET-3_Kelly-Sue-DeConnick.pdf.

Eisner, Will. *Comics and Sequential Art*. Tamarac, FL, Poorhouse Press, 1985.

Gaiman, Neil. Script for *Miracleman* #17. *Panel One: Comic Book Scripts by Top Writers*, edited by Nat Gertler, Tamarac, FL, About Comics, 2002, p. 3.

Groensteen, Thierry. *Comics and Narration*. Jackson, University Press of Mississippi, 2011.

Markus, Christopher, and Stephen McFeely, with revisions by Joss Whedon. *Captain America: The First Avenger*. Final shooting draft, 2010, p. 39. Scripts Collection, Margaret Herrick Library, Academy of Motion Picture Arts and Sciences, Beverly Hills, CA.

McFarlane, Brian. *Novel to Film: An Introduction to the Theory of Adaptation*. New York, Oxford University Press, 1996.

Miodrag, Hannah. *Comics and Language: Reimagining Critical Discourse on the Form*. Jackson, University Press of Mississippi, 2013.

Naremore, James, editor. *Film Adaptation*. New Brunswick, NJ, Rutgers University Press, 2000.

Nolan, Jonathan, and Christopher Nolan. *The Dark Knight*. Unpublished screenplay, posted at https://www.raindance.org/download/the-dark-knight/.

Riesman, Abraham. "The Superheroes Won: Cultural Critic Ta-Nehisi Coates Unpacks the Way Comics Have Conquered the World." *New York Magazine*, 20 April–3 May 2015, p. 108.

Riskin, Robert. *Lost Horizon*. Unpublished screenplay archived at the Internet Movie Script Database, https://www.imsdb.com/scripts/Lost-Horizon.html.

Steibel, Robert. "Who the Hell Was the Conscious and Clever Brains behind the Marvel Phenomenon?" *The Comics Journal*, 6 November 2013, https://www.tcj.com/who-the-hell-was-the-conscious-and-clever-brains-behind-the-marvel-phenomenon/.

Whedon, Joss. *The Avengers*. Script, 2nd Blue revisions, 3 August 2011, 119A, p. 114. Scripts Collection, Margaret Herrick Library, Academy of Motion Picture Arts and Sciences, Beverly Hills, CA.

Adaptation and Seriality: Comic Book to Television Series Adaptations

SHERRYL VINT

One of the significant challenges of adapting comic books to film is the difference between the serial narrative of the comic book form and the traditionally closed narrative form of film. A different set of challenges, however, attend to the process of adapting from comic book to television: both are serial forms, yet each has distinct audiences and different ways of engaging such audiences over an individual series' duration and across other titles in their respective medium. Television series have increasingly been a venue for comic book adaptation, from the CW series *Arrow* (2012–) and *The Flash* (2014–), to Fox's *Gotham* (2014–2019), loosely based on Ed Brubaker and Greg Rucka's *Gotham Central* comic, to the Netflix series *Daredevil* (2015–2018) and *Jessica Jones* (2015–), the latter based on Brian Michael Bendis's comic *Alias*. This chapter explores what might be at stake in the choice to adapt a comic book to the small rather than the big screen. What might this cultural moment and a recent example of a comic book to television adaptation tell us about the aesthetics and audiences of both media today?

The contemporary media landscape is replete with characters drawn from comic books, especially superheroes, on film and television. Previous eras have seen adaptations of comic books to both big and small screens, of course, from the campy antics of Adam West in *Batman* (1966–1968) or the nod toward the women's movement in the televised *Wonder Woman* (1975–1979) starring Lynda Carter.[1] Although comic readership has declined since the 1990s, the medium has simultaneously become more diverse in its topics and often darker in its themes. Big publishers DC and Marvel have more recently been joined by a plethora of indie publishers, such as Dark Horse and Image, leading both DC and Marvel to create their own indie imprints, Vertigo and Icon, respectively. At the cinema, superhero films grew from a minor player in blockbuster movies in the 1980s—launched by *Superman*

(1978)—to become their own box office force, dominated by Marvel, with *Avengers* and *X-Men* franchises continually in production.

Television in the Twenty-First Century

Marvel Studios and their integrated films based on the Avengers and its lead members—Captain America, Thor, Iron Man—dominate today's comic book adaptations. The key to Marvel's success is consistency of casting across a number of character-focused films, starting with Robert Downey Jr.'s charismatic performance in *Iron Man* (2008), to finally "assemble" the team in *The Avengers* (2012). New films were introduced in teasers following the credits of current films, including cameos by major stars, planting curiosity about the next phase in an integrated story. Marvel thus mitigated the usual obstacle of adapting a serial comic narrative into a closed medium, producing a set of interlinked stories that could simultaneously stand on their own and be read as part of an ongoing narrative; this balance of open and closed narrative approximates the seriality of comic books, which also often run story lines across titles, such as the "Death of the Family" story line in DC Comics, which required readers to purchase issues of *Batman*, *Batgirl*, *Batman and Robin*, *Catwoman*, *Detective Comics*, *Nightwing*, and *Teen Titans* to read the full narrative. Marvel gave fans the big-budget action set pieces that are important in both film and comics (effects sequences; full-page spreads) but also an ongoing serial narrative central to television as well as to comics.[2] They soon added television series set in the same universe, most centrally ABC's *Agents of SHIELD* (2013–), whose narrative is affected by events in the ongoing movie cycle.[3] In short, Marvel made films with the sensibilities of comic book creators.[4]

Marvel used royalties from related media, such as the early *Spider-Man* (2002, 2004, 2007), *X-Men* (2002, 2003, 2006), and *Blade* (1998, 2002, 2004) film trilogies, to sustain the corporation as comic book readership flagged (see Bushby). It then launched this new media cycle under its own control (Johnson 1). The open narrative form is characteristic of the new cinema of media convergence, according to Chuck Tryon, an "incompleteness" (19) that encourages viewers to seek out more of the narrative in subsequent products, not only the next film but also DVD and Blu-ray extras, videogames and ARGs (alternate reality games), and comic books themselves. Marvel has created an immersive web of texts whose aim is to satisfy consumers between installments of the major film franchise by suturing them more fully into the Marvel world in the meantime.

Such integration between film and television is characteristic of the recent media environment, and here one might hypothesize that comic books were an important point of connection, since superhero characters have successfully and frequently been adapted to both media. Previously such adaptations proceeded independently: while there might be some narrative continuity between their imagined worlds, both referring to the comic as a touchstone, different versions of the same character could appear simultaneously in film and television: for example, Brandon Routh's Superman in *Superman Returns* (2006) coexisted with Tom Welling's television portrayal on *Smallville* (2001–2011) without any attempt to integrate these worlds;[5] DC reproduced this structure in *Justice League* (2017), whose Barry Allen / Flash (Ezra Miller) coincided with Grant Gustin's version on the eponymous television series. In contrast, Marvel created a seamless world in which the same actors move across its properties, anchoring its flagship television series *Agents of SHIELD* with Phil Coulson (Clark Gregg), a minor character in *The Avengers*, and even securing a guest appearance by Samuel L. Jackson as Nick Fury in two crucial episodes that connected the narrative across media.[6] At one time this would have been unimaginable, given differences in budget, schedules, aesthetics, and actors that separated these media, buttressed by their very different cultural capital, with film regarded as having much more prestige.[7] This situation has changed, however, and television is rapidly gaining in critical acclaim and being sought out as a medium to work in by some of the most prominent Hollywood directors, such as David Fincher, Vincenzo Natali, Jonathan Nolan, Martin Scorsese, and Steven Soderbergh, and actors such as Don Cheadle, Kirsten Dunst, Anthony Hopkins, Jessica Lange, and Clive Owen.

Undoubtedly, the most important changes to the media landscape are the new circumstances through which television is produced, distributed, and watched. Once consumed on the network's schedule in a regime John Ellis argues was characterized by "scarcity" of choices, television is now the medium of consumer choice in a context of almost overwhelming numbers of network and cable stations, the emergence of independent productions funded by streaming services, and a vast catalogue of items to view on demand. People now watch television at times of their choice, often "bingeing" on multiple episodes at once. The move away from discontinuous seriality—viewed as an industry necessity in an era when advertising revenues were the mainstay and openness to occasional and new viewers a marketing axiom—and toward long story arcs, which began in the late 1990s, have come to define the most celebrated television shows today (see Creeber). Many series now tell a single story from beginning to end of a season or even across several seasons, sometimes with a more loosely plotted "middle"—as was the case for breakout hit *Lost* (2004–2010)—and at other times planning a tight progression across seasons, such as in *Breaking Bad* (2008–2013).

Amanda Lotz characterizes this new television as "revolutionized" and argues that "the changes in television that have taken place over the past two decades . . . are extraordinary and on the scale of the transition from one medium to another, as in the case of the shift from radio to television" (6). Two things stand out about such television: first, the shift toward seriality, and second, the emergence of new stakeholders, in the form of original content produced by streaming providers. The new style has much in common with the narrative structure of comic books, which often tell a single story through several issues that are later bound and sold as a volume, but which must also keep open the chance for a new volume/season. The affinities between the two media are highlighted by the choice made by a number of showrunners to finish their story in the comic medium when series cancellation prevented completion of an anticipated story arc, such as *Jericho* (series 2006–2008; published by IDW Comics 2013–2014) and *Revolution* (series 2012–2014; published on comicbook.com 2015). The *Buffy the Vampire Slayer* comic, based on Joss Whedon's television series (1997–2003), is popularly known as "Season 8," but that series' finale was planned; Whedon did complete his spin-off series *Angel* (1999–2004) in comics, when it was canceled before the planned narrative was complete.

Marvel's remarkable success with its transmedia franchises, which specifically include the integration of film, television, and digital games, suggests that comic books might be the ideal medium to adapt for this new landscape of television production and, moreover, that digital games—themselves often a source for film adaptation—are also a key component of new modes of media consumption. As Lotz analyzes, these changes in distribution venues require us to acknowledge that television must now be understood less in terms of the technology of the receiver and its place in our home and more as a particular kind of content that we deliberately seek out, whatever its platform: "Convenience technologies encourage active selection, rather than passive viewing of the linear flow of whatever 'comes on next' or 'is on,' and consequently lead viewers to focus much more on programs than on networks—all of which contributes to eroding conventional production practices in significant ways. . . . The viewing behaviors these technologies enabled, in tandem with the vast choice among outlets that viewers could now access, were vital to the shift of television from what Bernard Miège theorized as a 'flow' industry to something more like a 'publishing' industry" (Lotz 68).

In this context, content providers seek to establish a "brand" identity that encourages viewers to return to their venue as the place to reliably seek out distinct "prized content," Lotz's term for television we watch by design. It is not surprising that when Sony, who had partnered profitably with Marvel on earlier films such as the *Spider-Man* trilogy, entered the original content market, they chose to adapt a comic book, Brian Michael Bendis and Michael Avon Oeming's *Powers*.[8] This adaptation was originally released on PlayStation, their game console that functions as a streaming media player through a subscription to Sony's PlayStation Vue, and was later released for purchase on Amazon Prime streaming.

Reinventing Superheroes in *Powers*

Powers first appeared in 2000 in the six-issue story "Who Killed Retro Girl?" A playful take on the superhero stories that dominated the medium, *Powers* features Detective Christian Walker, formerly the superhero Diamond, who lost his powers in a fight with his nemesis, Wolfe, and became a homicide detective.[9] It spanned fourteen story arcs, more or less one per year, until it was reinvented as *Powers Bureau* in 2013, thus far comprising two volumes. The focus remains on Christian and his partner, Deena Pilgrim, but both undergo a number of changes across these years, including occasionally having other partners, being off the police force at times, and developing new powers for a period. While each arc tells an integrated story, the breaks between them are often substantial, and considerable time has passed when we rejoin the characters. For example, between "Supergroup" (2003) and "Anarchy" (2003), a year passes in narrative time—Christian has been kicked off the force for revealing FBI info in an interview—and so we are introduced to a different version of the character than the one we left.[10] The series is held together by the characters, whom we come to know deeply over time, but each arc features its own case that closes with that story line. For example, the mystery of "Who Killed Retro Girl?" is resolved at the end of the six-issue run. "Roleplay" (2002) tells a story of murdered college students, who were killed by the villain they hired to make their cosplay experience of being heroes more intense. "Supergroup" starts with the murder of a former member of hero group FG-3 and ends with the revelation that their entire public identity is a media construction: far from being childhood friends united in heroism, they are products of a government experiment whose work is funded in exchange for 30 percent of the merchandising from their hero persona; their mental instability comes to light and the government quietly erases its mistakes by killing them.

The comic version of *Powers*, then, is balanced between episodic and

Christian (Sharlto Copley) mentors Calista (Olesya Rulin) in *Powers*.

serial narrative, relying on the emotional connection to the world and its characters to bring readers back for the next volume. In this way, it matches the seriality typical of television as it evolved more toward story arcs in the 1990s. This mode of storytelling, however, is more episodic than the emerging and integrated narratives of what television scholar Jason Mittell calls "complex TV." The comic series does not quite return to the steady state that was once typical of television, in that characters do grow and change, but at the same time, beyond Christian and Deena, most characters, like the "guest stars" of an earlier era of television, are central to a particular arc's story but not part of the ongoing story world. The main characters in "The Sellouts," for example, feature only in that story, part of a superhero team called Unity. They are an ironic version of the main DC heroes of the Justice League of America,[11] and the story is about how Supershock, a version of Superman, has grown senile with age and increasingly disillusioned with a humanity that cannot seem to overcome its baser instincts—provoked, as a last straw, by a sex scandal tape of one of his Unity colleagues, Red Hawk.[12] Supershock turns on humanity and begins killing indiscriminately, and it is only when Ultrabright, a version of Wonder Woman, convinces him to see himself as a man, not a god, that he can be stopped, fading away once he stops believing in his own transcendence.

As this brief plot outline suggests, the self-contained stories of the *Powers* comic take much of their meaning from their immersion in a wider culture of superhero comics, a world whose norms are established for the readers and whose allusions are recognized if never directly stated. *Powers* stands out in this context because of the innovative way it uses its medium: rather than focusing on the heroes, it is about police detectives who are usually in the background of such narratives; the cases that Christian and Deena investigate have mundane rather than world-in-peril solutions—Retro Girl is killed by a deranged fan who wanted to preserve her at the height of her power rather than see her age and deteriorate; the chemist couple responsible for killing Damocles in "Gods" (2012) does so out of vengeance for an assault on them that is like the stories of humans impregnated by the gods, such as Zeus and Leda; the death of a hero out of costume in his suburban home in "Cosmic" (2007) proves to be merely an accident, caused by the crash landing of another power who is still learning how to fly and land. The comic thus looks askew at a narrative world that is already familiar to its established audience. The television series, however, seeks to connect with the established market of viewers already invested in non-ironic comic book heroes. Moreover, television needs to contract a regular cast of characters so that actors are readily available to them. Jason Mittell argues that "television's character consistency is more than just an industrial convenience, as one of the primary ways that viewers engage with programming is to develop long-term relationships with characters" (127). Thus, the television adaptation cannot rely on the same narrative techniques that suture comic book readers to *Powers'* ironic take on this world.

What propels the comic reader's interest in *Powers* is less these stories and more the way Bendis tells them: instead of grand battles in which the fate of the world is at stake, these tend to be petty disagreements driven by pride or avarice, with Bendis often rapidly sketching in the ideas for various powered figures—Queen Noir, Bug, the Lance, Z—and letting readers' imaginations and knowledge of the genre/medium fill in the blanks. He delights most, it seems, in narrating those scenes that are usually left out of the superhero stories: the marital squabbles, Retro Girl's autopsy and the difficulty of working on a "powered" body, the lawsuits that emerge from working through what it might mean to think about powered individuals in another otherwise realist context. A consistent theme that runs across most of the issues is a comparison of powers to Hollywood celebrity, a kind of metacommentary on how the world within the comic intersects with the world of the reader of the comic, so that *Powers'* heroes live in a world of media and merchandising, whereas typically comics imagine a world where, for example, Superman exists but the media merchandise we associate with this figure does not. The television series, in contrast, seeks to create an emotional bond between its viewers and the story world, and so it integrates a number of incidents from the comic in ways that highlight the interpersonal connections of those involved rather than the events themselves: Christian and Retro Girl have a romantic past that is rekindled; Deena gains a father with a past of police corruption; Deena becomes romantically involved with another police detective, Kutter; and overall the fight against super-hero crime is presented with an earnest sincerity worthy of a crime drama such as *NYPD Blue* (1993–2005).

Innovation versus Imitation

The most innovative part of the comic is its creative use of its own medium. Rather than the orderly way of laying out cells and panels, *Powers* follows in the footsteps of celebrated comics such as Alan Moore's *Watchmen* (1986) in pushing the visual elements of its medium. For example, in "Who Killed Retro Girl?" color is used to emphasize that this is not the comic book world we have come to expect: scenes of Retro Girl's autopsy are muted in twilight blues and dark grays, reinforcing Christian's emotional state and signaling that this will be a darker and grittier story. Scenes of Christian's past as Diamond are in brighter and lighter colors, visually showing how much the world has changed for him in his new circumstances. In issue two, some of the panels simulate live news coverage, and when the cameraman rushes to chase an ongoing event, the visual image is blurred as if a handheld camera produced it. Issue twenty shows part of its narrative in a drawing style meant to mimic the media image cultivated for FG-3 (brighter colors, rounder faces) as compared to their "real" life told in the *Powers* drawing style of the rest of the series (dark tones, angular anatomy), and issue twenty-six is partly taken up by pages that represent a Golden Age comic story of Unity, drawn in a grainy style and with yellowed tones to imitate the aging paper of old comic books. In issue nine, the visual story is suddenly disrupted by a figure drawn in three-dimensional, photo-realist style that contrasts dramatically with the two-dimensional drawing typical of comic books; this figure briefly pops in and is dismissively called a "dimensional jumper" by Christian before he disappears. The *Powers* comic thus foregrounds and plays with its medium, continually reminding us of the kinds of stories stereotypically told in this medium and generating its meaning through the ways it plays with and thwarts expectations.

The *Powers* comic reflects features that Mittell associates with complex TV and its new narrative strategies, one of which he calls operational viewing: we watch "not just to get swept away in a realistic narrative world (although that certainly happens) but also to watch the gears at work, mar-

Johnny (Noah Taylor) reinvented as Christian's darker half.

veling at the craft required to pull off such narrative pyrotechnics" (43). Comics are similar to complex TV in that one "cannot simply watch these programs as an unmediated window to a realistic storyworld into which you might escape; rather, complex television demands that you pay attention to the window frames, asking you to reflect on how it provides partial access to the diegesis and how the panes of glass distort your vision on the unfolding action" (Mittell 53). Yet the comic also remains more episodic than this new complex TV, and this is the key difference between it and the television adaptation. Rather than allowing characters and stories to drop in and out of a world, whose continuity is ensured only by our main characters, the series, especially in its first season, tightly weaves together moments from across all the issues of *Powers* published thus far to create an integrated narrative: Retro Girl is alive and a major character in Season 1; minor criminal Johnny Royalle becomes something of a brother figure to Christian, although they have ended up on opposite sides of the law, creating a strong emotional backstory; both become father figures to Calista, the young girl who takes up the mantle of Retro Girl, humanizing Johnny; Christian becomes obsessed with regaining his lost powers, making him something of an antihero and putting him on a character arc toward growth and redemption—and the list goes on, with many isolated episodes of the comic woven into an entwined narrative in the series.

PlayStation Network's *Powers* adaptation was canceled after two seasons, leaving the future of the entertainment service's originally scripted content in doubt. The series successfully incorporated some aspects of the new age of television in its focus on character and long narrative arc,[13] but it failed to note that today's television viewers also demand an active viewing experience that lets them enjoy *how* a narrative is made. This misstep seems surprising coming from a development team whose central business is digital games, given how important gaming has become to transmedia storytelling, especially in games adapted from television series that allow players to "extend their participation in these rich storyworlds beyond the one-way flow of traditional television viewing" (Mittell 35). Although the *Powers* series has scenes of characters playing video games, including a game based on the "real" powers in their world, no game adaptation for PlayStation users was ever released. In sum, it seems that Sony misread its audience and the contemporary television environment and thus missed the mark, relying on a sense of the similarities between comic and television seriality that is belied both by recent shifts in the television industry and by the metafictional qualities of *Powers*, making it an unlikely title to adapt to typical melodrama seriality.

In his work on transmedia, Henry Jenkins distinguishes between adaptation and extension of narratives, arguing that the former tells the story via a new medium while the latter extends the story world in the move to a new medium, although he acknowledges that both tendencies are at play in any adaptation. Marvel achieved tremendous success using transmedia storytelling for franchise building because it extends its story worlds with medium-specific experiences. *Powers*, in contrast, focused on merely adapting its story to television, telling a more tightly integrated narrative as is consistent with recent trends in television seriality but failing to be true to the comic's ironic tone. The transition in the latter half of Season 2 toward introducing a "next generation" of the Unity team, with younger cast members—reminiscent of the many current CW youth-oriented television adaptations of DC comics—suggests that the writers attempted to shift their work toward an extension of the *Powers* story world, but they did so without having first secured viewers' emotional investment in these new versions of the series characters. The adaptation too openly revealed that its transmedia storytelling was aimed at franchise building rather than narrative extension and failed to note that what is most innovative about contemporary television is not the stories it tells but how it tells them. Its failure amid so many successful television comic adaptations suggests that emotional connections to characters rather than serial narratives are what hold viewers' attention

The next generation of powers: Zora, the new Retro Girl; Tristan, the new Triphammer; a younger Unity.

in small-screen contributions to transmedia story worlds. Moreover, it suggests that medium matters in a transmedia context, and that only those narratives that master the specific strengths of each medium will successfully extend their story worlds across them.

Conclusion

It is, of course, risky to offer any broad conclusions based on the single example of this adaptation; one might simply conclude that the people who adapted *Powers* did so poorly and that explains its failure. There is an element of truth to this view, but nonetheless a few observations can be drawn from this example that seem to have generalizable implications. The most important is that a transmedia narrative environment does not indicate that the medium has become irrelevant as consumers pursue their desired narratives across different media. Rather, this example suggests that it is perhaps more important than ever to pay attention to the specificity of medium in a context wherein success means that one must utilize each to best advantage across a transmedia strategy. Marvel has clearly demonstrated its skill at this calculus, uniting its various properties through a single narrative but using different kinds of texts to bring distinct elements into focus. The films, of course, offer the spectacular effects sequences that have become so central to the blockbuster mode and also serve as the place where relevant paradigm-shifting narratives are made (Hydra's infiltration of SHIELD; the Sokovia Accords, for example). The network television series is a smaller-scale version of this globally focused narrative, reproducing a typical difference between big and small screens with smaller effects budgets and lower-salaried actors. And finally, the Netflix series are character-driven and focus on what are understood to be niche audiences—people of color, women—as they tell stories focused on the local as it has been transformed by the events of the film franchise. Marvel understands that films can be made more episodic and that television has become oriented toward more closed narratives in the move toward story arcs, but the media's political economics remain disparate even as their approaches to seriality converge.

From the point of view of seriality and ongoing changes to television as a mode, *Powers* was a good choice of a series to adapt. It had an established fan base, a distinct narrative world that could be created without a huge effects budget, and its experimental use of the comics medium and the superhero narrative made it a good match for the new kind of prized television that Mittell argues we consume via operational viewing, that is, a focus on how a narrative structure works. Thus, one might conclude that Sony utilized one element of the new landscape of television correctly in the integrated narrative it created for Season 1 out of more episodic issue runs of the comic series. At the same time, however, because *Powers* is a stand-alone narrative that connects to the rest of the comic book world via satire and allusion, rather than as a property open to the kinds of crossover stories that might serve as the seeds from which to build a transmedia franchise, Sony seems to have misread the new landscape of television in the choice to adapt *Powers*. Attempts to ameliorate this in Season 2 by rebooting the series with younger versions of the comics' characters missed the mark, simply rejuvenating a still-closed narrative world. *Powers*, then, is a comic book adaptation that might speak to the comic's audience—people who know and care about this world and its characters—but not one that speaks to its own television audience, who now have very different expectations of this medium than viewers of an earlier era in which television and comic seriality were more closely aligned.

Notes

1. The more recent adaptations draw on a history of radio and film serial adaptations that began almost as early as the comics themselves. Both DC's Superman and Batman generated serials, as did Marvel's Captain America.

2. Marvel added to these films, focusing on the "big" characters, such as Iron Man and Captain America, with a second phase that included films focused on lesser-known characters, such as *Guardians of the Galaxy* (2014) and *Ant-Man* (2015).

3. Once the "brand" was established, Marvel announced more films, some of which introduced characters new to the cinematic universe, such as *Doctor Strange* (2017) and *Black Panther* (2017), alongside new installments of the established film franchises. Through a licensing deal with Sony, *Captain America: Civil War* (2016) reintegrated Spider-Man back into the Marvel Universe. Media convergence through such licensing deals and through corporate acquisitions is an important part of this new phenomenon. Although this strategy was embarked upon when Marvel was functioning as an independent entity, Marvel Studios was bought by Disney in late 2009 and thus was already a Disney entity when the first integrated film was released in 2012.

4. Johnson notes that Marvel also successfully used this strategy of integration across multiple series for its animated television adaptations (7). He also argues, drawing on David Bordwell, that cinema has its own traditions of networked narrative, and thus "Marvel's cinematic intertextuality did not threaten textual traditions in the cinema so much as leverage compatibility with comic book storytelling" (7). I take his point, but his examples, such as the James Whale *Frankenstein* films, seem closer to the model of sequel than to this new integrated narrative across media perfected by Marvel.

5. In this case, the different temporal settings—adult Clark Kent, teenaged Clark Kent—offer a logical reason, but nonetheless the choice to imagine another time and version of Superman rather than seek integration reflects standard practice up until Marvel's *Iron Man*.

6. The recent television adaptation of the science fiction thriller *Limitless* (2011; series 2015–2016) attempted the same strategy by bringing in star Bradley Cooper to play his film character and thus situate the series as less an adaptation and more a continuation of the film's story world.

7. See Ellis for a discussion of the differences between film and television as media. His work, based on an earlier era of distribution, stresses that cinema is an "event" that we see on a screen larger than ourselves, while television is consumed in the home, often in a distracted state, on a small screen. For an analysis of a more recent era of "TV III" in which such differences are eroding, in part due to changes within both industries and in part due to a new context of consumption in which people watch both media in identical contexts through DVDs, streaming services, etc., see Nelson; and Hills and Creeber.

8. PlayStation Vue has partnerships with other established networks, and mainly serves as a streaming provider for their content. Sony also owns the streaming service Crackle, a site for online series and Hollywood films. PlayStation Vue seems to be aimed more strongly at penetrating the television market, while Crackle focuses mostly on partnerships with film studios. Crackle original productions began as online series, with *Chosen* (2013–2014) one of its early drama series; the *Powers* series was originally optioned by Fox for television adaptation, although the project was not pursued beyond the pilot, which was recast when the series moved to PlayStation. Crackle is driven by advertising revenue, whereas Vue relies on subscriptions.

9. Police procedural comics have become common since *Powers* first emerged, but it predates better known series, such as *Gotham Central* (first published in 2002). Frank

Miller's noir comic *Sin City* (1991–2000) debuted earlier but did not combine super-heroes with the detective stories.

10. Television can make such huge temporal leaps as well—famously, a single match cut skips a year within a single episode of *Battlestar Galactica* (2004–2009; "Lay Down Your Burdens, Part 2," 10 Mar 2006)—but they are rare.

11. It is worth noting that this is the first issue of the series to be published under the Icon imprint, the indie arm of Marvel, DC's traditional rival, and thus it is unsurprising that the critique focuses on DC characters; the previous issues were published under the artist-created Image label. In addition to Superman/Supershock, Wonder Woman/Ultrabright, the group consists of Red Hawk/Batman; his sidekick, Wing/Robin; Dragonfist/Green Arrow; and Nucleus/the Atom.

12. There is an elaborate in-joke about the presumed homosexual relationship between Batman and Robin, since the sex tape involves Red Hawk having sex with a (female) prostitute dressed as Wing, his (male) sidekick. Although the sex tape story and senility of Supershock are integrated into television's Season 2, the larger meta-commentary on superheroes and sexual orientation is omitted.

13. This is the case especially for the first season, in which genuine emotional connections are created among the characters and a backstory is developed that warrants our investment in these relationships. Season 2 is much less consistent in its characterization, shifting the focus between two major antagonists who remain so undeveloped that there is no emotional payoff in their defeat, and undermining how Retro Girl was established as the moral center of the series in the first season.

Works Cited

Bendis, Brian Michael, and Charlie Huston, creators. *Powers*. Circle of Confusion, Jinxworld, and Sony Pictures Television, 2015–2016.

Bendis, Brian Michael, and Michael Avon Oeming. *Powers: The Definitive Hardcover Collection, Vol. 1*. Marvel Comics, 2006.

———. *Powers, Vol. 4: Supergroup*. Marvel Comics, 2003.

———. *Powers, Vol. 6: Sellouts*. Marvel Comics, 2004.

———. *Powers, Vol. 10: Cosmic*. Marvel Comics, 2007.

———. *Powers, Vol. 14: Gods*. Marvel Comics, 2012.

Bushby, Helen. "How Cinema Boosted Marvel's Fortunes." *BBC News Online*, 4 July 2003, http://news.bbc.co.uk/2/hi/entertainment/3004396.stm.

Creeber, Glen. *Serial Television: Big Drama on the Small Screen*. London, BFI, 2005.

Ellis, John. *Seeing Things: Television in the Age of Uncertainty*. London, I. B. Tauris, 2002.

Hills, Matt, and Glen Creeber. "Editorial: TV III." *New Review of Film and Television Studies*, vol. 5, no. 1, April 2007, pp. 1–4.

Jenkins, Henry. "Transmedia 202: Further Reflections." *Confessions of an Aca-Fan*, 1 August 2011, henryjenkins.org/2011/08/defining_transmedia_further_re.html.

Johnson, Derek. "Cinematic Destiny: Marvel Studios and the Trade Stories of Industrial Convergence." *Cinema Journal*, vol. 52, no. 1, Fall 2012, pp. 1–24.

Lotz, Amanda. *The Television Will Be Revolutionized*. 2nd ed., New York, New York University Press, 2014.

Mittell, Jason. *Complex TV: The Poetics of Contemporary Television Storytelling.* New York, New York University Press, 2015.

Nelson, Robin. "HBO Premium: Channeling Distinction through TV III." *New Review of Film and Television Studies*, vol. 5, no. 1, April 2007, pp. 25–40.

Tryon, Chuck. *Reinventing Cinema: Movies in the Age of Media Convergence.* New Brunswick, NJ, Rutgers University Press, 2009.

PART TWO

PANELS AND FRAMES

Felix in—and out of—Space

J. P. TELOTTE

For some critics and historians, the story of early animation is largely one of character—its development, attraction, and centrality to the work of the cartoon. Donald Crafton, for example, has suggested that we can better understand cartoons of the period 1900 to 1928 through the lens of "performance art," that is, as a series of virtuoso actions by the animator or animators in which a central figure—a cat, mouse, clown, or some vaguely defined figure (such as Warner Bros.' early cartoon star Bosko)—effectively stands in or "figures" that creator and his artistry (Crafton 4). For others, such as Esther Leslie, animation in these formative years was essentially a variation on modernist art and its rebellion against the constrictive forces of an earlier cinematic order, or more specifically "the confutation of Hollywood's narratives and naturalism" (45). Thus, Leslie describes how what she sees as the most successful early cartoons embody an abstract sensibility, suggesting that "everything in the drawn world is of the same stuff" (23). Yet there seems a level on which both assessments are right, for the signal performance and an ontologic sameness are mutually characteristic of early animation, especially as practiced in the United States. As part of this reconsideration, I want to examine the cartoons of one of the most popular animated characters, Felix the Cat, considering how they draw upon both of these characteristics, while also measuring them against a later generation of cartoon art, as represented by sound-era Felix cartoons and the various comic strips and comic books that attempted to reinvent this figure and rebuild his popularity in the 1930s and beyond.

Animating Space

As I have argued elsewhere, we might also think of animation as being fundamentally about *space*—the space within which animation occurs and the
bringing to life or animating of that space, of all that constitutes the cartoon world and its characters. It is a perspective partly inspired by the work
of architect and art historian Anthony Vidler, who observed, in this same
early modernist period, and coincident with the many and varied "representational experiments of modernism" (*Warped Space* 7), a shift in attitude
toward another sort of representational/aesthetic space, that of architecture.
He chronicles how architecture began to be conceived of "as comprised of
'space' rather than of built elements like walls and columns" (143), and how
that new conception necessarily became intertwined with our own point of
view on and sense of involvement in space. But in a move that differentiates
his view of architectural modernism from Leslie's of cartoon modernism,
he also observes a tendency "to permeate the formal with the psychological" (Vidler, *Warped Space* 2), that is, to treat space as a representation or
projection of the human psyche, of character, as we sought out, in that new
"unwalled" condition, new ways to address the equally "unwalled" and un-
defined self: "to represent the space of modern identity" (Vidler, *Warped
Space* 1) that seemed to have lost many of its traditional supports, becoming
fragmented and dislocated.

In early animation this productive conflation of self and space seems to
reach a high level of exploration and achievement, especially in the Felix the
Cat cartoons—arguably the most popular and influential body of animated
work between 1919 and 1928. As Stefan Kanfer sums up, in that single decade of production "Felix's celebrity increased every year," and even "intel-
lectuals began to surround him with fulsome praise and overanalysis" (56),
while songwriters penned songs about him, Surrealist artists championed
him as an oneiric figure, and an appreciative public purchased a wide variety
of products bearing the likeness of this most merchandised of early cartoon figures. Cartoon historian Giannalberto Bendazzi explains this level
of popularity by suggesting that "in the panorama of its decade, Felix was
uniquely complex, being at the same time feline, human, and 'magical'" (57),
and he notes how "the smooth use of every element in Felix's graphic world
contributed to the character's magic" (57). Rather than embrace that vague
notion of "magic" at this point, though, I want to underscore Bendazzi's
larger sense of *combination* at work in the Felix films, for in these early cartoons the performance of the self depends precisely on the leveling out of
all things, on the demonstration of their sameness—or spatiality—within

the world of the cartoon. It is this combinatory effect, though, that largely disappears from the later sound films, cartoon strips, and comic books that also bear his name and that, instead, often sought to locate a "magical" element of his character.

Felix's Character and Authorship

Because the notion of figuration, as Crafton reminds, evokes both the cartoon's central figure and its animator/creator, one should first give some attention to the vexed question of authorship or creation that has always surrounded the Felix cartoons. Pat Sullivan, widely celebrated as Felix's creator, owned the studio that produced Felix, claimed to have invented the figure (even repeating a particular "origin" story for the figure), and negotiated contracts for the cartoons and comic strips. However, after his death it was learned that he had never registered the copyright in his name. In fact, as John Canemaker chronicles, Sullivan's lawyer found that the copyright was in the name of King Features Syndicate, which distributed both the films and the comic strips.[1] Moreover, Sullivan's chief animator, Otto Messmer, claimed to have created the Felix prototype for the short *Feline Follies* (1919), an animated part of a *Paramount Screen Magazine* film for which Sullivan's studio often produced content. Various studio employees have indicated that Messmer was responsible for most of the work on the Felix cartoons, particularly story and characterization, and animation historian Michael Barrier, after interviewing a number of Sullivan's staff, concluded that "Felix was wholly Messmer's creature" (31). Such conflicting claims, though, make assigning authorship, or considering the sort of figuration relationship Crafton suggests, somewhat problematic. At least in his early animated cartoons, Felix the figure simply escapes easy categorization, becoming, as his tail so often did in the cartoons, a lingering question mark for historians and commentators. But there is little contention about the various comic strips and comic books for which Messmer created most of the panels and stories beginning in 1923. These efforts, including a Sunday comic strip starting in 1923, daily comics beginning in 1927, and comic book appearances starting in 1943, would become mainstays of the Felix franchise until Messmer's assistant, Joe Oriolo, revived it as a television cartoon series in 1959.

In the early Felix films, the cat, too, escapes easy characterization. He is a baseball player—and better than any of his human teammates—in *Felix Saves the Day* (1922); an incompetent babysitter who loses the baby in *Felix Minds the Kid* (1922); a hero in the war against mice in *Felix Turns the*

Tide (1922); a failed rescuer of an overweight woman in *Felix Lends a Hand* (1922); a politician who leads the cat population to Mars in *Astronomeows* (1928). Apparently, he could be whatever the situation called for, and as Paul Wells notes, Felix, like the early Mickey Mouse, increasingly seemed to "take on a greater diversity of roles and levels of engagement" (25), to always seem, as noted before, a bit dislocated, a figure without a singular defining narrative or impulse. Moreover, in every role success and failure seem equally possible, in part because the character was so vaguely defined, so much a part of whatever fragmentary world was conjured up for each story—just as open or "unwalled" as the vaguely drawn spaces in which he was set down.

But two things were very quickly established and became almost iconic for the Felix films: the cat's peculiar walk and the "ideographic playfulness" (23), as Leslie terms it, that accompanies most of his actions. The former, immortalized in the 1923 British music hall song "Felix Kept on Walking," refers to the cat's tendency to pace back and forth, hands folded behind his back and usually on what seems empty space, figured as an undifferentiated white ground/background, as he tries to puzzle out a problem or an action in abstract space—as if separating himself from the depicted world. The latter denotes his consistent ability to turn visual signs of that thinking—images of the same substance as himself—into useful appliances or momentary solutions. Thus a series of question marks, placed one atop another, becomes a ladder in *Felix Saves the Day*, another is turned into a sap to defeat an ogre in *Felix in Fairyland* (1923), and two of them become a pair of skis in *Felix Gets the Can* (1924), while exclamation points become oars in *Two-Lip Time* (1926) and an airplane propeller in *Eats Are West* (1925). And throughout his films, Felix readily grasps, adapts, and similarly transforms other such graphic markers—musical notes, sight lines—or everyday objects into useful physical *things*, even *animate* objects, such as when hot dogs become sled dogs to pull his sled in *Felix Gets the Can* or soldiers in the war against mice in *Felix Turns the Tide*. In the process, such effects remind us that in this world not only is everything of "the same stuff," but also every *thing* might be seen as equally figurative, as if an embodiment or figuration of Felix's own animating abilities. Like an animator, he can *imagine* things into being.

But it is an animating ability that, as most commentators have tended to ignore, works both ways. For if Felix can himself act figuratively and inspire—or animate—other objects into a state of figuration, so too can he become just like those various objects he encounters, at times quite willfully but at others just accidentally, as if he too were being authored by his environment. A frequent, if only partial, example is when he meets someone,

Felix doffs his ears in *Futuritzy* (1928).

raises a paw to his ears, and then doffs the ears and top of his head as if a hat. Similarly, and as every commentator has noted, his tail proves easily detachable, as when it becomes a crank for turning a windmill in *Two-Lip Time*, a parasol in *Eats Are West*, or a telescope in *Felix Gets the Can*. But more to the point is his own transformative ability, as when, in trying to ward off a polar bear, he grabs two icicles, inserts them as tusks, and seemingly turns into a walrus in *Eskimotive* (1928), or when, to escape a pursuer, he flips upside down and seems to transform into an easily overlooked black bush, simply part of the landscape in *Felix in Fairyland* (1923) and numerous other films. *No Fuelin'* (1927) provides an instance of what I term accidental transformation, where, searching for wood to make a fire, Felix enters a bowling alley, is mistaken for a bowling ball, and, when thrown by a bowler, makes off with the pins. Another example can be seen in *Felix All Puzzled* (1925), when he is accidentally kicked by a mule, lands in Russia, rolls into a ball with his tail sticking into the air, and is immediately mistaken for a revolutionary's bomb, only then to be chased by various revolutionaries with *real* bombs.

In these and many other instances, Felix obviously reveals his kinship to what Leslie terms the "permutable world" of the cartoon (22), an object or even part of an object in the landscape, part of what constitutes the drawnness of the animated film, and a character that does not so much "figure" the animator as he is "figured" by the other characters, objects, or circumstances around him. In such instances, as well as those in which he is broken into pieces by some accident and must then literally pull himself together—as occurs in *No Fuelin'* and many other films—Felix becomes by turns figure *and* space, a character who exists not as a reference to the animator but as a product of that "same stuff" of which the narrative—if narrative it be—is made.

As a further example, one might consider a single cartoon, *Sure-Locked Homes* (1928), a late work that might also inform, with its dreamlike nature, why he was so soundly embraced by the Surrealists in this period. As the film begins a title card announces that night's "all-enveloping cloak" is arriving, and suddenly—and quite literally—night seems to fall in the form of large drops of black ink that drip from above, coloring most of the blank sky but leaving a circular white hole, an absence of dark that one quickly recognizes as the moon. Frightened by several figures in the night, including a night-shirt dropped by a laundryman that, floating on the night breeze, seems ghostlike, Felix returns to his home and locks the door—transforming a basket into a padlock and using his tail for a key. After breathing a visible sigh of relief, though, he finds a series of menacing shadows tracking him through the house—one in the form of a gorilla, another an elephant, a third a crocodile, then a bat. Capturing one of these menacing shadows in a spider's web, he locks it in a closet and fires a gun through the door, only to have the figure ooze out through a bullet hole and, just like that inky sky at the start of the film, gradually occupy almost the entire room, leaving just a small lit corner that is Felix. After a panicked call brings a policeman—physically, through the phone line—Felix discovers in an adjoining room that a baby, playing with a lamp, has apparently been making hand shadows, images that in turn have produced this scared version of the usually self-assured and quite logical cat, a figure who is himself rendered as a great dark spot on the screen when the irritated policeman clubs him and he seems to explode into a large black splatter.

This film is more than just a common demonstration of how the dark might play upon one's mind. It is a stylish and stylistic display of how character produces space and space produces character—in effect, how both seem of the same substance, or insubstantial substance, given the reflexive character of the narrative. The small child who has been producing and animating these insubstantial images, when revealed, turns and winks at the camera, as if admitting the key gag here, that his actions stand in not for the animator but for the whole world of the movies with their equally powerful—and at times equally naïve—play of light and dark, of image and ground, of figure and space, underscoring a point Vidler makes about all modernist space: that "the surroundings no longer surrounded, but entered the experience as presence" ("Explosion of Space" 15).

The attraction of the early Felix, I would argue, is built on this new spatial foundation, one in which figure depends on space and space on figure, in which their very interchangeability—and thus film's mutational ability—is the key source of the cartoon's gags. And yet that foundation would not prove very substantial, neither as the cartoons moved into a full sound format[2] nor as the character was translated into other media, such as comic strips and comic books. In 1936 a series of properly synchronized and Technicolor Felix sound cartoons was produced by the Van Beuren Studio and released by RKO Radio Pictures. Directed by former Disney animator Burt Gillett, these cartoons—*The Goose That Laid the Golden Egg*, *Neptune Nonsense*, and *Bold King Cole* (all 1936)—offer a pointedly changed character set down in a Disney-like three-dimensional world, with the different character and style yoked to the sort of fairy-tale elements that were hallmarks of the highly successful Disney Silly Symphony series (1929–1939).

Van Beuren's Felix Cartoons

While the Van Beuren cartoons were expensively done and technically up-to-date, they offered little of the original Felix character. In fact, Leonard Maltin judges that their "least interesting factor is the personality of Felix" (207). In presentation the character looks like the Felix of the late-silent and early-sound cartoons, although his size seems to shift frequently, largely because he is no longer a pet or stray cat, seeking to survive in the human world, but rather a cat anthropomorph, much like Mickey Mouse, Porky Pig, Flip the Frog, and other humanized animals of the period. In fact, *Neptune Nonsense* begins with Felix tending to what we assume are *his own* pets, as he walks through a house and feeds a bird in a cage, two dogs, and a goldfish—all of them much smaller than Felix—while in *The Goose That Laid the Golden Egg* he has a pet goose, the title character, which at one point he tucks under his arm, as also does the much larger pirate Captain Kidd when he steals the goose for his own gain. But more telling than such perspective problems is the nature of this cat character. Never a troublemaker, nor worried about his next meal, as was common in the earlier films, this Felix is what one might simply term a do-gooder, helping his lonely goldfish find a companion in the first cartoon; in the second, passing out gold coins produced by his magic goose to the poor; and in *Bold King Cole* helping the king rid his castle of ghosts. And when not actively aiding others, he is the butt of jokes—rather than the instigator—from other characters, such as a traffic-cop octopus in *Neptune Nonsense*, or he is subordinated to larger-than-life central figures like King Neptune, Captain Kidd, and Old King Cole—all of them simply far more "interesting" than this rather lifeless version of Felix.

And if figure and space helped to produce each other, or, as Vidler says, mutually "entered the experience" in the original Felix cartoons, in the Van Beuren efforts the world, too, seems to lack "character." Driven by a dominant sense of built space, Van Beuren's Felix cartoons suggest a solid world—a world of houses and castles, even under the sea in *Neptune Nonsense*—hardly the "universe of transformation, overturning and provisionality" that Leslie sees as dominating the earlier silent efforts in animation (vi). But more to the point, that space no longer seems connected to psyche, to character, to "the space of modern identity," as Vidler puts it (*Warped Space* 1). In fact, *Bold King Cole* seems an almost direct address to this notion by evoking the ghosts of the king's castle, who, tired of his constant boasting, arise from the various paintings and statues that memorialize their lives and try to scare such windiness out of him. Using a suit of armor to conduct and shoot lightning at them, Felix exorcizes these remnants of personality that imbue this space, leaving it a safe structure, no longer likely to haunt anyone or to provide a haven for psychic projection or representation.

The Comic Strip Felix

But that shift was already underway in the comic strips and then further solidified in the comic books that would sustain the "life" of the Felix character after his disappearance from film in 1936 and before his return as a television figure in the 1950s. As earlier noted, this movement was in itself significant, since the film industry had typically looked in the other direction; that is, it had regularly sought to find in the world of the comics popular characters that might prove viable as animated cartoon stars. This latter group comprises a long list of figures, including Little Nemo, Mutt and Jeff, Krazy Kat, the Katzenjammer Kids, Jerry on the Job, Old Doc Yak, Happy Hooligan, and Popeye—some wildly successful after their transition to film but others quickly forgotten. Felix, however, would become the first screen cartoon figure to make that difficult transition from animated to drawn comics, a transition that attests to his character's iconic power. But in the process of crossing that media boundary, the figural-spatial dynamics that were one of the cartoons' hallmarks would gradually disappear, leaving Felix

Felix transforms himself in a 1935 comic strip.

largely unable to transform his world and his world equally unable to inspire alterations in him.

As an illustration, consider a sampling of early Felix comic strips available on the Internet Animation Database as part of the "Classic Felix the Cat" webpage.[3] These strips, dating between 1923 and 1931, were variously pencilled by Otto Messmer or Jack Bogle but also in some cases finalized (i.e., done in ink) and personally signed by Pat Sullivan. The first, a twelve-panel strip, simply emphasizes Felix's role as a trickster, for when he is rebuffed in an effort to get a job as a mouse catcher, he steals a wedge of cheese, attracts some mice, throws the cheese into the house from which he was booted, and is soon after offered "a home for the rest of your life" by the now mouse-plagued homeowner. Similarly, a Christmas strip from 1925 shows Felix watching a group of poor children at Christmas and resolving to help them. That night he serenades the neighborhood with a literal caterwauling, only to have various objects, including toys, thrown at him, all of which he gathers up and, wearing a Santa beard and hat, presents to the children.

And that same trickster character is at the heart of a series of linked weekday strips from May 13–16, 1931, wherein Felix reads about an offer of a $50,000 prize for the first "non-stop flight to Timbuctoo." Going into his famous pondering walk, he sees a man carrying a sandwich-board advertisement, tricks him to fall into an open manhole, leaving behind the two sandwich boards, and then attaches the boards to an empty barrel. When the man eventually rises up from the manhole, there is a graphic display of stars whirling in a circle around his head, which Felix appropriates for a propeller so he can fly "off to Timbuctoo." The last of these three examples obviously adds to that trickster component an elaborate demonstration of Felix's transformative abilities, although both the plot and the various transformations—including the opening in which Felix appropriates a numeral "8" from a sign to use as glasses—are all lifted from an earlier animated cartoon, *The Non-Stop Fright* (1927). Otherwise, the key focus is on Felix's own abilities at figuring out and tricking an all-too-solid and hardly "provisional" world.[4]

Another, and more ambitious, film-based strip sequence is the multi-day "Roameo," based on another 1927 film of the same title. Drawing on an elaborate series of temporal and spatial shifts, this twenty-one-strip Felix adventure juxtaposes a constant element of the cat's character—that he is an inveterate girl chaser—with a world that always seems to, as one panel puts it, "carry him away." Thus, in the first two installments even as Felix works up the courage to propose to his feline girlfriend, he finds himself distracted by a Spanish cat, heard singing over the radio, later by an Eskimo kitten encountered at the North Pole, and then by a hula dancer met on a tropical island. In each case he seems quickly to fall in love, only to be "actually carried away by the music," as a caption notes, scared off by his señorita's knife wielding, chased away by a rock that proves to be a polar bear, or transported by an angry rival's spear throw—a throw that amazingly lands him back at home in the arms of his (original) sweetheart. Only once in these twenty-one roaming installments do we see Felix's signature transformative ability: when being counted out in a battle with a Spanish bull, he seizes the number "3," places it on his head, and turns it into horns to even the odds against the bull. But for the most part, he has become a character who repeatedly finds himself at the mercy of forces beyond his control or even understanding. In fact, the spear that carries him not only across several comic panels but also across the ocean comes from a character, his angry rival, that he never even sees. It simply works as a kind of providential force, bringing him back to his—and the entire adventure's—starting point, while suggesting a level on which the "built" world was, in this other medium, reasserting its power over and independence from character.

The Comic Book Felix

The shift can also be traced out in some of the Felix comic books that would be issued over the years by the Dell, Toby, and Harvey publishers. A sampling of these comic book stories, ranging from 1946 to 1954 and collected in Craig Yoe's *Felix the Cat: The Great Comic Book Tails*, reveals a character who is no longer a trickster and is practically never given to his famous walk; instead, it is the world itself that seems constantly to play tricks on Felix while defying his ability to walk through its puzzling nature. In "Starbust" (1946), for example, Felix wakes up in bed and announces, "This will be my lucky day!" But each page brings only a new accident or bit of trouble to confound that optimistic expectation: he slips on a bar of soap and falls down the stairs; he steps on a tack and drops his bottle of milk, breaking it; the lucky horseshoe hung over his door falls on his neck; he steps into an open manhole, and so on. Only an accidental run-in with a lion reverses his fortune, as he is able to pull an arrow from its paw, bandage the big cat, and receive its pledge to guarantee "nothing but good luck" for Felix from then on.

Similarly, "Mask Bawl" (1948) begins with Felix reading a thrilling adventure story, one that leaves him bored with his own "humdrum existence." On heading out into the "real" world for some adventure, though, he encounters a dragon, a knight in armor, an Indian, a couple of masked men with guns, a pair of sword-wielding pirates, a ghost, a witch, even a fairy who tries to comfort the frightened cat. But the issue is not, as he tries to reason out, his imagination playing tricks on him thanks to the book he has read, nor is it "a witch's spell," as he also thinks. Images scattered throughout the panels— a dark sky, an orange moon, falling leaves, jack-o'-lanterns, haystacks—clue the readers that it is Halloween, and the various figures he has encountered were all simply headed for a Halloween party, which Felix has managed to disrupt. Chased by the partygoers, he ends up back at home, vowing, "Bed is all the adventure I want in the future." There is nothing mysterious—or even adventurous—about this world; it is not a puzzle but a party, and one to which this version of Felix has not been invited, as these comic stories repeatedly work to contain and control the instability of both the cat and the world he inhabits.

In his study of comic book "grammar," Scott McCloud notes an essential dynamic at the heart of this form. While comics often offer strange images, and their individual panels serve to "fracture both time and space, offering a jagged staccato rhythm of unconnected moments," they also, at a most basic level, depend on the experience of "closure," allowing readers to connect those "jagged" effects and "mentally construct a continuous, unified reality" (McCloud 69). It is a dynamic effect that seems at the heart of these iterations of Felix the Cat, as individual panels, or in some cases three or four panels, introduce some new challenge—to experience or understanding— and the series of such challenges seems to suggest, to Felix and sometimes to the reader, just the sort of "unwalled" world that is most often found in the early animated cartoons. Yet the gutters between panels become emblematic of Felix's own limitations, his inability to see this world properly, to make the necessary connections, while the final panels in the comic books invariably sort things out *for him*.

Thus "Shadow Shudders" (1950), which recalls the 1928 film *Sure-Locked Homes*, has Felix frightened by a series of shadows cast by his kitten nephews, including one of a lion. While he initially passes these scary images off as tricks of his imagination or even as "phantoms," the lion seems quite substantial and chases him out of his house and all around the city. In the midst of the chase, though, he encounters a newspaper with the headline "Lion Es-

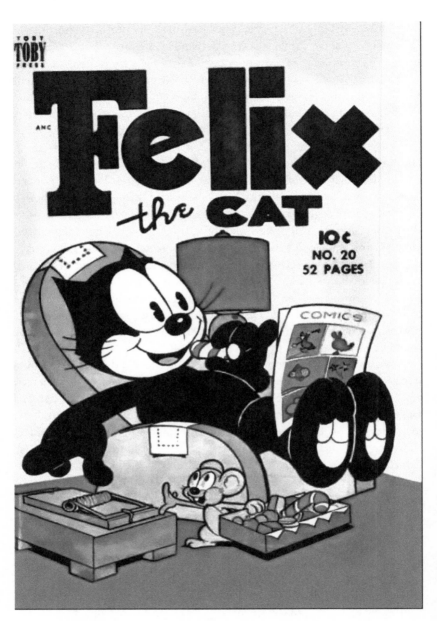

Felix at home in the domestic space of the comic book (Toby Press, 1950).

capes Circus," recognizes that it is a trained lion that he is dealing with, and gets it to jump through a hoop and into a nearby circus wagon. It is a simple trick and a reminder of his erstwhile capacity for being tricky and transformative, but it is also one only made possible by a world that rather easily explains itself—in this case with the help of a convenient headline—and with his help, regains its stability, even rewarding Felix with free circus tickets for himself and his mischievous nephews.

Such simple stories that are centered on Felix's mistaking of an otherwise normal world, though, ultimately make capital from the very absence of the cat's character. Apart from Felix's signature look, there is little to distinguish him from any other comic character, much less to project the modernist sense of a figure and a world mutually given to, as Leslie says, "transformation, overturning and provisionality" (vi). A later comic book development, though, suggests an awareness of this problem and an effort to restore part of that sensibility, as Felix becomes the owner of a mysterious magic carpet that obeys his every wish—although its literal obedience at times makes for comic troubles. The 1950 story "Vegeteria" introduces this development with Felix seated on the carpet and explaining, "My magic carpet takes me to the lands of fantasy." And in that tale he flies to the land of Vegeteria, where he manages to save its vegetable inhabitants from an invasion of potato bugs and beetles; in another 1950 story, "Candy Land," he lands in Candy Land, where he is imprisoned for being a "sweet-toothed cat" and must learn a lesson about too many sweets; "Flights of Fancy" (1951) has him transport a poor little girl who wants a book of fairy stories to Fairy Land, where she actually meets various storybook characters; in that same year's "Worse and Reverse," he explores "reverse" land, where fish catch cats and eat them and horses ride in carriages while cats pull them; and in "Roboteria" (1953) he goes to the planet Roboteria, a place inhabited by robots, where he is jailed for being a spy from a nontechnological world.

The various adventures in these and other stories obviously depend on the mechanism of the carpet to restore some of the "magic" that, as one might recall, Giannalberto Bendazzi cited as one of the reasons for the cartoon Felix's success in the 1920s. And that lesson was again followed when Joe Oriolo created a new series of Felix the Cat cartoons for television, starting in 1959. In these cartoons, a redesigned, more modern-looking Felix carried a "magic bag," or as Canemaker describes it, "a valise that changed into sundry objects and protected him from harm" (152). In effect, his own rather magical personality had become objectified, literally bagged up, only to be unpacked when the otherwise simplistic plots needed a sudden boost or gag.

That objectification—and the separation of figure from personality—though, only underscores the changes in both Felix and his world. In these new cartoons he was being produced by another world and another medium—and for a different audience, one of young children who might not understand how both character and world could prove equally shifty. Certainly television of the late 1950s did not see itself, as both film and early animation did, as part of the modernist moment, celebrating its liberations, its newly discovered "unwalled" nature. Gradually, but probably inevitably, in comic strips, comic books, and television incarnations Felix had moved into a space where walls of different sorts were set up, where "surroundings" once again "surrounded." Only the prospect of something magical—providence, a carpet, a magic bag—recalls that magical dimension of early animation, when there seemed to be a freedom to figure self and world anew, when the power to figure, to author, to animate aligned with the open space that was a key part of Felix's very personality and real attraction.

Notes

1. Canemaker, in *Felix: The Twisted Tale of the World's Most Famous Cat*, has untangled the "twisted" legal situation surrounding Felix's ownership, which surfaced only after Pat Sullivan's sudden death in 1933. See pp. 137–141.

2. Pat Sullivan resisted the industry move into sound cartoons, largely instigated by the success of Disney's Mickey Mouse films. However, he eventually allowed some of the silent films to have sound effects added and others to be made with postsynchronized sound, resulting, as Canemaker judges, in sound that was "sloppy, rarely matching the action on the screen" (129) and eventuating in the distributor's canceling the contract for more Felix cartoons.

3. Besides a sampling of early cartoon strips, "The Classic Felix the Cat Page" offers links to some of the best Felix cartoons, a list of Felix-inspired songs, examples of production and promotional art, and links to other Felix-related sites.

4. There is some irony in Felix's translation into a *magic* cat on television, since he was the first cartoon image broadcast on a medium that was itself originally seen as rather magical. In 1928 RCA Research Labs used an image of Felix—blurry, but iconic and easily recognized—for experimental transmissions from their prototype television camera.

Works Cited

Barrier, Michael. *Hollywood Cartoons: American Animation in Its Golden Age*. Oxford, UK, Oxford University Press, 1999.

Bendazzi, Giannalberto. *Cartoons: One Hundred Years of Cinema Animation*. Bloomington, Indiana University Press, 1994.

Canemaker, John. *Felix: The Twisted Tale of the World's Most Famous Cat*. New York, Pantheon, 1991.

"The Classic Felix the Cat Page." *Internet Animation Database*, www.intanibase.com /gac/felix/index.aspx. Accessed 7 January 2019.

Crafton, Donald. *Shadow of a Mouse: Performance, Belief, and World-Making in Animation*. Berkeley, University of California Press, 2013.

Kanfer, Stefan. *Serious Business: The Art and Commerce of Animation in America from Betty Boop to "Toy Story."* New York, Da Capo, 1997.

Klein, Norman M. *Seven Minutes: The Life and Death of the American Animated Cartoon*. New York, Verso, 1993.

Leslie, Esther. *Hollywood Flatlands: Animation, Critical Theory and the Avant-Garde*. London, Verso, 2002.

Maltin, Leonard. *Of Mice and Magic: A History of American Animated Cartoons*. Rev. ed., New York, Penguin, 1987.

McCloud, Scott. *Understanding Comics: The Invisible Art*. New York, Harper Collins, 1994.

Telotte, J. P. *Animating Space: From Mickey to WALL-E*. Lexington, University Press of Kentucky, 2010.

Vidler, Anthony. "The Explosion of Space: Architecture and the Filmic Imaginary." *Film Architecture: From "Metropolis" to "Blade Runner,"* edited by Dietrich Neumann, Munich, Prestel, 1999, pp. 13–25.

———. *Warped Space: Art, Architecture, and Anxiety in Modern Culture*. Cambridge, MA, MIT Press, 2000.

Wells, Paul. *Animation and America*. New Brunswick, NJ, Rutgers University Press, 2002.

Yoe, Craig, editor. *Felix the Cat: The Great Comic Book Tails*. IDW Publishing, 2011.

A Comic Book Life/Style:
World Building in *American Splendor*

MATT YOCKEY

Conventional considerations of film adaptations of comic books focus on comics as *visual* texts (what is drawn but not, importantly, what is written on the page) rather than as *written* texts. By concentrating on the visual register of both comic books and films at the expense of the written word, such analyses preclude important aspects of both comics and films as expressive vehicles for the circulation of affect, the production of feelings that cohere author and audience subjectivities by way of what is written and not simply what is drawn. Further, a closer look at the literary construction of comic book narratives potentially broadens our understanding of the transmedia synergies that at least partly inform how film adaptations of comic books are made and received. The aesthetic representation and production of affect, as determined by the subjectivities of author and audience, is central to the inherent dialectical nature of comics, of their production and consumption, and their subsequent remediation on film.

This chapter will consider how the 2003 film adaptation of Harvey Pekar's long-running autobiographical comic book *American Splendor*, also titled *American Splendor*, offers an opportunity to consider the value of what Daniel Yacavone calls the "forms of cinematic expression and immersion . . . a distinctly aesthetic form of cinematic affect" (xxiv). I will argue that what Yacavone terms a "*cineaesthetic* world-feeling" (xxiv) is evident in the film adaptation of *American Splendor* in its construction of an auteur via the written world in dialectical tension with the drawn world. Consequently, the value of the cinematic adaptation of *American Splendor* partly resides in how it confirms and complicates Yacavone's belief in a unique affective register in film. Because the governing voice of the *American Splendor* comic books is that of its writer and primary subject, Harvey Pekar, whose life stories are depicted by a variety of different artists, the film adaptation allows us to consider the filmmakers as another instance of artists offering their interpretative representation of Pekar's voice and subjectivity in collaboration with the author. Consequently, the film expands and deepens the relationship between Pekar and his audience by introducing a transmedia component to Pekar's constructed world. The film offers not simply another take on this world but elaborates on Pekar's key aesthetic concern with literary and cinematic realism by exploiting the temporal and aural qualities of cinema as a means of reflecting, actualizing, and extending the affective experience of the comic books themselves.

A World Narrated

The film *American Splendor*, directed by Robert Pulcini and Shari Springer Berman, is based on the modestly produced comic book series of the same name written by Pekar from 1976 to 2008 (Pekar died in 2010). Pekar's self-published comic book was unusual in both form and content: it was magazine size, black and white, and focused almost entirely on episodes from his mundane life as a file clerk at a Veterans' Administration hospital in Cleveland. Pekar described *American Splendor* thusly: "It's an autobiography written as it's happening. The theme is about staying alive. Getting a job, finding a mate, having a place to live, finding a creative outlet. Life is a war of attrition. You have to stay active on all fronts. It's one thing after another. I've tried to control a chaotic universe. And it's a losing battle. But I can't let go. I've tried, but I can't" ("Harvey Pekar Obituary"). Pekar's description highlights several elements that are essential to understanding *American Splendor* as a writer-driven world-building exercise: autobiography, the inherent drama of everyday life, and the iterative struggle to assert and maintain ontological truth in the face of a contingent universe. Consider, for example, his 1984 story "Hypothetical Quandary" (illustrated by Pekar's first and most famous collaborator, his friend Robert Crumb), in which we see Pekar over the course of sixteen panels on three pages ruminate about a missed opportunity with a "big publisher."

As Pekar gets into his car and drives to a bakery, the first six panels are dominated by thought balloons as he wonders how his life might change if he were to land such a deal and be able to live off of his writing. He initially concludes that his writing would likely suffer if he lost his "working man's outlook on life." He then considers a counterpoint: "As long as I'm alive I'll be finding interesting things to write about, meeting interesting people. . . . If I lived a different life I could still write about it." As he walks down the

Fresh bread: the cure for the disappointments and daily frustrations of life in Harvey Pekar's *American Splendor*.

street, his recently purchased loaf of bread in hand, Pekar's thoughts continue: "Knowin' myself, I could always find something to get shook up over and write about. Let's face it, I'm not gonna become a mellow man overnight no matter what happens! Oh well, it's all hypothetical. . . . That woman didn't call me back." He then smells the bread in his hand, and the last panel shows a satisfied smile on Pekar's face and a final thought balloon: "Ah, fresh bread!" That his consternation over not getting a lucrative publishing contract, and his subsequent internal debate about the possible outcomes of such an event, is finally seemingly satisfied by his happiness with a common loaf of fresh bread confirms that, on one level, *American Splendor* is very much concerned with how we all navigate the disappointments and daily frustrations of life.

What is essential to this story is the possibility inherent in the phone call Pekar did *not* receive and the inner turmoil it provokes in him, even as he goes about his daily business. Pekar denies his readers a scene depicting his initial contact with "that woman from that big publisher," which would serve as a conventional setup for his later disappointment. The inner life of the protagonist, initially depicted as in tension with his external reality (his inner tumult in no way outwardly evident in his journey to the bakery) is finally regarded as an essential component of that daily life; his quietly triumphant affirmation of the fresh bread confirms the (temporary) resolution of his latest life crisis. While Pekar is presumably going to the bakery simply because he needs a loaf of bread, the trip actually affords him the opportunity to mull over this latest (non)event in his life. Consequently, by representing this episode in his life in a comic book story, Pekar is confirming that the seemingly mundane activities of his life, through which he expresses his concerns about who he is in the present and who he might or might not become in the future, are of comparable value to his readers.

The remediation of Pekar's uncertainty about his own identity as a writer (it is significant that his concerns revolve around the familiar dilemma of retaining his authenticity versus achieving financial security) is valuable to Pekar himself not only as the explicit author of the story but, implicitly, as another reader of it after the fact (in their similarity to journal entries, Pekar's stories must be regarded on one level as being written for himself to read at some future date). Joseph Witek observes, "A 'Harvey Pekar' figure is not present in every piece in *American Splendor*, yet even in those stories and vignettes that are about other people, the author is present by implication as an observer or listener" (123). More to the point, all *American Splendor* stories implicitly confirm Pekar's presence as an observer alongside the reader, rather than simply as the witness-subject telling the story. The idea of Pekar as a reader himself is amplified by the fact that his stories are illustrated by others, allowing a distancing between author and text that foregrounds the subjectivity of the author in the contrast between the written words, as the direct expression of Pekar's thoughts, and the art, which is always someone else's interpretation of Pekar's lived experiences. Pekar's autobiographical approach is thus qualified by the fact that he does not illustrate his stories.

The tension produced by the intersection of written text (autobiography) and drawn text (biography) echoes the essential dialectical properties of comic book sequential art. As Thierry Groensteen observes of comic books, "Each new panel hastens the story and, simultaneously, holds it back. The frame is the agent of this double maneuver of progression/retention" (45). Sequential panels that present a narrative provide a sense of forward movement that is constantly also arrested by the individual static images, producing an affective tension in the reader, who constantly acknowledges this simultaneity of movement and stasis. Pekar's thematic concern with the dialectic of stasis/change in his own life (both materially and ontologically) is reflected in the tension between the words and the pictures in his stories and this essential condition of sequential art. This dialectic is further realized by Pekar's use of different artists to depict the events in his life, so that we recognize these different iterations of Pekar within the context of his governing subjectivity. The dynamic energy produced by these various tensions fuels readers' affective responses to Pekar's work and, in fact, acts as the glue that holds together the world Pekar constructs in his stories and that is actualized in their very production and consumption. Pekar constantly wrestles with the fleeting nature of life itself and the ongoing instability of one's place in the world, and through his representation of these struggles he produces a coherent worldview that, in its consumption by readers, becomes a textually built and affectively experienced world in and of itself.

The episodic and iterative construction of *American Splendor* (its internal continuity) directly informs an understanding of the comic book series as the presentation of a constantly unfolding built world. In fact, *American Splendor* complicates the conventional understanding of comic book seriality; its continuity revolves around the persona of Pekar (who sometimes appears in his stories in a thinly disguised form) and his otherwise disconnected anecdotes. They are simply stories from a man's life, and while certain "characters" reappear (most prominently Pekar's coworkers and his third wife, Joyce Brabner), the stories typically can be read in any order the reader chooses. And while Pekar produced stand-alone volumes chronicling significant events in his life (such as *American Splendor: Our Movie Year* and, with Brabner, *Our Cancer Year*), these too do not demand to be read according to the chronology of Pekar's life. The internal continuity of these stories is the constructed persona of Pekar himself, and its constant process of reconstruction (a process reified by the different artistic interpretations of Pekar's life and by his self-reflexive thematic interest in identity). According to Witek, "While many of Pekar's stories and vignettes are funny and interesting in their own right, the repetition of characters and scenes and the accretion of a variety of incidents make reading *American Splendor* a cumulative experience. . . . In a comic book that is thoroughly rooted in the life of a single person, the relativity of individual identity becomes a major thematic subtext" (137). It is this subtext that strongly informs the experience of *American Splendor* as a world-building enterprise, one in which the representation of the ongoing construction of Pekar's subjectivity is central to the internal coherency of his life as a recognizably discrete textual world. Thus, the authorial presence of the comic book writer, as opposed to writer-artist, separates Pekar's work from other autobiographical comic books in which the notion of a single-authored world is more easily accepted (as seen with the work of writer-artists such as Crumb, Justin Green, Joe Sacco, Julie Doucet, and Marjane Satrapi). Pekar's distinct voice governs the aesthetic and thematic trajectories of *American Splendor*, and like the comics themselves, the film adaptation of his work becomes yet another collaborative vehicle by which Pekar's ongoing project of identity formation is realized.

Walking the Line

Pekar's role as either an explicit or an implicit narrator is the primary element that informs an affective response to his work that consequently coheres it as a world experienced by Pekar and perpetually reexperienced by
both Pekar (as an abstract co-reader) and his audience. Jan Baetens argues
that Philippe Marion's observation that in comics "style, storytelling and
medium are inevitably and necessarily intertwined and mutually dependent" informs "a new type of analysis of these visual elements, one which
is no longer 'stylistic' (as in other, traditional forms of comic analysis), but
'*communicative*' or rather '*narrative*'" (Baetens 146). Baetens's consideration
(by way of Marion) of narrative content and comic book form in relationship to visual representation offers a useful perspective by which to account
for the affective value of *American Splendor*, in which various artistic styles
reinforce the inherent fluidity of Pekar's persona that is itself presented primarily as both subject and narrator in the intimate format of the independent comic book. Further, the plurality of different visual representations of
Pekar paradoxically confirms his governing authorial agency; every artist is
depicting Pekar and the events in his life (or events in other people's lives, as
told to Pekar). The different visual interpretations do not compete with one
another in a hierarchy of authenticity but confirm the constancy and multiplicity (a dialectic of subjectivity in general) of Pekar's identity.

Baetens further observes that "the visual form of all comic elements is
considered a 'trace,' that is a reflection, a symptom, an index, of the subjectivity of a narrator" (145). It is just the presence of this trace as evidence
of the writer (rather than of the artist) that is so strongly formulated in
the film adaptation of *American Splendor*. The film confirms that the synthesis of style, storytelling, and *two* mediums—comic books and film—
reinforces and extends Pekar's primary thematic concern with identity. In
this way, the film adaptation should be regarded as another important iteration of *American Splendor* as an affectively realized world experience that
reflects and extends the relationship of comic book author and reader. Ap-
plying Marion's ideas of "graphiation" ("the graphic and narrative enunciation of the comics") and "graphiateur" ("the agent responsible for it"), Baetens notes, "In the work of the 'trace,' author and graphiateur communicate,
and in this process Philippe Marion defines the reader as a graphiateur who
ignores himself, or a virtual graphiateur who, thanks to an empathetic process of identification, makes his old move of reliving life through the artist's
fictive object" (147, 153). This consideration of the reader as an agent in the
construction of textual meaning is best understood in terms not of self-

denial ("ignoring himself") or of reiteration ("reliving life") but of one for whom reading *American Splendor* is understood as a new experience that demands self-recognition. The reader affectively recognizes the familiar in Pekar's stories of the everyday, as well as their newness to him or her (even upon multiple readings; after all, the ongoing travails of Pekar chronicled in *American Splendor* reflect the experience of reading about them: our perspectives necessarily change, however incrementally, all of the time). Such an understanding on the part of the reader is complicated by the autobiographical narrative and biographical visual dialectic of the *American Splendor* comics. Thus, the film offers a further self-reflexive mediation on identity and identification in its open commentary on Pekar himself as a "fictive object," or, more usefully, as a social and aesthetic construct, the real and the fictive essentially entwined in the production of meaning of Pekar as author and character. Correspondingly, viewers' recognition of Pekar in these synthesized positions (author and subject) can produce self-recognition of their own constructed subjectivities, implicitly aligning the affective experience of the viewer with that of Pekar, who appears throughout the film to comment on the film's representation of his own comic book remediation of his life.

The film's reflexive consideration of identity confirms Yacavone's contention that "for the viewer the diegetic and nondiegetic belong equally to one and the same *perceptual or phenomenological reality* of a film" (22). According to Yacavone, this homogenizing affective experience of the diegetic and nondiegetic compels a viewer to acknowledge "the difference between the (fictional) world *in* a film and the strongly suggested existence of another, 'larger' world of a cinematic work," what he terms a film's "total aesthetic reality" (23). As an adaptation of an autobiographical comic book series, Pulcini and Berman's film is doubly invested in the suggestion of multiple worlds defined by the heterogeneous representation of a single author's worldview (which necessarily entails remediation of that author's self-perception). The film thus departs from what David Bordwell characterizes as classical film narration's mission to create "an apparently independent profilmic event" that "depends upon the notion of the invisible observer" (24). In its reflexive conflation of author-subject-audience subjectivities, the film adaptation of *American Splendor* marks Pekar, the directors, and viewers alike as visible and invisible observers *and* authors of the text's meaning. This process requires that, like Pekar himself does in writing his stories and handing them over to others to illustrate, the film's remediation of reality allows viewers to simultaneously recognize themselves within the text (in large part by way of its self-reflexive considerations of identity) and outside of it. In understanding how Pulcini and Berman's film confirms Yacavone's notion of a film's total aesthetic reality, it is important to consider that its self-reflexivity foregrounds his contention that films should be regarded as "both representational—in the most general sense of affording us with symbolically constructed models of experience and 'ways of knowing'—and presentational, as inseparably connected to aesthetic perception and appreciation" (Yacavone xviii).

The film's presentational mode is the primary strategy by which an affective experience is constituted for viewers, Yacavone's cineaesthetic world-feeling, which links them to Pekar as author, subject, and viewer. The film opens with one of its key aesthetic strategies, the presentation of a comic book device (in this case a comic book–style caption that reads, "1950: Our story begins . . .") within the cinematic frame (a shot of five children trick-or-treating). The visual invocation of a comic book trace is a constant throughout the film and includes captions, word and thought balloons, and comic book–styled panels. This reflexive deployment of comic book traces in the film extends the synthesis of style, storytelling, and medium as a narrational strategy into the domain of film, so that the viewer is immediately recruited as a self-aware participant in the affective experience of meaning making in and of the text.

Pulcini and Berman's immediate citation of a comic book trace in the form of this first caption serves the thematic purpose of the scene. The woman who answers the door acknowledges each masked child's Halloween identity ("We got Superman here, and Batman, and his sidekick, Robin, the Green Lantern"), until she gets to the final boy, who is not wearing a costume. When she asks bemusedly, "Who are you supposed to be?" the boy responds incredulously, "I'm Harvey Pekar." As the other boys mockingly murmur "Pecker" to one another, the woman challenges the young Harvey: "'Harvey Pekar'? That doesn't sound like a superhero to me." A flustered Harvey responds, "I ain't no superhero, lady. I'm just a kid from the neighborhood, alright?" He resignedly mutters, "Ah, forget this," and stomps away. The camera tracks him as he angrily plods down the street, and as he mutters to himself, "Why does everybody have to be so stupid?" a jazz score begins playing on the soundtrack, linking Pekar's subjectivity (both how he sees himself and how others see him) to a musical motif (jazz) that reflects one of Pekar's principal adult interests (he wrote jazz record reviews for many years). Thus Pekar's self-image and how the audience sees him are conflated, the synthesized subjectivities realized through the combination of direct address via a cinematically remediated comic book device (the opening caption that indicates the presence of both the filmmakers and Pekar as co-narrators), the narrative content (the scene's deconstruction of childhood nostalgia and its resultant affirmation of the constancy of Pekar's disgruntled persona), and the music (the soundtrack relies heavily on jazz throughout the film to convey Pekar's affective experiences and to produce a sympathetic affective response in viewers).

Pulcini and Berman then cut to a series of shots of actor Paul Giamatti as an adult Harvey stalking the same Cleveland streets of his youth, the match-on-action cut indicating that while Harvey is now an adult, how he and others see him is fundamentally unchanged. He rejects masks and embraces authenticity, an emotional "realness" that draws viewers closer to him, even as it tends to repel those around him. Thus, as the viewer continues to see people in Harvey's life react to him, the viewer potentially enjoys three points of identification: with Harvey the beleaguered protagonist, with these people in his life, and with Pekar the narrator, symbolically watching the film with us.

As the camera follows Giamatti walking, we see the opening credits. The directors then pull the camera out to reveal that the shot of Giamatti is in a filmic approximation of a comic book panel, the shot now embedded in a cinematic visualization of a comic book page. This panel, as with all the others that follow, is first seen very briefly as a still, monochromatic image in a cinematic approximation of a comic book panel that then is seemingly activated into live action by the panning (the presence of the directors as enunciators of the filmic text) and the viewer's gaze. The camera pans across and down this page, sequentially focusing on a series of panels that introduce the film to the viewer ("From off the streets of Cleveland comes . . . *American Splendor*"). The panel that contains the film's title presents it in the same style as the comic book logo, superimposing it over a long shot of a rather bleak urban landscape, with the tiny figure of the real Harvey Pekar walking from left to right. The shots of Giamatti and then the actual Pekar walking on the streets of Cleveland are both continuous and discontinuous. The real Pekar is clearly on a different street than Giamatti, and he walks much slower than Giamatti does in the previous series of shots. The camera then pans down to a panel that seems to be taken directly from an *American Splendor* comic book, a Crumb illustration of Pekar facing the viewer, saying (via word balloon), "My name is Harvey Pekar," repeating the declaration of identity that we have just seen the young Harvey make on the woman's porch, indicating that the signifier "Harvey Pekar" is both constant and fluid, as evidenced by the four iterations that we have encountered so far in the film (the actor playing Harvey as a child, Giamatti as Harvey, the real Harvey, and this comic book illustration). The camera pans right to a second Crumb panel of Pekar, who "says," "I'm a character in a celebrated

In *American Splendor* (2003), Pekar (Paul Giamatti) figuratively and literally walks a line between the real and the fictive—between cinema and comic books.

underground comic book." The camera continues to pan down and across a series of live-action panels (one of the real Pekar walking, another of Giamatti walking, and two different panels/shots of Cleveland without any figures in them), with captions crediting the supporting cast.

This sequence of panels conveys the narrative progress we associate with comic book panels, even as it undermines the representational narrative truth we associate with both comic book panels and film frames. That is to say, in its self-reflexivity, this opening sequence calls attention to the very processes of identity construction characteristic of both comic book and film production and consumption. Ultimately, Pekar is seemingly walking nowhere (we never see a specific destination or him stopping), and the tension inherent to this image of relentless but directionless walking presented in sequential panels and live-action footage serves as a visual metaphor for the film's theme of identity construction: the self as an ongoing production always in the dialectical state of progress/retention. As in "Hypothetical Quandary," Pekar is defined by his agitated mobility within the abstract spaces of Cleveland, a thinking Everyman, who, in the film's credit sequence, figuratively and literally walks a line between the real and the fictive and between the cinema and the comic books, mapping out the boundaries of his subjectivity in the process.

The camera continues its panning, and the next panel is another comic book illustration of Pekar (in medium shot) addressing the viewer (this one in the style of longtime *American Splendor* artists Greg Budgett and Gary

Dumm): "Different artists draw me all kindsa' ways." The camera pans right, and we see the real Pekar in a medium still shot facing the camera, with a word balloon that reads, "But hey, I'm also a real guy. . . ." Alternating panels of Giamatti walking and location shots of Cleveland are followed by another comic book illustration by Crumb, of Pekar facing the camera and jabbing a thumb at the panel to the right, with a word balloon that reads, "An' now this guy here's playing me in a movie." The camera pans right, and we see another panel showing Giamatti walking. The sequence continues with alternating shots of Giamatti walking and various Cleveland location shots. In the penultimate panel, another comic book–style illustration of Pekar addresses the viewer in a word balloon: "Anyway, if you're wonderin' how a nobody guy like me ended up with so many incarnations, pay attention. . . ." In this panel the viewer is positioned as a graphiateur who will necessarily actively participate in understanding how this multivalent sign "Harvey Pekar" came to be and will, consequently, contribute to the realization of this latest, cinematic incarnation.

In the final shot of the sequence, the film transitions out of the comic book panel format, reversing the viewer's entry into this stylized technique. This stylistic bookending is important, for it suggests that our introduction to Pekar depends upon an equal recognition of comic book and filmic iterations of him as a means of understanding the real person whose identity they confirm only when apprehended together. As we see Giamatti continue walking, we hear Pekar in voice-over narration: "Okay, this guy here, he's our man, all grown up and going nowhere. Although he's a pretty scholarly cat, he never got much of a formal education. For the most part he's lived in shit neighborhoods, held shit jobs, and is now knee-deep into a disastrous second marriage. So if you're the kind of person looking for romance or escapism, or some fantasy figure to save the day, guess what . . . ?" The film then wipes from Giamatti walking to Pekar in the studio recording the voice-over and concluding with the declaration, "You got the wrong movie." The visual and aural presence of the real Pekar, coupled with the revelation of the filmmaking process (the cinematic equivalent of a trace), reinforces Pekar's voice-over assertion that the film we are about to see is no conventional narrative fantasy. Here one recognizes that the enunciative power of Pekar's voice in the comics (in captions and word and thought balloons) is now realized in the purely cinematic use of sound. Here Pekar's voice is also performing the work of the jazz score, so that whenever one hears either the real Pekar or jazz music in the film, one knows that each confirms the affective authenticity of the text: they are traces of Pekar's authorial presence in the *American Splendor* world. Pulcini describes Pekar's voice as "post-beat jazzy" (Gordon) and reveals that Pekar himself was instrumental in building the film's soundtrack: "We asked Harvey to make a list of some of his favorite songs. He references the music actually a lot in his comics. We put together this list, and we had tons of music in the editing room. . . . And every once in a while we'd call Harvey and say, 'What would you be listening [to] in a scene like this?' And he'd say, 'Go pick this up'" (Head).

Pekar's voice is an abstraction in the comics and a phenomenological "object" of the film that coheres all transmedia adaptations of Pekar and extends his own authorial intent to privilege aural expression (whether his own voice or those of others, of music, of literature, of comics) as a key affective element of everyday life. Craig Hight observes, "The Pekar style is to capture the vernacular of language, to be faithful to the rhythms of idiosyncrasies of everyday conversation" (183). These rhythms then serve as a primary structuring device of Pekar's comics, so that readers "hear" his voice and those of others in concert with the sequential panels. In "Hypothetical Quandary," for example, the rhythms of the panels are in sympathetic alignment with the cadences of Pekar's train of thought. Neither is more important than the other. Thus, Pekar writes narrative jazz, his wry insights into daily living that typically resist conventional structure (he observed once, "I try to avoid pat endings; plot means nothing to me" [Witek 5]), a comic book equivalent to the rhythmic but unconventional structures of jazz music, such as the bebop of Charlie Parker, that Pekar preferred. According to Witek, Pekar "brings a musician's ear to the rhythms of daily speech and the nuances of ethnic dialects; many of the short pieces in *American Splendor* are simply celebrations of the way people talk" (130–132). Thus, a world is built through a narrational style that confirms Pekar's subjectivity.

Conclusion

This process of world building evident in Pekar's writing is wholly extended in the film adaptation of his work, so much so that "adaptation" is not sufficient to describe the film's effect of retelling many of the stories from his comics (which is something Pekar himself did in the comic books, sometimes having different artists draw different versions of the same story), adding new ones, and inserting the actual Pekar into the film itself. Like Pekar's comic books, the film *American Splendor* is finally an affect-generating textual dialogue between audience and author about, and constitutive of, the processes of identity formation. This speaks to Daniel Yacavone's consideration of "a narrative film's singular cinematic and artistic (i.e., wholly work-specific) reality, as a perceptual, cognitive, and affective one. One way to do this is to grant the *world-of* a cinematic work, as corresponding to this latter reality, and as transcending both the literal and the fictional in all sorts of different directions, toward all manner of objects of meaning, feeling, and attention that are *neither* fictional nor denoted directly" (25–26). The trans-mediality of *American Splendor* reflects and conveys the transmediality of author and reader subjectivity. In his recitation of episodes of the every-day, Pekar not only defines a worldview but presents it in such a way that it potentially generates corresponding feelings in his audience. The world that Pekar represents in his work is constructed around Yacavone's notion of an affective reality that exceeds the limits of both the literal and the fictional in its conflation of both.

According to Yacavone, "Film worlds are marked by complex and world-constitutive dynamics of transformation and immersion; these processes are not only relationally codependent but, via the anticipations of filmmakers and tacit understandings and expectations of audience members, mutually reinforcing" (xiv). The value of *American Splendor* lies much less in its nar-rative and much more in the subjective world it creates. This is essential to understanding the transmedia relationship between a comic and a film based on it. As a film adaptation of a long-running, serial comic book recounting episodes in Pekar's life, Pulcini and Berman's work offers a model for how film adaptations of comic books at their best can expand upon the subjec-tive world-building potential of each medium. In adapting a body of work that is inherently autobiographical, Berman and Pulcini exploit the essential autobiographical experience of watching a film adaptation of a comic book for those viewers who have read or will read the source material. In such recollections or anticipations, the viewer of the comic book adaptation af-fectively actualizes what Deborah Linderman identifies as "the laws of nar-rative motion" by which "the integrity (organicity) of the text is assured by its tendentious unfolding" (143). The film adaptation of a comic book fore-grounds what Linderman regards as a film's inherent overdetermination, its "'textness' . . . [which] is constituted by a system of perpetual and perpetu-ating deferrals of meaning" (144). Through the aesthetic re-presentation of Pekar's work, the film adaptation offers for the viewer an encounter with the processes of meaning making in his or her own life, a strategy that is at the root of the affective world-building experience of the film. While in the case of the film adaptation of *American Splendor* one can see how the autobio-graphic nature of the source material and the self-reflexivity of the film itself highlight this deferral of meanings as an essential aspect of the viewing ex-perience, it is essential to all encounters with transmedia texts.

As Yacavone observes, "The so-called aesthetic attitude is, properly speaking, a heterodox and complex affair in which a great deal of 'cognitive' and 'cultural' integration takes place and in which perception, intuition, imagination, reflection, and interpretation all play a part" (xviii). Pekar, as the narrator of the film, models and directs this aesthetic attitude. Through "Harvey Pekar," Pekar presents viewers with a protagonist fully invested in actualizing this aesthetic attitude by, in large part, discovering and representing aesthetic experiences in the everyday. There is an essential binary in the title *American Splendor* that destabilizes subjectivity as related to space (the ironic juxtaposition of "American splendor" and Pekar's quotidian world, as exemplified by the shots of Cleveland in the film's credit sequence). This speaks to the work's desire to locate aesthetic experiences in the everyday. The inherent dialectic of the mundane and the aesthetic is the project of *American Splendor*, realized by the work itself. The "cognitive" and "cultural" integration that Yacavone writes of is the integration of the protagonist into his world, of the author into that fictive world, of the author and his work into the real world, and of the readers into the fictive work *and* into the real world. This process aestheticizes being. Our own lives are regarded as an aesthetic experience in our recognition of the aesthetic attitude that defines the world of the *American Splendor* metatext as defined by Pekar as author. As Berman has said of her film, "It's a traditional biopic that self-destructs after a while. Which is very true to Harvey's spirit" (Gordon). And it is that "self-destruction" that is itself the very source for the construction of Pekar's textual world, the dialectic of identity that speaks to the essential progression/retention of self that defines everyone's ongoing world building.

Works Cited

Baetens, Jan. "Revealing Traces: A New Theory of Graphic Enunciation." *The Language of Comics: Word and Image*, edited by Robin Varnum and Christina T. Gibbons, Jackson, University Press of Mississippi, 2001, pp. 145–155.

Bordwell, David. "Classical Hollywood Cinema: Narrational Principles and Procedures." *Narrative, Apparatus, Ideology: A Film Theory Reader*, edited by Philip Rosen, New York, Columbia University Press, 1986, pp. 17–34.

Gordon, Bette. "Shari Springer Berman and Robert Pulcini." *Bomb*, no. 84, Summer 2003, http://bombmagazine.org/article/2570/shari-springer-berman-and-robert -pulcini.

Groensteen, Thierry. *The System of Comics*. Translated by Bart Beaty and Nick Nguyen, Jackson, University Press of Mississippi, 2007.

"Harvey Pekar Obituary." *Telegraph*, 13 July 2010, http://www.telegraph.co.uk/news /obituaries/culture-obituaries/books-obituaries/7888494/Harvey-Pekar.html.

Head, Steve. "Interview with the Directors of *American Splendor*." *IGN*, 28 August 2003, http://www.ign.com/articles/2003/08/29/interview-with-the-directors-of -american-splendor.

Hight, Craig. "*American Splendor*: Translating Comic Autobiography into Drama-Documentary." *Film and Comic Books*, edited by Ian Gordon, Mark Jancovich, and Matthew P. McAllister, Jackson, University Press of Mississippi, 2007, pp. 180–198.

Linderman, Deborah. "Uncoded Images in the Heterogeneous Text." *Narrative, Apparatus, Ideology: A Film Theory Reader*, edited by Philip Rosen, New York, Columbia University Press, 1986, pp. 143–152.

Pekar, Harvey. *American Splendor: The Life and Times of Harvey Pekar*. New York, Ballantine Books, 2003.

Witek, Joseph. *Comic Books as History: The Narrative Art of Jack Jackson, Art Spiegelman, and Harvey Pekar*. Jackson, University Press of Mississippi, 1989.

Yacavone, Daniel. *Film Worlds: A Philosophical Aesthetics of Cinema*. New York, Columbia University Press, 2015.

The Extraordinary Career of Modesty Blaise

JAMES CHAPMAN

Introduction

It would probably be fair to say that unlike their American counterparts, British comics have at best a very patchy history of successful adaptation into film and television. Norman Pett's Jane, the famously scantily clad strip-cartoon heroine of the *Daily Mirror*, appeared in two forgettable films separated by some four decades — *The Adventures of Jane* (1949) and *Jane and the Lost City* (1988) — as well as a television serial (1982) that blended live action and drawn backgrounds. Frank Hampson's *Dan Dare: Pilot of the Future*, the British *Flash Gordon*, was dramatized by Radio Luxembourg in the early 1950s, but various film projects, including one by Lindsay Anderson in the 1950s and another by producer Paul De Savary with James Bond star Roger Moore in the mid-1970s, remained unrealized, and it was not until 2004 that Britain's premier space-adventure hero made it onto television screens in the form of a CGI animated series that bore little resemblance to the artfully crafted original strip from the *Eagle*. And the two films of *2000 AD*'s taciturn lawman of the future — *Judge Dredd* (1995) starring Sylvester Stallone and *Dredd* (2012) with Karl Urban — disappointed the comic's aficionados without winning over the general cinema-going public.

Joseph Losey's film *Modesty Blaise* (1966) was perhaps the most culturally and artistically ambitious attempt to adapt a British comic strip for the cinema: a major film by a recognized auteur director that brought together some of the leading talents of British and European filmmaking in the 1960s. At the time *Modesty Blaise* was regarded very much as a film of its moment, a perfect expression of the zeitgeist of the period that social historian Arthur Marwick has called "the High Sixties" (7).[1] As the reviewer for the *Monthly Film Bulletin* remarked: "If a social historian were faced with the task of citing the film most representative of the spirit of the age, *Modesty Blaise* would be a strong contender. The film is a paean to the mid-sixties, the age of the ephemeral, the use-it-and-throw-it-away phenomenon, the era of the colour supplement, of paper plates and plastic toys and colourful gimmickry in the visual arts" (D.W. 89). Later critical assessments of the film have been less favorable. Leslie Halliwell, the doyen of British popular film historians, considered it "comic-strip adventures made by people with no sense of humour" (696). David Thomson feels that it was an "unnecessary" film and concurs with Halliwell that it marked "a break in Losey's seriousness, without indicating any sense of humour" (453). Robert Murphy is a slightly less harsh critic, acknowledging that the film "has undeniably impressive moments," though nevertheless he still concludes that "Losey seems to have had little understanding of the genre he attempts to subvert and his smart-alecky tricks backfire more often than not" (230–231). The most damning verdict on the film *Modesty Blaise* came from the creator of the original comic strip, Peter O'Donnell, who is quoted as saying, "It makes my nose bleed just to think of it" (Paterson 5).

The Texts of Modesty Blaise

The *Modesty Blaise* film was in fact the third "text" of Modesty Blaise, following her appearances in the newspaper comic strip (1963) and a novel (1965). Modesty Blaise—adventure heroine extraordinaire, who has been widely if somewhat erroneously described as "a female James Bond"—was the invention of writer Peter O'Donnell, who was commissioned to write a new daily comic adventure strip for the Express Group of newspapers in 1962. The period since the end of the Second World War had witnessed a transformation in British newspaper strips as the traditional "funnies" were complemented by a new style of adventure strip that was strongly influenced by the fluid and dynamic style of Alex Raymond's *Rip Kirby*, an American strip syndicated in the *Daily Mail* from 1947 that came to be regarded in Britain as a "how-to-draw comics primer for a whole generation of would-be comic artists" (Roach 12). *Modesty Blaise* can be seen within a lineage of contemporary adventure strips that also includes *Buck Ryan* (*Daily Mirror*, 1937–1962), *Tug Transom* (*Daily Sketch*, 1954–1966), and John McLusky's *James Bond* strip for the *Daily Express* (1957–1977). O'Donnell wrote adventure strips, including *Garth* and *Romeo Brown*, for the *Daily Mirror*—the latter was drawn by the first *Modesty Blaise* artist, Jim Holdaway—and penned stories for women's magazines. He later explained: "So in effect I was

Modesty Blaise, adventure heroine extraordinaire, in her comic-strip stylings.

working in two different genres, one featuring macho male heroes and the other involving romance, though there was always a strong element of adventure in the stories I wrote for the women's market. For some time before the call from [Express Group strip cartoon editor] Bill Aitken, I had been intrigued by the idea of bringing these two genres together by creating a woman who, though fully feminine, would be as good in combat and action as any male, if not better" (O'Donnell x).

Modesty Blaise chronicled the adventures of a former jewel thief turned crime fighter and international troubleshooter and her loyal Cockney sidekick, Willie Garvin. The strip was rooted squarely within the conventions of the adventure thriller, with story templates ranging from Cold War defection ("The Long Lever") and Mafia infiltration of the British underworld ("Take Over") to white slavery ("The Puppet Master") and—that perennial staple of the genre—a secret society with ambitions for world domination ("The War-Lords of Phoenix").

Modesty Blaise may be seen as a prototypical example of a multimedia franchise. In 1965 O'Donnell published the first of thirteen *Modesty Blaise* books—eleven novels and two short story collections—which allowed him scope for a greater degree of psychological depth than the daily comic strips.[2] "Crude, violent, quite exciting, and not totally unreadable," was one reviewer's verdict on the first novel (Richardson 23). There is some confusion as to whether *Modesty Blaise*, the first book, was a novelization of an early version of the film screenplay written by O'Donnell (as he claimed in interviews) or whether the film started out as an adaptation of the book.

But there was no doubting the popularity of *Modesty Blaise* across different media. The comic strip was reportedly syndicated to sixteen countries (Caute 207). And the novel was also licensed for publication in the United States, France, Germany, Denmark, Norway, Sweden, Finland, and Spain. *Modesty Blaise*, as one contemporary commentator observed, was "going to become not so much a strip as an industry. . . . A film is being made, starting next week, the paperback rights have been sold, and the first hardback printing of 20,000 has been 'heavily subscribed'" ("London Letter" 12).

The contexts for the advent of *Modesty Blaise* are to be found in a particular moment of British social and cultural history. The 1960s were a period of profound and far-reaching social change, especially in terms of attitudes toward class, gender, and sexuality. Modesty Blaise—in all her incarnations but especially in the comic strip and the books—reflects the changing mores of the time. Modesty is presented as a modern, emancipated heroine: she is intelligent, independently wealthy, physically capable, and skilled in both armed and unarmed combat. An introductory scene in the first comic story, "La Machine," in which Modesty fends off an overly amorous suitor with an elbow to the mouth and a heel on the neck, prompted Raymond Durgnat's remark that "Modesty Blaise, a female James Bond, is obviously a frigid sadist" (22). In fact, she is neither frigid nor a sadist: she takes lovers (Modesty's sex life is more explicitly acknowledged in the books than in the strip) and resorts to violence as a last resort. Her refusal to be domesticated ("Let's keep it that way and not get possessive, h'mm?" she tells one boyfriend in "The Gabriel Set-Up") positions Modesty within the same discourse of liberated femininity that, in their publicity at least, characterized the women of the James Bond films. Claudine Auger, who played Domino in *Thunderball* (1965), might have been describing Modesty Blaise when she said of the Bond women: "They can live without a man doing everything for them because they are independent. They like to decide their future destinies for themselves. They are highly sexual—but only with men worth their loving. They are free, you see, completely free" (Bennett and Woollacott 231).

The gender politics of the *Modesty Blaise* comic strip are exemplary of the tensions that invariably arise in the characterization of action heroines in popular culture. On the one hand, such characters—other contemporaneous examples include Cathy Gale and Emma Peel of the British telefantasy series *The Avengers* (1961–1969), while later examples appear in *Xena: Warrior Princess* (1996–2001) and *Alias* (2001–2006)—are claimed as representing a progressive idea of femininity that challenges conventional stereotypes: such action heroines are never passive damsels in distress and are often characterized as being more intelligent than their male colleagues and

Pulp sensibilities meet 1960s British pop aesthetics in the cover art for the 1965 novel version of *Modesty Blaise*.

counterparts. On the other hand, such characters are still often presented as sexualized objects who are positioned by the male "gaze": the writers and directors of *The Avengers* were all male, and most comic strip artists have been male. Modesty Blaise herself reflects this tension: she is often pictured in her underwear or in a tight-fitting bodysuit. On occasion she even strips naked: a tactic known as "the Nailer" that distracts her (male) opponents and allows Modesty and Willie to gain the advantage. The suggestion that the *Modesty Blaise* comic strip is entirely progressive in its gender politics therefore needs to be qualified.

David Buxton identifies the multiple texts of Modesty Blaise as an exemplar of the emergence of the "pop" aesthetic of the 1960s—a trend in the arts and popular culture that also included Pop Art, the new beat groups in music, *Playboy* magazine, television series such as *The Avengers* and *The Prisoner* (1967), and films such as the Bond movies and *The Ipcress File* (1965) (Buxton 76). The term "pop" itself is usually attributed to British artist Richard Hamilton, who, in a widely quoted manifesto of 1960 originally published in the catalogue to accompany a Pop Art exhibition at the Institute of Contemporary Arts in London, described it as "popular, transient, expendable, low cost, mass produced, young (aimed at youth), witty, sexy, gimmicky, glamorous, big business" (Hamilton 28). For Buxton, "one of the strengths of pop was its ability to take form in several different media: films, television series, novels and, last but not least, comics. Some pop texts like James Bond, *The Ipcress File*, and *Modesty Blaise* existed in two or three media forms" (Buxton 76). There are a number of parallels between *Modesty Blaise* (comic and books) and *The Ipcress File* (novel and film), including their foregrounding of conspicuous consumption and their characters' familiarity with fashionable consumables—Michael Caine, who starred in the film of *The Ipcress File*, was touted for the role of Willie Garvin in the *Modesty Blaise* film— as well as plot devices such as brainwashing ("The Puppet Master") and drugging with LSD ("The Hell-Makers"). Similarities to *The Avengers* can be found in the martial arts heroine with tailor-made combat suits—Honor Blackman's leather-clad Cathy Gale and Diana Rigg's Emma Peel—as well as the parade of diabolical master criminals and mad scientists.

Production and Reception Contexts

The production of the film *Modesty Blaise* demonstrates the complex and at times contradictory economic and cultural factors at work in the British film industry in the 1960s. The film was originally to have been produced by the British Lion Film Corporation, smallest and weakest of Britain's three major film companies, behind the Rank Organization and the Associated British Picture Corporation, which throughout the 1950s had been propped up by loans from the government-funded National Film Finance Corporation. Sidney Gilliat, who with his writing and producing partner Frank Launder was responsible for polished British thrillers such as *Night Train to Munich* (1940), *Green for Danger* (1946), and *Secret State* (1952), was to direct (Walker, *Hollywood, England* 298). Joseph Janni, the producer, was closely associated with the British new wave cinema of the early 1960s and had developed an acclaimed partnership with director John Schlesinger on *A Kind of Loving* (1962), *Billy Liar* (1963), and *Darling* (1965). Janni was a member of a consortium that had bought British Lion in 1964, and he maintained his interest in *Modesty Blaise* when disagreements within the consortium scuppered British Lion's production plans. The film was picked up by Darryl F. Zanuck's Twentieth Century-Fox as part of the studio's British production program alongside other big-budget films intended for the international market, including *Those Magnificent Men in Their Flying Machines* (1965) and *The Blue Max* (1966). Its reported budget of £1 million ($3 million) was three times that of the first James Bond film, *Dr. No* (1962) (Walker, *Hollywood, England* 302). Sidney Gilliat withdrew from the project when Janni resolved to cast Monica Vitti in the title role, and in so doing opened the way for Joseph Losey to take charge of the film. Therefore, a film that originally was to have been wholly British financed and made by the "old guard" of the British film industry was transformed into an example of the Hollywood-financed "runaway" productions that were becoming increasingly common and was made by an American exile director associated with the "new" cinema of the 1960s.

On the face of it, Losey would seem an unusual choice, to say the least, to direct a comic strip adventure film. His background was in the New York experimental theater scene of the 1930s, and his left-wing politics had caused him to be blacklisted by the House Un-American Activities Committee in the early 1950s. Losey spent the rest of his career as an exile filmmaker in Europe. He directed several films in Britain under various pseudonyms before achieving modest critical success in his own right with *Time without Pity* (1957), *The Gypsy and the Gentleman* (1958), *Blind Date* (1959), *The Criminal* (1960), and *The Damned* (1963). However, it was *The Servant* (1963), a brilliantly observed, cynical dissection of the British class system, that established Losey as one of the foremost figures in British cinema's cultural renaissance in the 1960s and began a collaboration with playwright Harold Pinter that also led to the equally critically acclaimed *Accident* (1967) and *The Go-Between* (1971). Losey was the epitome of a "serious" filmmaker who regarded film as a medium for telling complex, ambiguous stories and who cared little for the commercial demands of the box office. Immediately before embarking upon *Modesty Blaise* he had made *King and Country* (1964), a low-key, profoundly pessimistic film exposing the injustice of military executions during the First World War. It is difficult to imagine two films more different in content, tone, and style than *King and Country* and *Modesty Blaise*.

So what drew a director like Losey to a project like *Modesty Blaise*? He does not seem to have had much interest in the source text: indeed, there is no clear evidence that he had even read the comic strip. The film's publicity material suggested simply that Losey saw it as something different following a succession of more serious projects: "Joseph Losey, who has established a peerless reputation for off-beat subjects of serious intent such as *The Servant* and *King and Country*, diverts his talent for the unusual into a new vein with his direction of *Modesty Blaise*" (O'Brien 1). Another possibility is that Losey saw it as an opportunity to make a genre film with a difference. In an interview shortly before production commenced, he hinted strongly that he would not be approaching the subject matter in a conventional way: "Modesty Blaise is a fairytale and as such needs no explanation. It will be primitive, with moments of high camp, touches of pop art and slick humour" (Walker, "This Is How" 7). And another explanation still is simply that Losey wanted to work with Monica Vitti, who was something of an art house darling following her films with Michelangelo Antonioni: *L'Avventura* (1960), *La notte* (1961), *L'eclisse* (1962), and *Il deserto rosso* (*Red Desert*, 1964). Losey had previously worked with Jeanne Moreau on *Eve* (1962) and would later work with Julie Christie on *The Go-Between*: he seems to have been particularly drawn to directing a type of actress whose screen image combined beauty and intelligence. As he explained at the time: "I cannot work successfully with any player, male or female, unless I fall in love with them a little. Not sexually, you understand, but more than just affectionately. That's how it is with Monica Vitti" (Walker, "This Is How" 7).

Losey assembled a first-rate cast and crew for *Modesty Blaise*. Dirk Bogarde, whom he had directed in *The Servant* and *King and Country*, played the villain, Gabriel. At the time Bogarde was attempting to shake off his matinée-idol image with more challenging roles: his casting is further evidence of the film's serious intentions. Terence Stamp, one of the new generation of working-class British actors alongside Tom Courtenay, Albert Finney, and Richard Harris, and who had impressed as the young seaman in *Billy Budd* (1962), was preferred to Michael Caine for the role of Willie

Monica Vitti's blonde hair distinguishes her cinematic Modesty Blaise from the brunette versions of comic strip and novel.

Garvin, while authoritative character actor Harry Andrews was perfect as British secret service chief Sir Gerald Tarrant. Key members of the creative team included production designer Richard MacDonald, who had also worked with Losey on *The Servant* and *King and Country*, cinematographer Jack Hildyard, who had won an Academy Award for *The Bridge on the River Kwai* (1957), and jazz musician John Dankworth as composer. Dankworth provides another link to the "pop" movement, as he had composed the original theme music for the black-and-white episodes of *The Avengers*.

But the production of *Modesty Blaise* was beset with problems. Losey brought in Evan Jones, with whom he had worked on *The Damned*, *Eve*, and *King and Country*, to write the screenplay. Jones evidently thought little of the source material, which he described as "boring" (Caute 208). Indeed, Jones's first draft of the screenplay differed so significantly from the comic strip that Express Newspapers complained it broke the contractual agreement to preserve the "essential" characteristics of Modesty Blaise: specific complaints included making her fair rather than dark-haired and giving her "stuck-on tattoos" (Caute 208). Jones made some modifications to appease the lawyers, mostly in relation to Modesty's clothes and hair (Vitti at one point dons a black wig). The screenplay also ran afoul of censors on both sides of the Atlantic. The US Production Code Administration was concerned about the prominence of sex: it objected to scenes where Willie Garvin telephones Modesty while he is in bed with another woman and where Modesty poses as a prostitute in an Amsterdam window-brothel. The British Board of Film Censors was more worried about the amount of violence: in particular, it objected to a scene where Sir Gerald Tarrant seems indifferent to the shooting down of a civilian airliner (Caute 209). In the event, Losey seems to have departed from Jones's script, rewriting it extensively during shooting. Jones later complained that "the script was completely different in the finished film, and I disliked almost everything Joe did with it" (De Rahm 171). The shooting of the film was marred by poor relations on set that saw a falling-out between Losey and Jack Hildyard. And the film was not helped by Monica Vitti's lack of English and her refusal to dye her blonde hair.

Yet despite all the travails of its production, the critical reception of *Modesty Blaise* at the time was largely positive. Most reviewers found it fun and evidently understood it as a genre parody. The *Times* felt that it hit "the right tone: enjoying its own preposterousness, it still manages to work inside the conventions of the secret agent genre and keeps us on the edge of our seats even though we giggle." John Coleman (*New Statesman*) felt that it "resoundingly takes the mickey out of the sex-and-sadism of the original while delightedly embroidering round the original's lavish eccentricities and kinks." And Isabel Quigley (*Spectator*) contended that "*Modesty Blaise* is just what the Bond films should have been and weren't: witty, and visually a delight. . . . Funny and exquisitely accomplished, it is screen nonsense as it ought to be." Some critics felt that it was enjoyable but essentially shallow. For Kenneth Tynan (*Observer*), it was "very diverting to watch—a triumph of inventive obsolescence, with instant rust built into its modish glitter." Nina Hibbin (*Morning Star*), a fierce critic of the Bond films for their racist content, saw it as "Sunday color supplement chic gone delirious. . . . It is the James Bond myth turned upside down and inside out and blown up until it bursts. . . . [But] once the myth is exploded (and it doesn't take long), there's not much else to hold on to." Alexander Walker (*Evening Standard*) thought it "a film that sums up the mood of the times—and the tastes of its director—in every stetch of celluloid." Dennis Searle (*Women's Mirror*) called it "a guide-book to contemporary mores." Others, however, found greater depth in the film, such as Dilys Powell (*Sunday Times*), who described it as "Losey's brilliant satire on our modern dream-world." In contrast, David Robinson (*Financial Times*) felt that it was marked by "uncertainty" about what sort of film it wanted to be: "Is it an attempt to interpret in film terms the pop art idioms of the comic strip in which, in origin, Modesty Blaise belongs—to aim at the sort of effect that Godard achieved in *Alphaville* and *Pierrot le fou*? Or is its intention to send up the secret agent film which is already itself a send-up? Is it surrealist comedy, a satirical farce or a deconstructor's piece? Or all three?"[3]

Reading *Modesty Blaise*

Seen today, *Modesty Blaise* is something of a curate's egg of a film. On the one hand, it is visually a tour de force: a perfect cinematic realization of the Pop Art aesthetic with its bold colors, outré costumes, and set designs that combine sleek modernism (Modesty's high-tech apartment with its science-fictional trappings) and olde-worlde accoutrements (Gabriel's villain's lair is an abandoned monastery on a Mediterranean island). And there are brilliant visual jokes that recall some of the best moments of *The Avengers*, such as the scene where a bowler-hatted gentleman presses a doorbell with his umbrella and is immediately blown up as the house explodes. On the other hand, the narrative makes little sense: there are numerous non sequiturs— for example, Modesty's costumes and hair color change without explanation in a scene in the apartment of her boyfriend, Paul Hagan (Michael Craig)— and various plot points are left unexplained. And the tone of the film shifts uneasily between moments of sadism, such as Gabriel's sidekick-assassin Mrs. Fothergill (Rossella Falk) torturing and killing a victim by strangling him between her thighs, and moments of high camp: at the end of the film Gabriel is staked out under the blazing desert sun croaking in a parched voice for "champagne . . . champagne." If the casting of Monica Vitti and Dirk Bogarde suggests the film's art house ambitions, then the slapstick climax as the men of Sheik Abu Tahir (Clive Revill) arrive to rescue Modesty and Willie is more reminiscent of the crazy comedy of films like *Hellzapoppin'* (1942) or the James Bond spoof *Casino Royale* (1967).

Of course, it might be that the uneven tone and quality of *Modesty Blaise* suggest that Losey was uncomfortable with the material or that it was simply an outcome of the troubled production process. At the same time, however, there is another explanation: that Losey saw *Modesty Blaise* not as a conventional genre film but rather as a deconstruction of the genre. There are several indications that this might have been so. There are references to the comic strip *Modesty Blaise* in the film: Willie's apartment has a giant cut-out of Modesty as she appears in the strip, and at one point Gabriel mentions that another character "reads the comic strip." The idea that the Modesty of the film is the "real" Modesty who at points assumes the identity of the comic strip Modesty would explain why her appearance changes: Vitti appears wearing Modesty's trademark all-in-one combat suit and black hair and so "becomes" Modesty Blaise. The film's narration employs a self-reflexive device as Sir Gerald Tarrant and the Minister (Alexander Knox) comment on scenes they do not witness within the film's diegesis: "Have you warned Miss Blaise about pressing doorbells in Amsterdam?" And the film demonstrates a postmodern sensibility in its playfulness with genre conventions: there are references to the Bing Crosby–Bob Hope *Road* movies of the 1940s as well as to contemporaneous European cinema, such as the moment when Modesty and Willie break into song in a manner reminiscent of Jacques Demy's *The Umbrellas of Cherbourg* (1965).

If the playfulness of *Modesty Blaise* sits uneasily with Losey's reputation as a serious filmmaker, however, there have been attempts to reclaim the film for auteur theory. Andrew Sarris, for example, contends that "*Modesty Blaise* is a more serious enterprise than it seems precisely because of the strenuousness of its brevity. Losey is joking about matters concerning the relations of men and women, relations that affect him deeply" (97). It is perhaps something of a stretch to claim that Losey saw *Modesty Blaise* as a comment on the status of the exile, because Modesty's backstory as a wartime refugee is entirely missing from the film (Gardner 122). But elsewhere *Modesty Blaise* does reveal certain parallels with other Losey films. Bogarde's Gabriel, with his mother complex and uneasy relationship with his employee/mistress Mrs. Fothergill, seems like a parody of his Hugo Barrett in *The Servant*, while the "impossible romance" between Modesty and Willie anticipates Losey's exploration of a similar theme in *The Romantic Englishwoman* (1975) (Richards 63).

And the theme of class is never far below the surface in any of Losey's films. *Modesty Blaise* places greater emphasis on class than the comic strip: in particular, the establishment, as represented by Tarrant and the Minister, is characterized as manipulative as well as callous in the extreme ("No use crying over spilt milk" is the dismissive response to the death of the agent blown up in Amsterdam). Tarrant lures Modesty into working for the secret service by telling her that Willie has been sentenced to death following a revolution in South America: in the novel this is true and puts Modesty under a sense of obligation, but in the film it is quickly established as a lie. And Tarrant manipulates Modesty and Willie in so far as the shipment of diamonds they are hired to transport is really a decoy to flush the arch-criminal Gabriel into the open: their lives are placed in jeopardy as part of an elaborate deception ploy.

If the class politics of the *Modesty Blaise* film differ from the comic, so too do the film's gender politics. The Modesty of the film is a more coquett-ish — one might even say "girlish" — character than her comic strip counter-part. As played by Monica Vitti, she becomes more of an elegant clothes-horse than the comic strip Modesty: her constant costume changes at times threaten to turn the film into an extended fashion parade. At the same time, the violence of the comic strip becomes much more stylized: unlike, say, Honor Blackman in *The Avengers*, it is difficult to believe in Vitti as a physi-cal action heroine. On one level this might be an example of how inappro-priate casting can affect the content and tone of the film. On another level it might reflect the equivocation around gender that some commentators have detected in Losey's films. While Losey himself is generally regarded as a sympathetic director of women, the women in his films are often not sympathetically portrayed. *Modesty Blaise* was Losey's first film to place a woman at the center of the narrative (*Eve* is only a partial exception to this) and might be seen as an indicator of his future, more women-centered films of the 1970s. But the Modesty of the comic strip — combining as she did strength and femininity — is not the Modesty of the film.

Conclusion

For aficionados of O'Donnell's comic strip and novels, the film *Modesty Blaise* is generally seen as a missed opportunity: Monica Vitti is fundamen-tally miscast as Modesty, and the director seems to have little understand-ing for the source texts. It is tempting to speculate how the film might have turned out had it been left to other hands. It has always seemed to me that *The Avengers* in its John Steed–Emma Peel middle period caught the mood of the *Modesty Blaise* comic strip better than the film: what price a *Modesty Blaise* film scripted by Brian Clemens, directed by James Hill or Sidney Hay-ers, and starring Diana Rigg as Modesty? Film and comic historians, how-ever, must deal with texts as they are rather than as they would wish them to be. *Modesty Blaise* may be yet another example of the failure of British comics to adapt successfully into film; but it remains (to date) the only cine-matic incarnation of Britain's foremost comic strip adventure heroine.

Notes

1. While accepting that periodization is an arbitrary but necessary tool, Marwick posits the idea of a "long sixties" from ca. 1958 to ca. 1974, a period he further divides

into three phases: "The First Stirrings of a Cultural Revolution" (1958–1963), "The High Sixties" (1964–1969), and "'Everything Goes' and 'Catching Up'" (1969–1974).

2. The *Modesty Blaise* books, all written by Peter O'Donnell, are *Modesty Blaise* (1965), *Sabre Tooth* (1966), *I, Lucifer* (1967), *A Taste of Death* (1969), *The Impossible Virgin* (1971), *Pieces of Modesty* (1972), *The Silver Mistress* (1973), *Last Day in Limbo* (1976), *Dragon's Claw* (1978), *The Xanadu Talisman* (1981), *The Night of Morningstar* (1982), *Dead Man's Handle* (1985), and *Cobra Trap* (1996). *Pieces of Modesty* and *Cobra Trap* are short story collections. All the books were published in Britain by Souvenir Press, except *Pieces of Modesty*, which was published as a paperback original by Pan.

3. Reviews are sourced from the BFI Reuben Library's digitized clippings collection for *Modesty Blaise*, which for this period does not include page numbers: *Times*, 5 May 1966; *New Statesman*, 6 May 1966; *Spectator*, 13 May 1966; *Observer*, 8 May 1966; *Morning Star*, 7 May 1966; *Evening Standard*, 5 May 1966; *Women's Mirror*, 4 June 1966; *Sunday Times*, 8 May 1966; *Financial Times*, 6 May 1966.

Works Cited

Bennett, Tony, and Janet Woollacott. *Bond and Beyond: The Political Career of a Popular Hero*. London, Macmillan, 1987.

Buxton, David. *From "The Avengers" to "Miami Vice": Form and Ideology in Television Series*. Manchester, UK, Manchester University Press, 1990.

Caute, David. *Joseph Losey: A Revenge on Life*. London, Faber and Faber, 1994.

D. W. "Modesty Blaise." *Monthly Film Bulletin*, no. 389, June 1966, pp. 89–90.

De Rahm, Edith. *Joseph Losey*. London, Andre Deutsch, 1991.

Durgnat, Raymond. "An Apology for Comic Strips." *New Society*, 21 November 1963, p. 22.

Gardner, Colin. *Joseph Losey*. Manchester, UK, Manchester University Press, 2004.

Halliwell, Leslie. *Halliwell's Film Guide*. 6th ed., London, Grafton Books, 1987.

Hamilton, Richard. *Collected Words*. London, Thames and Hudson, 1982.

"London Letter: Forthcoming Attractions." *Guardian*, 9 July 1965, p. 12.

Marwick, Arthur. *The Sixties: Cultural Revolution in Britain, France, Italy and the United States, c. 1958–c. 1974*. Oxford, UK, Oxford University Press, 1998.

Murphy, Robert. *Sixties British Cinema*. London, British Film Institute, 1992.

O'Brien, Catherine. "Brief Facts about 'Modesty Blaise.'" Publicity release held by the BFI Reuben Library in the digitized clippings file for the film, n.d.

O'Donnell, Peter. "Girl Walking." *Modesty Blaise: The Gabriel Set-Up*, by Peter O'Donnell and Jim Holdaway. London, Titan Books, 2004.

Paterson, Mike. "Blaise of Glory: The Modesty Blaise Phenomenon." *Modesty Blaise: Top Traitor*, by Peter O'Donnell and Jim Holdaway. London, Titan Books, 2004.

Richards, Peter. "Real Ice, Man: Joseph Losey's *Modesty Blaise*." *Film Comment*, vol. 31, no. 4, 1995, pp. 60–64.

Richardson, Maurice. "Crime Ration." *Guardian*, 11 July 1965, p. 23.

Roach, David. "The History of British Comic Art." *True Brit: A Celebration of the Great Comic Book Artists of the UK*, edited by George Khoury, Raleigh, NC, Two Morrows Publishing, 2004, pp. 5–29.

Sarris, Andrew. *The American Cinema: Directors and Directions 1929-1968*. New York, Da Capo Press, 1996.

Thomson, David. *A Biographical Dictionary of Film*. London, Andre Deutsch, 1994.

Walker, Alexander. *Hollywood, England: The British Film Industry in the Sixties*. London, Michael Joseph, 1974.

———. "'This Is How I Will Transform Monica Vitti into Modesty Blaise.'" *Evening Standard*, 17 June 1965, p. 7.

Authenticity and Judge Dredd on Film

J. MARK PERCIVAL

What is an "authentic" film adaptation of a comic book? If this question is difficult to answer, consider the questions that must follow: How do we decide what is or is not "authentic" in comics adaptations? Why do the answers to these questions matter, and to whom? If one is to attempt to address these issues in any meaningful way, there must be a clear account of the ways in which the notion of authenticity is constructed and deployed around the production, mediation, and consumption of comic book film adaptations. Authenticity is not an essentialist value that can be associated unambiguously with any cultural artifact or activity. Rather, it is a social construction, a term whose meaning varies according to any given consensus among interest groups in a particular place, in a specific historical context. In this chapter I will explore the ways in which authenticity is constructed and manipulated in the production of two film adaptations of the British cult comic book character Judge Dredd, who first appeared in 1977 in the second issue of the UK weekly science fiction action-adventure anthology comic *2000 AD*.

Dredd, a future-dystopian law enforcer, has been adapted twice for the screen, in 1995 and in 2012. The first film, *Judge Dredd*, starring Sylvester Stallone, was not well received by critics or fans and was a relative commercial flop, despite eventually grossing a worldwide $113 million on an estimated $70 million budget (*IMDb, Judge Dredd*). The second, *Dredd*, starring Karl Urban, received mixed reviews but again fared badly at the box office, grossing around $41 million worldwide on an estimated budget of $35 million (*IMDb, Dredd*). Yet in 1987, Paul Verhoeven's *Judge Dredd*–influenced *RoboCop* was largely praised by critics and genre fans, grossing over $53 million in the United States alone on an estimated budget of $13 million (*IMDb, RoboCop*), so a hyper-violent, law-enforcing protagonist is not in itself a barrier to commercial success.

Cover of *Judge Dredd: Year One*, issue #1 (March 2013) (IDW), with art by Carlos Ezquerra.

Judge Dredd co-creator John Wagner and fan discourse more generally tend to position Sylvester Stallone's Judge Dredd as largely inauthentic and Karl Urban's Dredd as a significantly more credible version of the character. Yet the "authenticity" of *Dredd* was not enough for it to avoid an even less commercial first-run box office than its 1995 predecessor. In this chapter I want to look at some of the ways in which various constructions of authenticity emerge around both films and to consider the value of "authenticity" for particular films in an era of comic book film adaptations where the perceived *absence* of authenticity can be used to explain the market failure of a film.

Authenticity

In any discussion of music, film, comic books, or indeed any cultural artifact or event, one of the most significant qualities attributed to that object or happening is its authenticity. In popular music the authenticity of an artist might be understood as the performer's apparent honesty and "true" self-expression, either in terms of the music they make or the ways in which they live their lives. Consider long-running disputes in country music, hip-hop, or rock around artists who are argued to be "real" or "fake" or may have been judged by fans as having "sold out" to commercial imperatives. An early example of this might be the booing of Bob Dylan at the 1965 Newport Folk Festival and the Manchester, England, audience member's heckle of "Judas" at a May 1966 show, both of which expressed fan dismay at Dylan's perceived "selling out" of his authentic acoustic-folk and protest-singer roots. In film, the evolution of auteur theory valorizes selected directors as creative geniuses whose work is a true, "authentic" expression of their ideological, philosophical, or aesthetic perspective on life, culture, and the human condition, from Hitchcock to Tarantino and Jane Campion. In comics, expressions of the "authentic" are potentially even more varied than those in other cultural industries. From new creative teams arriving on long-running titles to whole fictional universe reboots, characters are periodically (re)presented as returning to a more "true" original state or to the "spirit" agreed to have been present in the earliest years of their existence. One example of this is writer-artist John Byrne's 1980s run on *Fantastic Four*, of which Marvel writer-editor Tom DeFalco noted, "Byrne went back to basics with the Fantastic Four and evoked the title's early days of Stan Lee and Jack Kirby" (200)—in other words, the period during which the title was considered by fans to have been at its most innovative.

There are of course many different, often contradictory ways of establishing consensus, however temporary, as to what is or is not "authentic," which is of course one of the reasons that investigating the construction and deployment of authenticity as a cultural value is so attractive to scholars. The question of how notions of authenticity are negotiated around comic book adaptations is arguably even more complex, given multiple sets of mainly arbitrary, socially agreed rules around truth, accuracy, and aesthetics in comics and film and in the adaptation process itself. Comics fans in particular engage in discussion and argument around the extent to which a film adaptation is successful in capturing the look, feel, and "spirit" of the characters about whose representation in the wider world they are passionate.

It is important to say a little more about what I mean when I discuss authenticity as both a social construct and a property that emerges from, among other things, interaction of the notions of social and cultural capital as developed by Pierre Bourdieu in *Distinction* (1984) and elsewhere. Authenticity is a socially constructed value that emerges from networks of social, cultural, and political interaction and can be attributed to any number of cultural products, including (but not limited to) popular music, film, television, literature, and video games. In the field of media and cultural studies authenticity is never considered to be an absolute value ("that thing is real; that one over there is fake"), intrinsic to the cultural object; rather, it is a way of establishing value and hierarchy in cultural discourse and is closely related to Bourdieu's ideas on taste, distinction, and various forms of non-economic capital. It is a value that is generated and attributed in different ways, at different times, by differently constituted social groups with different objectives (social, political, economic, and so on). In some ways it is always a risk to invoke Bourdieu, given the ubiquity of his ideas, but his discussion of two variations on the concept of capital are very helpful in many areas of cultural analysis: social capital (essentially, *who* you know in a given field and their status) and cultural capital (*what* or *how much* you know about a particular field). Both ideas are very helpful when considering the discourse around any literary adaptation and are particularly so when addressing films based on comic book characters and story arcs. In any given context there is always a balance and an interaction between social capital and cultural capital and their relationship to economic capital.

One of the key authenticity discourses around any film adaptation of an original literary source is the degree to which the adaption is "true" to the original text. How this truth is defined is usually contested, often in colorful disputes between individuals, groups, or institutions that, to a greater or lesser degree, wish to demonstrate their understanding of the intentionality or meaning of the source, the adaptation, or both. Given the diversity of areas around comic book adaptation in which authenticity can be disputed, agreed, and attributed, it is much more appropriate to address here "authenticities" in the plural. These spaces of dispute or consensus are where social and cultural capital are deployed in the pursuit of establishing authenticity of a particular argument or hierarchical position, but are also for attributing authenticities to adaptations and indeed to specific characteristics of those adaptations.

A helpful analysis of the ways in which the notion of authenticity is invoked and deployed is in Richard Peterson's work on the construction of authenticity in country music. Drawing on formal *Oxford English Dictionary* definitions of the term, Peterson discusses the ways in which these notions of authenticity are flexible, fluid, and often contradictory. Of the various strands of authenticity that Peterson examines, one is particularly useful here: a cultural product or phenomenon can be positioned as authentic when it is *authenticated* by an individual or institution that has the authority (cultural, social, political) to attribute authenticity to that product or phenomenon. In Bourdieu's terms, these authenticators would be figures with high levels of perceived cultural capital but also significant social capital. They are, in often diverse ways, understood as sources of informed, expert knowledge in their respective fields. Authenticators are also often part of social networks that include other creators or critics in related fields of cultural production. This combination of cultural and social capital allows for powerful (though rarely undisputed) claims for the validity of the authentication process and the authenticity attributed to both cultural objects and the creators of those objects.

All of this matters when looking at notions of authenticity around film adaptations of comic books, because this is the space in which issues of authenticity are raised and disputed, though rarely resolved. Comics present particular sets of problems for those involved in the adaptation process. Film adaptations of single books (say, *War and Peace*) or even of a series or franchise (for example, the *Harry Potter* novels) have clearly defined source material with narrative structures and character arcs likely to be significantly similar to those that work in the context of mainstream Hollywood films. Disputes around the authenticity of literary adaptations often focus on what is left out of the film versions, or on the significance of changes made to timelines or character arcs to accommodate a non-specialist audience and a 90-to-120-minute running time. There is no real question about which version of *War and Peace* or *Harry Potter and the Prisoner of Azkaban* to adapt; there is just the original, published text.

Comics, however, have many characteristics that present serious issues for filmmakers. Story arcs are predominantly episodic, with cliff-hangers every six to eighteen or so pages, depending on the format. In addition to the original creators of the characters, there are usually multiple authors, writers, and artists over many years, with different, often conflicting approaches to the strip. Characters may have been around for many decades, meaning many versions of costumes and multiple variations on character motivation and powers, any of which might work on the page but might be plainly ridiculous on screen. Some story lines, villains, supporting characters, and heroes can be logic-free and continuity challenging. And all of this before considering the 1980s arrival in comics of retroactive continuity adjustment (or "retconning"), which attempts to fix narrative holes or mistakes in previously published material to add to existing mythology or to change fictional historical events in the service of a contemporary narrative. Then there's the issue of multiple universe reboots in both Marvel and DC worlds, events that often change costumes, characters, origins, histories, and powers. Oh, and comics characters, with few exceptions (one of which is Judge Dredd) don't age in real time. Actors, however, do age in real time. So a film franchise running more than a few years will start to encounter problems with on-screen performers who can only credibly play, say, Iron Man or Captain America for so long. The plethora of interests involved in adapting comics leads to a proliferation of strands of authenticity and an often dizzying array of attempts to establish hierarchies of authenticities, the levels at which individuals and institutions operate within those hierarchies, and the power or influence those players have in attributing authenticity to particular adaptations.

Judge Dredd, *2000 AD*, and British Comics

James Chapman correctly argues that the history of comics in the United Kingdom has been significantly different from that of the industry in North America in terms of formats, audiences, and the kinds of stories that were told. From the 1930s onward, British comics were aimed for the most part at young children of five or six years of age and up and were almost always weekly, printed mostly in black and white or two color on poor quality newsprint paper. Even during the 1950s to 1960s heyday of more sophisticated comics aimed at a slightly older audience of boys (for example, *Eagle*, 1950–1969), the serial anthology format was standard, with a regular set of characters appearing in strips of between two and five pages per week.

In February 1976, publishing house IPC launched a new weekly boys contemporary adventure comic, *Action*, which attracted national tabloid newspaper outrage over its often violent and gory stories. It was controversial but also commercially successful and featured the talents of, among others, writer-editor Pat Mills, Scottish writer John Wagner, and Spanish artist Carlos Ezquerra. *Action* was canceled in late 1977, but earlier that year Mills had already moved ahead with creating a new anthology weekly whose science fiction–themed stories Mills hoped would add a fantasy element that would distract moral crusaders from the often violent and satirical content. *2000 AD* was a commercial success, it has had an unbroken run since February 1977, and its breakout character, Judge Dredd, has become an iconic institution in British comics. Dredd's parent comic became a breeding ground for British creators who have gone on to become major figures in the US comics industry, among them Alan Moore and Dave Gibbons (*Watchmen*), Mark Miller (*The Ultimates*), and Grant Morrison (*Animal Man, The Invisibles*).

Judge Dredd's co-creators were writer John Wagner and artist Carlos Ezquerra, with some input from *2000 AD* editor and writer Pat Mills, who scripted Dredd's first appearance, and Mike McMahon, who drew Dredd's first story around character and city designs by Ezquerra (Goodwin). The first strip appeared in issue #2 (or "prog 2" in *2000 AD*'s own terms), cover dated March 5, 1977, and just one of several future-set science fiction themed strips (Wilson). Wagner returned to Dredd with "prog 9" and Ezquerra returned the following issue. While there have been many artists and writers associated with Dredd over four decades of publication, it is the Wagner/ Ezquerra team that is credited with the creation and early development of the character, and it is Wagner who has continued to write key Dredd stories.

Over the course of the early run of stories, Dredd's first name is revealed to be Joseph, and on the rare occasions that it is used it is often shortened to Joe. Dredd's post-apocalyptic future world is populated by vast, violent urban sprawls (the Mega-Cities), irradiated wastelands, and mutants, with only the Judges representing the forces of the law, standing between order and chaos. Dredd is a street judge, combining the roles of police officer, judge, and administrator of the law, up to and frequently including a sentence of death. It is no coincidence that artist and character co-creator Carlos Ezquerra based Dredd's helmet in part on the shape of that of a medieval executioner, as he notes in Paul Goodwin's comprehensive 2014 documentary, *Future Shock! The Story of 2000AD*. Other aspects of Dredd's appearance were influenced by David Carradine's character Frankenstein in Paul Bartel's *Death Race 2000* (1975), while Wagner in part attributes Dredd's ruthless enforcement of justice to Clint Eastwood's character in *Dirty Harry* (1971).[1] Writer Neil Gaiman, also in Goodwin's documentary, observes that the text, subtext, and intertextuality of Dredd is "glorious, twisted social commentary. . . . It was the thing that was being commented on, while also being the commentary." *Judge Dredd*, the strip, was also often laced with dark humor and sociopolitical satire, which alongside the often spectacular visuals worked to establish the character Dredd as having almost unprecedented longevity in British comics.

Dredd on Film

Given the influence of film and television on Dredd's character and the strip's aesthetic, it was perhaps surprising that the first *Judge Dredd* screen adaptation didn't appear until 1995 in the form of Danny Cannon's *Judge Dredd*, starring Sylvester Stallone. The story of the first *Judge Dredd* film is covered in some detail in Martin Barker and Kate Brooks's *Knowing Audiences: Judge Dredd, Its Friends, Fans and Foes*. Barker and Brooks suggest that *RoboCop* actually pushed back development of the first *Judge Dredd* adaptation for several years because a *Dredd* film might have looked too similar to a property that had in fact itself drawn heavily from *Dredd*. In preproduction on the Stallone film the studio sought to humanize Dredd and to frame him as relatable in the same way that other contemporary action heroes were. Stallone's star status was also an issue. On the one very obvious hand, *2000 AD*'s insistence that the reader could never see Dredd's face was up against the studio's (and Stallone's) requirement that viewers should see the star. The moment in which Dredd's helmet comes off early in the film is seen by fans as the point when its authenticity starts to unravel. On the other hand, Stallone had other ideas about the eventual tone of the film: in a retrospective interview for *Uncut* magazine in 2008, he said, "It probably should have been much more comic, really humorous, and fun," which would have made it even more at odds with the dark and violent satire of the comic than the cut of the film that appeared in 1995.

The plot of *Judge Dredd* is essentially an amalgam of a number of early Dredd *2000 AD* story arcs and characters, but in essence, Dredd (Stallone) is framed for murder by his escaped criminal (and of course evil) clone brother, Rico (Armand Assante). Dredd fights to prove his innocence by traveling through the Cursed Earth radiation desert beyond the walls of Mega-City One to emerge triumphant in an act-three confrontation with his "brother," which ends as Rico falls to his presumed death from the Statue

Sylvester Stallone as Judge Dredd in *Judge Dredd* (1995).

of Liberty. In this pared-down version of the plot there is little to trouble fans of the original strip, but there was much in the detail of the film's tone, script, and character that was problematic for fans, critics, and, as it turned out, film audiences more generally.

There was no sequel to *Judge Dredd* (1995), and as the years passed it seemed unlikely that Dredd would ever return to the cinema screen. But another Dredd adaptation was eventually announced in 2008 and released in 2012. Writer-producer Alex Garland was known for his novel *The Beach* (1996), later a film (2000) directed by Danny Boyle and starring Leonardo DiCaprio. More importantly for Dredd fans, however, he was screenwriter of the neo-zombie film *28 Days Later* (2002) and the bleak science fiction of *Sunshine* (2007), both directed by Danny Boyle. *Dredd*'s director, Pete Travis, had a relatively low-key track record, having worked mainly in UK television drama. *Judge Dredd* co-creator John Wagner was announced in 2011 as consultant on the project, which contributed significantly to a burgeoning fan expectation of a much better screen version of Dredd than the Cannon/Stallone vision. Karl Urban would star as Dredd alongside Olivia Thirlby as rookie telepathic Judge Anderson, up against Lena Headey's damaged and vindictive drug lord, Ma-Ma. Released in September 2012, the film sees Dredd and Anderson investigating several deaths in one of Mega-City One's huge Block residences and quickly engaging in violent conflict with Ma-Ma. Dredd and Anderson defeat Ma-Ma's forces, and in an echo of the climax of 1995's *Judge Dredd*, Ma-Ma is thrown by Dredd to her very definite death from the uppermost level of the Block.

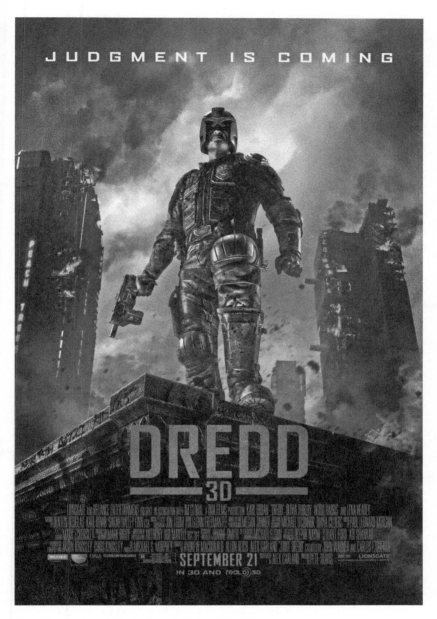

Karl Urban took over the titular role in *Dredd* (2012).

Overall, the tone of the film is dark and largely devoid of humor or satire, though it is peppered with often very fleeting visual and verbal references to Dredd on the printed page and some story arcs that in their original form were often deeply satirical and darkly funny. The vast majority of such references (the "Easter eggs" that have come to characterize most comic book screen adaptations) would be meaningless to the casual viewer but are highly prized by genre fans. This, of course, is the *point* of movie Easter eggs but also part of a web of signifiers of authenticity for fans of the source material.

Dredd and the Authenticators

Aaron Taylor argues that there has been effective co-optation by the Hollywood Marvel superhero franchises of fan engagement with the source texts, and that a consequence of this process has been the repositioning of key film production talent as *creator-fans*. One such creator-fan is Joss Whedon, director of *The Avengers* (2012) and *Avengers: Age of Ultron* (2015) but also creator and showrunner of cult genre TV show *Buffy the Vampire Slayer* (1997–2003) and its spin-off, *Angel* (1999–2004). Taylor observes that there were regular allusions to comic books and comics characters throughout the runs of both shows, and it is for this reason (among others) that Whedon was an obvious fan-pre-approved choice to direct the first *Avengers* film.[2]

Judge Dredd opened in the summer of 1995, years before the development of the process that Taylor has identified, and there is also a striking absence of authenticator approval around the film. Fleetway, the then publisher of *2000 AD*, produced an official comic book adaptation of the film, a relatively new twist on cross-media appearances of characters and story at the time (comic book to screen, screen to comic book). Despite art by Carlos Ezquerra, the comic of the film was poorly received by *2000 AD*/Dredd fans, in part because Dredd, firmly established as the faceless and relentless embodiment of the law, had to appear without his helmet. Ezquerra, according to Barker and Brooks, was "forced" into this position (217), so even the presence of Dredd's co-creator failed to lend authenticity to the Stallone film. Director Danny Cannon's only significant previous feature was *The Young Americans* (1993), starring Harvey Keitel and with an estimated budget of $3 million (*IMDb, Young Americans*). Thus, in 1995 Cannon was clearly not positioned as a creator-fan, at least in terms of his track record on screen. However, in the contemporaneously filmed twenty-minute US TV featurette, *Stallone's Law: The Making of Judge Dredd*, which appeared on the 1999 DVD release of the film, Cannon talks about being a fan of the source material, and even Sylvester Stallone expresses enthusiasm for the comics. The extent to which this promotional short contributed to any sense of authenticity around the film is impossible to assess today, but given the negative response to the film from critics and fans, it seems that if this was the intention it was not successful, despite intercuts of original Dredd comic book artwork. So, for Stallone's *Judge Dredd* there is no hint of proto-creator-fan authenticity from director or star, or of authentication from Dredd's creators or publishing house.

As writer-producer on *Dredd* (2012), Garland shows a clear understanding of the importance of fan approval for his film, in part because the Stallone film so clearly failed in this respect and in part, no doubt, because of the success of Marvel Studios in balancing fan aspirations with mainstream blockbuster franchise demands, from *Iron Man* (2008) onward. A key example of Garland's appreciation of the significance of fan approval is the pre-release August 2012 screening of *Dredd*, as reported by Dredd fan Steve Hargett in his blog, *Judge-Tutor Semple*. Present at the screening were both of Dredd's comic strip co-creators, Wagner and Ezquerra, along with the film's star, Karl Urban, writer-producer Alex Garland, and a number of key players in the UK *2000 AD* Judge Dredd fan community. This event works in several important ways, not only to establish Taylor's notion of co-optation of fan-community approval in building early positive promotion for the film, but also to associate the filmmakers closely with the original creators of Dredd and their canonical knowledge of the fictional world within which Dredd operates. As noted earlier in this chapter, Garland had brought Wagner in as a script consultant and had apparently responded positively to Wagner's suggested changes, which were intended to make the screen Dredd more like the Dredd fans knew from *2000 AD*. Outside the *Judge Dredd* universe, Garland brought with him a significant degree of genre cultural capital as writer of the downbeat science fiction film *Sunshine* and writer-producer of *28 Days Later*. In the same way that Whedon was a directorial choice with a high level of fan preapproval (along with the associated cultural capital and aura of authenticity), Garland was a figure whom Dredd fans were likely to trust to do a good job on a Dredd adaptation.

In a 2012 interview with YouTube fan channel Talk Comix, Dredd co-creator Wagner is very positive about the then forthcoming *Dredd*. He says, "I think they've done a really nice job. . . . Karl Urban is a very good Dredd, Olivia Thirlby is a terrific Anderson. The plot is basically Dredd; there's nothing that happens in that movie that's not Dredd. In the first movie [*Judge Dredd*] you'd be hard pressed to find something that was [Dredd]." Wagner has at least one positive comment to make around the production design and the visual aesthetic of the Stallone version, but he qualifies his compliment by making it clear that the look of the film should have been good given the money spent on it: "Their production values were great," he says, "[but] they had the budget for it." So, while this is a moderate and qualified after-the-fact endorsement of the Stallone film, it is clearly not authentication as such. In terms of approval for the then forthcoming 2012 film, however, Wagner is clear and unequivocal. If authenticity of adaptation is measured in apparent fidelity to the source material *and* in the approval of the author of the original text, Wagner's comments neatly meet both of those requirements.

The Talk Comix interview is arguably an example of Taylor's idea of the co-optation of fan base as a promotional strategy for a film around which fan expectations were high. Additionally, Wagner is clearly positioned, from a *Judge Dredd* comics fan perspective, as the most important authenticator for any adaptation of his creation. He is a respected and much-loved figure in British comics, a regular guest at UK comics conventions, and as Dredd co-creator, his involvement with the 2012 *Dredd* was a major signifier of authenticity not only for the film as cultural object but also for the key figures in the film's production, most notably Garland.

During the launch and promotion of *Dredd* in Great Britain, then, Wagner was a crucial part of the process, much more so than in similar events around the Marvel Cinematic Universe (MCU) films, where the stars are normally foregrounded alongside key production figures like Kevin Feige, president of Marvel Studios and producer/executive producer on the series of Marvel franchise films, starting with *Iron Man* in 2008. Wagner's significance as key signifier of authenticity is clear in the prelaunch and launch period of the film but also continues into the home-media life of *Dredd*. In the special features of the *Dredd* DVD/Blu-ray release, Wagner is present alongside Garland in the interviews segment. Interviewed on set, Garland demonstrates his deep background knowledge of the original *2000 AD* strip and discusses his childhood experiences of reading it. Although Wagner actually says very little and Garland dominates the discussion, the body language between the two men suggests a comfortable familiarity. Whether Wagner's apparent reticence is a consequence of what he said (or did not say) on that day, or if it was the result of the editing process, is a matter of speculation. Nevertheless, his presence next to Garland even when simply acknowledging Garland's comments lends significant authority to Garland as *author*, and therefore lends authenticity to the film itself.

In one of the DVD interview segments, Garland contrasts his film to the 1995 *Judge Dredd*, introducing another level of authenticity signification, that of the plucky outsider versus the inertia of the Hollywood mainstream. He suggests that the potential audience for *Dredd* might have had "their expectations defined by that first film, and we can . . . come out as [a] whole different thing. Much more hard-core and edgy, there's drugs and violence and brutality. There's something very rough about it. I hope it comes out of left field." By implication, his film is the alternative to the mainstream blockbuster that preceded it, more adult in theme and content, and so *better* and more true to the source material.

The same batch of UK DVD extras presents a short clip of director Pete Travis discussing Garland's script and not only Garland's status as a fan of the comic book origins of Dredd but also his ability to craft a story that will attract film fans unfamiliar with *2000 AD*. Travis goes on, though, to say that "hopefully, the story will appeal to people who are familiar with the comic. I think that we really want them to like it, and I hope that they will." This interview clip works in two ways. First, it again positions Garland as a figure whom the fan base can trust with the material: he is a fan, just like they are (as was Whedon for Marvel fans). Second, it contributes to the slightly counterintuitive impression that the director is not in this case the most significant author of the film, and that it is in fact the screenwriter-producer who is the auteur. A contemporary interview in *Empire* magazine with Travis suggests that both men collaborated much more closely on set than is usual for director/writer pairings, which further contributes to the perception of Garland as authentic (and authenticated) author of the final product.

Conclusion

The construction of authenticity as a perceived attribute of cultural objects and phenomena is fluid and dependent on the social, cultural, and political contexts within which they are created and disseminated. *Judge Dredd* story arcs have often been positioned by creators, fans, and critics as social commentary on the real world in which the character's host comic book, *2000 AD*, exists. *2000 AD* itself is often understood as an outsider, challenging a staid mainstream comics publishing environment. This is apparent in many popular and critical accounts but nowhere more clearly than in Goodwin's documentary, *Future Shock*. Simon Frith, a major figure in popular music scholarship, discusses the construction of a "folk" discourse around rock music, a discourse of authenticity that allows rock fans (and performers) to see themselves as part of a resistant, rebellious outsider community despite the apparently contradictory presence of a multimillion-dollar industry that is central to the global creative industrial entertainment economy (Frith 26). Comic book fans and creators also manage to embrace this contradiction, aided perhaps by comics' gradual ascendance of the popular cultural hierarchy since the mid-1980s, the development of the graphic novel, and the mainstream success of several superhero franchise series films featuring characters from a number of comics publishers.

This chapter has addressed some of the processes through which authenticity (or its absence) is attributed to two film adaptations of *Judge Dredd*, a process in which I have emphasized the role of the *authenticator* as the individual or institution with the cultural authority to grant an aura of authenticity to a film project. When *Judge Dredd* arrived on cinema screens in 1995 there were few of the social media and other channels of digital communication available to comic book fans awaiting *Dredd* in 2012. While the internet existed in 1995, and fans were early adopters of the technology in the form of discussion boards, email, and other forms of messaging, these were far from being mainstream activities in the consumption of popular cultural texts. What was perhaps more different then was the perceived status of fans and indeed comic book creators in Hollywood: in 1995 neither fans nor creators seemed to possess either the social or the cultural capital to make it possible for them to have any significant influence on the development of comic book screen adaptations. As Aaron Taylor correctly points out, since the opening salvo in the creation of the Marvel Cinematic Universe with *Iron Man* in 2008, there have been mostly successful attempts to co-opt fans into the promotional work of superhero comic book cinema adaptations. *Dredd* (2012) went several steps further in this process by explicitly and publicly including *Judge Dredd* creators in the creative and promotional process of the film, from preproduction through launch to home-media release. Their cultural capital for fans is enormous: the presence of Wagner and Ezquerra raises the apparent cultural and social capital of the filmmakers and of Alex Garland in particular, who was able to confirm his status as the most appropriate creator-fan to bring Dredd to the screen in the most authentic way possible. The commitment of star Karl Urban to the central conceit of Dredd, that the audience never see his face, was clearly icing on the authenticity cake.

Why, then, if *Dredd* worked hard to be the best, most *authentic* screen vision of the character, was its performance at the box office so disappointing? There is no easy answer to this question. Barker and Brooks, in their attempt to speculate on the relative failure of the earlier film adaptation, listed a number of possible factors: the increased number of competing films released in 1995; the presence of the third *Batman* film, *Batman Forever*, in the market; and confusion and conflict in the production and promotion of the film. None of these factors are about authenticity as such, but the film was widely considered to be a failure in terms of representing Dredd on screen as he "should" appear. *Dredd* (2012), by contrast, got so much more right in terms of doing what it needed to do in the development of its aura of authenticity, from association with original character creators to presentation of a unified front of film-creator fandom (despite unsubstantiated and rapidly denied rumors of conflict between writer-producer Garland and director Travis). There are other potential contextual factors: Joss Whedon's *The Avengers* was released earlier in 2012, as was a non-superhero film, *The Raid: Redemption*, a low-budget martial arts action movie (premiered in festivals in late 2011) with enough similar plot elements to *Dredd* that the casual cinemagoer might have seen *Dredd* as derivative. What is more interesting here are the ways in which *Dredd* successfully extended and developed the processes through which authenticity is associated with a comic book adaptation, not only in the text itself but also in the contextual production and promotional processes around it.

I began this chapter with three key questions. First, what is an "authentic" film adaptation of a comic book character or story? Second, how do we decide what is or is not "authentic" in comics adaptations? And finally, why do the answers to these questions matter, and to whom? The processes of authentication I have addressed here suggest that, for *Judge Dredd* at least, adaptations can be understood as authentic in both textual and contextual terms, and in the ways in which text and context interact. Textual elements of *Dredd* (2012) are authenticated contextually not only by fans (highly active bloggers and prominent fan-scene participants) and creator-fans (Alex Garland), but crucially also by *Judge Dredd*'s original comic book creative team. From this perspective *Dredd* is an "authentic" adaptation. *Judge Dredd* (1995) contains textual elements (in this case, production design) partially authenticated retrospectively by Dredd creator John Wagner. From the same perspective of authenticity as a value that depends on *authentication*, the Stallone film is at best a film that displays some authentic characteristics but is not understood by fans and original character creators as an *authentic* adaptation.

The perceived authenticity of comic book adaptations matters in these examples at least, and in similar ways in other (perhaps all) comic book adaptations. What is significantly more difficult to decide, though, is whether an "authentic" adaptation is a good *film*. Those arguments must play out in future scholarship.

Notes

1. In the early years of *2000 AD*, Dredd lived in an apartment in a tower block named after Rowdy Yates, a character played by Clint Eastwood in the 1960s TV western *Rawhide*.

2. For a sense of the regularity with which comic book allusions crop up in Whedon's "Buffyverse" (*Buffy the Vampire Slayer* and *Angel*), see Stewart.

Works Cited

Barker, Martin, and Kate Brooks. *Knowing Audiences: Judge Dredd, Its Friends, Fans and Foes*. Luton, UK, University of Luton Press, 1998.

Bourdieu, Pierre. *Distinction*. London, Routledge, 1984.

Chapman, James. *British Comics: A Cultural History*. London, Reaktion Books, 2011.

DeFalco, Tom. "1980s." *Marvel Chronicle: A Year by Year History*, edited by Catherine Saunders, Heather Scott, Julia March, and Alastair Dougall, London, DK, 2008, pp. 194–245.

Eagle. Vol. 1, Hulton Press/IPC, 1950–1969.

Frith, Simon. *Performing Rites: On the Value of Popular Music*. Cambridge, MA, Harvard University Press, 1996.

Goodwin, Paul, director. *Future Shock! The Story of 2000AD*. DVD. Metrodome, 2014.

Hargett, Steve. "Why *Dredd* (2012) Is a Good Comic Book Adaptation." *Judge-Tutor Semple*, 2013, https://judgetutorsemple.wordpress.com/2013/01/21/why-dredd-2012-is-a-good-comic-book-adaptation-spoilers-medium-out-of-context/.

IMDb. Box Office/Business for *Dredd* (2012). Last modified 1995, http://www.imdb.com/title/tt1343727/business?ref_=tt_dt_bus.

———. Box Office/Business for *Judge Dredd* (1995). Last modified 2013, http://www.imdb.com/title/tt0113492/business?ref_=tt_dt_bus.

———. Box Office/Business for *RoboCop* (1987). Last modified 1988, http://www.imdb.com/title/tt0093870/business?ref_=tt_dt_bus.

———. Box Office/Business for *The Young Americans* (1993). Last modified 1993, http://www.imdb.com/title/tt0108633/business?ref_=tt_dt_bus.

Miller, Frank. *300*. Milwaukie, OR, Dark Horse Comics, May–September 1998.

Peterson, Richard. "Authenticity: A Renewable Resource." *Creating Country Music: Fabricating Authenticity*, Chicago, University of Chicago Press, 1997, pp. 205–220.

Rotten Tomatoes. "*Dredd* (2012)." https://www.rottentomatoes.com/m/dredd. Accessed 17 October 2016.

———. "*Judge Dredd* (1995)." https://www.rottentomatoes.com/m/judge_dredd. Accessed 17 October 2016.

———. "Tomatometer Criteria." https://www.rottentomatoes.com/help_desk/critics. Accessed 17 October 2016.

Stewart, Kevin J. "12 Great Comic Book References in *Buffy* & *Angel*." *WhatCulture*, 28 September 2013, http://whatculture.com/tv/12-great-comic-book-references-in-buffy-angel.

Sylvester Stallone. Magazine interview. *Uncut*, no. 131, April 2008, p. 118.

Talk Comix. "Interview with John Wagner at Glasgow Con 2012." *YouTube*, uploaded 18 July 2012, https://www.youtube.com/watch?v=J-poxzZW1rQ.

Taylor, Aaron. "Avengers Dissemble! Transmedia Superhero Franchises and Cultic Management." *Journal of Adaptation in Film and Performance*, vol. 7, no. 2, 2014, pp. 181–194.

2000 AD. IPC/Fleetway/Rebellion, 1977–present.

Wilson, Nathan. "Judge Dredd." *Salem Press Encyclopedia of Literature*, January 2015, http://search.ebscohost.com/login.aspx?direct=true&db=ers&AN=103218747&site =eds-live&custid=s1234290&authtype=ip,shib.

CGI as Adaptation Strategy: Can a Digitally Constructed Spider-Man Do Whatever a Hand-Drawn Spider-Man Can?

JAMES C. TAYLOR

The opening title sequence of *Spider-Man* (2002) presents a digitally rendered space filled with the iconography associated with Spider-Man. A virtual camera soars and swerves around spiderwebs, glimpses of the eponymous superhero, of the supervillain Green Goblin, and New York City. This opening acts as a mission statement for the film and its sequels (2004 and 2007), announcing an intent to use computer-generated imagery (CGI) to realize Spider-Man's familiar traits in spectacular new ways.

Director Sam Raimi's first *Spider-Man* film is often seen as a watershed moment in the proliferation of CGI and superhero narratives in Hollywood cinema. Analysis of the ways in which the film deploys CGI, and how the sequels develop these techniques, can reveal much about the opportunities that digital filmmaking technologies present superhero comic book adaptations. The drawn images of comics and photographic images of live-action film provide a central ontological distinction between the media. CGI transcends physical restrictions of practical special effects, providing new avenues for the cinematic re-creation of fantastic comic book content. But there are differences in the origin, qualities, and reception of drawn, photographic, and digitally rendered images that obstruct the adaptation of content between them.

This chapter will first interrogate ontological and conceptual relations between the three image types, identifying points of overlap and divergence that impact their compatibility. I will proceed to analyze strategies in the films that address common criticisms of CGI not believably integrating into live-action cinema. Each area of analysis will compare techniques used in the films to those found in *Spider-Man* comics. I will go beyond discussions of transferring imagery between media and consider ways in which the films' uses of CGI evoke recurring themes of *Spider-Man* comics. Concentrating exclusively on the *Spider-Man* trilogy enables further exploration of CGI's potential narrative function. I will outline ways in which CGI augments diegetic narrative threads running through the trilogy while complementing these threads with a narrative about its own construction.

Image Ontology

Photographic images are commonly considered to be objective, while drawn and digital images are subjective. This distinction is rooted in the nature of an image's production. André Bazin argues that the photographic image is objective due to being produced through an automatic process that occurs without human intervention (12–14). This line of thinking attributes the quality of indexicality to the photographic image, since the process imprints an indexical representation of profilmic material ("a figure, object or scene that actually was in front of a camera in the real world" [Purse 6]) on celluloid. Pascal Lefèvre explains that, conversely, drawn images present the artist's subjective perspective on reality (8). Lev Manovich situates digitally constructed images in this subjective category, arguing that due to being manually constructed by human artists, they have less in common with traditional photographs than with painting (295). Yet the fact that many modern films are shot on digital cameras, and comics are drawn using digital processes, eliminates material distinctions between image types; each is formed from intangible numerical data. The different methods of production, however, and the ontological qualities they affix, largely remain. Digital photography still captures profilmic phenomena with a camera, digital techniques for creating comics art typically emulate traditional drawing methods whereby the artist forms lines and shapes on a two-dimensional surface, while CGI entails rendering three-dimensional objects and space.

An image's ontology frequently provides a principal criterion in discourses of realism. Bazin's oft-quoted assertion that "the photographic image is the object itself" (14) equates the photographic image with its physical referent, and consequently indexicality with realism. Lefèvre argues that the subjective stylization of drawn images suppresses expectations of realism, which explains why certain content, such as hyperbolic violence, is more readily accepted in comics than film (9). Perceived ontological distinctions between drawn and photographic images therefore suggest that certain content cannot easily transition from comics to film.

Even if, for now, one maintains that content is bound to form, the ability to combine different kinds of images in a single medium enables ontologi-

Drawn skyscrapers merge into a photographic representation of New York in *Giant-Size Astonishing X-Men* #1 (2008).

cally complex composites that are rich in meaning. The practice of compositing different profilmic elements together, or with artificial elements, to provide an illusion of indexicality, when in fact a camera did not capture the finished shot in one take, was accomplished using analog methods from the early days of cinema (Purse 4–5). The history and nature of compositing undermines the commonly held binary separation of celluloid photography and digital images, revealing that both can offer a hybrid indexicality (5–6). For example, the compositing process in the *Spider-Man* trilogy means that photographic representations of New York are interspersed in, and mapped onto, a digital construct of the city. A variety of digital, profilmic, and digital/ profilmic hybrid bodies populate this space.

While images in comic books are generally constructed from scratch, drawn and photographic elements can be combined, as is evident in John Cassaday's depiction of Spider-Man in *Giant-Size Astonishing X-Men* #1 (2008). In the foreground, Spider-Man is drawn in an acrobatic pose above the roofs of skyscrapers. In the background, the drawn skyscrapers merge into a photographic representation of New York. The geometric precision of the drawn skyscrapers enables them to segue into the photographic ones, while the diagonal angle in which Spider-Man's body is positioned matches the tilted perspective from which the skyscrapers are presented.

The intermingling of artificial and photographic elements in Raimi's *Spider-Man* films and Cassaday's panel evokes thematic concerns central to superhero texts. Peter Coogan identifies "superpowers" and "the urban setting" as core conventions of the superhero genre (203). While the former's fantastic nature and the latter's grounding in modernity are seemingly at odds, their interactions create allegorical meaning. As Dan Hassler-Forest outlines, superheroes "represent not only a fantasy of overcoming the obvious limitations of the human body within the physically and mentally overpowering vertical landscapes of the modern metropolis; they can also be read as the literal embodiments of modernist aspirations" (174). The ways through which Spider-Man inhabits Manhattan in Raimi's films and Cassaday's panel fuel both of these dichotomous readings. The ontological disjunction between Spider-Man's drawn or digitally rendered body and Manhattan's indexical qualities situate hero and city as oppositions. Spider-Man's superhumanly acrobatic form provides him with the power to freely traverse, and thus conquer, the oppressive structures of industrialization. Conversely, stylistic continuities between body and cityscape, such as seamless segues between artificial and indexical elements, present them as reciprocal realizations of modernity's promises fulfilled.

Jason Bainbridge argues that the superhero genre's blending of fantasy and reality is particularly prominent in Marvel comics due to New York's centrality to the publisher's universe. Having popular superheroes like Spider-Man, the Fantastic Four, and the X-Men inhabit New York distinguishes Marvel from rival publisher DC, whose biggest superheroes are typically located in fictional cities. DC's fictional cities can be allegorical counterparts of real cities — for example, "[Superman's] Metropolis is often referred to as New York by day and [Batman's] Gotham as New York by night" (Bainbridge 163) — but are always at one more remove from reality than Marvel's. Cassaday's panel and other Spider-Man stories exemplify the Marvel Universe's and New York's fusion, the wall-crawling superhero having a symbiotic bond with the city throughout his history (Bainbridge). The stylistic synthesis of superhero and city in Raimi's films does not just communicate a prevailing concern of the superhero genre, but more specifically adapts a key theme of *Spider-Man* comics.

While retaining ontological specificity allows different image elements to generate meaning when composited together, image types should not be thought of in binary terms as being either objective and photographic or subjective and stylized. Subjectivity intervenes before a photograph is taken, with the photographer deciding camera placement and framing. Human agency can continue to shape the photographic image after it has been captured. "For example," writes Stephen Prince, "flashing film prior to development or dodging and burning portions of the image during printing will produce lighting effects that did not exist in the scene that was photographed" (34). These subjective alterations have existed since the birth of photography, although they have been expanded as the medium has developed and entered the digital age. Meanwhile, drawn images and CGI can strive to achieve the impression of photorealism.

Whether photographic, drawn, or digitally rendered, images can appear in a range of styles. Scott McCloud places a variety of different styles of comics art on a triangular diagram between points of realism, symbolism, and abstraction (52–53). The infinite array of possible styles that fall between these points "represents the total *pictorial vocabulary* of comics or of *any* of the visual arts" (51; emphasis in the original). The proposed availability of any style to any visual art suggests that no content is unavailable to each image type, so long as an appropriate style is chosen. Traditionally, different production processes inhibit photographic images from taking on symbolic and abstract qualities as easily as drawn images. However, as Liam Burke's detailed discussion of a "comic aesthetic" in cinema demonstrates, the ability of digital filmmaking technologies to freely manipulate the filmic image has led to many twenty-first-century comic book adaptations having highly stylized aesthetics that recall their source medium (169–227).

Cultural associations of drawn images with subjectivity generally and comics specifically with extravagant fantasy arguably permit heavy stylization in films that present themselves as comic book adaptations. These permissions exist in tension with the pervasive cultural tendency to equate the photographic image with realism, which potentially restricts the degree to which CGI can mold and stylize imagery in live-action film. The ontological properties of film are such that realism should not be thought of as solely dictated by an image's appearance. Cinema's capacity to present movement offers a kind of realism not apparent in still images, while the specific qualities of movement in live-action cinema present a new set of criteria that determine CGI's construction.

Movement

Tom Gunning proposes that a concept of cinematic realism based on movement rather than indexicality is more instructive when theorizing cinema in the age of digital imaging, as it is inclusive of forms of filmmaking that are not based on filming profilmic phenomena. Gunning builds on Christian Metz's discussion of motion and temporality being central to cinema's "impression of reality." Metz argues that while the photographic image connotes pastness, the moving image offers a sense of presence (Metz 5–6). Gunning adds that "motion always has a projective aspect, a progressive movement in a direction, and therefore invokes possibility and a future. . . . We could say that through a moving image, the progress of motion is projected onto us" (Gunning 42–43). Motion occurs in both space and time, whether in film or reality. One cannot contemplate moving images in the same way that one does still images, because to engage with moving images is to be involved in their progression into the future, which advances in tandem with the progression of reality. Gunning asserts that our participation in motion is a visceral sensation, as we do not just see but also feel it (39). Since this participation occurs regardless of the kind of movement that is being presented, "motion therefore need not be realistic to have a 'realistic' effect, that is, to invite the emphatic participation, both imaginative and physiological, of viewers" (Gunning 46). Following Gunning, one participates in digitally rendered fantastical movements in the same way as profilmic movements. Kinetic phenomena that do not exist physically, such as Spider-Man's acrobatics, thus provide an impression of reality.

Gunning's inclusive conceptualization of cinematic movement in the abstract sense ignores specific qualities of movements. These qualities are of great importance when we consider the expense, time, and artistry devoted to ensuring digitally rendered forms in Hollywood films move in ways that adhere to laws of physics. This commitment suggests that due to the cinematic image's kinesis aligning with the audience's experience of time and motion, there is also an imperative for the particularities of CGI's movements to match this experience. Prince's notion of "perceptual realism" provides a useful framework for the criteria informing special effects artists' attempts to create realistic CGI: "A perceptually realistic image is one which structurally corresponds to the viewer's audiovisual experience of three-dimensional space. . . . Such images display a nested hierarchy of cues which organize the display of light, color, texture, movement, and sound in ways that correspond with the viewer's own understanding of these phenomena in daily life" (32). Both profilmic and digitally rendered material in "realist" or "fantasy" films can exhibit these correspondences to the viewer's audiovisual experience of the real world (32). Movement plays a vital role in this process. Even though no real human can swing from organic webbing emitted from their wrists or naturally leap multiple stories, fantastic movements like these are presented realistically by corresponding with our understanding of how Earth's gravitational pull affects matter.

Due to still images in comics lacking actual movement and temporality, and therefore not automatically assimilating into a reader's experience of reality, movement is presented through unique suggestive means. These methods have participatory qualities distinct from cinema's, while presenting specific movements alongside more abstract sensations of motion. McCloud explores how comics enlist the reader as a collaborator who activates diegetic motion (65). Spatial devices like motion lines, a series of figures mapping different stages of a movement, and transitions between juxtaposed panels indicate characters' and objects' trajectories. Readers mentally complete these movements. The static images have no temporality other than that which they imply and with which the reader imbues them. Andrei Molotiu defines "iconostasis" as "the perception of the layout of a comics page as a unified composition" (91) rather than a narrative sequence. Molotiu's concept of "sequential dynamism," in which energized relations between compositional and other elements propel the reader's eye along various trajectories that can align with or deviate from the sequential narrative flow, can complement iconostasis (89). Molotiu analyzes pages from early *Spider-Man* comics drawn by Steve Ditko that deploy these strategies to create expressive compositions imbued with kinesis.

A double splash page from *The Amazing Spider-Man: Volume 2* #33 (2001), drawn by John Romita Jr., combines elements of the aforementioned strategies. An array of overlapping figures presents different moves in Spider-Man's battle against supervillain Morlun. While captions arranged in a steepening arc direct the reader's eyes from the top left to the bottom right, movement occurs chaotically in all directions, creating competing trajectories. Individual figures depict specific movements, such as punches and grapples. At points movements continue from one figure to the next, such as in the bottom right, where Spider-Man hits Morlun with a chunk of rubble, only to see Morlun unharmed as the rubble shatters around him in the image to the right. In general, however, the overlapping figures bear no explicit causal relation to one another. By refusing to present a clear temporal flow of events, the page functions as a unified composition that conveys expressive kinesis rather than progression. The combination of specific moves, suspended from a clear temporal flow, with an abstract sense of motion, showcases the ability and unrelenting stamina of both characters, while suggesting a potentially endless battle.

Although ontologically distinct from comics, the projective temporal flow and specific qualities of Spider-Man's digital body's movements in the

Movement through suggestive means in *The Amazing Spider-Man: Volume 2* #33 (2001).

film trilogy can create similar effects. As Spider-Man first swings from a sky-scraper in pursuit of a criminal after Uncle Ben's murder, the virtual camera circulates tumultuously around his airborne body.[1] The disorienting com-peting motion of camera and body involves the viewer in an energetic flurry while creating particular sensations such as giddiness and vertigo that are augmented by relations between body and space. Arcs formed as Spider-Man gains momentum on downward swings that propel him back upward recall those of a pendulum, thus simulating the effect of gravity on the move-ments of weighted objects. Spider-Man's initially clumsy but increasingly assured negotiation of obstacles — buildings, streetlamps, bridges — tests his superpowers in a familiar environment to acclimatize both superhero and audience to his movements. The camera reflects Spider-Man's growing ac-quaintance with his abilities by gaining a greater sense of stability as the se-quence develops — for instance, by following from behind as he progresses down the street. The street's linearity enables a clear mapping of Spider-Man's spatial trajectory and gauging of his speed. He overtakes cars mov-ing in the same direction, the narrative of pursuit emphasizing temporal urgency. While comics can convey Spider-Man's energy and showcase his agility by holding him in stasis, cinema offers comparable sensations and displays by having him move through space and time in ways that are at once expressive, spectacular, and perceptually realistic.

Cinematic movement's affective sensations must therefore be considered alongside its perceptual qualities when analyzing the realism of CGI. But in focusing on the visceral experience and visual reception of moving images, respectively, neither Gunning nor Prince discuss intellectual processes in which audiences are engaged. Scholars such as Dan North and Aylish Wood argue that CGI, and special effects more generally, does not just involve audiences in an image's narrative content, but prompts conceptual awareness of the technology through which it was created. Sustained long takes that bounce and circle around the hero are a key way that the *Spider-Man* trilogy showcases digital filmmaking technologies. The longest of these occur in the first film's last, and second film's penultimate, shots, which last roughly thirty and forty seconds, respectively. Orit Fussfeld Cohen contends that the artifice of digital effects can be concealed through fast editing, which "prevents the spectator from perceiving the conjoined, digitally manipulated compound shot as a computer-generated product" (55). Following Cohen, it might be said that the prolonged takes of Spider-Man conversely foreground their digital composition. The free-flowing, unbroken movements of the camera and Spider-Man's body emphasize their lack of physical restraints such as cranes and wires. This narrative about the digital construction and navigation of complex composite spaces entwines with the diegetic narrative concerning Spider-Man's mastery of space. As North similarly outlines, the powers of the technology and of Spider-Man are in a reciprocal relationship, as they draw attention to each other, engaging audiences in both simultaneously (166–169).

The Digital Body

The dual narrative about the power of the special effects and of Spider-Man is undermined if the CGI's realization of the superhero's body fails to satisfy the viewer. Two primary criteria that impact the reception of digital bodies emerge from Lisa Purse's discussion of critical responses to digital bodies in Hollywood cinema: the body must believably inhabit its surroundings, and the body must act and emote like a human or humanlike being (60–63). These criteria return us to discourses of perceptual realism. In each case, insufficient correspondences between digital bodies and real-world experience disrupt a film's verisimilitude. Many of the critics Purse surveys identify these failings in the *Spider-Man* films. However, the films employ two

Spider-Man surfs on a digitally rendered door in *Spider-Man 3* (2007).

sets of narratively resonant strategies to mitigate inadequacies in these areas. First, Spider-Man and his environment are drawn toward representational alignment as they interact. Second, Tobey Maguire's physical and emotive presence is stressed to inscribe the hero with humanity. Each strategy evokes core themes of *Spider-Man* comics, thus circumventing restrictions that expectations of perceptual realism place on live-action films freely adapting comic book content.

Purse proposes that photorealism is not a fixed quality but can be seen as "a continuum between looser and more strident performances of photographicness" (60). The negative reception of Spider-Man's digital body stemmed from its cartoonishness occupying the opposite side of the continuum from its urban surroundings (60). As the trilogy progresses, however, the environment takes on an increasing degree of elasticity that is more consistent with Spider-Man's body, bringing Spider-Man and his surroundings together on the photorealistic continuum.

In the first film, space gains its highest degree of malleability within the diegesis when Green Goblin attacks the World Unity Festival. Digitally rendered segments of buildings fall toward the streets, presenting a direct threat to civilians' profilmic bodies. Space takes on greater elasticity upon being digitally dismantled in *Spider-Man 2*. When Otto Octavius's fusion machine is activated, metal is drawn toward it, causing structures to contort. The first time this happens, windowpanes bend inward until the glass shatters, digitally rendered shards propelled toward and killing Rosalie Octavius. In this case, as in the first film, digital environmental elements act antagonistically. The second film also features some instances of characters using dynamic environments to their advantage. For example, while fighting up the side of a clock tower, Spider-Man and Doctor Octopus both use a clock hand as a projectile. Spider-Man's digital body makes much more productive use of transformative space in *Spider-Man 3*. When Spider-Man saves Gwen Stacy as she falls down the side of a skyscraper, he weaves through tumbling, digitally rendered rubble that turns from obstacle to aid as he catapults and springs off pieces to gain speed. Elsewhere, while chasing Sandman, Spider-Man surfs on a digitally rendered door that has been removed from an armored van. He attaches to the van and to passing cars with strings of webbing to gain velocity from being towed. In both scenes, tactile interactions between Spider-Man's body and environmental elements foster spatiotemporal unity.

Granting Spider-Man and his urban locale comparable dynamism, and making the city an ally, combines with compositing of digital and profilmic elements to evoke Spider-Man and New York's symbiosis. Harmonious relations between superhero and city have been conveyed by imbuing New York with plasticity since Spider-Man's first comic book adventures. Scott Bukatman observes that in Ditko's compositions "the physical space of the actual city became utterly unstable. Walls became floors and verticality was close to being entirely lost in his swirling circular forms" (207). CGI enables New York in the *Spider-Man* trilogy to obtain a comparable degree of transformability, the city's geometry subverted as crumbling walls and detached doors become mobile platforms. Spider-Man's increasingly positive harnessing of malleable environments as the trilogy progresses narrates the consolidation of his bond with the city as he masters his powers. This diegetic narrative is again interlinked with the complementary extratextual narrative about the special effects advancing from film to film.

Although integrating superhero into environment, bringing Spider-Man and New York into representational alignment does not make him emotionally expressive. Spider-Man's costume provides a further barrier, completely concealing the human form. Aaron Taylor discusses ways in which the *Spider-Man* trilogy deploys Maguire's performance to surmount the expressive restriction of the digitized body and superhero's costume. Performances of physical humor in grounded scenes when the actor wears the costume, and having Spider-Man remove his mask, both reveal not general human qualities but the idiosyncrasies of Maguire as performer (Taylor 281–283).

Spider-Man's digital body does the acrobatic heroics while Maguire's body emotes.[2] This dichotomy conveys the segregation of superhero and civilian identities that Peter Parker endeavors to uphold. A recurring concern of *Spider-Man* texts is the impossibility of separating these two identities. Peter was introduced to comic books, in *Amazing Fantasy* #15 (1962), as a nebbish teenage outcast. Upon gaining superpowers he seeks to transcend his adolescent anxieties by becoming Spider-Man, whose costume hides Peter's youthful features. Peter thus constructs the Spider-Man identity to negate his marginalized civilian identity. Yet Spider-Man cannot be the flawless hero to which Peter aspires. Peter's general social restriction as a teenager continues in Spider-Man's persistent persecution by the adult establishment, from the media to the police. Meanwhile, Peter's personal hardships contribute to and multiply Spider-Man's problems.

Interactions between different pictorial and alphanumeric forms frequently communicate fraught relations between the Spider-Man and Peter Parker identities in the comics, as evident from the first depictions of the character. The cover of *Amazing Fantasy* #15 presents Spider-Man swinging confidently, chest thrust out, a criminal squirming under one arm. Everything about this striking image, drawn in bold lines by Jack Kirby, who is widely celebrated for his muscular heroes in kinetic compositions, exudes heroism. But the cover also features speech balloons that offer a different perspective. Spider-Man exclaims, "Though the world may mock Peter Parker, the timid teen-ager . . . it will soon marvel at the awesome might of . . . Spider-Man!" These words hint at hubris, while indicating anxieties that the bombastic costume conceals. A further disjoint is evident between Kirby's cover and Ditko's interior art, which utilizes thinner lines and frailer figures. On the opening splash page of the Spider-Man story, a lanky Peter stands apart from peers who mock him. Behind Peter is a panel within the panel, containing a silhouette of an assertive figure, a web, and a spider, all looming over Peter. These omens promise greatness while foreboding danger. Contrasting styles and signs are juxtaposed in these opening glimpses of Spider-Man and Peter to evoke tensions, such as hero and victim, power and burden, that the character is caught between.

In the *Spider-Man* trilogy, the intermingling of Spider-Man's digital body and Peter/Maguire's physical presence provides a comparable means of presenting the inescapable interlacing of identities. The uncanniness of Spider-Man's flawlessly agile digital body provides a potent representation of the infallible hero that Peter sees as an escape from his daily troubles. Scenes when Maguire's unmasked face is composited onto Spider-Man's digital body reveal that the superhero does not escape, but rather is infused with and driven by Peter's humanity. This technique peaks in *Spider-Man 3* when a lengthy airborne battle is staged between two unmasked opponents: Peter in civilian clothes and Harry Osborn as Green Goblin. Both combatants' bodies oscillate between digital, profilmic, and hybrid digital/profilmic forms throughout the fight. Maguire's expressions amplify the intensity of specific moments. For example, after the disclosure of his adversary's identity, Peter's digital body clings to a tumbling chunk of wall before the camera moves inward to reveal a blend of bewilderment and terror across Maguire's face. Peter's and Harry's emotions resonate outside of the immediate mo-

244 Panels and Frames

ment, providing a culmination of all the feelings they have exchanged over the preceding films. Having both characters unmasked situates this battle as an emotional (and technological) climax of the trilogy. Furthermore, rendering Peter's civilian body through the CGI usually reserved for his idealized superhero self underscores how, just as Peter's problems torment Spider-Man, Spider-Man's actions impact Peter's life.

Conclusion

When considering the applications of CGI in adapting content from comics to film, one must go beyond questions of the potential to faithfully transfer imagery. The particular ways digital filmmaking technologies place different elements in dialogue with one another provide a more fruitful area of exploration. CGI can be composited with profilmic material, expressive and perceptually realistic kinds of movement can occur simultaneously, while narratives about the characters' and digital filmmaking technologies' abilities complement each other. This intermingling of elements is particularly appropriate for the adaptation of superhero comic books. The genre comprises fundamental tensions, notably fantasy/urban and superhero/ civilian. Comics create meaning by juxtaposing pictorial and other forms. The points of thematic exchange inherent to superhero comics' content are not so much bound to as *enabled by* form that is itself plural. The unique presentational and conceptual pluralities that CGI facilitates in film can be harnessed to adapt superhero narratives' thematic tensions. Individual superhero films configure CGI to articulate their chosen superhero's particular thematic inflections. A digitally rendered Spider-Man has different tools at his disposal than his hand-drawn counterpart but uses them to spin familiar webs in which he is ensnared, struggling to reconcile great power and great responsibility.

Notes

1. In this essay, I will often refer to movements created by a virtual camera simply as camera movements. Aylish Wood determines that since virtual cameras perform the same basic movements as physical cameras (tracks, pans, zooms, etc.), it is appropriate to discuss them using the same terminology (166).

2. A stunt double's body is also used in certain scenes; however, the films endeavor to hide this body's existence, whereas the digital body and Maguire's body declare their presence.

Works Cited

Bainbridge, Jason. "'I Am New York' — Spider-Man, New York City and the Marvel Universe." *Comics and the City: Urban Space in Print, Picture and Sequence*, edited by Jörn Ahrens and Arno Meteling, New York, Continuum, 2010, pp. 163–179.

Bazin, André. "The Ontology of the Photographic Image." *What Is Cinema?* Vol. 1, edited and translated by Hugh Gray, Berkeley, University of California Press, 2005, pp. 9–16.

Bukatman, Scott. *Matters of Gravity: Special Effects and Supermen in the 20th Century.* Durham, NC, Duke University Press, 2003.

Burke, Liam. *The Comic Book Film Adaptation: Exploring Modern Hollywood's Leading Genre.* Jackson, University Press of Mississippi, 2015.

Cohen, Orit Fussfeld. "The New Language of the Digital Film." *Journal of Popular Film and Television*, vol. 42, no. 1, 2014, pp. 47–58.

Coogan, Peter. "Genre: Reconstructing the Superhero in *All Star Superman*." *Critical Approaches to Comics: Theories and Methods*, edited by Matthew J. Smith and Randy Duncan, New York, Routledge, 2012, pp. 203–220.

Gunning, Tom. "Moving Away from the Index: Cinema and the Impression of Reality." *Differences: A Journal of Feminist Cultural Studies*, vol. 18, no. 1, 2007, pp. 29–52.

Hassler-Forest, Dan. *Capitalist Superheroes: Caped Crusaders in the Neoliberal Age.* Winchester, UK, Zero Books, 2012.

Lefèvre, Pascal. "Incompatible Visual Ontologies? The Problematic Adaptation of Drawn Images." *Film and Comic Books*, edited by Ian Gordon, Mark Jancovich, and Matthew P. McAllister, Jackson, University Press of Mississippi, 2007, pp. 1–12.

Manovich, Lev. *The Language of New Media.* Cambridge, MA, MIT Press, 2001.

McCloud, Scott. *Understanding Comics: The Invisible Art.* New York, Harper Perennial, 1994.

Metz, Christian. "On the Impression of Reality in Cinema." *Film Language: A Semiotics of Cinema*, translated by Michael Taylor, New York, Oxford University Press, 1974, pp. 3–15.

Molotiu, Andrei. "Abstract Form: Sequential Dynamism and Iconostasis in Abstract Comics and Steve Ditko's *Amazing Spider-Man*." *Critical Approaches to Comics*, edited by Matthew J. Smith and Randy Duncan, New York, Routledge, 2012, pp. 84–100.

North, Dan. *Performing Illusions: Cinema, Special Effects and the Virtual Actor.* London, Wallflower Press, 2008.

Prince, Stephen. "True Lies: Perceptual Realism, Digital Images, and Film Theory." *Film Quarterly*, vol. 49, no. 3, 1996, pp. 27–37.

Purse, Lisa. *Digital Imaging in Popular Cinema.* Edinburgh, UK, Edinburgh University Press, 2013.

Taylor, Aaron. "Playing Peter Parker: Spider-Man and Superhero Film Performance." *Make Ours Marvel: Media Convergence and a Comics Universe*, edited by Matt Yockey, Austin, University of Texas Press, 2017, pp. 268–296.

Wood, Aylish. *Digital Encounters.* London, Routledge, 2007.

Scott Pilgrim's Precious Little Texts: Adaptation, Form, and Transmedia Co-creation

JOHN BODNER

The *Scott Pilgrim* series was published in black and white in six volumes beginning in 2004,[1] and it is difficult to overstate the impact of this serial graphic novel on the Canadian comic landscape specifically and on the wider world of North American comics in general. The work was, until the final volume, solely produced by the cartoonist Bryan Lee O'Malley with the independent comic publisher Oni Press.[2] The work has won one Eisner Award (2010) and several awards or nominations for the Joe Shuster and Harvey prizes. In 2010 the series reached sales of one million copies in print in North America alone, and the work has been translated into thirteen languages. As Heidi MacDonald noted, by sales, *Scott Pilgrim* is in the company of mega-sellers such as Jeff Smith's *Bone*, Neil Gaiman's *Sandman*, and Alan Moore's major works. Perhaps more importantly, the work imported several graphic and storytelling innovations into the mainstream of North American comics.

This chapter explores three interrelated aspects of the comic and film narratives. First, I analyze O'Malley's *Scott Pilgrim* books as a complex, polyvocal, and experimental narrative that utilizes the language of comics in ways that were novel at the time of O'Malley's writing. Second, I explore the production history of the comic and its adaptation to film to outline the co-creation and interwoven nature of both tales. Third, I provide a close reading of the film itself to suggest several novel ways to understand the transcoding of comic language into film. Thus, this investigation offers a pragmatic interpretive exploration that advances Robert Stam's deconstruction of originality in adaptation studies, arguing that the *Scott Pilgrim* "source text" is already an adaptation, deeply intertextual and dialogic, which is itself partially co-created through the very act of Edgar Wright's adaptation into film.

To begin, the series is a multigeneric, postmodern pastiche of media narrative and graphic traditions, the most striking of which is the incorporation of manga facial structure and overall character design into a North American comic; with oversized eyes, flat faces, small chins, generally implied noses, and delicate bodies, Scott Pilgrim and the other characters are depicted, in the language of Scott McCloud, along the iconic ("cartoony") axis of graphic depiction typical of a pattern first developed by Osamu Tezuka (McCloud 52–53). There is some disagreement over the origin of the style, with O'Malley noting that he was influenced by American mainstream comics, early anime, and manga (Sava), or claiming the eye style came from Disney and the 1964 stop-action movie *Rudolph the Red-Nosed Reindeer* (McCulloch). Outside of the fight scenes — some of which quote from manga, like Kazuo Koike's *Lone Wolf and Cub* (bk. 4, ch. 24, pp. 184–188) — there are few other incorporations of Japanese visual language, like facial graphic emblems, *chibi* transformations (there is one minor one), or hyperrealistic masking techniques (Cohn; McCloud 43). O'Malley admitted after the work was in print for several years that the technique also creates a necessary ambiguity to the ethnicity of the characters (O'Malley, "Q: This Isn't Meant to Be").[3] A second major influence on the work involves the graphic and narrative techniques of video games, specifically 8-bit graphic games from the 1980s, like Nintendo properties such as *Mario Bros.* (1983), and early 1990s transitional 16-bit games, like *The Secret of Monkey Island* (1990). While video games today form the source texts for a number of transmedia products, from films to novelizations, *Scott Pilgrim* stands at the beginning of the emergence of what has come to be known as "geek culture" (see Oswald).

Plot and Characterization

While O'Malley simply calls his work a "romance story," it is also a comedy that has, at its core, a bildungsroman of the main character through his relationship with Ramona Flowers and the subsequent physical battles with her seven evil exes. At the beginning of both the comic and the film, the eponymous character is an unemployed, arrested-development twenty-three-year-old (twenty-two in the film) who plays bass in an amateur three-piece rock band, Sex Bob-omb. His economic immaturity is marked by our introduction to his shared basement apartment,[4] where "commentary boxes" label all of the possessions as belonging to his roommate, Wallace Wells, with the exception of a coat and a "lame poster" (bk. 1, ch. 1, p. 9). His emotional immaturity is indicated by his asexual relationship with the seventeen-year-old Knives Chau. Across several scenes he also appears to substitute a historically informed personal identity (and memory thereof) with identity formation through pop-culture affiliation[5]—a point explored throughout the comic but largely abandoned in the film.

The reader is meant to assume that the story's perspective is Scott's through the comic version of free indirect discourse that O'Malley constantly undermines by employing (through various overt and subtle techniques) the Bakhtinian double voice in order to highlight the unreliability of Scott (as lens) (Bakhtin). Beyond simply the heteroglossia created by the dialogue of various characters, several of these techniques are unique to the comic medium. The first is the use of commentary boxes. Within these boxes authorial voice is used in both traditional and subversive ways. First, it provides basic information on places, time jumps, and people in a neutral manner. However, a subset of these labels provides information that undercuts Scott's perspective and/or provides ironic effects, as with the labeling of Wallace's possessions mentioned before. Second, the text box provides a space for an authorial voice to address the reader directly in the second person, which is sometimes used to counter the hegemony of Scott's perspective—usually with the point of creating humor through juxtaposition (bk. 1, ch. 4, pp. 21, 83; bk. 3, ch. 16, p. 3). Third is the use of text as picture, which subverts the commentary box's informative role. For example, as Scott stands across the street from his new job, O'Malley renders the word "WORK" in 8-bit video game font, a quarter of the panel large. The font, size, and placement reference the iconic "fight" graphic from the original *Street Fighter* (1987) one-on-one fighting game, thus creating a parody of Scott's worldview (bk. 4, p. 88). More radically, O'Malley transforms the text "LOVE" into a pictorial icon as it leaves the lips of Knives Chau, only to be fanned away by Scott as the bubble-cloud letters almost touch him.

This fantastic style reinforces an observation by O'Malley (McCulloch) and later Wright (Wright and Pope) that much of the text as graphic is merely the internal perspective of how Scott understands himself and the world. More radically, Wright suggests that everything that happens after Ramona delivers a package at Scott's door (bk. 1, ch. 4, p. 1) occurs only in Scott's head. This position is reinforced by Scott's delusion that he fought a supervillain's horde to win Kim's love in high school rather than simply beating up a small, unassuming classmate. As I will outline, the commentary box remains vital to Wright's formal project to recreate the comic in filmic form. Here it is enough to note that as much as Wright utilizes captions and text boxes in recreating comic graphic language in his film, O'Malley is himself conspicuously experimenting with the formal and narrative possibilities within his intertextual pastiche.

Scott Pilgrim's Precious Little Life (2004). The font choice of the word "WORK" references the 8-bit graphics of the original *Street Fighter* video game.

Within the comic the instability of the text, and the comedy this affords, is reinforced and enacted through the proliferation and overabundance of graphic and narrative styles, genres, and graphic traditions, including 8-bit and arcade video games, manga (of various genres), Hong Kong kung fu films (specifically, those produced in the 1960s–1970s by Golden Dawn and Shaw Brothers), mainstream comic books, anime, 1980s action movies, and American romantic comedies. The abundance of overlapping and inter-woven narratives is partially supported by the larger literary genre to which the story belongs, magical realism. In both the comic and the film the narra-tive remains, despite several foreshadowing dream sequences, strictly mun-dane until Scott Pilgrim meets Ramona Flowers (an American expatriate recently arrived in Toronto) at his door in book 1 (ch. 4, p. 3), where it is revealed (nestled inside of a Canadian/American cross-cultural joke) that Ramona uses Scott Pilgrim's consciousness as a subspace bypass to more efficiently deliver packages for Amazon. The revelation that the larger genre of the work is magical realism fully occurs in the first fight scene of book 1. Visually, the battle is a melange of video game iconography and martial arts manga choreography, but, more importantly, the battle between the first evil ex-boyfriend, Matthew Patel, and Scott Pilgrim wholly shatters the mundane plane by introducing fireballs, daemons, superhero abilities, and a general distribution of some or all of these powers among most characters in the story. Thereafter, the mundane and the fantastic are carefully balanced within the narrative both textually and visually—a point that will become important in arguing for an expanded understanding of the technique of recreating the verisimilitude of comics within the formal filmic language first proposed by Michael Cohen.

Padmini Ray Murray observes that the underlying structure of the tale is based on traditional combat video game narratives where the character gains experience and strength by defeating increasingly difficult opponents, often called "boss battles" (131–132). Murray's key insight is to recognize that alongside such rewards as gold (Canadian denominations of coin) or material benefits (weapons, extra life), Scott Pilgrim gains emotional and psychological rewards in a slow march of maturation until, in the end, Scott and Ramona "win" each other through the defeat of Gideon.[6] Murray's pattern is much clearer in Wright's film, which reduces the comic's much more multistranded maturation story by directing the narrative flow into a clear unidirectional stream that narratively echoes the popular expression of Joseph Campbell's monomyth hypothesis. In contrast, O'Malley's comic presents much more elliptical storytelling that often arrests the headlong movement to the next boss battle in favor of building relationships with readers and between characters, such as Scott's bandmates, Steven Stills and Kim Pine; his roommate, Wallace Wells; and his former girlfriends, Knives Chau and Envy Adams. Other events, like Scott getting a job and an exploration of the character of Kim, who retreats "up north" at the end of book 4, are given a significant amount of space. O'Malley admits in an interview with Oliver Sava that the serial nature of the story created narrative problems: "I don't know [at the end of book 1] if I really knew what any of my characters were. I drilled down into them as I went along. . . . He [Scott] became more defined as I went along. . . . I just kind of created problems and then I have to create a solution. That's the thing about doing a serialized book. You don't necessarily have everything planned out" (Sava). In contrast, the film streamlines but reduces character interactions and developments.

For my purposes, the most significant difference in plot and characterization centers on Ramona Flowers. In the comic, book 6 is largely a condensed story arc wherein Ramona recreates, in an accelerated fashion, her own maturation from a woman who always leaves relationships to someone who will stay and fight. Her defeat of Gideon is a metaphor for her own emotional success. In contrast, the film reduces her to the role of captive and prize to be won, and her self-actualization is (confusingly and reductively) kinetically performed in her fight with Knives Chau and her singular groin strike against Gideon. Thus, rather than having a partially balanced set of character arcs, the movie gives us one. While I have outlined the traditional graphic and narrative features that need to be considered when approaching the text as text, and the text as adaptation, I want to further problematize a simple reading of adaptation by considering the lineage of both texts' production.

Publication History and Narrative Form

Where O'Malley's comic is, through its complex intertextual experimentation with various graphic traditions, already a deeply dialogic and unstable text,[7] a brief breakdown of the publishing and production history for the comic and the movie demonstrates how the co- or parallel creation of the texts undercuts discourses of fidelity and originality in favor of a poststructuralist and emergent view of production and adaptation (Stam).

Book 1 of *Scott Pilgrim* was published in 2004, with the subsequent volumes released in 2005, 2006, 2007, 2009, and 2010. O'Malley was the sole creator until book 6.[8] Production of the film began in 2005, with filming beginning in March 2009. The movie premiered in Canada on July 27, 2010, in Toronto. In 2012 Oni Press released a colorized version of the comic that should be treated as a variant text and remains outside the scope of this chapter.[9] *Scott Pilgrim* is rare in the history of comic adaptations in having a source text actively created while the movie is being developed and filmed.[10] The act of parallel creation deeply affects both texts.

As noted in several interviews and paratexts, O'Malley and Wright (along with cowriter Michael Bacall) began working on the film after the publication of books 1 and 2, employing a plot outline provided by O'Malley (although, importantly, the outline did not include an ending). While not credited as a writer, O'Malley was involved in the film throughout production, from casting to the use of his reference photographs and locations to designing such items as the characters' distinctive T-shirts (Wright and O'Malley). Thus, the film is not merely based on the comic but partially constructed by O'Malley himself. Importantly, and more substantial to this discussion, he also saw a rough cut of the film before he finished book 6 (McCulloch). Elements from the film script and rough cut appear in books 4 to 6. In the DVD commentary with director of photography Bill Pope, Wright comments that some dialogue from the film appears in the comic, but neither he nor O'Malley in interviews provide specific examples (Wright and Pope). Wright's comment that the final set piece influenced a scene in the comic is easier to source since the film's step pyramid is mirrored in book 6 (ch. 37, p. 166) and is distinctly different from Ramona's subspace/headspace depicted earlier, in book 4 (ch. 24, p. 156). The film also affected the variant color version, about which O'Malley noted, "I basically just told [colorist] Nathan [Fairbairn] to watch the first half hour of the movie a million times and do his own version of the palette of the movie" (Sava).

Outside of the film, O'Malley admits to constructing his text partially in response to online discourse about the comic book. The idea of a dialogic relationship between fans and creators mediated by productive spaces online is well documented in the work of Henry Jenkins (*Fans, Bloggers; Textual Poachers*), but emerging at the beginning of Web 2.0, O'Malley is among the first generation of comic book creators nurtured online and affected by parallel narratives therein (Murray 130). For example, O'Malley recalls at times modifying his work

> based on stuff that people were speculating [about] online. I was kind of playing with the audience at this point, and I was playing with Kim more— because she was a fan favorite—and putting her in more situations. People thought that Scott might end up with Kim, and I was like, "It's not going to happen, but I'm going to fuck with you until the end. . . ." Before volume five—this is another fan response thing—people didn't like Ramona. People were all anti-Ramona. . . . So I wanted to just really dig into Ramona. I was like, "I need to make people love Ramona, because I love her." (McCulloch)

While much of the emergent nature of the text arising out of dialogue with various fan discourses remains hidden, the comic series itself appears unstable for other reasons. For example, various devices that were dominant in the first two volumes disappear, like an extratextual narration on how to play a song depicted on the page (bk. 1, ch. 1, pp. 8–9) and an in-text guide where Stephen Stills directly addresses the reader to deliver a cooking class (bk. 2, ch. 9, pp. 9–12) as the rest of the cast remains within the diegesis. These seemingly fundamental elements in the formal structure of the text disappear, and the authorial second-person voice is used far less frequently, as the story progresses. O'Malley explains the shifts: "As the story goes on, I started to concentrate more on narrative and I started to veer away from that sort of thing. It's just my development as a writer" (Sava). Likewise, the significant shift in his drawing style of the characters in book 4 is also explained as being related to his maturation as an artist. Perhaps, more significantly to the following discussion on the formal features of the film, O'Malley's composition of the page and the introduction of panels/frames is much more complex, and he abruptly introduces the page-as-frame itself (Groensteen 28): "Well, it's like the world of *Scott Pilgrim* gets smaller here. And it's reflected in the pages' layouts. I started using more margins. His world is shrinking a little bit. Especially when you get to the last chapter in which Ramona leaves. It has these heavy margins all around. His world is getting smaller" (Sava).

The film itself appears more stable and more consistent in its tone and techniques, although there is one significant event that hints at its instability. Until three months before its release the film had a different ending. Wright claimed at the time that the reshoot was to film minor "pick-ups" and to include some small elements from book 6; however, the reshoot changed the ending from Scott restarting his relationship with Knives to walking through a subspace door with Ramona (Miller). Beyond rumors that the ending did not test well with advance audiences, or the simple recognition of the instability of the filmic text,[11] the episode demonstrates that the film and the comic must be treated as parallel co-creations with overlapping influences across elements like plot, graphic representation (icon), and characterization. Or, as O'Malley commented in an interview: "They designed the pyramid, and I was like, 'I need to have a pyramid in my book.' So I was, in one way, building on the movie, and in the other way, I was free to diverge as much as I wanted" (Sava).

Film Form and the Language of Comics

Insofar as co-creation of the comic and the film undermines issues of fidelity and originality, as Liam Burke has noted, fidelity itself remains a discourse that underpins both fan/vernacular aesthetics of consumption as well as the formal and aesthetic nature of production (17–18). In my concluding section I outline the innovation in filmic techniques developed by Wright to transcode not simply the language of comics but the aesthetic experiments of O'Malley himself. The contemporary period of comic studies has seen an explosion in approaches, but it is safe to say that since the work of Scott McCloud in the United States and Thierry Groensteen in France, a great deal of energy and debate has focused on the form of comics, whether understood as a language, a system, or discrete units. In this section I will instrumentally use several features from this school of comic studies but sidestep the wider debate on whether neo-semiotics (Groensteen), pragmatic formalism (McCloud), or various relationships between discrete units like image/text (Harvey; Mitchell) constitute a definitional program for understanding the totality of the medium.

If one agrees with Linda Hutcheon that the heart of the crisis of adaptation is filmic naturalism, then one can see two distinct traditions in contemporary comic adaptations (Hutcheon 32). The first, embraced by Marvel Studios, Sony Pictures, and Warner Bros./DC Films, recreates naturalism through the increasing flexibility of digital special effects to produce a revolutionary depiction of comic content completely within the codes and conventions of mainstream film; these adaptations are fundamentally Jack Kirby without the language Jack Kirby worked in. The second tradition of adaptation is represented by Wright's *Scott Pilgrim vs. the World*, along with a small number of films like *Dick Tracy* (1990), *The Mask* (1994), and Frank Miller and Robert Rodriguez's *Sin City* (2005).[12]

I argue that of the small number of filmmakers who reject conventional filmic adaptation, Edgar Wright has constructed the most formally comic book–like film, not only by integrating the language of the medium into the diegetic or visual content (through a complex process of "transcoding"), but also, more significantly, by integrating the language and formal features of sequential art itself (Hutcheon 42–43). In order to demonstrate this process, I build off of two insights in Michael Cohen's analysis of the movie adaptation of *Dick Tracy*. First, Cohen argues that *Dick Tracy* replicates "comic aesthetics" through techniques that destroy the naturalism of conventional cinema to create what he calls a "fiction effect." Important in Cohen's analysis is that this effect is antagonistic to realism and succeeds insofar as it is a complete system involving everything from sets to characters to color to action. I argue later that Wright's magic realism technique provides a challenge and an opportunity to expand on the mechanisms of constructing comic aesthetics. Cohen's second observation is that the comic aesthetic is partially created through the use of shot/frame to recreate comic panels. I return to this point in more detail later. Here, it is enough to note that the technique of transcoding the movie frame as a comic frame is accomplished (partially) through the static camera (Cohen 32–33). In analyzing Wright's film, I will critique Cohen's point, but his idea of stasis (rather than a total fiction effect) is, I believe, a key mechanism for creating a comic aesthetic, which I demonstrate in the following close reading of the film.

Wright's first and most obvious technique in replicating the comic aesthetic is to directly quote from O'Malley's comic by switching from live action to the actual panels themselves as Ramona narrates the backstory of her relationship with Matthew Patel and Todd Ingram. This technique is surprisingly rare,[13] and can be found in an early example when a character flips through the source-text comic in Corrado Farina's *Baba Yaga* (1973),[14] an adaptation of the irregular serial comic *Valentina* (1965–1996) by Guido Crepax. Unlike the comic-as-storyboard approach of *Watchmen* (2009) or *Sin City*, Wright's second technique is consistently but judiciously to quote panel content throughout the film—generally choosing moments of stasis within the film to match the comic medium's static iconic order. More precisely, Wright transcodes by using the illusion of stasis in film to mirror the illusion of movement in comics.

Third, Wright takes up O'Malley's complex use of the comment box, marks (action lines), and onomatopoeia text as sound effects to become one of the few filmmakers to use the technique since the much-derided *Batman* television series (1966–1968).[15] Like O'Malley, he uses comment boxes to label time, place, elements, people. Doing so, while atypical, is common enough in film not to deconstruct realism;[16] however, the following uses represent micro incursions into the fabric of the diegesis. For example, one type of label externalizes subjective perspectives, with "a b o u t t o e x p l o d e" appearing as an agitated Scott enters the after-party, the label prefiguring a (nonphysical) fight with Ramona. Another technique commonly employed by O'Malley, the ironic authorial voice, is used only twice, as in the scene when, after Todd punches the highlights out of Knives Chau's hair, Envy approvingly says to Todd, "You are incorrigible." Todd replies, "I don't know the meaning of the word," and a commentary box helpfully appears to inform us that "he really doesn't." The effect is twofold: integrating a formal technique that is iconic within comic book language causes the viewer to constantly recognize the language itself while temporarily displacing (but not dispelling) the realism underlying the film.

By far the most complex use of text is Wright's integration of onomatopoeia sound effects. Wright uses three categories of text/sound to produce approximately forty-two instances in the film. What is curious is that in only one instance does the text substitute for an actual sound effect, which occurs when Todd's hair deflates after being "de-veganized" and we see the word "SAG." In all other instances the sound effect duplicates an already provided sound cue. Where it is purely duplicating sound, its purpose is, again, to denaturalize the text by parodying a distinct formal feature of comics' language. As with his mirroring of stasis in iconic panel content, in two scenes Wright also appears to be engaged in a much more complex use of text: the first battle of the bands and Lucas Lee's "grind" down the rail at Casa Loma. In both scenes, specific, and high-volume, noise (the band onstage and the video game soundtrack, respectively) is used to drown out all other pos-

Scott Pilgrim vs. the World (2010). Director Edgar Wright replicates content from comic book panels as images within the film.

sible sound—necessitating the use of text.[17] This allows Wright to mimic the silence of comics, in which text is also required to represent sound. Even in places where text merely duplicates sound effects there is still a more complex project than merely replicating a cute trope. Commenting on the use of sound in manga, Robert S. Peterson notes that "the strategy to include

sounds is not intended to produce redundancy, rather to slow the reader down and create greater visual depth and texture to the scene" (166). With an important exception that I will discuss, obviously the pace at which one views a film scene is fixed, but the density of reading that scene can be increased along with the concomitant engagement that writers like McCloud claim is unique to the active reading/deciphering of comics (McCloud 89).

Finally, marks are used in two ways and function, on the formal level, similarly to my analysis of text. First, they denote sound; second, and more abstractly, they focus attention along eye lines ("stare lines," to coin a phrase). In this they replicate preexisting information (sound, visual) delivered in another medium (film) but do so as a pastiche of comic language and to denaturalize the scenes in which this technique appears.

The most complex formal technique of integrating comic language is Wright's transcoded construction of comic panels. The supremacy of the panel in replicating a comic aesthetic is central since, as Groensteen has argued, comics are a system of meaning constructed partially out of the "arthrology" and "spatio-topia" of their panels (21–22).[18] Cohen's analysis of *Dick Tracy* argues that the impression of panels is created through camera stasis and depth of field. Cohen's analysis is not wrong, but as he himself admits, continuity editing can obliterate the panel impression—as he notes happens throughout the film, except in the two instances he writes about (Cohen 35). It is also necessary to attend to transitions, or as Wright comments: "Lots of people have mentioned the transitions throughout, and also what's nice, a lot of people have mentioned like even just beyond replicating the panels but like how it feel[s] like reading a comic book" (Wright,

Bacall, and O'Malley). Building on his visual language in *Shaun of the Dead* (2004) and *Hot Fuzz* (2007), Wright's transitions use several techniques, but in *Scott Pilgrim*, when they are employed in a shot that seeks to replicate the comic panel, they reinforce the panel's presence by replicating its companion—the "gutter."[19] He accomplishes this task with cuts that are exceedingly quick or that open into shots that displace conventional temporal logic (anticontinuity editing), or with cuts that utilize a purposefully barely visible wipe effect. As with McCloud's observation of the role of the gutter in comics, Wright's use of transition and shot selection disrupts the absolute closure of film and consequently increases the comic aesthetic, since "comics are closure" (McCloud 67).

Wright disrupts closure through transition in a number of ways that mirror his use of other comic techniques, from the simple to the complex. First, he copies O'Malley's post-Knives-Chau-breakup page by using natural objects (a tree as we move into the scene and then a stanchion on a streetcar) to create borders, which have the added benefit of replicating Groensteen's "iconic solidarity," where multiple images exist (in this case temporarily) in relationship to each other so we can watch the juxtaposition of Chau's sadness with Scott's brimming joy as Ramona appears next to him in her own frame (Groensteen 19). The use of objects like the tree or characters crossing in front of the camera to introduce the wipe transition is common in the film and acts as the inked line that makes the panel border.[20] A second feature of this scene is that it employs Cohen's static camera to initially create the comic frame.

A more complex example of transition replicating comic aesthetics appears in the scene where Scott Pilgrim is ordering a package from Amazon so that Ramona will deliver it. Scott sits in front of the computer in medium frame; next, the view cuts to Wallace in medium close-up, then back to medium-framed Scott sitting cross-legged in front of the door. The story has not yet introduced supernatural elements, and Scott's movement from one side of the room to the other cannot logically take place within a naturalistic reading of the temporal structure of these moments. The entirety makes sense in a comic reading, however, if each moment is read as a separate physical frame that denotes a temporal unit that the reader can decode because of the spatio-topia of the comic page (Groensteen).[21] The effect, as Wright noted before, is that the scene essentially "feels" like a comic book. For those viewers who are unfamiliar with the formal pastiche, Wright's accomplishment is that the scene also works as comedy and foreshadowing of the magical realism turn in the story.

In a third scene one sees how transition allows for the sense of the panel to be created for Cohen's immobile camera. The scene takes place at Julie's party, where Scott is asking guests about Ramona. Bookended by two shot/reverse-shot sequences, in the middle are four short moments, all shot from the same position over Scott's left shoulder—a slight camera move in and then a quick cut to the next person, now slightly closer to the camera, a slight track in, and repeat until the final person is in medium close-up. The quick cuts drop the viewer into the moment of speech, which creates a disjointed continuity that closely resembles the subject-to-subject transitions in comic panels as the reader skims over the page (McCloud 74). As O'Malley notes, the effect is akin to reading a comic quickly:

> Wright: Maybe it doesn't feel like reading a comic if you're a slow reader . . .
> O'Malley: . . . the way you flit through from scene to scene you're . . . in the next scene before you know it. (Wright, Bacall, and O'Malley)

Later in their conversation both artists talk about how they would read comics and manga (respectively) "super fast," and then Wright notes, "I would go back and look at the artwork." In attempting to denaturalize the filmic text, Wright has produced a comic aesthetic that replicates the quick-reading strategy open to all comic book readers because of the architecture of the page (Groensteen 60–61; Cohn, "Navigating Comics"); however, Wright also suggests a way in which technologies are pulling film and the tactics of filmic reading closer to the mode of comics, noting that when viewers get to the action scenes they should "slow it down to frame advance and it will be like a Frank Miller book" (Wright, Bacall, and O'Malley). While outside the scope of this study, first the VHS and now Blu-ray and DVDs, as well as increasingly cheap and accessible video editing software, have allowed a radical decoupling of film from its basic temporal architecture, such that viewers (cum producers) increasingly experience film as discrete units over which one can linger, return, pause, skip, or skim—in essence, a comic book.[22]

Conclusion

Wright's complex and experimental visual techniques provide a way to expand the discussion of transcoding comic books' formal features into film. Few films will be able or willing to replicate Wright's quoting of the most indexical of comics' formal features, like text boxes or onomatopoeic sound effects, but this inquiry into Wright allows for a partial widening of the possibilities in adaptation transcoding. First, one recognizes Cohen's central thesis on the static camera as central to the language of transcoding the formal features of the comic book panel; but now, with the work of Wright, one can integrate the filmic category of transition and its ability to replicate the border and gutter to imply the panel as well.

Many of the trends I discuss here have since become ubiquitous and inform key aspects in the production and consumption of comic books and their adaptation in film. For example, Kelly Sue DeConnick and Valentine De Landro's *Bitch Planet* is being actively constructed within an online dialogue with various paratexts from interpretive essays, letters to the writer/ artists, blogs, fan art, and fan fiction ("Social Feed"). While some of the instability in O'Malley's work is explained by his maturation as an artist and by the traditional dialogue across intertextual texts through his use of pastiche, the elements of co-creation by artists through their participation in paratexts will become an increasing element in comic book analysis in the future, and with it, a general orientation of the unstable and emergent will need to be integrated into the field.

In the production, co-production, adaptation, and continued transmedia narrative production of *Scott Pilgrim* (a stage play has been recently discussed), O'Malley's and Wright's texts act as exemplars of the current state of global cultural production and reception of popular fiction. Thus far, however, Wright's and O'Malley's formal experimentation remains an isolated example of a process whereby two texts are deeply implicated in each other's production, which has the overall effect that, like the magical realism of the tale itself, both the comic and the film acknowledge each other's presence and hold them in tension and possibility before the reader and viewer.

Notes

1. The references in this chapter are to the black-and-white Oni first edition. The series uses continuous chapter numbering, with a variable number of chapters in each book. Books 1 to 3 use a full bleed with no pagination, whereas books 4 to 6 contain a combination of full bleeds and pages as frames and panels. The periodic margin on the bottom of the page allows for numbering. When referencing items in books 1 to 3, I cite the work as follows: book, chapter, page number within chapter. When citing books 4 to 6, I omit chapter information and use the running pagination.

2. The press specializes in independent, book-length, or limited-series non-superhero stories. Like the underground and independent publishers before them, creators retain full copyright of their creations.

3. In his collected works, Fred Pattern suggests that the first clear manga influence in North America occurred in Wendy Pini's independent comic book series *ElfQuest* (1979) (Pattern 19). From his own biographic information and despite his relative geo-

graphic isolation in Timmins, Ontario, O'Malley would have been the first generation born into a North American pop culture mediascape that included accessible anime on television and manga in comic book shops in the 1980s (Pattern).

4. O'Malley has noted in several interviews that the housing, jobs, and general lived circumstances of his characters mirror his own time in Toronto. The pattern of employment, housing, and general socioeconomic profile creates an accurate ethnographic snapshot of his generation that effectively grounds the story in its convincing mundanity (see Finn; Cote and Bynner).

5. The urban flaneur and its various historically informed manifestations, whether gentrifiers or hipsters, has, since Walter Benjamin, marked a key shift in identity formation, of which O'Malley is a keen ethnographer within the comic, from music, to T-shirts, to tea (Beauregard).

6. Here the logic of violence as a performance and crucible of self has less resonance with historic video games and more with the aforementioned *Lone Wolf and Cub* and is again dissimilar from mainstream superhero comics.

7. I have chosen the term *unstable* to distinguish *Scott Pilgrim*'s specific material instability in its mode of production and emergent form within and through paratexts as distinct from either novelistic theories like Bakhtin's dialogism or Brian McHale's postmodernist interpretation of text(s).

8. The assistance appears to be confined to more labor-intensive aspects of the art, with John Kantz credited with screen tone and background and Aaron Ancheta doing crowd scenes and inking assistance.

9. The colorist is Nathan Fairbairn, with O'Malley acting as editor.

10. George R. R. Martin's *A Song of Ice and Fire* series, adapted in HBO's *Game of Thrones* (2011–2019), is another example; Season 6 of the television show outpaced the books, and the latter never caught up to the former. A second caveat to my point is that all serial comic books, insofar as they are potentially endless, will always be created through and beyond any movie project; however, *Scott Pilgrim* was designed and executed as a limited serial.

11. William D. Routt, who in 1995 recognized the proliferation of technology and the advancement in restoration projects, is one of the first to note how variants and the instability of film texts have spawned a new field of film studies.

12. *Sin City* is instructive on a couple of fronts. First, the film abandons naturalism by digitally recreating Miller's chiaroscuro rendering. After this, however, the project is less radical than one might think, since Miller's original comic is a pastiche of the visual and narrative conventions of the relatively contained filmic language of film noir. The movie version only has to reverse engineer the larger genre tropes (Hutcheon 43). Note: The origin of this line of analysis is credited to Crystal Rose in personal communication with the author.

13. This is not to confuse the technique of displaying comic books themselves in adaptation movies or the genre of "motion comics."

14. Alternate titles: *The Devil Witch*; *Kiss Me, Kill Me*.

15. There is no clear "action lines" mise-en-scène in *Batman*, but by Season 2 in the series the intertitle cards containing the onomatopoeia also contain animated action lines that, because the cards are edited on the punch, act as action lines to the now absent but still present motion of the blow.

16. Curiously, thanks to texting, the "comment box" is increasingly appearing in film and on television, as with the BBC's *Sherlock* (2010–present).

17. There are accompanying Foley sounds in the grind scene, but they are almost half the volume of sound effects in other scenes.

18. Groensteen's formal system is based on an iconic solidarity between objects ("icons") in space ("spatio-topia") and arthrology, or articulation of various iconic forms.

19. On the visual techniques of Wright, see Zhou.

20. Knives Chau's movement from being framed by her mirror to the moment-to-moment cuts of her texting Young Neil is another example.

21. The larger issue of chronotopes in comics is beyond the scope of this chapter but is addressed elsewhere by Sue Vice.

22. A similar revolution in video game capture technology has allowed for not only asynchronous narrative production and consumption but also similar modes of reading/producing the text itself.

Works Cited

Bakhtin, Mikhail. "Discourse in the Novel." *The Dialogic Imagination*, edited by Michael Holquist, translated by Caryl Emerson and Michael Holquist, Austin, University of Texas Press, 1981, pp. 259–422.

Beauregard, Robert A. "The Chaos and Complexity of Gentrification." *Gentrification of the City*, edited by Neil Smith and Peter Williams, Boston, Unwin Hyman, 1988, pp. 35–54.

Burke, Liam. *The Comic Book Film Adaptation: Exploring Modern Hollywood's Leading Genre*. Jackson, University Press of Mississippi, 2015.

Campbell, Joseph. *The Hero's Journey: Joseph Campbell on His Life and Work*. Edited by Phil Cousineau, San Francisco, Harper Row, 1990.

Cohen, Michael. "Dick Tracy: In Pursuit of a Comic Book Aesthetic." *Film and Comic Books*, edited by Ian Gordon, Mark Jancovich, and Matthew P. McAllister, Jackson, University Press of Mississippi, 2007, pp. 13–36.

Cohn, Neil. "Japanese Visual Language: The Structure of Manga." *Manga: An Anthology of Global and Cultural Perspectives*, edited by Toni Johnson-Woods, New York, Continuum, 2010, pp. 187–203.

———. "Navigating Comics: An Empirical and Theoretical Approach to Strategies of Reading Comic Page Layouts." *Frontiers in Psychology*, no. 4, 2013, pp. 1–15.

Cote, James, and John M. Bynner. "Changes in the Transition to Adulthood in the UK and Canada: The Role of Structure and Agency in Emerging Adulthood." *Journal of Youth Studies*, vol. 11, no. 3, 2008, pp. 251–268.

Finn, Janet. "Text and Turbulence: Representing Adolescence as Pathology in the Human Services." *Childhood*, vol. 8, no. 2, 2001, pp. 167–191.

Groensteen, Thierry. *The System of Comics*. Translated by Bart Beaty and Nick Nguyen, Jackson, University Press of Mississippi, 2007.

Harvey, Robert C. *The Art of the Funnies: An Aesthetic History*. Jackson, University Press of Mississippi, 1994.

Hutcheon, Linda. *A Theory of Adaptation*. 2nd ed., London, Routledge, 2012.

Jenkins, Henry. *Fans, Bloggers, and Gamers: Exploring Participatory Culture*. New York, New York University Press, 2006.

———. *Textual Poachers: Television Fans and Participatory Culture*. New York, Routledge, 1992.

Kioke, Kazuo, and Goseki Kojima. *Lone Wolf and Cub*. Translated by Dana Lewis. Milwaukie, OR, Dark Horse Comics, 2000–2002.

MacDonald, Heidi. "Scott Pilgrim's Finest Sales Chart: 1 Million in Print." *The Beat*, 17 September 2010, http://www.comicsbeat.com/scott-pilgrims-finest-sales-chart-1 -million-in-print/.

McCloud, Scott. *Understanding Comics: The Invisible Art*. New York, Harper Perennial, 1994.

McCulloch, Joe. "A Conversation with Bryan Lee O'Malley—SPX 2008." *Comics Comics*, 27 June 2010, http://comicscomicsmag.com/?p=3631.

McHale, Brian. *Postmodernist Fiction*. New York, Methuen, 1987.

Miller, Neil. "Scott Pilgrim Reshoots and Why You Shouldn't Worry." *Film School Rejects*, 4 May 2010, https://filmschoolrejects.com/scott-pilgrim-reshoots-and-why-you-shouldnt-worry-ea1221e1fec9#.w6qge7aav.

Mitchell, W. J. T. *Iconology: Image, Text, Ideology*. Chicago, University of Chicago Press, 1986.

Murray, Padmini Ray. "Scott Pilgrim vs the Future of Comics Publishing." *Studies in Comics*, vol. 3, no. 1, 2012, pp. 129–141.

O'Malley, Bryan Lee. "Q: This Isn't Meant to Be an Insult or a Rant or [. . .]." *Radiomaru*, 25 June 2013, http://radiomaru.tumblr.com/post/53857149606/q-this-isnt -meant-to-be-an-insult-or-a-rant-or.

———. *Scott Pilgrim, Vol. 1: Scott Pilgrim's Precious Little Life*. Portland, OR, Oni Press, 2004.

———. *Scott Pilgrim, Vol. 2: Scott Pilgrim vs. the World*. Portland, OR, Oni Press, 2005.

———. *Scott Pilgrim, Vol. 3: Scott Pilgrim and the Infinite Sadness*. Portland, OR, Oni Press, 2006.

———. *Scott Pilgrim, Vol. 4: Scott Pilgrim Gets It Together*. Portland, OR, Oni Press, 2007.

———. *Scott Pilgrim, Vol. 5: Scott Pilgrim vs. the Universe*. Portland, OR, Oni Press, 2009.

———. *Scott Pilgrim, Vol. 6: Scott Pilgrim's Finest Hour*. Portland, OR, Oni Press, 2010.

Oswald, Patton. "Wake Up, Geek Culture. Time to Die." *Wired*, 27 December 2010, http://www.wired.com/2010/12/ff_angrynerd_geekculture/.

Pattern, Fred. *Watching Anime, Reading Manga: 25 Years of Essays and Reviews*. Albany, CA, Stone Bridge Press, 2004.

Peterson, Robert S. "The Acoustics of Manga." *A Comic Studies Reader*, edited by Jeet Heer and Kent Worcester, Jackson, University Press of Mississippi, 2009, pp. 163–171.

Routt, William D. "Textual Criticism in the Study of Film." *Screening the Past*, 7 July 1997, http://edu.au/humanities/screeningthepast/firstrelease/firjul/wdr.html.

Sava, Oliver. "Bryan Lee O'Malley Walks through the Newly Colored *Scott Pilgrim* Series." *The A.V. Club*, 28 April 2015, http://www.avclub.com/article/bryan-lee -omalley-walks-through-newly-colored-scot-218613.

"Social Feed." *Bitch Planet* tumblr, bitchpla.net, ongoing.

Stam, Robert. "Beyond Fidelity: The Dialogics of Adaptation." *Film Adaptation*, edited by James Naremore, New Brunswick, NJ, Rutgers University Press, 2000, pp. 54–78.

Vice, Sue. "'It's About Time': The Chronotope of the Holocaust in Art Spiegelman's *Maus*." *The Graphic Novel*, edited by Jan Baetens, Leuven, Belgium, Leuven University Press, 2001, pp. 47–60.

Wright, Edgar, Michael Bacall, and Brian Lee O'Malley. "Commentaries." DVD, disc 2. *Scott Pilgrim vs. the World*, directed by Edgar Wright, Universal Studios, 2010.

Wright, Edgar, and Bill Pope. "Commentaries." DVD, disc 2. *Scott Pilgrim vs. the World*, directed by Edgar Wright, Universal Studios, 2010.

Zhou, Tony. "Edgar Wright — How to Do Visual Comedy." *YouTube*, uploaded by Every Frame a Painting, 26 May 2014, https://youtu.be/3FOzD4Sfgag.

Transmedia Adaptation and Writing in the Margins: A Graphic Expansion of George Romero's *Night of the Living Dead*

AVIVA BRIEFEL

"Genre," Christine Gledhill writes, "is first and foremost a boundary phenomenon. Like cartographers, early genre critics sought to define fictional territories and the borders which divided, for example, western from gangster film, thriller from horror film, romantic comedy from the musical" (221). In this chapter, I will take the notion of "boundary phenomenon" literally, as a description of the process through which one genre, comics, draws from the boundaries of another, the horror film. Double Take's compilation *Ultimate Night of the Living Dead* (2015–) is a multivolume exploration of what happens, or might have happened, at the margins of George Romero's 1968 landmark film. The graphic collection takes on a spatial approach to adaptation, which consists of pushing through the boundaries established by the cinematic text and exploding its aesthetics of containment. In doing so, *Ultimate* transforms *Night of the Living Dead* from a narrative that visibly seeks to police its margins into a multidirectional network based on extension and permeability.

This spatial approach to expanding horror, I want to suggest, functions as a strategic way of at once demonstrating and enacting the political reach of the horror genre. By now, critical studies of horror take its subversive potential as a given — it is a mode that has the potential to destabilize social norms through its aesthetics of shock and violence. As Laura Frost writes, "We expect horror to play the role of provocateur: the genre that will go where no genre has gone before, however taboo" (16). But what is less apparent, perhaps, is how horror's provocations are disseminated throughout culture and how their meanings are received and renegotiated. By opening up the inaccessible spaces of Romero's film, *Ultimate Night of the Living Dead* provides a vivid object lesson in the transmissions and re-creations that horror can put into action.

Networks of Horror

Night of the Living Dead, released by the Walter Reade Organization in 1968, has a deceptively simple plot: a group of humans tries to survive a zombie attack and ultimately fails. The film begins with a brother and sister, Johnny (Russell Streiner) and Barbra (Judith O'Dea), who travel to a graveyard in the Pennsylvania countryside to pay their respects to their deceased father and are soon attacked by a lone "ghoul" (the term used for zombies in the film). Johnny is killed, while Barbra escapes and runs to an abandoned farmhouse, where she encounters Ben (Duane Jones), an African American man who has just escaped from a major ghoul attack himself. As Barbra withdraws into a catatonic state of shock, Ben reinforces the house against the horde of zombies congregating outside of it. The two living characters soon find that the house is occupied by other humans, who have been hiding out in the basement: a middle-aged married couple, Harry and Helen Cooper (Karl Hardman and Marilyn Eastman), with their young daughter (Kyra Schon), who has been injured by a zombie; and a teenage couple, Tom and Judy (Keith Wayne and Judith Ridley). The humans struggle to survive, all the while listening to radio and television reports that provide conflicting accounts on why the dead are coming back to life and eating the living. The film ends tragically: Tom and Judy are consumed by zombies following a failed escape; Harry Cooper is devoured by his now zombified daughter, who then stabs her mother with a garden trowel; Barbra is dragged away by an undead Johnny; and Ben, who has survived the night, is shot the next morning by a roaming militia that (supposedly) mistakes him for a zombie.

The film has had an impressive afterlife, generating myriad remakes, adaptations, and reimaginings; as Ben Hervey writes, "*Night*, even more than most films, is what it has become" (25).[1] Launched in September 2015, Double Take's *Ultimate Night of the Living Dead* is the most recent project to undertake an extensive rewriting of the film. The collection consists of ten-volume explorations, created by several comic artists, of the world imagined by Romero. Each volume in the series focuses on a section of the terrain presented or suggested by the film and magnifies it into its own narrative. Some of the volumes take up characters and situations introduced in *Night*—*Rise*, for example, centers on what happens to Johnny when he is separated from Barbra at the beginning of the film, while *Soul* follows Ben's experiences beyond the film's final frames. Other volumes introduce new characters and situations, all of which are located on the outskirts of Romero's diegetic world, ranging from the events at a local supermarket in *Dedication* to the crisis at a nearby hospital in *Medic*. While each volume presents its own discrete narrative, it connects to the others through related events, characters, and places. Every few months, a new installment of ten volumes comes out both in print and digitally, continuing each story. At the time of my writing this chapter, three installments have appeared, and I will focus on these while recognizing that the comics' narratives are ongoing.

By extending the world of Romero's film in multiple directions, *Ultimate* functions as a network, which Caroline Levine describes through its capacity for "unending expansion: once there is a link between two nodes, there is a network, and it can grow simply by linking to new nodes. Thus, the network form affords a certain infinite extensiveness" (117). This structure is apparent both in the serial nature of the project—ten narratives evolving and intersecting for an undetermined number of installments— and in the map that accompanies each print issue. The map represents an intersection of roads, streets, and institutions (the church, the university, the hospital), each of which becomes associated with a particular narrative and set of characters. In turn, the reader can imagine further intersections between the various nodes as characters travel from one location to another—starting off at the cemetery on Main Street, for example, Barbra and Johnny eventually gravitate to the hospital on Franklin Road. As in the film, media information plays a central role in each story, as televisual images and radio broadcasts pervade different spaces with information (or a lack thereof) about the zombie outbreak. Doctor Grimes, who also appears on television in the film version, emerges in various installments, both as an image broadcast on multiple screens and as a character in his own right. One of the narrative strains, *Remote*, underscores the importance of the media as a crucial network node by following the struggles of Samantha Stanton, a radio reporter who must continue the broadcast despite her being the last remaining survivor at her station. Reading each issue thus becomes a matter of following a single narrative and determining its manifold connections to the others.

With its multidirectional wanderings, *Ultimate* takes on the spatial logic of zombies in their resistance to the specificity of place. As Hugh S. Manon writes, "Compared to a ghost, which typically inhabits a highly particularized locale, zombies roam widely. They are tied not to a spectral home base— a certain room in an old hotel or a specific burial site—but instead occupy a particular area or range. The appearance of zombies at a given locale can only ever be incidental, the result of them having traversed a field of adjacent spaces" (323–324). In the film and the comic collection, zombies are consummate wanderers; we see them trudging slowly from one location to another and violating diegetic and formal barriers as they burst through walls

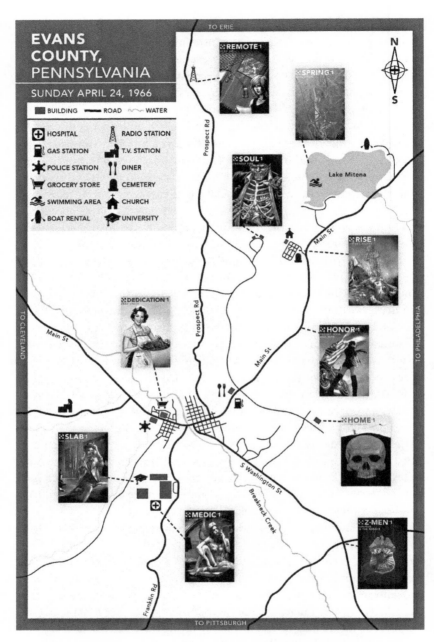

Literally mapping story lines in Double Take's *Ultimate Night of the Living Dead* (2015).

and frames. The cemetery scene at the beginning of Romero's film emphasizes the zombies' rupturing of spatial and aesthetic boundaries. As Johnny
teases Barbra about her childish fear of the cemetery, a mere detail of a figure
appears in the background, which after a brief sequence of shots looms large
in the foreground as an attacking ghoul. What this emergence from margins
to center represents, according to James McFarland, is an enactment of a
struggle for visibility and presence played out at the level of form: the zombie as "stain stands for an insistent aspect of the object that otherwise could
not achieve representation" (49). The rest of the film plays out the aftermath
of this struggle, as these undead "stains" proliferate and mark their refusal
to stay off-screen. By repeatedly magnifying details from the original film
and bursting into places where *Night* refused to venture, *Ultimate* adopts the
zombie as a formal strategy for opening up narrative space.

The comic assertively sets itself up against the aesthetics of enclosure that
mark Romero's film. Despite — or because of — its narrativization of zombies
as frontier-defying creatures, *Night* opts for a structural logic of claustrophobia. This aesthetic is apparent in the first few images of the film, which show
an extreme long shot of the car taking Johnny and Barbra to the cemetery.
Whereas Ben Hervey compares the "almost agoraphobic" scene of the beginning to the claustrophobia of the ending (30), in which Ben is confined
to the basement, I would argue that the film makes us aware of our entrapment in the meticulous suturing of one part of the road to the next that
makes up the credit sequence. The road in the first several shots extends
from one part of the frame to the other, signaling a potential for extensive
wandering that is counteracted with a cut on motion to the rest of the road
in the next frame. The suturing together of the road scenes marks a sharp
contrast to the maps of the comic series, whose roads extend outward in
multiple directions.

The ensuing scenes in the farmhouse, which initially represents a space
of refuge and ultimately a death trap for the characters, heighten this sense
of confinement. With the exception of relatively short views of the fields
outside the house, and of the spaces shown on the television, this is where
we spend the majority of the film. The sense of isolation and entrapment is
expressed cinematically, as the film frame becomes conflated with the im-
prisoning house itself. Much of *Night* shows Ben, sometimes accompanied
by other characters, nailing boards to doors and windows, scenes that are
shot through a tight framing that foregrounds what Stephen Heath terms
the cinematic "constraint of the rectangle" (391). The labor that the characters put into keeping the zombie world outside of the house exaggerates the
film's "constant welding together" of "screen and frame, ground and back-

Roads to nowhere? Editing in *Night of the Living Dead* (1968) counteracts the notion that roads offer escape.

ground, surface and depth" (Heath 397), this time with the intent of creating an insular world.

The formal confinement of the road and house scenes has several visual counterparts throughout the film, which enact its aesthetics of enclosure on a micro level. At various points, the mise-en-scène reveals a horizontal structure, a possible extension outward, blocked on either side by another structure. Aside from various images of lateral boards interrupted by vertical ones or doorframes, this configuration is apparent in shots of Barbra lying catatonically on the couch with a lamp and armrest or another character framing her, the Coopers' daughter lying on a table in the basement bookended by her mother and her mother's handbag, and the memorable image of the television propped on and framed by two chairs. These shots at once reinforce the importance of the horizontal axis in a film that is about roaming zombies attempting to cross the barrier from the outside to the inside, while establishing the limits of that horizontality—it inevitably comes up against a buffer, be it the side of a frame or the wall of a house. These restraints are particularly tangible in the shots of the television on the chairs, as the broadcasts represent our only visual connection to the outside world and themselves signal an altogether different spatiotemporality. As Vivian Sobchack observes, "Although the entire action of the film only occurs one night from dusk to dawn and over a small localized geographic area, the exterior news scenes on the telecasts seem shot in daylight while the action we watch at the farmhouse occurs in darkest night" (189). By repeatedly returning to the shot of the two chairs framing and restraining the television set, Romero emphasizes that the televisual bears no more possibility of liberation than the barred windows and doors of the home.[2]

The film's aesthetics of confinement stand in marked contrast to its evergenerating afterlife of remakes and critical interpretations. The latter in particular rupture its confined horizontalities through the metonymic slide of meanings that critics have assigned to the film. They have discussed *Night of the Living Dead* as a narrative about racial inequality and violence, an allegory for the Vietnam War (see especially Higashi; Randell), a meditation on hippie culture (Becker), and a representation of environmental apocalypse (Soles), to list only a few examples. At least early on, Romero was famously resistant to the political implications of casting an African American actor in the male lead, stating, "It was an accident. The whole movie was an accident" (qtd. in Hervey 24). Nonetheless, the scenes of an African American

"This just in": there is no escape in *Night of the Living Dead*, where even the television screen is constrained by the chairs on either side.

male striking a white woman, as Ben does in response to Barbra's panic early on, and of a white militia shooting and then incinerating Ben on a pyre, are unavoidably evocative of American racial fears and realities. For Adam Lowenstein, the final sequence, with its grainy images of the militia disposing of Ben's body, presents "inescapable connotations" of racial violence; the "message" is "instantly readable" (159, 160). Lowenstein compares this ending to other horror and science fiction films, which demand more active interpretive work from their audiences to make connections to contemporary or historical traumas.

There is yet another aspect of *Night* that opposes its aesthetics of enclosure: its own referentiality. In Kyle Bishop's words, it presents a prime example of "assemblage filmmaking" through its compilation of multiple narratives and sources, including Robert Matheson's novel *I Am Legend* (1954), Jack Finney's novel *The Body Snatchers* (1955), Daphne du Maurier's story "The Birds" (1952), and Alfred Hitchcock's cinematic adaptation of this story (1963) (271).[3] *Night* also draws extensively from EC and DC comics, with their graphic depictions of violence, outlandish plots, and general irreverence (Hervey 106; T. Williams 10). The fact that *Ultimate* returns the film to the comic tradition represents yet another aspect of its attempts to position the original as part of a larger textual network, by enacting the logic of exchange that defines zombies. As Steven Shaviro contends, the very structures of contagion and spectatorship contained by the zombie genre provokes lateral chains of associations: "A chain of mimetic transference moves from the zombies, to the man who dies and returns as a zombie, to the other man who watches him die and return, to the audience fascinated by the whole spectacle" (Shaviro 97).

Ultimate uses the associative and wandering logic of zombies to break through the artificial boundaries of Romero's film. It challenges the aesthetic insularity of *Night* by transporting readers into the film's margins and off-screen spaces. So, for instance, in *Home* we spend time in Beekman's Diner, a location that is only briefly mentioned in the cinematic Ben's account to Barbra of his having escaped a zombie attack. In *Spring*, we visit the lake where Tom and Judy were most likely setting off to swim before the ghouls drove them to the house, and in *Medic* we witness the graphic reanimation of the amputated corpse described by Doctor Grimes in a television interview. In all of these cases, and in many others, the series grants a fleshed-out, full-color image of what was merely referenced verbally in the black-and-white film, thereby suggesting a usurpation of the visuality of cinema by comics. This sense of a takeover is especially tangible in the digital version of the comics, in which the reader can animate images by clicking from one frame to the next, a mode of visual control from which traditional film spectators are exempt. As Paul Gravett writes, "The interactivity and multi-modality of digital comics have led to the notion of the reader not only having control of the reading experience of a comic, but also having a choice of more than one path to follow" (128). Readerly choice—of the order in which to read the comics, of whether to encounter them digitally or on paper, of which narrative to prioritize over another—is essential to *Ultimate*'s reconfiguration of *Night*.

The comic takeover of the film narrative involves a careful balance of homage to the original with a broadening of its parameters. In the words of one of the comic's writers, Jeff McComsey, the process of adaptation entailed using the film "as a kind of Rosetta stone for ideas" (qtd. in Crump). The reader can experience the joyful sense of being able to revisit a beloved original in every blowing up of a detail mentioned by the film or reenactment of a scene from a different angle. At the same time, the series acknowledges that absolute repetition is impossible, that exploring the margins so carefully blocked by the film involves a radical transformation of the narrative. To create a network of nodes out of *Night* is to venture into hypothetical space, a "what if?" mode that must alter the narrative as a whole. This idea is enacted in the first installment of *Rise*, "Sister's Keeper," which reimagines Barbra and Johnny's on-screen relationship.

The beginning of this installment is almost identical to the opening of the film, as the siblings visit their father's grave, exchange teasing banter, and are then attacked by a zombie that had been wandering in the background. As in the film, the zombie pushes Johnny into a gravestone, while Barbra escapes. But whereas in *Night* Johnny ultimately returns as a ghoul and drags his sister away, here the comic transitions from Barbra's discovery of the house to the graveyard, where Johnny opens distinctly human eyes—he has not been killed after all. In the next several frames, we return to familiar landmarks, including the siblings' abandoned car and the farmhouse, but this time from his point of view. Thus, from an altogether new perspective, we glimpse the burning truck where Tom and Judy had perished in attempting to get gas and flee to a safety station, the zombies eating the couple's body parts, and the doors and windows of the farmhouse that the zombies are trying to break through. The corresponding scene in the film ruptures the insularity that the characters (and the narrative as a whole) had so carefully maintained: the outside is coming in. By showing the same scene from the outside, this time through Johnny's sentient gaze, the comic offers a palliative to *Night*'s anxiety about breaking borders. As Barbra repeats the same terrified screams on seeing her brother as she does in the film—"Johnny . . .

no!"—his reassuring gaze, legible to us alone, shows that another story is about to take place. He pulls his sister into the margins that the film closes from us and transforms the story from one of fratricide into fraternal survival as Barbra and Johnny band together to combat zombies. In a gentle jab at the original, she hugs her brother and remarks, "They said you were dead," to which he responds, "Who said that?" The hypothetical and expansive space of the margins claims the authority to rewrite what came before.

Ultimate's extension of the boundaries of *Night* is politically charged. References to racial identity and struggle, as well as to racism, are scattered throughout the series, suggesting that the zombie outbreak is inseparable from the political and social climate of late-1960s America, when the film and comic take place, as well as to contemporary readers' own fraught racial environment almost five decades later. In "Dead Air," the first issue of *Remote*, for instance, the radio station delivers an update on race riots, communicating that "an uneasy calm has settled over the predominantly Negro community of Watts in Los Angeles. Policemen armed with shotguns patrol the streets, trying to prevent any outburst of rioting." In the first issue of *Z-Men*, which centers on the Secret Service in light of the zombie outbreak, President Lyndon Johnson comments that the reports coming from Pennsylvania are probably the result of "black militants stirring up some shit." This climate of racial tension is populated by additional African American characters who take on central roles in the intersecting narratives, thus expanding the realm of racial representation of Romero's film, in which Ben is the only identifiably black character depicted on screen. With its multiple representations of racial identity and racism, *Ultimate* undermines the idea that race in the film is only an "accident" of casting. Even if the casting itself was the result of circumstances, its implications are far-reaching.

The first installment of *Soul*—ironically titled "Friendly Fire"—brings the issue of race and interpretation to the foreground with its retelling of Ben's story. Like *Rise*, which centers on Johnny and Barbra, this series initially establishes its fidelity to the film, only then to take a very different path. The issue begins with Sheriff McClelland (resembling the film character, played by George Kosana) and his militia killing zombies in the fields outside the house where Ben has survived the night. After spotting him in the window, the sheriff gives one of his men the order to "hit him in the head. Right between the eyes," which he does. The moment is rapidly followed by a view of the black-and-white television (still propped on two chairs) in the living room, in which a reporter questions McClelland about how he identifies ghouls before shooting them: "For example, the man in the house, the one you just had Deputy Vincent shoot. He was pretty far away. How do you know he was a ghoul?" to which the sheriff responds, "The way I got it figured, pretty much everybody in this vicinity is contaminated." This televised exchange verbalizes the question that many viewers find to be silently encoded in the film: did McClelland mistake Ben for a zombie, or did he spot a black male and decide that it didn't matter *who* he was? A few frames later, the comic's expansive perspective shows a reporter in the newsroom advising his on-site coworker, "Watch yourself out there, Bill. These rednecks will shoot anything but what they're aiming at," followed by a frame of a man—who turns out to be President Johnson—looking at the events on a stack of television screens and saying, "Christ Almighty. They just shot an unarmed black man on national television." By enlarging the frame around Ben, *Ultimate* urges us to think about context rather than viewing the character's death as an isolated and accidental (in terms of shooting or casting) incident.

But it turns out that Ben is not dead. Like Johnny, he survives the event that was supposed to finish him off. After a series of frames that show what Ben *would* have been subjected to had he died—being dragged by a meat hook onto a burning pyre—we see him open his eyes and yell, "I'm alive in here!" McClelland hears him and tells his men to hold their fire, an order that initially invites us to challenge the sheriff's alleged racism—maybe he was truly unaware of the fact that Ben was a living human. Once again, however, by expanding the frame of the text both formally and narratively, the comic compels us to understand situations in a broader context: whether the shooting was accidental or not, both Ben and McClelland are trapped within the racist framework of late-1960s America. After his initial relief at Ben's survival, the sheriff begins to ask him increasingly probing questions about his actions during the zombie attack that betray his suspicion of the character. When Ben tells him about the truck he used to escape from Beekman's Diner, McClelland responds probingly, "So you stole it?" and interrogates him about the deaths of the various characters in the farmhouse. By the third installment of *Soul*, McClelland decides to arrest Ben, stating all the while, "Not that I don't trust you or anything," and leads him out in handcuffs. Racism emerges here in a different form—not as a violent lynching but as a more mundane example of the relentlessness of racial profiling, a theme that resonates strongly in early twenty-first-century America.

The focus on off-screen spaces and events also grants Ben an agency that surpasses his role in the film. As he tells his story to the increasingly suspicious McClelland, we see familiar events from *his* perspective. For instance, whereas in the film Ben first appears from Barbra's point of view, as a startling presence that emerges from the outside world, here we witness his slow approach to the farmhouse from his gaze, which reveals his driving hands and cracked windshield. When he describes boarding up the house, we also see the scene from his perspective, revealing only his hands and the objects he handles. Although the film does allow us glimpses into Ben's viewpoint, the comic makes it impossible for us to forget that we are viewing the world and events through his eyes. Strikingly, its re-presentation of events also suggests that his agency is pronounced when most of his body occupies off-screen space, and only his hands are visible to him and to us. This strategy demonstrates yet another way in which the comic series highlights the political and aesthetic implications of its own mode of "marginal" storytelling. Reaching out into the borders of the original allows for a productive exploration of its subtexts, ones that will inevitably generate narratives of their own.

Conclusion

The generative logic of *Ultimate Night of the Living Dead* attests to the productive possibilities of adaptations as aesthetic and critical fields of inquiry. By taking its readers through hypothetical journeys into the margins of Romero's text, the comic collection demonstrates that playing with *form* can have a radical effect on our understanding, and interpretation, of content. In an essay for *Film Quarterly*, Evan Calder Williams writes that we might pay closer attention to how the horror genre plays with form in politically significant ways: "There are forms, techniques, details, and affects that threaten to throw off their role as backdrop. Does this always happen? Of course not. It is a flickering prospect that runs through the genre. . . . It is this horror, that of the secondary material that refuses to quit the scene or do its job, that deserves to be defended and elaborated" (E. Williams 33). Rather than infringing on *Night of the Living Dead*'s territory, *Ultimate Night of the Living Dead* positions itself as a companion text that works jointly with the original to call forth the powerful, but often evasive, monsters wandering at the margins of horror narratives. Double Take's important collection attests to how other media, in this case comics, can venture into the horror film to draw out this secondary material by mapping out spaces beyond the film frame. Given the political climate in which the series was created, culminating in the presidential election of Donald Trump, we need to take this intervention seriously. It outlines an example for how horror can generate vibrant and far-reaching political networks that, through its aesthetics of shock and protest, can begin to map our shadowy path to the future.

Notes

1. It bears repeating that the figure of the zombie did not originate with this film but extends as far back as west central Africa in the seventeenth century (Lauro 16); as Sarah Lauro explains regarding the tendency to assign Romero with credit for having "discovered" the zombie, "Romero is to the zombie what Columbus is to America" (97).

2. As several critics have observed, this is in part due to the conflicting and illogical nature of the news and advice afforded by the broadcasts. Sobchack writes, "In a deadly quiet and parodic reversal of radio and TV appearances in traditional SF films, the radio and TV in this film demonstrate a total lack of connection with the characters in peril" (188).

3. For Barbara Bruce, the film also enters into intertextual dialogue with Sidney Poitier's oeuvre, including—of course—*Guess Who's Coming to Dinner* (1967).

Works Cited

Becker, Matt. "A Point of Little Hope: Hippie Horror Films and the Politics of Ambivalence." *Velvet Light Trap*, no. 57, Spring 2006, pp. 42–59.

Bishop, Kyle. "Assemblage Filmmaking: Approaching the Multi-Source Adaptation and Reexamining George Romero's *Night of the Living Dead*." *Adaptation Studies: New Approaches*, edited by Christa Albrecht-Crane and Dennis Cutchins, Madison, NJ, Fairleigh Dickinson University Press, 2010, pp. 263–277.

Bruce, Barbara S. "Guess Who's Going to Be Dinner: Sidney Poitier, Black Militancy, and the Ambivalence of Race in Romero's *Night of the Living Dead*." *Race, Oppression and the Zombie: Essays on Cross-Cultural Appropriations of the Caribbean Tradition*, edited by Christopher M. Moreman and Cory James Rushton, Jefferson, NC, McFarland, 2011, pp. 60–73.

Crump, Andy. "Jeff McComsey Talks *Ultimate Night of the Living Dead* & the Zombie Genre." *Screen Rant*, 18 September 2015, https://screenrant.com/jesse-mccomsey -ultimate-night-living-dead-interview/.

Frost, Laura. "Black Screens, Lost Bodies: The Cinematic Apparatus of 9/11 Horror." *Horror after 9/11: World of Fear, Cinema of Terror*, edited by Aviva Briefel and Sam J. Miller, Austin, University of Texas Press, 2011, pp. 13–39.

Gledhill, Christine. "Rethinking Genre." *Reinventing Film Studies*, edited by Christine Gledhill and Linda Williams, New York, Oxford University Press, 2000, pp. 221–243.

Gravett, Paul. *Comics Art*. New Haven, CT, Yale University Press, 2013.

Heath, Stephen. "Narrative Space." *Narrative, Apparatus, Ideology: A Film Theory Reader*, edited by Philip Rosen, New York, Columbia University Press, 1986, pp. 379–420.

Hervey, Ben. *Night of the Living Dead*. New York, Palgrave Macmillan, 2008.

Higashi, Sumiko. "*Night of the Living Dead*: A Horror Film about the Horrors of the Vietnam Era." *From Hanoi to Hollywood: The Vietnam War in American Film*, edited by Linda Dittmar and Gene Michaud, New Brunswick, NJ, Rutgers University Press, 1990, pp. 175–188.

Lauro, Sarah. *The Transatlantic Zombie: Slavery, Rebellion, and Living Death*. New Brunswick, NJ, Rutgers University Press, 2015.

Levine, Caroline. *Forms: Whole, Rhythm, Hierarchy, Network*. Princeton, NJ, Princeton University Press, 2015.

Lowenstein, Adam. *Shocking Representation: Historical Trauma, National Cinema, and the Modern Horror Film*. New York, Columbia University Press, 2005.

Manon, Hugh S. "Living Dead Spaces: The Desire for the Local in the Films of George Romero." *Taking Place: Location and the Moving Image*, edited by John David Rhodes and Elena Gorfinkel, Minneapolis, University of Minnesota Press, 2011, pp. 317–337.

McFarland, James. "Philosophy of the Living Dead: At the Origin of the Zombie-Image." *Cultural Critique*, no. 90, Spring 2015, pp. 22–63.

Night of the Living Dead. Directed by George Romero, Image Ten, 1968.

Randell, Karen. "Lost Bodies / Lost Souls: *Night of the Living Dead* and *Deathdream* as Vietnam Narratives." *Generation Zombie: Essays on the Living Dead in Modern Culture*, edited by Stephanie Boluk and Wylie Lenz, Jefferson, NC, McFarland, 2011, pp. 67–76.

Shaviro, Steven. *The Cinematic Body*. Minneapolis, University of Minnesota Press, 1993.

Sobchack, Vivian. *Screening Space: The American Science Fiction Film*. 2nd ed., New York, Ungar, 1988.

Soles, Carter. "'And No Birds Sing': Discourses of Environmental Apocalypse in *The Birds* and *Night of the Living Dead*." *Interdisciplinary Studies in Literature and Environment*, vol. 21, no. 3, Summer 2014, pp. 526–537.

Ultimate Night of the Living Dead. Various authors, Double Take, 2015–present.

Williams, Evan Calder. "Sunset with Chainsaw." *Film Quarterly*, vol. 64, no. 4, Summer 2011, pp. 28–33.

Williams, Tony, editor. *George A. Romero: Interviews*. Jackson, University Press of Mississippi, 2011.

Agency and Intertextuality: *Tank Girl*, Subcultural Aesthetics, and the Strong Female Protagonist

SCOTT HENDERSON

While it is not unexpected that much focus in discussions of comic-to-film adaptation is placed on visual elements, given the graphic nature of both formats, there remains a need to consider the intertextual, or transmedia, engagement that film and comics can have with other forms of popular culture media. Readers of comics are also viewers of film, and vice versa, and both are inevitably consumers of other popular media. Additionally, characters within comic and film narratives are often portrayed engaging with various forms of "real world" popular culture. The verisimilitude of filmic worlds often relies on real-world points of reference, whether it is via product placement or fictional characters encountering real-world celebrities, all serving to make the fictional world more plausible. Comic books have included the absurdity of Batman and Robin meeting the Beatles while attempting to solve the "Paul is dead" mystery (in *Batman* #222, June 1970) or Kiss appearing in Marvel's *Howard the Duck* (issue #12, May 1977). These fictional encounters with nonfictional people and events blur the lines between story world and the everyday life of readers. These transgressions also rely on the assumed cultural knowledge of the audience, whose own cultural capital is verified and rewarded, enriching their reading or viewing experience and allowing them potentially greater engagement with the text.

It is the nature of this external engagement, and the manner in which cultural references bring additional meaning to texts that are no longer self-contained, that is the focus of this chapter. In particular, the primary concern here is with the influence of popular music and popular music culture on both comic books as well as corresponding film adaptations, with particular attention given to the ways in which these references have informed the representation of strong female protagonists. Three comic books will be considered, all of which first appeared in what would best be defined musically as a post-punk era, and all of which engage directly with that genre of music both stylistically and narratively. *Love and Rockets*, the earliest example here, first appeared in 1981, when the Hernandez brothers—Gilbert, Jaime, and Mario—self-published the first issue. The comic was among the first of the so-called alternative comics movement of the 1980s and traced the lives of groups of intersecting Latina/o characters in a fictional Central American town named Palomar as well as in Los Angeles. *The Ballad of Halo Jones* was a series that appeared in the weekly British comic *2000 AD* and that focused on three different decades in the life of its titular hero, detailing her transformation from bored teenager to space soldier. *Halo Jones* extended over three "books," each appearing in installments in *2000 AD* between 1984 and 1986. It was written by noted comic book author Alan Moore, with illustrations by Ian Gibson, who is noted for his contributions to another *2000 AD* series, *Judge Dredd*. The last of the three, and the only one to have thus far been adapted into a film, is *Tank Girl*, created by Jamie Hewlett and Alan Martin and first appearing in UK alternative comics weekly *Deadline*, actually debuting in that publication's first edition in 1988. *Tank Girl* follows the story of its eponymous hero, so named for the tank she drives and also uses as a home. While her real name is Rebecca, her Tank Girl moniker is the name most frequently used in her series of adventures across a post-apocalyptic Australian landscape. The comic is filled with cultural touchstones, primarily of British culture, despite its setting, with references to popular music frequently included.

The significant role played by the soundtrack in Rachel Talalay's 1995 feature film *Tank Girl*, as well as aesthetic references to elements of music culture, particularly what would best be described as a punk aesthetic, is central to the development of the film's main character, and is illustrative of the ways in which not only *Tank Girl* but all three of these comics are able to employ transmedia elements as a crucial part of meaning making. While neither *Love and Rockets* nor *The Ballad of Halo Jones* has (yet) been adapted for cinema, each comic successfully adapts elements and references from popular music culture in creating its narrative worlds and developing its characters. Like *Tank Girl*, it is the representation of resilient women protagonists that is strongly influenced by the ideologies and styles of the adapted post-punk and punk music references.

Love and Rockets and *The Ballad of Halo Jones* are illustrative of the emergence of strong women characters within independent comics. Despite both titles, as well as *Tank Girl*, being created by male artists, there is a conscious effort in each to reframe how women are to be represented in comics. This is an issue addressed directly by Alan Moore in his postscript to the Titan Books collection of the chapters comprising Book One of *Halo Jones*:

References to punk style shape Alan Moore's strong female protagonist in *The Ballad of Halo Jones* (1984).

I didn't want to write about a pretty scatterbrain who fainted a lot and had trouble keeping her clothes on. I similarly had no inclination to unleash yet another Tough Bitch With A Disintegrator And An Extra 'Y' Chromosome upon the world. What I wanted was simply an ordinary woman such as you might find standing in front of you while queuing for the check-out at Tesco's, but transposed to the sort of future environment that seemed a prerequisite of what was, after all, a boy's science fiction comic. Hence, *The Ballad of Halo Jones*. (Moore 59)

As Maggie Gray has pointed out, Moore had previously indicated dissatisfaction with the portrayal of women in comic books in a three-part article he had written in 1983 entitled "Invisible Girls and Phantom Ladies." The article was published in Marvel UK's *The Daredevils*, and, as Gray notes, "it comprised a detailed overview of the portrayal of women in both American and British comics, as well as sections on bondage imagery, hentai manga, women creators (particularly from the 70s underground) and the role of women in the comics industry." *Love and Rockets* also foregrounds stories featuring women protagonists. The comic itself is divided into two broader story worlds, each offering the authorial vision of one of two Hernandez brothers, Jaime and Gilbert (a third brother, Mario, has been an occasional contributor). Jaime's focus is on the world of Huerta/Hoppers, a fictionalized community in Southern California, while Gilbert's focus is Palomar, a fictional Latin American village. The latter's story lines are imbued with a strong sense of magic realism, and the main character is Luba, a sexually energetic woman who eventually becomes mayor of Palomar. Jaime's stories focus on a group of Latina/o youths. As Jonathan Risner describes it, the story line "often revolves around the intermittent romance between Margarita Luisa 'Maggie' Chascarillo and Esperanza 'Hopey' Leticia Glass and largely foregoes superhero crusades, even sometimes playfully parodying the genre" (39). Maggie's job at the beginning of the series is as a "pro-solar mechanic," and she often travels the world repairing spaceships (effectively the "rockets" in *Love and Rockets*). Yet the narrative is rarely concerned with the rockets themselves or the men who fly them, who are portrayed as either ineffectual or as objects of Maggie's affection (and sometimes both), and instead focuses far more on the daily activities, relationships, and anxieties of Maggie and her friends.

Both *The Ballad of Halo Jones* and *Love and Rockets* foreground the ordinariness of their main characters and their encounters with the everyday in their respective worlds. For Halo, it is initially life in the Hoop, which is essentially a ghetto floating in the Atlantic Ocean off the coast of a future

Manhattan. Home to a largely unemployed populace, it is a place threatened by rebellion and rocked by ocean waves. Rather than focus on the uprisings, or the environment, or even an explanation of this future world, Book One instead concentrates on a day in the life of Halo and her friends, with the main activity being a routine shopping expedition. This everyday-life activity allows Moore and Gibson to introduce readers to the main characters, their relationships, and their environment, but without foregrounding the action and adventure scenarios of mainstream comic books. In his postscript in Book One, Moore addresses the disappointment felt by some readers, suggesting "there were those readers who complained that very little happened in the strip. Personally, I think what they actually meant was that very little *violence* happened in the strip" (Moore 59). Halo also ages as the series develops. Unlike most comic book heroes, who remain ageless while the world around them is updated with every reboot, Halo's age is updated in each successive book. Moore had originally planned nine books, taking Halo into her nineties, but only three were produced before he had a falling out with the publishers. The three take Halo from her teens in Book One to her thirties in Book Three. While the action does steadily increase, first as Halo joins a space crew as a stewardess and finally as she becomes a soldier fighting in a distant war, the emphasis is less on action and more on effect. Book Three begins with an unemployed Halo reluctantly being recruited into the army and then follows her through basic training and into battle. While there are prolonged sections that offer battle action, much more of the book addresses the psychological effects that war has on Halo, again subverting the expectations of action-based comic books.

Love and Rockets also allows its characters to age, tracing the relationship between Maggie and Hopey from their teenage years into middle age. One story line, "Wigwam Bam," addresses Hopey's realization that she may be becoming too old for a punk rock lifestyle. In addition to aging, the characters also struggle with everyday issues. Maggie, for example, is portrayed as being concerned with her fluctuating weight and changing body as she ages, while multiple characters are portrayed as reflecting on their youth as they get older. Also, the series employs many flashbacks depicting characters at various ages of their lives. None of this is marked by gendered stereotypes but rather is portrayed with realism. Maggie's concerns about her body image are not offered up as an indication of any gendered focus on the body, but rather as an individual's insights into the effect that aging has on all bodies. As the "Locas" stories of Jaime progressed, the series moved away from Maggie's role as a mechanic and instead focused on her personal life, as well as made occasional forays that developed stories of some of the series' minor characters. While the comic is punctuated with moments of personal drama, it avoids the expectations of action that are the purview of most mainstream comics.

While the post-apocalyptic landscape and its many challenges and threats prevent *Tank Girl* from focusing solely on the ordinariness of its protagonist's life, it is not all that dissimilar to its predecessors. This is more acutely true of the comic book, whereas the film adaptation is more concerned with larger-scale action. While the notion of a woman driving a tank through the post-apocalyptic Australian outback suggests that *Tank Girl* would be focused on action, much of that is displaced in the comic books through the protagonist's focus on her own pleasures, including sex, partying, and drinking. Many of the early adventures of Tank Girl involve encounters that disrupt her personal life. While she does undertake missions for an unnamed clandestine organization, Tank Girl is eventually fired from this role due to her tendencies to pursue her own baser pleasures rather than the mission at hand. Again, as with *The Ballad of Halo Jones* and *Love and Rockets*, typical comic action serves as a distraction from a focus on everyday life and desires. In the case of Tank Girl, her agency is much more prominent, while her day-to-day life does tend to have more moments of action. Similar to *The Ballad of Halo Jones*, the world into which the viewer is plunged in *Tank Girl* is an uncertain one, with readers immediately dropped into the world with no means of orientation and therefore left to figure things out on their own. Familiar cultural cues, such as *Tank Girl*'s aesthetic style, references to popular culture, and the use of new bulletins and other references, all enable the reader to piece together an understanding of the world of the comic.

In *Halo Jones*, the series opens with Halo lying in bed, with speech bubbles offering bits of information from news reports. For the reader, there is then an affinity established immediately with Halo; her subaltern status as a teenager in a world of high unemployment and civil unrest leaves her as powerless and uncertain as the comic's readership, who are essentially dropped into this unfamiliar narrative world with no explanation or orientation. The instability of the world and the struggles of Halo and her friends to negotiate it in completing the shopping reveal aspects of the narrative world to readers, while at the same time extending that identification with Halo, who is the one source of meaning and information afforded readers as she herself works to respond to her ever-changing environment. *Love and Rockets*, while most directly focused on day-to-day lives, also provides disorienting elements to the reader, whether it is via the magic realism in the Palomar episodes or the intersections between mundane life in Hoppers and Maggie's somewhat futuristic role as a rocket mechanic.

Jamie Hewlett and Alan Martin's *Tank Girl* (1990) combines punk culture, a tough female lead character, and a post-apocalyptic landscape to achieve cult status.

In all three titles, it is the presence of familiar cultural references and their adaptation that assist in grounding readers and aiding them in identifying with the protagonists. The most common reference in all three of these comics is to popular music culture, and more specifically to the music and the aesthetics linked with punk and post-punk alternative culture. The use of everyday life in each of these comic books allows characters to engage with popular music as part of the cultural terrain in which they exist. Each of these titles also shares a legacy related to the rise of independent or alternative comics. These spaces allowed for a move away from the expectations and conventions of the mainstream. This is an ideology in common with that of the independent and alternative music industries of the same era, with a mixture of producers, artists, distributors, fans, and others all largely working to support each other while challenging the hegemony of the mainstream industry. Gray acknowledges that these shared ideologies were key to bringing Moore into the *2000 AD* fold: "It was this unorthodox attitude at *2000AD* that convinced Alan Moore, who had previously only published in the underground press, fanzines and music papers, that there was a space for politically radical and artistically unconventional material in mainstream comics."

It is unsurprising that there has been such crossover between the two media, and as the quote from Gray identifies, the music press was one of the venues in which Moore's early work had appeared. There was certainly an alignment in terms of fans of both media. A number of alternative, post-punk bands made reference to the independent comic industry. For example, British band Pop Will Eat Itself included the lyric "Alan Moore knows the score" as part of their 1989 song "Can U Dig It?," while the name of another band, Mega City Four, adapts the *Judge Dredd* locale of Mega-City One. In 1985, former members of the band Bauhaus formed a group called Love and Rockets, taking the name from the Hernandez brothers' comic book. This interplay also works the other way, with references to bands or to alternative music genres making their way into the comic books. In *The Ballad of Halo Jones* one of Halo's friends, Ludy, is depicted playing with her band, Ice Ten, and it is suggested that the band's success would be the means for Ludy to escape life on the Hoop. Despite unfamiliar instruments and a range of alien musicians, music and concert attendance is still depicted as part of youth life in this future world. Ludy's band is reported as being signed to what is termed a "sublabel" by the name of "Lo-Fi," suggesting the nature of the band's sound and its affinities with independent, alternative aesthetics, even though their actual sound cannot be heard on the pages of a comic book. The Hoop is likely an unfamiliar (and in some literal ways) alien world for readers; thus, the employment of familiar cultural references becomes an important narrative anchor that makes this world more accessible and understandable. While not adaptation of another text, there is an adapting of familiar cultural cues and narratives that aid these written works. The notion that success in the music industry can be a means of escaping a dreary existence is as familiar to youth of the Hoop as it is to contemporary youth. In addition to the direct musical references in *The Ballad of Halo Jones*, the aesthetic style, particularly of the youth characters, is drawn from punk and post-punk culture in terms of the hairstyles, clothing, and the general look of the characters. With the comic emerging in the United Kingdom at the time that such fashions were common among youth, the aesthetic choices seem another means of allowing for audience identification with the alienating world of the comic. Nineteen eighties youth culture borrowed, in examples such as band names or lyrical references, from these depictions of the future, while the comics employed recognizable tropes of youth culture to allow their diegetic locales to resonate with readers.

Popular music is even more central to the Locas story line in *Love and Rockets*. As indicated earlier, one of the central characters, Hopey, is a member of a series of punk rock bands, and their gigs and the surrounding social scene is a recurring aspect of the comics. Alongside Hopey's fictional bands, various characters in the comic and numerous audience members depicted at band shows are seen wearing T-shirts of real bands, positioning the fictional stories of Locas within the real world occupied by readers. The familiarity of the references being made in the comic provides a connection with readers, and it is extended via the use of youth styles in the depiction of characters. Haircuts, clothing, accessories, and other aspects of fashion are drawn from punk and post-punk imagery, clearly placing the action of the comic books into a contemporary setting.

Tank Girl is explicit in its popular music allusions, both in terms of its style, which owes a great deal to the graphic design styles that emerged during punk, and via references to specific bands and artists. In fact, each issue of the comic book included a "soundtrack" listing in the issue's credits. This suggested to readers what music they might wish to listen to while reading the installment, as well as what the writers might have been listening to or been inspired by. But not all of the soundtracks are drawn from the punk and post-punk genres. Early examples suggest Ennio Morricone (chapter 3 of book 1) or even the Bay City Rollers (in "The Australian Job, Part Two"). The latter comic opens with Tank Girl's tank crashing into a yacht in Sydney Harbour, suggesting that the soundtrack here may be an ironic comment on the styles and tastes of those on board the yacht, reaffirming Tank Girl's

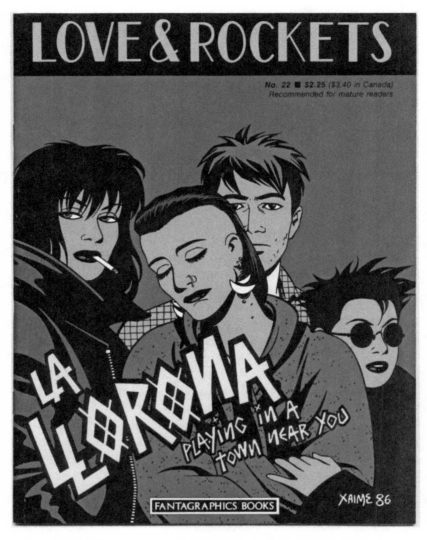

Punk culture features heavily in *Love and Rockets* (1986), including a story line following the touring adventures of fictitious band La Llorona.

more alternative credentials. The "soundtrack" of the *Tank Girl* comics thus aligns with the way in which soundtracks are deployed in contemporary cinema: songs are selected for the cultural meaning they bring to a scene, whether it is in setting the tone of the action, providing extradiegetic comment on the action, or helping to establish character. This use of music also relies on the cultural knowledge of viewers (or readers, in the case of the comic book example). They are expected to recognize the aesthetic or lyrical cues being provided via the choice of song. In this regard, the choice of punk and post-punk or "alternative" music genres is important in all three of the comic books referenced here. Not only do they situate themselves as distinct from the mainstream, but there is also important resonance in relation to genre and the popular association of these alternative music genres with nonhegemonic representations of gender.

All three of the comic book examples here rely on a correspondence between their music-influenced aesthetic style and the depiction of strong female protagonists. Despite the absence of an audio component in comic books, each of these texts adapts popular music references effectively into its narrative, enabling readers to make meaning via the cultural cues provided. In the case of *Tank Girl*, the film adaptation is then able to employ the musical references much more directly in its soundtrack. As M. Keith Booker has noted, while the film itself was a commercial failure, its strength was in its aesthetic rather than narrative aspects: "The film also exuberantly embraces the anarchic punk spirit of the comic book, which helps what could have been a truly awful film attain a certain zany energy. The pointless plot is punctuated by a number of highly entertaining moments thanks, partly, to the sheer excess of Lori Petty's campy performance as the ass-kicking title character" (Booker xxi).

While, as Booker indicates, Talalay's *Tank Girl* captured the spirit of the comic book, its narrative did not match the styles and structures of the source material. As Imelda Whelehan and Esther Sonnet note, the "individual comic episodes retain a vague narrative coherence (but one that may be thematic rather than motivational)," and the comic's "storylines are discontinuous and the identity of Tank Girl itself is fragmented" (Whelehan and Sonnet 34). The film instead has a more cohesive narrative, anchored by a voice-over provided by Tank Girl (Lori Petty) that functions to assist viewers in understanding its diegetic world. As opposed to the uncertainty in the comic book, where the cultural references offered become moments of familiarity, the genre attributes foregrounded in the film provide a greater sense of stability. The film's narrative makes use of diverse elements of the world of the *Tank Girl* comic but unifies them as Tank Girl seeks revenge against a powerful corporation, Water and Power, and its leader, Kesslee (Malcolm McDowell). As Whelehan and Sonnet note, "unlike the comic which clearly centres on Tank Girl as an unheroic or even accidental anti-hero, whose exploits are just as likely to end in drunkenness, sex or the accidental dismembering of male adversaries, the cinematic version of the protagonist is situated from the outset with an emotional and even moral justification for her future actions" (41). The genre that influences this structure is undoubtedly the western, as Tank Girl seeks revenge for the massacre of her lover, the shooting of her water buffalo (depicted and treated as akin to a horse in the classic Western), and the kidnapping of a young girl from her household. The actions of Water and Power are not unlike those of monopolistic cattle barons in the western, thus Tank Girl's revenge narrative is one familiar to viewers, while the post-apocalyptic Australian landscape calls to mind other familiar stories, such as George Miller's original *Mad Max* series of the 1970s and 1980s, which itself seems an inspiration for the comic books.

Despite critiques such as that of Whelehan and Sonnet, the *Tank Girl* film also has been heralded by some as offering a feminist critique, particularly in its depiction of its protagonist. Dominique Mainon and James Ursini refer to the film as "stridently feminist in theme, minus the cliché victim/avenger complex. Her character is likable, funny, sexy, and original. Her 'sidekick' Jet Girl (Naomi Watts) is an intelligent and talented mechanic, who starts as a victim in a male-run prison colony but with the inspiration of Tank Girl learns to assert herself and break free" (157–158). So while Whelehan and Sonnet are correct that the film's narrative descends into cliché, it is the aesthetic elements, particularly Petty's performance as Tank Girl, that open up greater possibilities for a feminist reading. Not dissimilar to the earlier examples, cultural references to popular music serve as familiar cues for readers. In the case of the *Tank Girl* film, the references serve to underscore the ways in which patriarchal control is undermined by Tank Girl. Subcultural cues position Tank Girl as a disruptive force who will have familiarity for viewers. As I have argued elsewhere, "just as Tank Girl refuses to surrender her independence despite constant threats and attacks from Water and Power's military forces, so the film's soundtrack refuses to unify with the narrative" (Henderson 154). In much the same way that the comic book's narratives are often derailed, image and particularly sound in the film provide a disruption to the generic narrative structure. With montages of comic book imagery, an abrasive soundtrack, Petty's array of punk-inspired costumes, among other moments of excess, the film's narrative does not feel closed but instead is decidedly intertextual. It can be argued that this intertextual openness refutes the more patriarchal leanings of a closed, genre narrative. Tank Girl provides many ruptures in the film that refute masculine authority, while the film's aesthetics simultaneously contest the dominant authority of a closed narrative.

Central to this aesthetic is the film's soundtrack and the corresponding punk imagery employed within the film's visuals. The imagery borrows from the comic book's aesthetics and adds to them in foregrounding the punk appearance of Petty's Tank Girl, as well as in invoking the early 1990s riot grrrl

Tank Girl (1995). Borrowing from its comic book source, a punk aesthetic informs the costumes of Tank Girl (Lori Petty) and Jet Girl (Naomi Watts).

movement. The soundtrack was overseen by alternative musician Court-ney Love, a contested figure within the riot grrrl movement,[1] but whose early work with her band, Hole, was undoubtedly an influence on riot grrrl, while her subsequent career is sometimes cast within the shadow of the movement. The majority of the songs on the soundtrack are from female or female-led alternative or post-punk singers and bands. The song played over the film's titles/opening sequence is Devo's "Girl U Want." While not a female-led band, Devo's brand of post-punk irony undermines pop music's foregrounding of male desire by making it both mechanical and ridiculous. While the song's lyrics may suggest that Tank Girl is "the girl you want," the song's style and pedigree suggest that this film has no intention of treating male desire unironically. The connections to popular music culture are fur-thered by the fact that the comic's co-creator and illustrator, Jamie Hewlett, went on to become a key member of the alternative animated band Goril-laz. The band incorporated a mix of hip-hop, post-punk, and electronica, all fronted by an animated group drawn in Hewlett's trademark style and strongly resembling his work in *Tank Girl*.

The relationship between music and gender is a key one for the film. While popular music's representation of gender is indicative of the ways in which sexual roles are often determined by mass cultural texts, punk and its generic successors, such as riot grrrl, have often provided alternatives to the gender norms established within the mainstream. Simon Frith and Angela McRobbie's pioneering 1978 article "Rock and Sexuality" clearly outlines the dominant constructions offered while also pointing to the possibilities for female agency that then emerging genres such as punk had opened up: "Punk was the first form of rock not to rest on love songs, and one of its effects has been to allow female voices to be heard that are not often allowed expression on record, stage, or radio—shrill, assertive, impure individual voices, the sounds of singers like Poly Styrene, Siouxsie, Fay Fife of the Rezillos, Pauline of Penetration; punk's female musicians have a strident insistency that is far removed from the appeal of most postwar glamour girls" (Frith and McRobbie 384). While punk did not entirely live up to this early promise, the discordant sounds and alternative modes of production and consumption did provide a space in which other emerging genres (or subgenres) derived from punk were able to give greater space to female voices. This was particularly true of riot grrrl.

In its representation of its protagonist and via its soundtrack, *Tank Girl* engages directly with the meanings associated with riot grrrl. Lucy O'Brien identifies how "ironically the term Girlpower arose from the explosive Riot Grrrl movement, the 1990s daughter of punk rock" (462). Riot grrrl responded to long-held attitudes about women and rock, particularly the divide between consumer and producer, again echoing the ideologies of independent comic book production. In its effective use of music in adapting the comic book to film, *Tank Girl* is able to establish an affinity with the ideologies of the source material. The riot grrrl subculture put production at its forefront. Fans were encouraged to participate by forming their own bands or starting their own fanzines, becoming activists, or finding other means of actively pursuing and promoting the riot grrrl agenda. When the mainstream media began to misrepresent the movement, riot grrrls closed ranks and enforced a media boycott. They remained producers of their own media but avoided engagement with the mainstream and the possibilities for misrepresentation that it offered. Mavis Bayton has described the riot grrrl musical aesthetic as "determinedly lo-fi and committed to amateurishness so that what counted was raw energy and spirit rather than musicianship" (75). This "lo-fi amateurishness" (a reminder of the reference in *The Ballad of Halo Jones* to the "Lo-Fi sublabel") also served to keep the riot grrrl sound out of the control of commercial interests by shunning the expected musical norms for recorded music, allowing it to retain its authenticity as an active subjective voice.

The disruptive nature of the music in the film adaptation works as a form of cinematic excess. As described by Kristin Thompson, excess exists when "a film displays a struggle by the unifying structures to 'contain' the diverse elements that make up its whole system" (488). These moments of excess and the ability of the system to fully contain the component parts are evident in *Tank Girl* as the insertion of comic book imagery, Tank Girl's asides to the audience, and the soundtrack refuse to be contained by the narrative. While the optimism about punk exhibited by Frith and McRobbie was disproven, the reappropriation of punk aesthetics and production practices within the riot grrrl subculture is certainly distinct from the ways in which mainstream texts make use of punk merely as a stylistic cue, often for youthful rebellion or threat. Rather than reducing "punk" to a cultural stereotype, as has often been the case with representations in mainstream cinema, *Tank Girl*'s use of riot grrrl aesthetics creates an open text that resists cohesion, an action that then aligns with the film's (and comic's) disruptive intentions.

Punk went from what has been described by critics such as Dick Hebdige as a homologous subculture with its own signs, signifiers, connections, and meanings to becoming a signifier itself—most notably, of danger and rebellion. The threat that punk (and other subcultures) hold for the dominant culture is the existence of their own systems of meaning, the homology that Hebdige describes. This sort of transformation is evident in popular representations of punk, where the subculture goes from one with its own meanings to standing more generally for a concept ("threat") within the mainstream. Numerous Hollywood films picked up on such representations. In Susan Seidelman's *Desperately Seeking Susan* (1985), for example, suburban New Jersey husband Gary is brought by Madonna's character, Susan, to a New York dance club as part of his search for his missing wife. The club's "otherness" is represented to Gary and the film audience through a number of stereotyped punks, both on the elevator into the club and on the dance floor. The absurdity of a group of "punks" dancing (and not ironically!) to Madonna's "Into the Groove" is overlooked. The film itself is an interesting critique of suburbia and hegemonic gender roles; but at the same time, in this instance, it reduces punk to an equation with threat (and is clearly lacking any musical homology).

Ostensibly, punk created a ready-made set of signs that could be borrowed from, any of which could be used to signify the popular notions of the subculture (Mohawks, safety pins, and torn clothing being among the most prevalent of these).[2] In *Tank Girl* the employment of punk and riot grrrl styles is discordant and resists the tendency to posit punk as a commodity or a signifier solely of rebellion. Petty's constantly changing costumes defy any fixed meaning. This includes, at one point, a bowler hat and eye makeup that make her resemble one of the "droogs" from Stanley Kubrick's 1971 film *A Clockwork Orange*, a role made famous by Malcolm McDowell, the actor playing Tank Girl's nemesis, Kesslee. This is akin to the sorts of esoteric cultural references found throughout the original comic book series. These are references familiar to the knowing reader/viewer, and as such create an excess by pointing to meanings that exist outside of the diegetic world.

While the film adaptation of *Tank Girl* was both a commercial and a critical disappointment, including among many of the comic book's fans, as well as its creators, Hewlett and Martin, who were dissatisfied with studio interference, it is possible to see how the employment of popular music permits the adaptation to retain much of the fragmented nature of the source material. While the inclusion of a more cohesive narrative does seem a studio imposition, or at least one imposed by the structures and expectations of genre cinema, the film's excess provides an intertextual openness that aligns Tank Girl's own antipatriarchal stance with that of the film itself. In fact, for all three of the comic books analyzed in this chapter, it is the use of extra-textual reference, particularly to popular music culture, that enables each narrative's protagonists to resist the patriarchal expectations of comic book narratives. In appropriating the possibilities of music genres such as punk and riot grrrl, and their promise of less constrictive gender roles, these texts are able to offer strong female characters, while serving as reminders of the truly transmedia nature of contemporary popular culture.

Notes

1. Catherine Strong cites a *New Musical Express* article that positions Love as "an influential forerunner of the Riot Grrrl movement" (407) rather than a member of the movement, while Love herself distanced herself from riot grrrl in a 2005 interview in *Spin* (Reilly). Love's position as a controversial figure is reinforced in Nick Broomfield's 1998 documentary *Kurt & Courtney*.

2. This is not to negate that punk and punk's ideologies and aesthetics continued to exist beyond its initial explosion. The DIY ethic certainly continued and fed indie music scenes, led to the formation of labels, and has influenced other bands and movements, including, of course, the aforementioned riot grrrls.

Works Cited

Bayton, Mavis. *Frock Rock: Women Performing Popular Music*. Oxford, UK, Oxford University Press, 1998.
Booker, M. Keith. *"May Contain Graphic Material": Comic Books, Graphic Novels, and Film*. Westport, CT, Praeger, 2007.
Frith, Simon, and Angela McRobbie. "Rock and Sexuality." *On Record: Rock, Pop and*

the Written Word, edited by Simon Frith and Andrew Goodwin, New York, Pantheon, 1990, pp. 371–389.

Gray, Maggie. "Hanging Out with Halo Jones: 'Possibly the First Feminist Heroine in Comics'?" *The Free School*, 14 March 2011, https://freefreeschool.files.wordpress.com/2011/03/hanging-out-with-halo-jones-pdf.pdf.

Henderson, Scott. "Youth, Excess and the Musical Moment." *Film's Musical Moments*, edited by Ian Conrich and Estella Tincknell, Edinburgh, UK, Edinburgh University Press, 2006, pp. 146–157.

Kearney, Mary Celeste. *Girls Make Media*. New York, Routledge, 2006.

Mainon, Dominique, and James Ursini. *Modern Amazons: Warrior Women on Screen*. Pompton Plains, NJ, Limelight, 2006.

Moore, Alan. "Guns, Guys and Gore." *The Ballad of Halo Jones Book One*, by Alan Moore and Ian Gibson, London, Titan Books, 1986, p. 59.

O'Brien, Lucy. *She Bop II: The Definitive History of Women in Rock, Pop and Soul*. London, Continuum, 2002.

Reilly, Phoebe. "Courtney Love: Let the Healing Begin." *Spin*, vol. 21, no. 10, October 2005, pp. 70–74.

Risner, Jonathan. "'Authentic' Latinas/os and Queer Characters in Mainstream and Alternative Comics." *Multicultural Comics: From "Zap" to "Blue Beetle,"* edited by Frederick Luis Aldama, Austin, University of Texas Press, 2010, pp. 39–54.

Strong, Catherine. "Grunge, Riot Grrrl and the Forgetting of Women in Popular Culture." *Journal of Popular Culture*, vol. 44, no. 2, 2011, pp. 398–416.

Thompson, Kristin. "The Concept of Cinematic Excess." *Film Theory and Criticism: Introductory Readings*, 5th ed., edited by Leo Braudy and Marshall Cohen, Oxford, NY, Oxford University Press, 1999, pp. 487–498.

Whelehan, Imelda, and Esther Sonnet. "Regendered Reading: Tank Girl and Postmodernist Intertextuality." *Trash Aesthetics: Popular Culture and Its Audience*, edited by Deborah Cartmell, I. Q. Hunter, Heidi Kaye, and Imelda Whelehan, London, Pluto Press, 1997, pp. 31–47.

Black Panther: Aspiration, Identification, and Appropriation

JEFFREY A. BROWN

In the early 1970s the Black Owned Communication Alliance (BOCA) ran a series of public service advertisements calling for greater racial diversity in the media. One of the ads depicted a young African American boy striking a heroic pose, towel around his neck as a makeshift cape, looking at himself in the bathroom mirror. But in the reflection, all the boy sees is a generic white superhero looking back at him. "What's wrong with this picture?" the headline asks: "A child dreams of being the latest superhero. What could be wrong with that?" The copy underneath provides answer: "Plenty, if the child is Black and can't even *imagine* a hero the same color he or she is." The advertisement is a concise expression of the lack of diverse super-heroes and the inherent inequality of heroic models available for children of color during that still tumultuous post–civil-rights era. Much has changed in the world of superheroes since this BOCA advertisement was first pub-lished (and, in many ways, much has not changed). There has been a signifi-cant increase in racial diversity among the ranks of mainstream superheroes from both Marvel and DC Comics, as well as numerous independent pub-lishers. New superheroes of color have redefined the comic book landscape in recent years: the Miles Morales version of Spider-Man, both the David Zavimbi and Luke Fox versions of Batwing, the Kamala Khan take on Ms. Marvel, Amadeus Cho as the new Hulk, Jaime Reyes as the Blue Beetle, and Kong Kenan as the Super-Man of China, to name just a few.

Though the range of ethnicities depicted in comic books is changing, in this chapter I want to consider the still important issue of identification raised by the BOCA advertisement, specifically in relation to Marvel's Black Panther. The popular character debuted just a few years prior to the BOCA ad, influenced by both the civil rights movement and the blaxploitation film genre, and Black Panther has recently reached new heights through his

What's wrong with this picture?

A child dreams of being the latest superhero. What could be wrong with that?

Plenty, if the child is Black and can't even *imagine* a hero the same color he or she is.

It's like this: children learn by what they see. And if it weren't for Black media, a Black child wouldn't see the world as it really is...

with Black men and women doing positive things besides playing basketball and singing songs.

What can you do to make sure our kids have self pride? Decide which media shows them Blacks as Blacks *really* are.

And that's where BOCA comes in. BOCA, the Black Owned Communications

Alliance is an organization of Blacks working for Blacks.

We don't want your money. We want you to use the power you have to get what you deserve— a real picture of you. Your hopes. Your problems. Your needs.

We also want your opinion. So write us. We want to hear from you so we can set the picture straight.

BOCA The Black Owned Communications Alliance
P.O. Box 2757 Grand Central Station, New York, New York 10017

An early 1970s ad from the Black Owned Communication Alliance drives home the point that African American youth needed more diverse fictional role models.

best-selling comic books and the record-breaking feature film *Black Panther* (2018). Unlike most costumed superheroes, Black Panther is treated very consciously in modern depictions as a character burdened by racial representation. The writers and artists of his comic books, and the directors and actors from the films, are well aware of how important Black Panther is as an iconic black hero and as a positive symbol of African and African American life. Chadwick Boseman, who portrayed Black Panther so successfully in the movies, indicated the concern with crafting progressive representations of black people when he told *Time* magazine that a driving ethos behind the making of the film was answering the question, "How can we be represented in a way that is aspirational?" (qtd. in Smith 45). Indeed, as one of the most prominent and longest-lasting black superheroes, Black Panther reveals the complicated history of race and costumed characters and demonstrates the importance of heroic identification and aspiration both *along* and *across* racial lines. Moreover, because the modern Black Panther is an object of identification for fans from a variety of ethnic and national backgrounds, the character exposes the cultural and political tensions that arise at the intersections of admiration and appropriation.

In 1966 Black Panther became the first black superhero in mainstream comics, making his debut as a guest star in Marvel's *The Fantastic Four* #52. "Introducing the Sensational Black Panther!" the cover declared over an image of a mysterious figure clad in an all-black costume and cape leaping into action alongside the Invisible Girl, the Thing, the Human Torch, and Mister Fantastic. Created by the legendary team of Stan Lee and Jack Kirby, the writer and artist pair that had reinvented Marvel comics and reinvigorated the entire industry in the 1960s, Black Panther was part of Marvel's efforts to make superheroes more relatable. Though the white creators Lee and Kirby have denied that Black Panther was inspired by the burgeoning radical Black Panther Party that was also founded in 1966, readers have never missed the implied connection. In his secret identity, Black Panther is T'Challa, a prince and later king of Wakanda, an imaginary African nation of tremendous wealth and advanced technology. As part of his royal lineage, T'Challa is imbued with the increased strength, speed, agility, and stamina of a mythical panther god. Black Panther is duty bound to use his abilities to defend his nation and to protect the helpless wherever he encounters them.

Black Panther spent several years as a member of Marvel's preeminent superteam in *The Avengers*. He then became the focus of his own series, taking over the lead of *Jungle Action* with its fifth issue in 1973, until the series was canceled with issue #24 in 1976. The character finally received his own self-titled comic book, *The Black Panther*, in 1977, which lasted only fifteen issues before being canceled due to low sales figures. Despite some difficulties sustaining an ongoing series, Black Panther became a popular figure with a strong following among comic book fans. Black Panther continued to guest star in other heroes' books and team adventures, eventually earning a number of reboots and miniseries, including *Black Panther* vol. 2 (1988), vol. 3 (1998–2003), vol. 4 (2005–2008), and vol. 5 (2009–2010). Most recently, and leading up to the character's introduction to the Marvel Cinematic Universe, he has headlined another edition of his own critically acclaimed series *Black Panther* (2016–present), as well as variations and spin-offs like *Black Panther: World of Wakanda* (2016–2017), *Black Panther: Long Live the King* (2017–2018), *Black Panther and the Crew* (2017), and *Rise of the Black Panther* (2018).

The creation of Black Panther helped clear the way for several other early black superheroes, including Marvel's the Falcon in 1969, Luke Cage in 1972, Brother Voodoo in 1973, Black Goliath in 1975, and Storm (in *The X-Men*) in 1975, as well as DC Comics' Tyroc (in *The Legion of Superheroes*) in 1976 and Black Lightning in 1977. This small wave of black superheroes in the 1970s began to address the lack of heroic images available for black children to imagine as a reflection of themselves. In large part, many of these characters were also inspired by the low-budget, but highly profitable blaxploitation films of the time period. Movies like *Sweet Sweetback's Baadasssss Song* (1971), *Shaft* (1971), *Super Fly* (1972), and *Black Caesar* (1973) expressed and capitalized on racial politics and the desires of a substantial audience to see heroic images of black characters at the cinema. As Tommy Lott states in his history of black film theory, "some Hollywood studios discovered that there was a large Black audience starving for Black images on the screen" (43). Likewise, in his overview of media depictions of African Americans, Ed Guerrero observes that blaxploitation films "were made possible by the rising political and social consciousness of black people — taking the form of a broadly expressed black nationalist impulse at the end of the civil rights movement — which translated into a large black audience thirsting to see their full humanity depicted on the commercial cinema screen" (69). In addition to demonstrating the potential profitability of heroic black characters in the media, the blaxploitation films solidified a depiction of black heroes in stereotypical terms as streetwise tough guys and outlaws, fighting evil whites and drug dealers in defense of their urban ghetto neighborhoods and racking up plenty of sexual conquests along the way. While many of the black comic book superheroes that emerged in the 1970s mirrored the stereotypes made popular by the blaxploitation films, *Black Panther* managed to avoid many, but not all, of these limiting tropes.

Where Luke Cage was a jive-talking ex-con, hustling work in Harlem as a hero for hire, T'Challa's fictional royal heritage positioned him as a more noble and distinguished figure. Though Black Panther has enhanced physical strength, he was not defined solely by his body as a superpowered variation on the old stereotype of the black "brute." Instead, T'Challa is repeatedly described as a genius and a scientist—a thinker as much as a fighter. T'Challa is wealthy, mannered, well-spoken, and educated at the finest universities in the West. As Black Panther, he does not have to rely on brute strength alone; he is a trained fighter with magically enhanced abilities. Still, as an African character, Black Panther was aligned with stereotypes of a dark, exotic, and animalistic racial Other. Black Panther's first solo appearances were in *Jungle Action*, thus solidifying his association with a particularly rudimentary image of Africa as a dark and uncivilized continent. In his discussion of early black superheroes Rob Lendrum notes that Black Panther was often referred to in the comics via racialized terms like "a jungle beast with the garb of a *savage* cat" (367). Comic books are a medium that has historically been steeped in stereotypes of all kinds; it would have been nearly impossible for the first mainstream black superhero to escape every racially aligned trope and misconception. Still, Black Panther did fight crime, corruption, and supervillains both in America and in Wakanda during his time in *Jungle Action* and *The Black Panther*. Importantly, the character was also treated with dignity and respect by all of the more established heroes within the fictional Marvel Universe.

A large part of the modern appeal of Black Panther is due to the writers and artists who recognized the groundbreaking character's racial and political significance. Celebrated black writers like Christopher Priest, Reginald Hudlin, and Ta-Nehisi Coates embraced the opportunity to present Black Panther as a complex character challenged not just by supervillains but also by the responsibilities of his African kingdom, as well as issues like racism, colonialism, and xenophobia. These complicated and overtly political themes established as an integral part of Black Panther's world in the comics carried over into the character's feature film in 2018. The modern *Black Panther* comics also took the character in a range of new directions, including a marriage to Storm, the mutant weather goddess who is a member of the X-Men, T'Challa being replaced as the Black Panther for a time by his sister, Shuri, as well as dealing with alien invaders, tribal warfare, and a class revolt in Wakanda. Critics have praised the modern comic book incarnation of Black Panther's series as "strong. It's scary and it's inspiring. It dives head first into a conflict without any preparation or introductions, much like any great work of fiction should" (Cardona); and as possessing "a deep, interesting cast of characters, a fully realized world, and interesting politics at play. Its vibrancy is also a demonstration of how diversity can breathe new life into old concepts" (Holub). These modern *Black Panther* scribes have improved upon Lee and Kirby's original vision of the character by fleshing out his persona and his world as unique among the roster of Marvel's superheroes.

The early depictions of Black Panther in the 1960s and 1970s owed a lot of their success to the character's uniqueness as the first, and one of the few black superheroes. The twenty-first-century version is more popular than ever due, in large part, to his grounding in a culturally specific environment. In an interesting discussion of what makes a black superhero "truly Black," Kenneth Ghee speculates that the character needs to be "culture bound." "This critically important variable must be considered before we can determine if an *individual* Black fictional hero (created by Whites) is truly a Black hero at all," Ghee argues. "This is also the sociological function of any redeeming hero mythos; that is working to save *his own* people *first*, in the context of saving humanity, in other words 'culture bound'" (231). Ghee insists that just as all superheroes must fight for their culture, so must the black superhero; but where the dominant white superheroes like Superman and Captain America fight on behalf of dominant white society by default, to be "truly black" a superhero must focus on defending members of his own community first and foremost. This logic does not preclude saving people from a variety of backgrounds, but it does ensure a connection to black communities and an address of racial issues that affect specific groups. With Black Panther's modern adventures firmly grounded in Wakanda, his status as eminently "culture bound" is foregrounded. Moreover, as an Afrofuturist fantasy of technological and cultural perfection, Wakanda's location in Africa does not alienate African Americans; rather, it plays into a magical and romanticized conception of a motherland untouched by outside forces.

Despite Black Panther's newfound popularity in comic books at the start of the twenty-first century, he remained relatively low profile in a larger cultural context. Characters like Superman, Batman, Spider-Man, and Iron Man are recognized worldwide and have benefited from decades of media exposure and merchandising. Black Panther, on the other hand, was never a household name beyond the confines of comics fandom and some African American groups. But the inclusion of Black Panther in the Marvel Cinematic Universe elevated the character to the level of top-tier superhero. Introduced with a pivotal role in the blockbuster film *Captain America: Civil War* (2016), Boseman's performance of Black Panther all but stole the movie from the other, higher-profile superheroes.[1] Then the phenomenal success of the solo film *Black Panther* in 2018 turned the character into a cultural phenomenon. Directed by Ryan Coogler, *Black Panther* earned a record-setting $202 million in the United States over its opening weekend and would go on to gross over $1.5 billion worldwide, making it one of the top-ten grossing movies of all time. Moreover, *Black Panther* quickly became the most successful film by a black director, scripted by black writers, and featuring a predominantly black cast. As a high-profile film that embraced its blackness on a number of levels, *Black Panther* shouldered a lot of responsibility to deliver more than just a blockbuster. "Beyond box office and critics, the people have responded with enthusiasm and raves, attending showings of the movie decked out in African garb or Black Panther cosplay," noted a feature article in the *Daily Beast* about the importance of the film to children. "On social media," the article stated, "the unfettered enthusiasm has been met with constant dissection of what the film means and what it gets right or wrong. There's a lot of talk about representation—what it means for young black kids to see black faces that are heroic and beautiful, strong and independent, not defined by their proximity to whiteness" (Williams).

Mainstream press headlines declared the film a landmark cinematic achievement and an important racial milestone: "*Black Panther* Is More Than a Superhero Movie" (*Atlantic*), "*Black Panther* Is a Triumph, and a Breakthrough Superhero Movie" (*Boston Globe*), "*Black Panther*: Why This Film Is a *Moment*" (BBC News), "More Than a Movie, *Black Panther* Is a Movement" (CNN). Moreover, in recognizing the racial significance of the film, *Black Panther* was featured as a cover story in a wide range of magazines, from *Essence* and *Ebony* to *Variety* and *Entertainment Weekly* and from *Rolling Stone* to *Vogue*. The commercial and critical success of *Black Panther* proves that, as Lott and Guerrero described of the earlier blaxploitation films, black audiences are still "starving" and "thirsting" for big-screen heroic images. As the cover story in *Time* magazine pointed out, there have been black heroes in feature films before, but "Black Panther matters more because he is our best chance for people of every color to see a black hero. That is its own kind of power" (Smith 45).

Most superhero movies are still grounded in a post-9/11 fantasy of rewriting history so that colorful American heroes can save New York (or Gotham or Metropolis or Xandar) from devastating terrorist attacks (see Costello; Gilmore). But *Black Panther* charts new narrative and political ground by incorporating themes specific to American racial dilemmas. The central conflict of the film is an ideological one between T'Challa and Erik Killmonger (Michael B. Jordan) over Wakanda's long-standing refusal to engage with other nations. Killmonger regards Wakanda's isolationism as a cowardly dis-

Chadwick Boseman's T'Challa provides audiences the chance to see a black hero in *Black Panther* (2018).

regard for the horrors suffered by black people through centuries of colonialism, slavery, discrimination, and genocide. Killmonger, who grew up on the streets of Oakland rather than in the palaces of Wakanda, has witnessed and experienced racial atrocities firsthand. With Wakanda's stockpile of the powerful alien metal vibranium, and the incredibly advanced technology it provides, Wakanda could have given the rest of Africa, and non-whites around the world, a fighting chance against their enemies. As Killmonger's father, N'Jobu, explains to King T'Chaka (T'Challa's father, the previous Black Panther, and N'Jobu's brother) when N'Jobu is found to be involving himself in the racial turmoil of America: "Their leaders have been assassinated. Communities flooded with drugs and weapons. They are overly policed and incarcerated. All over the planet, our people suffer because they don't have the tools to fight back. With vibranium weapons they can overthrow all countries, and Wakanda can rule them all, the right way!" N'Jobu is killed by T'Chaka soon after his impassioned speech, but Erik grows up to pursue the same goal of using Wakanda's might to conquer the world on behalf of an exploited African diaspora. Or, as Killmonger declares after temporarily usurping the throne from T'Challa: "I've waited my whole life for this. The world is going to start over. I'MA BURN IT ALL!"

Much of the film's strength is derived from portraying Killmonger as not merely another crazy supervillain—like *Captain America*'s super-Nazi, the Red Skull, or *Batman*'s insane anarchist, the Joker. Ryan Coogler's direction positions Killmonger as an understandable result of his personal and cultural experiences. Killmonger's ideological perspective on racial injustices is presented as undeniably valid. In fact, Killmonger's threat to T'Challa ulti-mately exposes both dark family secrets and the disgrace of Wakanda's self-serving isolationism. In the end, T'Challa reverses centuries of Wakanda tradition and vows to help the disenfranchised beyond their own borders. "You were wrong—all of you were wrong—to turn your backs on the rest of the world," T'Challa tells his ancestors when he is on a mystical plane of existence. "We let the fear of discovery stop us from doing what is right. No more! . . . He [Killmonger] is a monster of our own making. I must take the mantle back. I must right these wrongs!" *Black Panther* is the rare super-hero film where the bad guy's motivation is shown as relatively justified and reasonable.

Still, the film does maintain Killmonger's status as a villain by stressing the danger of his extremism. Killmonger does not just want to liberate the colonized, he wants to be a colonizer. He would plunge the world into open warfare rather than pursue peace. As Okoye, the leader of the royal guard, tells Killmonger: "You are so full of hatred, you will never be a true king!" Killmonger's anger and hatred blind him to any other way, thus position-ing T'Challa's more measured approach to helping the impoverished Afri-can diaspora as the truly heroic solution. Where Killmonger wanted to arm African Americans with advanced weapons, T'Challa opts for establishing Wakandan educational facilities in the same Oakland ghetto where his uncle was killed. The film does not ignore the very real racial problems that have plagued our world for centuries, but it does champion a peaceful resolution as the best hope for progress.

Black Panther is a landmark black movie, but it also transcends being a movie that appeals primarily to one specific racial demographic. Yes, the film is a celebration of black heroism and an Afrofuturist depiction of an advanced Pan-African culture, unscathed by a history of colonial exploita-tion and race conflicts. Yes, the film incorporates sensitive issues of systemic racism, isolationism, financial and technological inequalities, and the logic of resisting oppression by any means necessary. But *Black Panther* is also an exciting, engaging, and accessible superhero movie full of amazing special effects, well-choreographed fight scenes, and incredible action sequences. As part of the multi-billion-dollar Marvel Cinematic Universe and under the ownership of Disney, *Black Panther* is both a significant moment in black popular culture *and* a commercial blockbuster meant for the broadest audi-ence possible. The cover story in *Time* magazine noted that as a superhero film "*Black Panther* marks the biggest move yet in this wave: it's both a black film and the newest entrant in the most bankable movie franchise in his-tory" (Smith 45). Indeed, one of the defining strengths of the movie is that audiences from a diverse range of cultural backgrounds can enjoy the story and identify with the characters. The film has appealed to black and white audiences in American and international markets, thus reaching its incredible worldwide box-office success. Both the film and its titular hero proved a crossover triumph of epic proportions.

As a blockbuster movie *Black Panther* followed the synergistic, multimedia marketing plan already established through Disney's promotional achievements with earlier Marvel properties and the *Star Wars* franchise. The now standard avalanche of toys, T-shirts, watches, cereal boxes, soft drinks, hats, buttons, Lego sets, jewelry, and stuffed animals crowded store shelves and were snapped up by eager consumers, thus generating hundreds of millions more in ancillary profits. "Success on screen can potentially mean plenty of money to be made off screen as well," the industry website *Market Place* noted; thus "Hasbro announced it's making more *Black Panther* toys than it has for any other Marvel character's first movie" (Balonon-Rosen and Adams). Despite the incredible number of products associated with the film, the demand for merchandise was so great that within weeks of its release thousands of stores across North America were already sold out of *Black Panther* toys (Fickenscher), although Disney ultimately managed to meet the incredible demand.

This extensive but typical merchandising campaign capitalizes on the desire of fans, especially children, to possess a piece of the fantasy and identify with the larger-than-life hero they aspire to be. Disney's marketing of their superhero toys and costumes caters to this idea of identificatory play. For example, a television commercial for the *Black Panther* line of toys featured three children, one wearing a Black Panther mask, another brandishing a distinctive claw, and the third using a replica of Shuri's blaster. "Make way for a new kind of warrior," the narrator intones, the children leaping, crouching, and shooting Nerf-style bullets as their backyard transforms into a Wakandan backdrop. "Make way for the hero in you. Be Marvel. Be more." The commercial begins with a young black male pulling a Black Panther mask over his face and ends with him coming face-to-face with Black Panther himself (or at least a CGI version of the character). With this toy campaign the concern expressed in the BOCA advertisement is finally and definitively countered. Now, when a black "child dreams of being the latest superhero," that boy or girl can easily "*imagine* a hero the same color he or she is."

Part of the important power of imagination, particularly in children's play fantasies, is that it does not have to be restricted to the rules of the real world. Indeed, many nonwhite children (and adults, for that matter) have no

A new kind of warrior, and a new way of imagining being a hero.

problem imagining themselves as Superman, Batman, Captain America, or any other character that appeals to them. A mountain of photographic evidence of black fans dressing up as their favorite superheroes, many of whom are white in the comics, can be found online and through media coverage of events such as "28 Days of Black Cosplay" and New York's annual Schomburg Black Comic Book Festival.[2] But I also agree with Kenneth Ghee's point that "a Black child should, at the very least, be able to imagine a positive superhero or mythological archetype and icon from his/her own race or culture instead of always having to look to another culture for his/her pretend play and idolism" (228). Imaginative play *as*, and identification *with*, superheroes has been demonstrated to help children learn to cooperate and resolve conflicts (Bauer and Dettore), to develop a strong sense of morality (Martin), to promote body acceptance (Young, Gabriel, and Hollar), to improve perseverance (White et al.), and even to choose healthier foods (Wansik, Shimizu, and Camps). "Becoming a superhero, flying over the school, helps children develop essential skills for later success," Timothy A. Kinard summarizes in his review of early childhood lessons. "Superhero play is not merely preparation for the future. It is a deep philosophical, psychological, sociological, anthropological exploration of life. It happens in the now, but at the same time it is a sustained, timeless exploration of the human condition" (Kinard 22). Thus, it is important that children of color have access to these same values and developmental traits, and that they believe these incredible heroes can come in a variety of skin tones.

With the *Black Panther* movie—and, to a lesser extent, television series like *Luke Cage* (2016–2018) and *Black Lightning* (2018–present)—black children have imaginative access to a wildly popular black superhero and to ready-made merchandise that encourages identificatory play as Black Panther. The press coverage of the *Black Panther* phenomenon repeatedly stressed ecstatic viewers claiming in person or over social media how great it was to see a big-screen superhero who looked like them. In fact, because *Black Panther* was so overwhelmingly embraced by black audiences, a relatively unique concern about children playing superheroes began to creep into public discussions: Is it okay for white kids to dress up as Black Panther? Children of all different ethnicities and nationalities were swept up in *Black Panther* mania and wanted to play with the toys, wear the T-shirts, and don the official mask and costume. But the current climate of racial politics in American culture makes something as simple as a child's "dreams of being the latest superhero" a thorny issue, albeit in reverse of the original dynamic from the BOCA advertisement.

In group chats, on Twitter, in blogs, and through entertainment-focused websites, parents fretted and argued about whether it was acceptable for nonblack children to dress up as Black Panther, or if it was a form of cultural appropriation. The mainstream press also reported on the concerns expressed by some parents. "White parents are trying to make sure they are not culturally appropriating when they take their children to see *Black Panther* over the weekend," noted the *Daily Mail*, "especially if those children want to dress up like the main character. . . . Some parents are worried that allowing their children to wear the Black Panther masks or costumes could be considered cultural appropriation, or even black face" (Miller). Likewise, in a *New York Times* article originally titled "Who's Allowed to Wear a Black Panther Mask?" that was cautiously changed to "The Many Meanings of Black Panther's Mask," Kwame Opam wrote: "Black Panther costumes—whether the character's full raiment or just his claws and mask—are on toy shelves in anticipation of the film's Feb. 16 release. At best, the character get-ups speak to the enthusiastic embrace of a black superhero. At worst, they could be perceived as an unwitting form of cultural appropriation, which has in recent years become a subject of freighted discourse" (Opam).

Criticisms about *who* is represented in the media and *how* they are portrayed have become standard concerns. Activists, special interest groups, media watchdogs, fans, and even creators have debated issues of appropriation, as well as stereotyping, whitewashing, and exploitation. The public debates over representations are valuable and progressive correctives to centuries of misrepresentations and outright racism. Superhero comic books have a long history of depicting nonwhite characters in very stereotypical ways: for example, the nearsighted and bucktoothed Japanese soldiers battled by Captain America during World War II, the jive-talking blaxploitation heroes of the 1970s, and the dozens of foreign characters whose super identities are based on cultural assumptions, like DC Comics' sexy Brazilian bombshell, Fire, and their cold Norwegian blonde, Ice.[3] Likewise, Disney, Marvel's parent company, has often been accused of appropriating elements of other cultures for their own profit with films like *Pocahontas* (1995), *Mulan* (1998), *The Princess and the Frog* (2009), and *Moana* (2016) (see Kutsuzawa; Yin; Samuel). The current trend of live-action film and television superheroes has also become a lightning rod for controversy by whitewashing some characters, such as the Middle Eastern villain R'as al Ghul in *Batman Begins* (2005) being played by Irish actor Liam Neeson or British actress Tilda Swinton cast as an ancient Tibetan monk in *Doctor Strange* (2016). The concern in relation to white children dressing up as Black Panther stems from a recognition of the importance and uniqueness of the character of a complex black superhero who is "culturally bound," in Ghee's terms. White kids playing Black Panther could be perceived as cultural appropriation or, more specifically, as what Richard A. Rogers categorizes as cultural exploitation: "the appropriation of elements of a subordinated culture by a dominant culture without substantive reciprocity, permission, and/or compensation" (477). Where "cultural appropriation" broadly implies an adoption of the manners, customs, or material objects of another group, which could include a subaltern group's use of a dominant society's traits, "exploitation" more clearly describes the practice of a dominant group assuming markers from a more marginal group without regard for historical or cultural importance.

Unfortunately, cultural exploitation happens all the time in our society and is based on unequal access to traditional forms of power. But to lump nonblack children dressing up as Black Panther in with ideas of appropriation and cultural exploitation would be to miss the importance of heroic identification both along and across racial lines. The case of *Black Panther* and imaginative childhood play is very different from other forms of white people embracing popular culture associated with black artists and communities. White fascination with black cultural forms has a long and complicated history in America. As Eric Lott has argued, even something as blatantly racist as white minstrels performing in blackface suggested a fascination with blackness at the same time that it was a means to ridicule blacks and soothe white fears of black men. In the modern era, white youths have embraced rap music and hip-hop fashions grounded in urban black experiences. Drawing a line from minstrel shows to white suburban kids embracing gangster rap, as well as hip-hop fashions, language styles, and physical mannerisms, Bill Yousman argues: "White youth adoption of Black cultural forms in the twenty-first century is also a performance, one that allows Whites to contain their fears and animosities towards Blacks through rituals not of ridicule, as in previous eras, but of adoration" (369). But, as Yousman goes on to note, while these contemporary aspects of black popular culture forms are enjoyed by white youths through a type of adoration, expressions like gangster rap, with its descriptions of violence, drug use, criminal wealth, and women as bitches and hoes, also demonstrate an acceptance of racist stereotypes and beliefs. "Thus, although the motives behind the performance may initially appear to be different, the act is still a manifestation of White supremacy," Yousman continues, "albeit a White supremacy that is in crisis and disarray, rife with confusion and contradiction" (369). Fortunately, the version of Black Panther presented in the film has popularized a black hero who is a world away from gangster rap, or any other limiting stereotypes. In fact, within the dynamics of the film Killmonger's language, mannerisms, and political stance echo the style of gangster rap, which is ultimately rejected as an inappropriate position to emulate.

Tellingly, some of the film's creators who were driven in part by the question of "How can we be represented in a way that is aspirational?" expressed their ultimate reward as coming from seeing children dressed up as Black Panther. In an interview with *BuzzFeed News* Sterling K. Brown, who plays T'Challa's uncle, N'Jobu, said he was proud to take his own boys to see the film and to see them dress up, but that he will also be excited to see white kids costumed as Black Panther at Halloween because that will indicate a real crossover. The film's star, Chadwick Boseman, agreed and thoughtfully added that he had already begun to experience that breakthrough: "I've seen little white kids dressed up as T'Challa. I've seen pictures and I've seen it in person. You know, I've seen, like, family members' kids, friends' kids. They show up on Halloween and they're the Panther and they understand that I'm the Panther, and they want to show me. People call me and say, 'We wanted to buy him Spider-Man, but he kept saying Black Panther'" (qtd. in Wieselman). Black Panther's most important superpower may ultimately be his ability to inspire all children to overcome assumptions about race and differences.

Indeed, this sense of progressive inclusion is essential to the movie's overall message. When T'Challa rejects Wakanda's history of isolationism and begins to work for cultural advancement on a global level, his actions are framed as the wise, responsible, and humane choice made by an ideal superhero. T'Challa's understanding of Killmonger's justified anger on behalf of the subaltern, combined with his rejection of Killmonger's desire to rule over the oppressors, positions T'Challa as a "culturally bound" hero and a voice of change. Where Killmonger sought to reverse the status quo of racial divisions, T'Challa ultimately seeks to overcome those divisions and to unite people regardless of race or nationality. King T'Challa's address to the United Nations at the conclusion of *Black Panther* clarifies the moral imperative of people accepting each other despite any perceived differences: "Wakanda will no longer watch from the shadows. We can not. We must not. We will work to be an example of how we, as brothers and sisters on this earth, should treat each other. Now, more than ever, the illusions of division threaten our very existence. We all know the truth: more connects us than separates us. But in times of crisis the wise build bridges, while the foolish build barriers. We must find a way to look after one another, as if we were one single tribe."

Notes

1. Many review headlines singled out Black Panther: "Why Black Panther's Debut in *Captain America: Civil War* Is So Important" (*Time*), "Black Panther Is the Most Exciting Hero to Join the Marvel Cinematic Universe in Years" (*Business Insider*), "Spider-Man and Black Panther Win *Captain America: Civil War*" (*Telegraph*).

2. For examples, see cosplayingwhileblack.tumblr.com, blacknerdproblems.com, and worldofblackheroes.com.

3. For considerations of comic books and racial issues, see Howard and Jackson; Gateward and Jennings; Fawaz.

Works Cited

Balonen-Rosen, Peter, and Kimberly Adams. "For *Black Panther* What Happens When Culture Meets Commodity?" *Market Place*, 2 March 2018, https://www.market place.org/2018/03/02/business/merchandising-black-panther-what-happens -when-culture-meets-commodity.

Bauer, Karen L., and Ernest Dettore. "Superhero Play: What's a Teacher to Do?" *Early Childhood Education Journal*, vol. 25, no. 1, 1997, pp. 17–21.

Cardona, Ian. "Black Panther: A Nation under Our Feet Merits a Place on Political Bookshelves." *Comic Book Resources*, 2 September 2017, https://www.cbr.com /black-panther-nation-under-our-feet-political-masterpiece/.

Costello, Matthew J. "Spandex Agonistes: Superhero Comics Confront the War on Terror." *Portraying 9/11: Essays on Representations in Comics, Literature, Film and Theatre*, edited by Veronique Bragard, Christophe Dony, and Warren Rosenberg, Jefferson, NC, McFarland, 2011, pp. 30–43.

Fawaz, Ramzi. *The New Mutants: Superheroes and the Radical Imagination of American Comics*. New York, New York University Press, 2016.

Fickenscher, Lisa. "There's a Shortage of *Black Panther* Toys at Stores." *New York Post*, 8 April 2018, https://nypost.com/2018/04/08/theres-an-embarrassing-shortage-of-black-panther-toys/.

Gateward, Francis, and John Jennings. *The Blacker the Ink: Constructions of Black Identity in Comics and Sequential Art*. New Brunswick, NJ, Rutgers University Press, 2015.

Ghee, Kenneth. "Will the 'Real' Black Superheroes Please Stand Up?! A Critical Analysis of the Mythological and Cultural Significance of Black Superheroes." *Black Comics: Politics of Race and Representation*, edited by Sheena C. Howard and Ronald L. Jackson II, New York, Bloomsbury, 2013, pp. 223–237.

Gilmore, James, N. "A Eulogy of the Urban Superhero: The Everyday Destruction of Space in the Superhero Film." *Representing 9/11: Trauma, Ideology, and Nationalism in Literature, Film, and Television*, edited by Paul Petrovic, New York, Rowman and Littlefield, 2015, pp. 53–63.

Guerrero, Ed. *Framing Blackness: The African American Image in Film*. Philadelphia, Temple University Press, 1994.

Holub, Christian. "Black Panther: A Nation under Our Feet, Book One: EW Review." *Entertainment Weekly*, 31 August 2016, https://ew.com/article/2016/08/31/black-panther-nation-under-our-feet-book-one-ew-review/.

Howard, Sheena C., and Ronald L. Jackson II, editors. *Black Comics: Politics of Race and Representation*. New York, Bloomsbury, 2013.

Kinard, Timothy A. "Flying over the School: Superhero Play—Friend or Foe?" *YC: Young Children*, vol. 69, no. 2, 2014, pp. 16–23.

Kutsuzawa, K. "Disney's *Pocahontas*: Reproduction of Gender, Orientalism and the Strategic Construction of Racial Harmony in the Disney Empire." *Asian Journal of Women's Studies*, vol. 6, no. 4, 2000, pp. 39–65.

Lendrum, Rob. "The Super Black Macho, One Baaad Mutha: Black Superhero Masculinity in 1970s Mainstream Comic Books." *Extrapolation*, vol. 46, no. 3, 2005, pp. 360–372.

Lott, Tommy L. "A No-Theory Theory of Contemporary Black Cinema." *Cinemas of the Black Diaspora: Diversity, Dependence, and Oppositionality*, edited by Michael T. Martin, Detroit, Wayne State University Press, 1996, pp. 40–45.

Martin, Justin F. "Children's Attitudes toward Superheroes as a Potential Indicator of Their Moral Understanding." *Journal of Moral Education*, vol. 36, no. 3, 2007, pp. 239–250.

Miller, Abigail. "White Parents Agonizing over Whether to Allow Their Children to Wear a Black Panther Costume." *Daily Mail*, 14 February 2018, https://www.dailymail.co.uk/news/article-5392691/White-parents-worry-kids-wear-Black-Panther-mask.html.

Opam, Kwame. "The Many Meanings of Black Panther's Mask." *New York Times*, 13 February 2018, https://www.nytimes.com/2018/02/13/style/black-panther-children-costumes.html.

Rogers, Richard A. "From Cultural Exchange to Transculturation: A Review and Reconceptualization of Cultural Appropriation." *Communication Theory*, vol. 16, no. 4, 2006, pp. 474–503.

Samuel, Kameelah Martin. "Disney's Tia Dalma: A Critical Interrogation of an 'Imagineered' Priestess." *Black Women, Gender & Families*, vol. 6, no. 1, 2012, pp. 97–122.

Smith, Jamil. "A Hero Rises: The Superpower of *Black Panther*." *Time*, February 2018, pp. 43–47.

Wansik, B., M. Shimizu, and G. Camps. "What Would Batman Eat? Priming Children to Make Healthier Fast Food Choices." *Pediatric Obesity*, vol. 7, no. 2, 2012, pp. 121–124.

White, Rachel, et al. "The 'Batman Effect': Improving Perseverance in Young Children." *Child Development*, vol. 88, no. 5, 2017, pp. 1–9.

Wieselman, Jarett. "*Black Panther* Stars Can't Wait to See White Kids Dressed as T'Challa for Halloween." *BuzzFeed*, 10 October 2017, https://www.buzzfeednews.com/article/jarettwieselman/black-panther-stars-cant-wait-to-see-white-kids-dressed-as.

Williams, Stereo. "What *Black Panther* Means to Black Boys and Girls." *Daily Beast*, 18 February 2018, https://www.thedailybeast.com/what-black-panther-means-to-black-boys-and-girls.

Yin, Jing. "Popular Culture and Public Imaginary: Disney vs. Chinese Stories of Mulan." *Javnost*, vol. 18, no. 1, 2011, pp. 53–74.

Young, Ariana F., Shira Gabriel, and Jordan L. Hollar. "Batman to the Rescue! The Protective Effects of Parasocial Relationships with Muscular Superheroes on Men's Body Image." *Journal of Experimental Social Psychology*, vol. 49, no. 1, 2012, pp. 173–177.

Yousman, Bill. "Blackophilia and Blackophobia: White Youth, the Consumption of Rap Music, and White Supremacy." *Communication Theory*, vol. 13, no. 4, 2003, pp. 366–391.

Contributors

JOHN BODNER is an associate professor of folklore in the Social/Cultural Studies program at Memorial University of Newfoundland, Grenfell Campus. Alongside his ethnographic-based research, Bodner writes on the nexus of folklore, popular culture, and comic books.

AVIVA BRIEFEL is a professor of English and cinema studies at Bowdoin College. She is the author of *The Deceivers: Art Forgery and Identity in the Nineteenth Century* (2006) and *The Racial Hand in the Victorian Imagination* (2015) and coeditor of *The Horror Film after 9/11: World of Fear, Cinema of Terror* (2011).

JEFFREY A. BROWN is a professor in the Department of Popular Culture and the School of Critical and Cultural Studies at Bowling Green State University. He is the author of numerous academic articles about gender, ethnicity, and sexuality in contemporary media, as well as four books: *Black Superheroes: Milestone Comics and Their Fans* (2000), *Dangerous Curves: Gender, Fetishism, and Popular Culture* (2011), *Beyond Bombshells: The New Action Heroine in Popular Culture* (2015), and *The Modern Superhero in Film and Television* (2016). His most recent book is *Batman and the Multiplicity of Identity: The Contemporary Comic Book Superhero as Cultural Nexus* (2019).

SCOTT BUKATMAN is a professor of film and media studies at Stanford University. He has been published in many anthologies and journals, including *October, Critical Inquiry, Camera Obscura*, and *Science Fiction Studies*. His books include *Terminal Identity: The Virtual Subject in Postmodern Science Fiction* (1993), *Blade Runner* (1997), *Matters of Gravity: Special Effects and Supermen in the 20th Century* (2003), *The Poetics of Slumberland: Animated*

Spirits and the Animating Spirit (2012), and *Hellboy's World: Comics and Monsters on the Margins* (2016).

LIAM BURKE is a senior media studies lecturer and major coordinator at Swinburne University of Technology, Melbourne, Australia. He has published widely on comic books and adaptation, including the book *The Comic Book Film Adaptation: Exploring Modern Hollywood's Leading Genre* (2015) and the edited collection *Fan Phenomena: Batman*. His most recent book is the coedited collection *The Superhero Symbol* (2019). Burke is a chief investigator of the Australian Research Council–funded project Superheroes and Me.

JAMES CHAPMAN is a professor of film studies at the University of Leicester, United Kingdom, and editor of the *Historical Journal of Film, Radio and Television*. He specializes in the history of British popular culture of the twentieth century, and his books include *Saints and Avengers: British Adventure Series of the 1960s* (2002), *Licence to Thrill: A Cultural History of the James Bond Films* (2007), *British Comics: A Cultural History* (2011), and *Swashbucklers: The Costume Adventure Series* (2015).

BLAIR DAVIS is an associate professor of media and cinema studies in the College of Communication at DePaul University in Chicago. He is the author of *The Battle for the Bs: 1950s Hollywood and the Rebirth of Low-Budget Cinema* (2012), *Movie Comics: Page to Screen, Screen to Page* (2018), and *Comic Book Movies* (2018). Davis has served on the executive board of the Comics Studies Society, and in 2017 he edited an "In Focus" section for *Cinema Journal* on the graphic novel *Watchmen* as well as a roundtable section on comics and methodology for the inaugural issue of *Inks: The Journal of the Comics Studies Society*.

BARRY KEITH GRANT is an emeritus professor of film studies and popular culture at Brock University in Ontario, Canada, and an elected fellow of the Royal Society of Canada. He is the author or editor of two dozen books on film and popular culture, including *Film Genre: From Iconography to Ideology* (2007), *Shadows of Doubt: Negotiations of Masculinity in American Genre Films* (2011), *Monster Cinema* (2018), and the four editions of *Film Genre Reader*, two editions of *The Dread of Difference: Gender and the Horror Film*, and *Notions of Genre: Writings on Popular Film before Genre Theory* (2016), all published by University of Texas Press. He was the editor in chief of the award-winning four-volume comprehensive *Schirmer Encyclopedia of Film*

(2007), and he also edits the film and media studies list for Wayne State University Press.

SCOTT HENDERSON is dean and head of Trent University Durham GTA and is a professor in the Communication and Critical Thinking program. Previously he was an associate professor in the Department of Communication, Popular Culture and Film at Brock University in Ontario, Canada. His research focuses on issues of identity and representation in popular culture. He has published work on such diverse topics as local music scenes, YouTube and youth identity, gay and lesbian film, British cinema, film soundtracks, Canadian cinema and popular culture, and Canadian radio policy.

JULIAN HOXTER is an associate professor of cinema and a screenwriting coordinator in the School of Cinema at San Francisco State University. Hoxter is the coauthor of a book on American screenwriting in the new millennium, *Off the Page: Screenwriting in the Era of Media Convergence* (2017), and editor of a volume on the history of the screenwriting craft, *Screenwriting* (2014). He has also published two single-author textbooks on screenwriting: *Write What You Don't Know: An Accessible Manual for Screenwriters* (2011), and *The Pleasures of Structure: Learning Screenwriting through Case Studies* (2015).

MIRIAM KENT is a lecturer in film and media studies at the University of East Anglia. Her forthcoming monograph, based on her recently completed PhD thesis, explores the representations of women in Marvel superhero films. Her research combines the theoretical approaches of feminist film theory, comics studies, gender studies, queer theory, and postcolonial theory.

J. MARK PERCIVAL is a senior lecturer in media at Queen Margaret University, Edinburgh, Scotland. He has written about Scottish indie music production, popular music and identity, and mediation of popular music and is currently working on representations of music and musicians in Silver and Bronze Age superhero comics. Mark presented music shows for BBC Radio Scotland from 1988 to 2000 and was a Mercury Music Prize judging committee member in 1998 and 1999.

CHRIS REYNS-CHIKUMA is a professor at the University of Alberta, where he teaches courses in French on francophone cultures (especially *bande dessinée*) and in English on comics (especially superheroes and graphic novels). His research in recent years has focused on comics, including *bande dessinée* and manga. His most recent publications are on Etienne Davodeau (*Contemporary French Civilization*), Lewis Trondheim (*Image [&] Narrative*), and, in collaboration with Jean Sébastien, French e-comics.

JASON ROTHERY is a freelance writer, theater artist, and lapsed academic. He holds a BFA in creative writing from the University of British Columbia and an MA in humanities from York University in Toronto.

AARON TAYLOR is an associate professor of new media and Board of Governors research chair at the University of Lethbridge, Alberta, Canada. He is the editor of *Theorizing Film Acting* (2012) and coeditor of *Screening Characters* (2019). His essays on performance, film authorship, and comics have been published in numerous journals. His work also appears in several anthologies, including *Rethinking Disney* (2005), *Great Canadian Film Directors* (2007), *Acting and Performance in Moving Image Culture* (2012), *Stages of Reality* (2012), *The Works of Tim Burton* (2013), *Millennial Masculinity* (2013), *Make Ours Marvel* (2017), *Close-Up: Great Screen Performances* (2019), and *Contemporary Serial Television* (2019).

JAMES C. TAYLOR is a teaching fellow in the Department of Film and Television Studies at the University of Warwick, United Kingdom. He recently completed his doctoral thesis, which examines the aesthetic strategies through which superhero comic books are adapted into blockbuster films.

J. P. TELOTTE is a professor of film and media studies in the School of Literature, Media, and Communication at Georgia Tech. Coeditor of the journal *Post Script: Essays in Film and the Humanities*, Telotte has authored more than a hundred scholarly articles on film, television, and literature and authored or edited a number of books. Among his more recent publications are *The Mouse Machine: Disney and Technology* (2008), *Animating Space: From Mickey to WALL-E* (2010), *Science Fiction Film, Television, and Adaptation: Across the Screens* (2012), *Science Fiction TV* (2014), and *Science Fiction Double Feature* (2015).

SHERRYL VINT teaches at the University of California, Riverside, where she directs the Science Fiction and Technoculture Studies program. She coedits the journal *Science Fiction Studies* and was a founding editor of *Science Fiction Film and Television*. She is the author of *Bodies of Tomorrow* (2007), *Animal Alterity* (2010), and *Science Fiction: A Guide for the Perplexed* (2014);

coauthor of *The Routledge Concise History of Science Fiction* (2009); editor of *Science Fiction and Cultural Theory* (2015) and a special issue of *Paradoxa* entitled *The Futures Industry* (2017); and coeditor of *The Routledge Companion to Science Fiction* (2009), *Fifty Key Figures in Science Fiction* (2009), *Beyond Cyberpunk* (2010), and *The Walking Med: Zombies and the Medical Image* (2016).

BENJAMIN WOO is an assistant professor of communication and media studies at Carleton University, Ottawa, Canada. He is the author of *Getting a Life: The Social Worlds of Geek Culture* (2018), coauthor of *The Greatest Comic Book of All Time: Symbolic Capital and the Field of American Comic Books* (2016), coeditor of *Scene Thinking: Cultural Studies from the Scenes Perspective* (2015), and the director of the Comic Cons Research Project.

MATT YOCKEY is an associate professor in the Department of Theatre and Film at the University of Toledo. His work has appeared in a number of journals, including *European Journal of American Studies, Transformative Works and Cultures, Studies in Comics, Journal of Fandom Studies,* and *Velvet Light Trap.* His "TV Milestones" monograph on the *Batman* television series was published by Wayne State University Press in 2014. He is the editor of *Make Ours Marvel: Media Convergence and a Comics Universe* (2017).

Index

Page numbers in *italics* indicate illustrations